263/7799

ORGANIZATION AND TECHNOLOGY IN CAPITALIST DEVELOPMENT

ECONOMISTS OF THE TWENTIETH CENTURY

General Editors: Mark Perlman, *University Professor of Economics, University of Pittsburgh* and Mark Blaug, *Professor Emeritus, University of London; Consultant Professor, University of Buckingham and Visiting Professor, University of Exeter*

This innovative series comprises specially invited collections of articles and papers by economists whose work has made an important contribution to economics in the late twentieth century.

The proliferation of new journals and the ever-increasing number of new articles make it difficult for even the most assiduous economist to keep track of all the important recent advances. By focusing on those economists whose work is generally recognized to be at the forefront of the discipline, the series will be an essential reference point for the different specialisms included.

A list of published and future titles in this series is printed at the end of this volume.

Organization and Technology in Capitalist Development

William Lazonick

Professor of Economics
Barnard College
Columbia University in the City of New York,
US

Edward Elgar

Published by
Edward Elgar Publishing Limited
Gower House
Croft Road
Aldershot
Hants GU11 3HR
England

Edward Elgar Publishing Company
Old Post Road
Brookfield
Vermont 05036
USA

A CIP catalogue record for this book is available from the British Library

Library of Congress Cataloging-in-Publication Data
Lazonick, William.
 Organization and technology in capitalist development/William Lazonick. — 1st ed.
  p. cm. — (Economists of the twentieth century)
 Includes bibliographical references and index.
 1. Great Britain—Economic conditions—1945– 2. Technological innovations—Economic aspects—Great Britain. 3. Industrial organization—Great Britain. 4. United States—Economic conditions—1981– 5. Technological innovations—Economic aspects—United States. 6. Industrial organization—United States.
 I. Title. II. Series.
 HC256.6.L394 1993
 338'.064'0941—dc20   92–2430
                                                       CIP

ISBN 1 85278 742 2
Printed and Bound in Great Britain by
Hartnolls Limited, Bodmin, Cornwall.

Contents

Introduction: Placing History at the Service of Economics

The essays collected in this volume were written over the decade of the 1980s, a period during which I pursued my project of constructing a historically relevant theory of advanced capitalist development. As a graduate student and then assistant professor in the Harvard Economics Department during the 1970s, my main concern had been to find a perspective on the operation of advanced industrial economies that could displace the impotent, but somehow dominant, neoclassical theory. Beginning with a paper written during my first semester as a graduate student in 1970 (later published as Lazonick 1974), my attention had been focused on Marxian theory as a possible alternative to neoclassical orthodoxy, or at least as a point of departure for discovering an alternative. My treatment of Marxian theory was critical; I was not prepared to accept it as relevant for the late twentieth century without first examining its validity for the early nineteenth century – the historical period from which Marx drew his political inspiration and (supposedly) his empirical evidence. During the last half of the 1970s, therefore, I had immersed myself in a detailed study of organization and technology in the British cotton textile industry in an attempt to understand the empirical validity of the Marxian analysis of the British Industrial Revolution (see Lazonick 1979 and 1987a).

By 1980 I was still engaged in the study of the cotton textile industry, but my interest had turned to the debate among economic historians over twentieth-century British economic decline. By analyzing the dynamic interaction of organization and technology in the comparative development of the cotton textile industries of Britain and the United States, I found a way of making a critique of the arguments of a group of economic historians whose market-oriented vision of a successful capitalist economy derived more from their theoretical training in neoclassical economics than from their historical analysis of changes in international industrial leadership.

I developed the critique through my own case study of cotton textiles as well as in collaboration with Bernard Elbaum, a one-time fellow graduate student at Harvard who was doing similar research on international competition in iron and steel. Around 1981 we wrote a position paper on the decline of the British economy in which we outlined what we came to call the institutional rigidity hypothesis. We argued that 'Britain was impeded from making a successful transition to mass production and corporate organization in the twentieth century by an inflexible nineteenth-century institutional legacy of atomistic economic organization' (Elbaum and Lazonick 1986:15). Fragmented by horizontal competition and vertical specialization, British industrialists failed to confront and transform the market relations that limited their abilities to develop and utilize mass-production technologies.

We then circulated our position paper among scholars doing research on British industry and institutions, and thus ultimately gathered together the contributors to our edited volume, *The Decline of the British Economy*. There then ensued a couple of years of intellectual interchange among this group of scholars which culminated in a 1983 conference on British economic decline. A subsequent version of our original position paper, much revised by this interchange, was published in the *Journal of Economic History* (Elbaum and Lazonick 1984), and appears as Chapter One of this volume. A slight revision of this piece also appeared as the introductory chapter to our edited book.

In showing that, whatever its competitive advantages in the nineteenth century, market coordination of the British economy could not meet the global competitive challenges of the twentieth century, we confronted the neoclassical belief in the efficacy of the market-coordinated economy. What I have subsequently called the 'myth of the market economy' (Lazonick 1991a) had a firm intellectual grip on the 'new' (or, more accurately, neoclassical) economic historians who had entered the debate over British decline. Among these economic historians, the one who had focused his research on the cotton textile industry was Lars Sandberg. Along with Donald McCloskey, Sandberg had also written the most sweeping statement of the accomplishments of the neoclassical economic historians in arguing against the entrepreneurial failure hypothesis of British decline (see McCloskey and Sandberg 1971). In an article that had first appeared in the *Quarterly Journal of Economics* in 1969 (Sandberg 1969, reprinted and revised in Sandberg 1974:ch. 2–3), Sandberg had performed a sensible, albeit static, analysis of the factor costs that determined the choice of alternative spinning technologies in Britain just before World War I. He treated the choice of technology as a constrained optimization problem, and asked whether the managers of British cotton spinning factories acted as cost-minimizers in the technological choices that they actually made.

My methodological reaction to this approach was that, following Joseph Schumpeter (1947), the critical issue in analyzing British decline was not whether British managers optimized subject to constraints but whether the constraints that they faced in the British environment discouraged them from making investments in advanced technology. The task of the economic historian was then to identify the constraints on technological change, and to ask why, as economic actors, British industrialists would not or could not overcome the constraints (see Lazonick 1981a and 1981b).

At the same time, in studying Sandberg's 1969 article, I noticed some empirical mistakes in it, and decided to redo the analysis to set the record straight. (When I located some of the secondary sources that Sandberg had used in Baker Library at the Harvard Business School, I discovered that the last person to check the books out of the library had been Sandberg himself, some twelve years earlier!) In addition to the sources that Sandberg used, I drew on some different data sources in an attempt to construct a more internally consistent data set and to fill in some gaps in Sandberg's factor cost data (for example, such momentous empirical facts, culled from railroad rate books, as the cost of shipping empty bobbins by railway in Lancashire circa 1912).

The result was 'Factor Costs and the Diffusion of Ring Spinning in Britain Prior to World War I', first published in the *Quarterly Journal of Economics* (1981a) and reproduced as Chapter Two in this volume. In researching and writing this piece my interest was not so much to pursue my main project – to elaborate a historically relevant theory of capitalist development – but simply to meet the neoclassical economic historians on their own intellectual ground. But, in redoing Sandberg's constrained optimization analysis, I was also able to articulate an important methodological position concerning the uses and abuses of the constrained optimization technique. If the process of economic development is about how constraints on technological choices are overcome, then the constrained optimization analysis, performed at a point in time, permits the researcher to identify the factors at a particular time and place that are constraining investments in more advanced technologies. With this knowledge, the researcher can then ask why such constraints existed in one time and place but not in another time and place when and where the advanced technology was adopted, and what social forces had to be put in place to transform the critical constraints.

In 'Industrial Organization and Technological Change: the Decline of the British Cotton Industry', originally published in *Business History Review* (1983a) and reproduced as Chapter Three in this volume, I performed the dynamic analysis. I showed that during the last half of the nineteenth century, when the British cotton textile industry was virtually unchallenged in international competition, the organization of the industry became increasingly vertically specialized and horizontally fragmented. Market relations coordinated the activities of thousands of cotton broking, spinning, weaving, and marketing firms. I then went on to show how, when challenged by international competition based on textile technologies capable of achieving much higher levels of throughput than the traditional technologies used in Britain, the market-coordinated British industry had great difficulty in reorganizing itself through horizontal concentration and vertical integration to permit the adoption of high-throughput technologies. The industry's market-coordinated structure prevented an innovative competitive response.

As in the more general argument on the decline of the British economy in Chapter One, the analysis of the decline of the cotton textile industry relied heavily on both the Schumpeterian concept of innovation as a disruption of the 'circular flow' of market forces in which enterprises merely adapt to their environment, and the Chandlerian concept of the 'visible hand' of business organization that, through vertical integration of production and distribution facilities, permitted enterprises to attain high levels of throughput from their productive resources and consequent economies of scale.

In *The Visible Hand*, Alfred Chandler (1977) had analyzed this process in US industries in which, because of their capital-intensity, vertical integration was accompanied by high levels of horizontal concentration. Relative to these 'Chandlerian' industries, the cotton textile industry – the industry that had been the subject of my study – was horizontally fragmented. Nevertheless, the US cotton textile industry was much more vertically integrated than the British cotton textile industry, and was able as a result to adopt new spinning and weaving technologies that, when used in combination, could yield high throughput and economies of scale. During the 1940s and 1950s, moreover, the US cotton textile industry became much more horizontally concentrated, whereas the British industry remained fragmented. In cross-national perspective, even the experience of a relatively labor-intensive industry such as cotton textiles confirmed Chandler's analysis.

Since 1986 revised versions of Chapters One and Three of this volume have been used as Harvard Business School case studies in the extremely successful course, The Coming of Managerial Capitalism. In addition, my articles on cotton textiles (those included as Chapters Two and Three here as well as Lazonick 1981c, Lazonick and Mass 1984) generated an appreciable amount of debate among economic historians. To some extent the debates focused on esoteria of spinning technology – whether mule spinning machines designed to spin warp yarns could be converted to spinning weft yarns (Sandberg 1984; Lazonick 1984), and whether the paper tubes that could be used on the spindles of ring spinning machines performed the same function as the paper tubes that could be used on the spindles of mules (Saxonhouse and Wright 1984 and 1987; Lazonick 1987b). Larger issues were, however, at stake.

In my debate with Sandberg, the larger issue was the adequacy of the constrained-optimization technique for analyzing changes in technological and economic leadership. In the end, I believe that Sandberg recognized that a dynamic methodology was warranted, although he may have had his doubts whether my approach was the one to follow.

In my debate with Saxonhouse and Wright, the larger issue concerned the determinants of global competitive advantage. Much of my argument concerning the organizational determinants of British relative decline in cotton textiles took the US cotton textile industry as the relevant model of industrial success. Yet, as Saxonhouse and Wright correctly noted, the US cotton textile industry had only limited success in capturing foreign markets, and was indeed protected in its home market. The national industry that beat out British cotton textiles during the interwar period was that of Japan, and the Japanese industry was, according to Saxonhouse and Wright, even more vertically specialized than the British industry. The source of Japanese competitive advantage, they asserted, was not the use of managerial coordination to introduce high-throughput technologies as Mass and I had argued, but simply cheap labor (Saxonhouse and Wright 1984:519).

Meanwhile, around 1985 after writing my reply to Saxonhouse and Wright (Lazonick 1987b), I realized that, if I wanted to advance my larger project of constructing a historically relevant theory of capitalist development, I had better extricate myself from the study of the cotton textile industry. A two-year stay as a research fellow at the Harvard Business School from 1984 to 1986 (as it turned out a period during which I also made a transition from being a non-tenured associate professor at Harvard University to being a tenured professor at Barnard College, Columbia University) gave me the opportunity and the stimulus to expand the scale and scope of my research agenda. Some five years or so later, I published two books: *Competitive Advantage on the Shop Floor* (1990a) and *Business Organization and the Myth of the Market Economy* (1991a).

The first half of *Competitive Advantage on the Shop Floor* draws on my cotton textile research on industrial relations and technological change, and forms a historical prelude to the second half of the book, written between 1986 and 1989, that compares the general evolution of shop-floor organization and technology in Britain, United States, and Japan. *Business Organization and the Myth of the Market Economy*, written between 1986 and 1990, elaborates the British, US, and Japanese comparison into a full-blown argument concerning the increasingly important role of managerial coordination at the level of the business enterprise for successful capitalist development. Bolstered by the historical argument, the book then mounts an extended analysis of how and why Anglo-American economists have, during the twentieth century, clung to the myth of the market economy – the myth, enshrined in the economics textbooks, that attributes economic prosperity to the market coordination of economic activity.

Nevertheless, even the task of completing these two books could not keep me from continuing my explorations into the spinning of yarn and the weaving of cloth. In 1989 the editors of *Business History* invited me to write a piece summarizing the debates in which I had been involved on the British cotton textile industry and international competition. I recruited my longtime associate, Bill Mass (who had continued to do research on textile machinery) to collaborate with me in writing the survey. The resultant article, 'The British Cotton Industry and International Competitive Advantage' (Mass and Lazonick 1990) reproduced in this volume as Competitive Advantage' (Mass and Lazonick 1990), reproduced in this volume as Chapter Four, deals with 1) an explanation of how the British cotton textile industry 2) why its leadership persisted until World War I, despite its relative technological backwardness from the 1880s; 3) why it was displaced as the world leader by the Japanese cotton textile industry during the interwar period; and 4) how the British cotton textile industry responded to the competitive challenge. In addition, given our own analysis of each of these four issues, we then examined what (if anything) the 'new' economic historians had to say about these matters.

Our most interesting discovery in writing this article was the extent to which Japan's rise to global leadership in cotton textiles from the 1910s into the 1930s was only partially based on cheap labor. Of critical importance to the success of Japan were both the organization of its industry, from the purchasing of cotton to the marketing of cloth, and the development of an indigenous technological capability. Access to relatively cheap labor did not hurt Japan's competitiveness on global markets. But cheap labor cannot explain why, by the 1930s, the Japanese cotton textile industry was dominating world markets, whereas the Indian cotton textile industry could only survive behind tariff barriers. In 'The British Cotton Industry and International Competitive Advantage', Bill Mass and I provided some preliminary answers to Japan's spectacular rise to dominance in this industry. At the time of writing, the subject is part of an ongoing research project (see Lazonick, Mass, and Rao 1992).

During the 1980s the main thrust of my comparative research was on how, during the first decades of this century, the United States surpassed Britain as a global competitor. My most recent research on comparative industrial development has focused on how, over the past few decades, Japan surpassed the United States as global leader (see Lazonick 1990a: ch. 9–10; Lazonick 1991a: ch. 1). This comparative research emphasizes that, across national economies, the different social environments result in different economic outcomes. But it also emphasizes that, even within a particular region of a particular nation over a relatively short time span (say, a decade or two), the social environment is subject to change.

This point is illustrated in Chapter Five of this volume, 'The "Horndal Effect" in Early U.S. Manufacturing', co-authored with Tom Brush (1985). The 'Horndal effect' is a term that, following the Swedish economist, Erik Lundberg (1961), Anglo-American economists adopted in the 1960s to mean sustained productivity growth without technological change (see Arrow 1962; Leibenstein 1966; for subsequent empirical work about what actually happened at Horndal, see Genberg 1992). In an article originally published in 1973, Paul David claimed to have found a case of the Horndal effect in a textile mill in Lowell, Massachusetts from the 1830s to the 1850s, and, following the lead of Arrow (1962), he attributed the sustained productivity growth to 'learning-by-doing'. He supported this assertion by fitting a time trend to four data points over a period in which there was a general increase in labor productivity (David 1973 and 1975).

I was not at all convinced by David's argument. The late 1840s and early 1850s were years in which Irish immigrants, quite new to factory work, began to replace Yankee workers in the textile mills of Lowell. Was a learning-by-doing argument relevant for a period in which a new workforce was replacing an older workforce? Would not one expect that the newly arrived Irish workers would have less power than the established Yankee workers to control the level of effort that they supplied to the production process? Was it not plausible to posit that a portion of the observed productivity increase was the result of an augmentation of the ability of employers to extract effort from their workers with the coming of the Irish?

To test what we called the 'production-relations hypothesis', Brush and I collected monthly data on, among other things, productivity, work experience, work conditions, and ethnicity of every worker who had worked in the main weaveroom of the factory in question – Lawrence Mill No. 2 in Lowell – over a period of some twenty years. The data set contained in excess of 13,000 observations. Our analysis of this data set provided support for both the learning-by-doing and the production-relations hypotheses as determinants of the textile mill's productivity growth.

We cautioned, however, that, despite the extreme microeconomic character of our analysis, our results were sensitive to how one interpreted the underlying phenomena measured by several key variables. The case study should, therefore, give pause to those who would draw conclusions from even more aggregated quantitative data without questioning whether the quantitative measures actually merited the qualitative meanings that were being attached to them.

In other words, in doing quantitative empirical work on productivity growth, one must give serious thought to the theory one is using to frame the analysis and interpret the results. In my view, a training in mainstream economics did not, and to this day does not, provide the historian, much less the economist, with such a critical perspective (see Lazonick 1991a). In the case of our analysis of the Horndal effect, what one needs is a theoretical framework for analyzing the impact of social organization (including the exercise of social power) on productivity. On this issue, mainstream economics simply does not provide one with a relevant theory or a relevant methodology.

In *Competitive Advantage on the Shop Floor*, I applied a methodology that integrated theory and history to the study of the social determinants of productivity growth. This work drew heavily on a variety of academic disciplines, including labor history. During the 1970s and 1980s a leading historian of shop-floor social relations in the United States was David Montgomery (1979 and 1987). He and his students documented the struggles of workers in the late nineteenth century and first half of the twentieth century in the United States to maintain a degree of control over the organization of work on the shop floor in opposition to increasingly powerful employers bent on securing more output per unit of labor time.

In revealing the historical record, Montgomery also sought to relate shop-floor struggles to the political movements of labor outside the workplace. This research is invaluable for anyone studying the causes and consequences of economic development in the United States in the twentieth century. But as I argue in 'The Breaking of the American Working Class', written as a review of Montgomery's book, *The Fall of the House of Labor* (Lazonick 1989), and included in this volume as Chapter Six, Montgomery failed to integrate the role of technological change into his analysis of the evolution of labor–management relations. He did not see how, by permitting more output per unit of labor time without necessarily requiring that workers supply more effort to the production process, the introduction of 'effort-saving' technologies on the shop floor created a terrain of cooperation between labor and management.

In 'The Basic Analytics of Shop-Floor Value Creation' (which first appeared as an appendix to my book, *Competitive Advantage on the Shop Floor*, and which appears in this volume as Chapter Seven), I demonstrate the interaction of labor–management relations and effort-saving technological change. Besides the lessons that I learned from my own studies of the determinants of the relation between effort and pay, the formal analysis presented in Chapter Seven was inspired by reading Frederick W. Taylor's, *The Principles of Scientific Management* (1967).

As I have detailed elsewhere (Lazonick 1983b and 1990a: ch. 7), Taylor's failed attempts to use piece-rate incentives to elicit more effort from workers cannot be understood unless it is recognized that his task was to generate higher levels of productivity through the introduction of effort-saving machine technologies. These technologies contained the potential to produce more output per unit of time with the same amount of work effort. But workers would only cooperate in supplying the effort to achieve high levels of throughput if they had reasonable expectations of securing what they considered to be fair shares of the productivity gains. Employers, for their parts, would only invest in the effort-saving technologies if they had reasonable expectations of securing sufficient levels of effort from workers to transform the higher fixed costs of the new technologies into lower units costs than could be achieved on the basis of the existing technologies. The role of 'scientific management' was to regulate this sharing of productivity gains between employers and employees so that the investments would be made and the efforts would be forthcoming that could in fact generate the productivity gains.

Taylor himself failed in this task because, in an era in which American employers were bent on eliminating the power of unions in the mass-production industries in which effort-saving technology was most applicable, he could never assure workers that they would in fact receive a fair share of future productivity gains. Only the experience of long-term employment security and income growth within particular companies could provide workers with the confidence that they would be rewarded for their hard work. And it was mass-production enterprises that had already secured dominant market shares in their industries that could best offer such employment conditions – as indeed occurred during the boom years of the 1920s. But, whatever the intentions of dominant employers, the promise of 'permanent employment' for blue-collar workers became a victim of the Great Depression of the 1930s (Lazonick 1990a: ch. 7–9). From the 1940s, the return of prosperity once again permitted dominant enterprises to make realistic assurances to workers of long-term employment security and income growth, although now these assurances were made even more realistic by the presence of mass-production unions, with their insistence on seniority in determining employment and even promotion.

It is essential to emphasize that, whether before or after the Great Depression, the companies that were best able to exercise control and generate value on the shop floor were those that, through technological innovation, had already secured dominant shares of their product markets. Technological innovation in turn required organizational innovation. As Alfred Chandler (1977) has shown, the companies that were able to gain dominant market shares were those that built managerial structures to plan and coordinate the movement of their enterprises into new product markets and the introduction of new process technologies. A company that undertook an innovative investment strategy could not hope to gain the cooperation of its blue-collar employees on the shop floor if it did not first gain the cooperation of its technical specialists responsible for product and process innovation. 'Strategy, Structure, and Management Development in the United States and Britain' (1986), first presented to the Fuji Business History Conference in 1985, and reproduced here as Chapter Eight, outlines how, after the turn of the century, major US business corporations put in place training systems and incentive systems to build cohesive organizations of professional managers.

In 'Strategy, Structure, and Management Development', I also contrast the building of these organizational capabilities in US enterprises with the relative failure to do so in Britain. In the United States, where, after the Great Merger Movement of the turn of the century, asset ownership became increasingly separated from managerial control, the most hardworking, ambitious, and creative technical specialists could look forward to upward mobility within the corporation, with the possibility of eventually entering into the ranks of top management. A prime purpose of management development within the enterprise was to ensure that, through job rotation and promotion, the most promising technical specialists would be transformed into managerial generalists. The result was the behavioral and cognitive integration of technical specialists into the managerial structure of the enterprise. This integration made the managerial structure a powerful collective force, capable of planning and coordinating the movement into new product markets, the development of new process technologies, and the achievement of high levels of throughput on the shop floor.

In contrast, even in the British industrial enterprises that emerged from the Second Industrial Revolution with large market shares, there was an evident social segmentation between top management and technical specialists that impeded the development and utilization of productive resources. In 'Strategy, Structure, and Management Development', I show how, even in new industries such as chemicals and electrical engineering, this segmentation within the enterprise evolved in the first half of the twentieth century as a legacy of the social institutions that had characterized Britain during its era of industrial leadership in the last half of the nineteenth century.

Just as British industry found it difficult to respond to the American (as well as

German and Japanese) challenge in the first half of the twentieth century, so US industry is finding it difficult to respond to intensified global competition now. In the last chapter of this book, 'Organizational Capabilities in American Industry: The Rise and Decline of Managerial Capitalism', originally published in *Business and Economic History* (1990b), I outline the role of organizational capabilities in the rise of the United States to industrial leadership during the first half of this century. I then suggest how, in the face of global competitors with even more powerful organizational capabilities, the social institutions (including the social organization of the enterprise) that underlay the rise of the United States to industrial leadership have, over the past two decades or so, begun to erode. This piece was originally written for a volume, edited by Howard Gospel (1991) on innovation and training in industry in the United States and Japan. I subsequently delivered the version of the paper reproduced in this book as a keynote address at the Business History Conference, an organization that in recent years has sought to bring business history and economics in symbiotic relation with each other (for my subsequent Presidential address to the Business History Conference on 'business history and economics,', see Lazonick 1991b; for an edited volume on organizational capabilities and competitive advantage, see Lazonick 1993).

In sum, the essays gathered together in this volume reveal the evolution of my thinking, research, and writing on the importance of organizational capabilities both for understanding the realities of capitalist development and for criticizing the irrelevancies of mainstream economics. For too long now, economists, intellectually imprisoned by individualist ideology and static methodology, have shunned the study of how people consciously and collectively combine their skills and efforts to transform their economic environment and generate economic growth. As an economist working in the Anglo-American traditions, it has been incumbent on me to criticize the market mentality and the ahistorical analysis that underpins mainstream economics. But my agenda goes well beyond negative criticism. Rather, I view my intellectual task as one of (to borrow a powerful phrase from Schumpeter 1942) '*creative* destruction'. The creative task is what makes the work worthwhile. What ultimately matters is not the outmoded vision of the economy and economics that our thinking, research, and writing help to destroy but the more relevant vision of the economy and economics that these intellectual endeavors help to create.

References

Arrow, Kenneth J. (1962), 'The Economic Implications of Learning by Doing', *Review of Economic Studies*, **29**, April.

Chandler, Jr., Alfred D. (1977), *The Visible Hand: The Managerial Revolution in American Business*, Harvard University Press.

David, Paul (1973), 'The "Horndal Effect" in Lowell, 1834–1856', *Explorations in Economic History*, **10**, February.

David, Paul (1975), *Technical Choice, Innovation, and Economic Growth*, Cambridge University Press.

Elbaum, Bernard and William Lazonick (1984), 'The Decline of the British Economy: An Institutional Perspective', *Journal of Economic History*, **44**, June.

Elbaum, Bernard and William Lazonick, eds (1986), *The Decline of the British Economy*, Clarendon Press.

Genberg, Mats (1992), 'The Horndal Effect: Productivity Growth without Capital Investment in Horndalsverken between 1927 and 1952', Ph.D. dissertation, Uppsala University, April.

Gospel, Howard F., ed. (1991), *Industrial Training and Technological Innovation: A Comparative and Historical Study*, Routledge.

Lazonick, William (1974), 'Karl Marx and Enclosures in England', *Review of Radical Political Economics*, **6**, Summer.

Lazonick, William (1979), 'Industrial Relations and Technical Change: The Case of the Self-Acting Mule', *Cambridge Journal of Economics*, **3**, September.

Lazonick, William (1981a), 'Factor Costs and the Diffusion of Ring Spinning in Britain prior to World War I', *Quarterly Journal of Economics*, **96**, February.

Lazonick, William (1981b), 'Competition, Specialization, and Industrial Decline', *Journal of Economic History*, **41**, March.

Lazonick, William (1981c), 'Production Relations, Labor Productivity, and Choice of Technique: British and U.S. Cotton Spinning', *Journal of Economic History*, **41**, September.

Lazonick, William (1983a), 'Industrial Organization and Technological Change: The Decline of the British Cotton Industry', *Business History Review*, **57**, Summer.

Lazonick, William (1983b), 'Technological Change and the Control of Work: The Development of Capital–Labor Relations in U.S. Mass Production Industries', in Howard Gospel and Craig Littler, eds, *Managerial Strategies and Industrial Relations*, Heinemann.

Lazonick, William (1984), 'Rings and Mules in Britain: Reply', *Quarterly Journal of Economics*, **99**, May.

Lazonick, William (1986), 'Strategy, Structure, and Management Development in the United States and Britain', in Kesaji Kobayashi and Hidemasa Morikawa, eds, *Development of Managerial Enterprise*, University of Tokyo Press.

Lazonick, William (1987a), 'Theory and History in Marxian Economics', in Alexander J. Field, ed., *The Future of Economic History*, Kluwer-Nijhoff.

Lazonick, William (1987b), 'Stubborn Mules: Some Comments', *Economic History Review*, second series, **40**, February.

Lazonick, William (1989), 'The Breaking of the American Working Class', *Reviews in American History*, **17**, June.

Lazonick, William (1990a), *Competitive Advantage on the Shop Floor*, Harvard University Press.

Lazonick, William (1990b), 'Organizational Capabilities in American Industry: The Rise and Decline of Managerial Capitalism', *Business and Economic History*, second series, **19**.

Lazonick, William (1991a), *Business Organization and the Myth of the Market Economy*, Cambridge University Press.

Lazonick, William, (1991b), 'Business History and Economics', *Business and Economic History*, second series, **20**.

Lazonick, William, ed. (1993), *Organizational Capabilities and Competitive Advantage*, Edward Elgar.

Lazonick, William and Thomas Brush (1985), 'The "Horndal Effect" in Early U.S. Manufacturing', *Explorations in Economic History*, **22**, January.

Lazonick, William and William Mass (1984), 'The Performance of the British Cotton Industry, 1870–1913', *Research in Economic History*, **9**.

Lazonick, William, William Mass and Mohan Rao (1992), 'Textile Technology Transfer, Development, and Diffusion: An International Perspective on National Industrialization', photocopy, Harvard University, January.

Leibenstein, Harvey (1966), 'Allocative Efficiency vs. "X-Efficiency"', *American Economic Review*, **56**, June.

Lundberg, Erik (1961), *Produktivitet och Räntabilitet*, Norstedt and Söner.

Mass, William and William Lazonick (1990), 'The British Cotton Industry and International Competitive Advantage: The State of the Debates', *Business History*, **32**, October.

McCloskey, Donald and Lars Sandberg (1971), 'From Damnation to Redemption: Judgments on the Late Victorian Entrepreneur', *Explorations in Economic History*, **9**, Fall.

Montgomery, David (1979), *Workers' Control in America*, Cambridge University Press.

Montgomery, David (1987), *The Fall of the House of Labor*, Cambridge University Press.

Sandberg, Lars (1969), 'American Rings and English Mules: The Role of Economic Rationality', *Quarterly Journal of Economics*, **83**, February.

Sandberg, Lars (1974), *Lancashire in Decline*, Ohio State University Press.

Sandberg, Lars (1984), 'The Remembrance of Things Past: Rings and Mules Revisited', *Quarterly Journal of Economics*, **99**, May.

Saxonhouse, Gary and Gavin Wright (1984), 'New Evidence on the Stubborn English Mule and the Cotton Industry, 1878–1920', *Economic History Review*, second series, **37**, November.

Saxonhouse, Gary and Gavin Wright (1987), 'Stubborn Mules and Vertical Integration: The Disappearing Constraint?', *Economic History Review*, second series, **40**, February.

Schumpeter, Joseph A. (1942), *Capitalism, Socialism, and Democracy*, Harper.

Schumpeter, Joseph A. (1947), 'The Creative Response in Economic History', *Journal of Economic History*, November.

Taylor, Frederick W. (1967), *The Principles of Scientific Management* [First published in 1912], Norton.

PART I

ORGANIZATION AND TECHNOLOGY IN THE BRITISH ECONOMY

[1]

The Decline of the British Economy: An Institutional Perspective

BERNARD ELBAUM AND WILLIAM LAZONICK

This paper attributes the relative decline of the British economy in the twentieth century to rigidities in its economic and social institutions that had developed during the nineteenth-century era of relatively atomistic competition. Inherited and persistent constraints impeded British firms from acquiring the market control, authority in labor relations, or managerial hierarchy necessary to avail themselves fully of modern mass production methods. At the societal level there was an interrelated failure to transform the character of British educational and financial institutions, labor-management relations, and state policy in order to promote economic development. By performing better in these respects late-industrializing countries were able to surpass Britain in economic growth.

THE British economy, once the workshop of the world, seems to have fallen victim to some century-long affliction. For lack of an adequate generic diagnosis, many observers have termed this affliction the "British disease."[1] There are signs, however, that the disease may be spreading, and the recent competitive reverses of American industry in the face of Japanese and European challenges have sparked renewed interest in explanations of economic growth and decline. The Japanese success in particular has recently received most of the attention from economists and policy makers, but there is yet, we would argue, much to be learned from Britain's economic failure.

In Britain itself, the ideology directing current government policy assumes that the nation's decline has been due to the obstruction of the self-regulating market economy by trade union power and state inter-vention. This ideological perspective finds intellectual reinforcement in orthodox economic theory that, in both its liberal and conservative variants, views the capitalist economy as fundamentally an atomistic market economy. According to economic orthodoxy, the perfection of market competition and economic prosperity go hand in hand.

Although this proposition goes back to the time of Adam Smith, it has

Journal of Economic History, Vol. XLIV, No. 2 (June 1984). © The Economic History Association. All rights reserved. ISSN 0022-0507.

Bernard Elbaum is Assistant Professor of Economics, Boston University, Boston, Massachu-setts 02215, and William Lazonick is Associate Professor of Economics, Harvard University, Cambridge, Massachusetts 02138. This paper synthesizes new research on British industrial decline, much of which will appear in a forthcoming Oxford University Press volume edited by Elbaum and Lazonick. They wish to thank the participants at the Anglo-American Conference on the Decline of the British Economy (held at Boston University on September 30-October 1, 1983) for their help in shaping the perspective presented here, and to Lance Davis and Michael Edelstein for their comments at the 1983 Economic History Association meetings.

[1] See, for example, G. C. Allen, *The British Disease* (London, 1976).

never been adequately supported by comparative examination of the historical experiences of capitalist economies. In particular, the issue of Britain's decline has largely been avoided by neoclassical economic historians who have been preoccupied with demonstrating that turn-of-the-century British managers "did the best they could" by optimizing subject to given constraints.[2] Neoclassical economists who have confronted the problem of explaining national decline simply assume that the mainspring of the wealth of nations is free market competition and proceed as a matter of course to blame Britain's economic misfortunes on either market imperfections or "noneconomic" factors such as the cultural peculiarities of businessmen or workers.[3]

By contrast, the historical perspective presented below attributes the decline of the British economy to the rigid persistence of economic and social institutions from the nineteenth-century era of relatively atomistic competition. In such countries as the United States, Germany, and Japan, successful twentieth-century economic development has been based on mass production methods and corporate forms of managerial coordination. But in Britain adoption of these modern technological and organizational innovations was impeded by inherited socioeconomic constraints at the levels of the enterprise, industry, and society. Entrenched institutional structures—including the structures of industrial relations, industrial organization, educational systems, financial intermediation, international trade, and state-enterprise relations—constrained the ability of individuals, groups, or corporate entities to transform the productive system.

Britain's problem was that economic decision makers, lacking the individual or collective means to alter prevailing institutional constraints, in effect took them as "given." In failing to confront institutional constraints, British businessmen can justifiably be accused of "entrepreneurial failure."[4] But the cause of the failure was not simply cultural conservatism, as some historians have implied. If British society was pervaded by conservative mores, it was in this respect certainly no worse off than Japan or continental European countries that were precapitalist, tradition-bound societies when Britain was the workshop of the world. The thesis of entrepreneurial failure casts no light on why Britain, the first industrial nation, should have been less

---

[2] Donald N. McCloskey, ed., *Essays on a Mature Economy: Britain After 1840* (London, 1971); Donald N. McCloskey and Lars Sandberg, "From Damnation to Redemption: Judgments on the Late Victorian Entrepreneur," *Explorations in Economic History*, 9 (Fall 1971), 89–108; R. C. Floud, "Britain 1860–1914: A Survey," and L. G. Sandberg, "The Entrepreneur and Technological Change," both in *The Economic History of Britain since 1700*, ed. Roderick Floud and Donald McCloskey, vol. 2 (Cambridge, 1981).

[3] See, for example, Richard E. Caves, "Productivity Differences among Industries," in *Britain's Economic Performance*, ed. Richard E. Caves and Lawrence B. Krause (Washington, D.C., 1980).

[4] David Landes, *The Unbound Prometheus* (Cambridge, 1969), chap. 5; Martin Wiener, *English Culture and The Decline of the Industrial Spirit, 1850–1980* (Cambridge, 1981).

successful than later industrializers in shedding customary attitudes that encumbered economic performance.

Britain's distinctiveness derived less from the conservatism of its cultural values per se than from a matrix of rigid institutional structures that reinforced these values and obstructed individualistic as well as concerted efforts at economic renovation. In our view, the causes and consequences of such institutional rigidities remain central to understanding the long-term dynamics of economic development as well as the current crisis of the British economy.

THE CONSEQUENCES OF COMPETITIVE CAPITALISM

In the third quarter of the nineteenth century, the British economy experienced a "long boom" that represented the culmination of the world's first industrial revolution. After three centuries of international conflict for the control of world markets and after seven decades of intense capital investment in productive capacity, Britain emerged unchallenged in the world economy. On the basis of national domination of world markets, there was much in the way of opportunity for aspiring merchants and manufacturers. As they entered into commerce and industry, the structure of British industry became extremely competitive. By today's standards, Britain's major nineteenth-century staple industries—textiles, iron and steel, coal mining, shipbuilding, and engineering—were all composed of numerous firms with small market shares. Their industrial structures were also characterized by a high degree of vertical specialization: distribution of intermediate and final products relied upon well-developed market mechanisms, often involving specialized merchant firms.

The managerial organization and technology employed by nineteenth-century British firms were comparatively simple. Characteristically, firms were run by owner-proprietors or close family associates. Managerial staffs were small, and methods of cost accounting and production control were crude or nonexistent. The development of industrial techniques typically relied upon trial and error rather than systematic in-house research. Most enterprises were single-plant firms that specialized in particular lines of manufacture of intermediate or final products. Industries exhibited a high degree of regional concentration based upon geographical advantages as well as external economies provided by local access to skilled labor supplies, transport facilities and distribution networks, capital, and product markets.

Up to the 1870s the long-term financing for these business ventures came from country banks, personal family fortunes, and retained earnings. After the collapse of the country banks in the Great Depression of the 1870s, financial institutions had little involvement in the long-term finance of British industry. The purchasers of share capital tended instead to be individuals—among them many shopkeepers and skilled workers—who invested their savings locally. With British firms able to tap local as well as internal sources of long-term financing, there is no evidence that they were short of capital in the decades prior to World War I. The last decades of the nineteenth century also saw the extension of national banks and the development of a highly liquid national capital market. But industrial firms were reluctant to risk loss of control by issuing equity on the national market or incurring long-term debt. Financial institutions provided only short-term working capital to British industry (mainly through overdraft accounts), and as a result never developed the institutional expertise to serve the demand for long-term capital that did arise. Instead they exported most of their capital, usually in exchange for fixed-interest bonds, to finance large-scale (typically government-backed) foreign projects such as railroads. A consequence of these arrangements was the separation of provincial industrial enterprise from national financial institutions based in the City of London, a characteristic feature of the British economy well into the twentieth century.[5]

Another outcome of British capitalism as it developed in the last half of the nineteenth century was the consolidation of job control on the part of many groups of workers in industry. During the "long boom," individual capitalists, divided by competition, opted for collective accommodation with unions of skilled and strategically positioned workers rather than jeopardize the fortunes of their individual firms through industrial conflict while there were profits to be made. The labor movement also made important legislative gains that enhanced the ability of workers to organize unions, build up union treasuries, and stage successful strikes.

A distinguishing feature of the British labor movement was its two tiers of bargaining strength. Workplace organizations enjoyed substantial local autonomy in bargaining, backed by the leverage that national unions could exert on employers during disputes. From the fourth quarter of the nineteenth century, as intermittent but often prolonged recessions occurred and as foreign competition began to be felt by many industries, capitalists were unable to replace the job control of shop-floor union organizations by managerial control. Despite the introduction of many skill-displacing changes in technology, the power of the union organizations that had developed earlier had simply become too great. Attempts by Parliament and the judiciary to undermine the trade union movement—most notably by means of the Taff Vale decision—resulted in the emergence of a distinct political party representing the interests of labor.

---

[5] Michael Best and Jane Humphries, "The City and the Decline of British Industry," in *The Decline of the British Economy*, ed. Bernard Elbaum and William Lazonick (Oxford, forthcoming).

THE CHALLENGE OF CORPORATE CAPITALISM

Elsewhere, from the late nineteenth century (notably in Japan, Germany, and the United States) corporate capitalism was emerging to become the dominant mode of economic organization. Corporate capitalism was characterized by industrial oligopoly, hierarchical managerial bureaucracy, vertical integration of production and distribution, managerial control over the labor process, the integration of financial and industrial capital, and systematic research and development.[6]

Oligopoly, by helping to stabilize prices and market shares, facilitated long-run planning, particularly where large-scale capital investments were involved. Managerial coordination of product flows within the vertically integrated enterprise permitted the achievement of high-speed throughputs that reduced unit costs. Vertical integration of production and distribution provided the direct access to market outlets that was a precondition for the effective utilization of mass production methods. Managerial control over the labor process in turn facilitated the introduction of new, high-throughput technologies. Integration of financial and industrial capital, along with managerial bureaucracy, made possible the geographic mobility of capital and the rapid expansion of capacity to produce for new or growing markets. Systematic research and development, particularly in such science-based industries as electrical and chemical manufacturing, provided the mainspring of technological innovation. Across countries, the degree of coordination of economic activity by the state and large financial institutions varied, with significant implications for economic performance. But the experience of successful capitalist economies in the twentieth century demonstrates the ubiquitous importance of the visible hand of corporate bureaucratic management.

In order to compete against the corporate mass production methods being developed in Germany, Japan, and the United States, British industries required transformation of their structures of industrial relations, industrial organization, and enterprise management. Vested interests in the old structures, however, proved to be formidable (if not insurmountable) obstacles to the transition from competitive to corporate modes of organization. Lacking corporate management skills and opportunities, British industrialists clung to family control of their firms. Even where horizontal amalgamations did take place, the directors of the participating firms insisted on retaining operational autonomy.[7] In any case, very few of these managers had the broader

[6] Alfred D. Chandler, Jr., *The Visible Hand* (Cambridge, Massachusetts, 1977); Alfred D. Chandler, Jr., and Herman Daems, eds., *Managerial Hierarchies* (Cambridge, Massachusetts, 1980).

[7] Leslie Hannah, *The Rise of the Corporate Economy: The British Experience* (Baltimore, 1976); Alfred D. Chandler, Jr., "The Growth of the Transnational Industrial Firm in the United States and the United Kingdom: A Comparative Analysis," *Economic History Review*, 2nd ser., 33 (Aug. 1980).

entrepreneurial perspectives or skills needed to develop modern corporate structures.[8]

The British educational system hampered industry by failing to provide appropriately trained managerial and technical personnel. On the supply side, the existing system of higher education was designed almost explicitly to remove its "aristocratic" students as far as possible from the worldly pursuit of business and applied science.[9] On the demand side, there was comparatively little pressure to transform this system as highly competitive businesses could not afford to hire specialized technical personnel and were further reluctant to support industry-wide research institutes that would benefit competitors as much as themselves.[10] Given the lack of interest of business and the educational establishment in fostering managerial and technical training, it is not surprising that the British state, rather passive towards industrial development in any case, took little initiative to make education more relevant to economic development.

Nor was leadership for industrial transformation forthcoming from other sectors of the British economy. The financial sector kept its distance from direct involvement in industry, preferring instead to maintain its highly liquid position by means of portfolio investment, mostly abroad. The orientation of Britain's bankers towards liquidity and protection of the value of the pound sterling was reinforced by the undisputed position of the City of London as the financial center of the world. The concentration of banking in the City also gave rise to a relatively cohesive class of finance capitalists with much more concerted and coherent power over national policy than industrial capitalists, who were divided along enterprise, industry, and regional lines.

In the absence of a shift to corporate enterprise structure, British industrialists also had little incentive or ability to challenge the shop-floor control of trade union organizations. In the United States and Germany a critical factor in the development of high-throughput production was the ability of management to gain and maintain the right to manage the utilization of technology. In most of Britain's staple industries, by contrast, managers had lost much of this "right to manage," reducing their incentive to invest in costly mass production technologies on which they might not be able to achieve high enough throughputs to justify the capital outlays. During the first half of the twentieth century, British unionism was able to consolidate its positions of control at both the national and workplace levels, aided by the

---

[8] William Lazonick, "Industrial Organization and Technological Change: The Decline of the British Cotton Industry," *Business History Review*, 57 (Summer 1983), 195–236.

[9] Julia Wrigley, "Seeds of Decline: Technical Education and Industry in Britain," in *The Decline of the British Economy*.

[10] David Mowery, "British and American Industrial Research: A Comparison, 1900–1950," in *The Decline of the British Economy*.

growing strength of the Labour Party and the emergency conditions of two world wars.

Lacking the requisite degree of control over product and input markets, British managers confronted severe obstacles in adapting their enterprise structures to take advantage of new market opportunities. As a result, in the late nineteenth and early twentieth centuries firms continued for the most part to manufacture traditional products using traditional technologies.

How these firms structured production depended very much on the prospects for selling their output. Contrary to typical textbook theory, Britain's competitive firms did not as a rule assume that the market could absorb all the output they might produce at a given price. Indeed they produced few manufactures in anticipation of demand. Almost all production was to order, much of it for sale to merchants for distribution to far-flung international markets.

In the heyday of British worldwide economic dominance, these arrangements proved advantageous to British firms. Unlike many of their international competitors, who had access only to much more confining markets, Britain's international marketing structure meant that British firms could get enough orders of similar specifications to reap economies of long production runs, and had a large enough share in expanding markets to justify investment in (what were then) up-to-date and increasingly capital-intensive plant and equipment. But the tables were turned by the spread abroad of tariff barriers and indigenous industrialization. Because Britain had already industrialized, its domestic market for such staple commodities as textiles or steel rails had reached a point of at best moderate growth potential. Under these circumstances, British firms could not find at home a market that could match the dramatic rates of expansion of the foreign markets foreclosed to them. Indeed, given its dependence on international markets, British industry was severely constrained to keep its own domestic markets open to the products of foreign firms.

Taking advantage of their more secure and expansive domestic markets, foreign rivals, with more modern, capital-intensive technology, attained longer production runs and higher speeds of throughput than the British. By virtue of their reliance on the corporate form of organization—in particular on vertical integration of production with distribution and more concentrated market power—Britain's rivals were better able to rationalize the structure of orders and ensure themselves the market outlets required for mass production. From secure home bases these rivals also invaded market areas and product lines where the British should have been at no comparative disadvantage.

Forced to retreat from competition with mass production methods, British firms sought refuge in higher quality and more specialized product lines where traditional craftsmanship and organization could still command a competitive edge—in spinning higher counts of yarn and weaving finer cloth, making sheets and plates of open hearth steel, and building unique one-off ships. Unfortunately for the British, in a world of expanding markets, the specialized product of the day all too often turned out to be the mass production item of tomorrow. The arrival of mass production methods and the pace and timing of decline varied among the major staple industries, with British shipbuilding, for example, still holding a commanding competitive position as late as World War II. But all eventually met a similar fate.[11]

INSTITUTIONAL RIGIDITY

From the standpoint of the neoclassical model of competition, these developments would lead one to expect a British response to competitive pressures that would imitate the organizational and technological innovations introduced abroad. In fact, the British only adapted patchwork improvements to their existing organizational and productive structure. Facing increasingly insecure markets and lacking the market control requisite for modern mass production, the British failed to make the organizational renovations that could have allowed them to escape competitive decline.

With the massive contractions of British market shares that occurred in the 1920s and early 1930s, firms in the troubled staple industries alternated between scrambling for any markets they could get and proposals for elimination of excess capacity and concentration of productive structure. In a period of contraction the market mechanism was anything but an efficient allocation mechanism, in part because existing firms remained in operation as long as they could hope for some positive return over variable costs, their proprietors living, so to speak, off their capital. Coordinated attempts to eliminate excess capacity were confounded by numerous conflicts of interest between owner-proprietors, outside stockholders, management groups, customers, banks and other creditors, and local union organizations. In particular the involvement of the national banks in the attempts to rationalize industry was aimed more at salvaging their individual financial positions than at developing a coherent plan for industry revitalization. In light of the failure to achieve coordination the rationalization programs that were implemented in the interwar period were half-hearted and of limited effectiveness.

During the interwar period and beyond, the rigid work rules of British

---

[11] Edward Lorenz and Frank Wilkinson, "Shipbuilding and British Economic Decline. 1880–1965"; Bernard Elbaum, "British Steel Industry Structure and Performance before World War I"; William Lazonick, "The Decline of the British Cotton Industry"; Stephen Tolliday, "Industry, Finance, and the State: Steel and Rationalization Policy"; all in *The Decline of the British Economy.*

unions remained an impediment to structural reorganization. Entrenched systems of piece-rate payment often led to higher wage earnings in more productive establishments, deterring firms from scrapping old capacity and investing in new. Union rules also limited management's freedom to alter manning levels and workloads, which in mechanical, labor-intensive industries such as textiles had particularly adverse effects on the prospective benefits of new technology.[12] In general, management could be sure that the unions would attempt to exact a high price for cooperation with any plans for reorganization that would upset established work and pay arrangements. On the other hand, amidst industrial decline the strong union preference for saving jobs even at low wage levels was an additional conservative influence on a generally unenterprising managerial class.

Given this institutional structure, Britain's staple industries were unable to rationalize on the basis of the profit motive. They relied too much—not too little—on the market mechanism. To be sure, there were some highly successful enterprises such as Imperial Chemical Industries and Unilever that emerged in new industries during the interwar period.[13] But in terms of our perspective on capitalist development, these firms are the exceptions that prove the rule: success was ultimately based on control over product and input markets and the ability to transform internal managerial and production structures to maintain control. Furthermore, even the new industries were not immune to the wider institutional environment. The slow growth of demand in new product market areas hampered the emergence of large firms and created a need for consolidation of industrial structure. In chemicals, fabricated metals, and electrical machinery, newly amalgamated firms suffered from a dearth of appropriately trained managerial personnel and, initially, experienced serious difficulties in overcoming vested interests and in establishing effective coordination of their enterprises. In automobile manufacturing, competitive performance was undermined after World War II by a long-established management strategy of using labor-intensive techniques that helped breed control of shop-floor activities by highly sectionalized union organizations.[14]

THE IMPACT ON GROWTH

If difficult to quantify precisely, the overall impact of these institutional rigidities on British economic performance was undoubtedly

[12] Lorenz and Wilkinson, "Shipbuilding and British Economic Decline," and Lazonick, "The Decline of the British Cotton Industry."

[13] William Reader, *Imperial Chemical Industries: A History*, 2 vols. (Oxford, 1972); Charles Wilson, *The History of Unilever: A Study of Economic Growth and Social Change*, 2 vols. (London, 1954), and *Unilever 1945–1965: Challenge and Response in the Post-War Industrial Revolution* (London, 1965).

[14] Wayne Lewchuk, "The British Motor Vehicle Industry: The Roots of Decline," in *The Decline of the British Economy*.

considerable. Throughout the pre-World War I years, the staple industries remained economically preponderant. According to the 1907 Census of Production, the largest of these industries—coal, iron and steel (including non-electrical machinery and railway equipment), textiles, and shipbuilding—alone made up roughly 50 percent of total net domestic industrial production and 70 percent of British exports. During the long boom of the third quarter of the nineteenth century there was a rapid increase in British output per head that drew important impetus from growth and technological advance in the staple industries.[15] Subsequently, from 1873 to 1913 a marked slowdown in aggregate productivity growth occurred, with some evidence that growth was particularly sluggish from the late 1890s to World War I.

Detailed industry-level evidence is useful for assessing the accuracy of the aggregate data and the reasons for the prewar productivity slowdown. British cotton enterprises, for example, did not reorganize the vertical structure of production in order to adopt more advanced technologies. Instead they chose to compete on the basis of traditional organization and techniques by cutting raw material costs and intensifying workloads.[16] The resultant cost-savings, augmented by the benefits of well-developed external economies, enabled the cotton industry to expand its output and exports despite stagnating labor productivity in the 15 years or so before World War I. In the British steel industry there was significant ongoing productivity advance in the newer sectors of open hearth steelmaking. Bessemer practice, however, was comparatively stagnant after 1890 as firms were deterred from investing in new, large-scale facilities by a sluggish domestic market, overseas protection, an increasing threat from foreign imports, and fragmented industrial structure.[17]

British growth in output per head not only slowed in the last quarter of the nineteenth century, but also began to lag relative to latter-day industrializing economies that were developing the institutional bases for corporate capitalism. British growth rates first fell behind those of other countries in the 1870s and 1880s. Serious losses in international competition were first sustained between 1899 and 1913 and were interlinked with the failure of British industry to match the productivity advances achieved abroad by fully availing itself of the benefits of mass production methods. With the exception of wartime intervals, the gap in relative productivity growth performance between Britain and most of its competitors has remained substantial ever since.

During the interwar period the competitive weaknesses of the staple

---

[15] R. C. O. Matthews, C. H. Feinstein, and J. C. Odling-Smee, *British Economic Growth, 1856–1973* (Stanford, 1982), p. 26.

[16] William Lazonick and William Mass, "The Performance of the British Cotton Industry, 1870–1913," *Research in Economic History*, 9 (Spring 1984).

[17] Elbaum, "British Steel Industry Structure and Performance."

industries became evident, while the productivity performance of the British economy as a whole remained poor by international standards. There remains, however, considerable controversy over the connection between the performance of the staple industries and that of the aggregate economy. According to one influential perspective, the weak performance of the interwar economy was largely due to the relative lack of mobility of resources from the "old" to the "new" industries.[18] This argument, however, is open to criticism on several grounds. It assumes that the old industries imposed effective supply constraints on the growth of the new—a rather dubious proposition given the high unemployment levels, ongoing capital export, and the housing boom that characterized the interwar period. If there were supply constraints on the growth of the new industries it was because of the failure of financial and educational institutions to infuse industry with sufficient long-term venture capital and the types of personnel required.

This argument also implies that the basic problem of the British economy was one of structural adjustment out of industries in which comparative advantage had been lost and possibilities for technical advance had for the most part been exhausted. Yet there is little evidence that shifts in comparative advantage were the root of the competitive problems of Britain's staple industries. Some international competitors in these industries, facing prices for labor and resources greater than or equal to the British, were nonetheless more successful because they adopted major technical advances. Recent evidence also indicates that interwar productivity gains in Britain's staple industries were comparable to those in the new industries (although much of the measured gains in productivity reflect the closure of obsolescent capacity).

The staple industries contributed significantly to Britain's relatively poor interwar growth performance mainly because they still bulked large in the economy and lagged behind seriously in international standards of technological and managerial practice. In 1924 staple manufacturing industries still accounted for 45 percent of all manufacturing net output. By 1935 this figure had fallen to 35 percent but remained at roughly that proportion into the late 1940s.[19] With persistent excess capacity in the staple industries, firms that had long ago written off their plant and equipment always stood ready to "ruin the market" for firms that might otherwise have invested in the modernization of plant and equipment and enterprise structure. Divided by competition, the firms of Britain's staple industries were unable on their own to rationalize capacity.

[18] Derek H. Aldcroft and H. W. Richardson, *The British Economy, 1870–1939* (London, 1969).
[19] G. N. von Tunzelmann, "Structural Change and Leading Sectors in British Manufacturing, 1907–1968," in *Economics in the Long View*, ed. Charles P. Kindleberger and Guido di Tella (New York, 1982), vol. 3, pp. 28–30.

THE BARELY VISIBLE HAND

What British industry in general required was the visible hand of coordinated control, not the invisible hand of the self-regulating market. Given the absence of leadership from within private industry, increasing pressure fell upon the state to try to fill the gap. Even before World War I, calls were made for greater state intervention. By the interwar period the British state had assumed a distinctly more prominent role in industrial affairs, macroeconomic regulation, and provision of social and welfare services.[20]

With further growth of state intervention after World War II—extending to nationalization of industry and aggregate demand management—critics have pointed accusing fingers at the government for failing to reverse, and even for causing, relative economic decline. At various times and from various quarters the state has been blamed for undermining private-sector incentives and the natural regenerative processes of the free market economy, for absorbing resources that would have been employed more productively in manufacturing, or for failing to provide British industry with a needed environment of macroeconomic stability and a competitively valued exchange rate.

In historical perspective, however, state activism must be absolved from bearing primary responsibility for Britain's relatively poor economic performance. In the late nineteenth century, at the outset of relative decline, the most singular features of the British state were its small size and laissez-faire policies. Even in the post-World War II period, British levels of government taxes, expenditures, and employment were not particularly high by European standards. Indeed, a distinctive feature of British state policy throughout recent history has been its reluctance to break from laissez-faire traditions. It is only in the second instance that state policy is implicated in British decline, by virtue of its failure to intervene in the economy more decisively in order to take corrective measures. The consequences of this failure of state policy first became evident in the interwar period.[21]

THE LIMITS OF INTERWAR INTERVENTION

The Irrationalities of Rationalization Policy

State intervention between the wars included programs aimed at rationalizing the depressed staple industries in order to rid them of excess capacity and facilitate modernization. The problem of excess capacity had been exacerbated by the vast and imprudent expansion of

---

[20] Charles Feinstein, ed., *The Managed Economy* (Oxford, 1983).

[21] Peter Hall, "The State and Economic Decline in Britain," in *The Decline of the British Economy*.

investment and overdraft borrowing during the short but frenetic boom of 1920/21. The prolonged state of depressed trade that followed in the 1920s placed the banks' loans in serious jeopardy. At that time the Labour government was also considering direct intervention as a means of reorganizing the failing industries and alleviating industrial depression. This combination of circumstances prompted the Bank of England to step in.

For the Bank, rationalization was an economically viable and politically desirable alternative to more far-reaching forms of government intervention that threatened to go as far as nationalization and "encroaching socialism." Bank of England Governor Montagu Norman conceived of intervention as limited, temporary, and exceptional. The Bank's approach was highly consensual and "quasi-corporatist." Firms were encouraged to form trade associations and develop their own plans for industry rationalization. Within the trade associations, firms were authorized to negotiate common pricing policies, mergers, and production quotas. Even then individual firms were reluctant to have the Bank of England intervene, and it was only the stick of bankruptcy and the carrot of support for tariff protection that enabled it to do so.[22]

When the Bank intervened more directly, it was as a merger promoter rather than as an investment bank. Where the market did not respond, the Bank was unwilling to put up its own funds. With the Bank and Treasury allied in keeping a tight hold on the public purse strings, the public funds devoted to backing rationalization schemes were negligible. Yet the Bank found that its efforts at voluntary persuasion had little influence over the allocation of market sources of finance.[23]

As for the government, its interwar industrial policies were confined largely to monitoring industrial affairs through the Import Duties Advisory Committee, established under the 1932 tariff legislation, and to legislative schemes aimed at reducing excess capacity in industries such as textiles. Like the Bank of England, the Advisory Committee pursued influence through conciliation and suasion, seeking no powers of centralized control over industry. Lacking the requisite authority to shape industrial development, the committee found itself overseeing a process of industrial quasi-cartellization that ensured profits for weak and strong firms alike. Government legislation generally responded to the wishes of industry trade associations with similar results.

Public attempts at rationalization left British industry with the worst aspects of both competitive and monopolistic worlds. Productive structure remained highly fragmented and inefficient, while quasi-cartellization and tariff barriers (or imperial preference) protected existing producers from competitive pressure. Rather than achieving its objec-

[22] Best and Humphries, "The City and the Decline of British Industry"; Lazonick, "The Decline of the British Cotton Industry"; Tolliday, "Industry, Finance, and the State."
[23] Tolliday, "Industry, Finance, and the State."

tive of promoting industry rationalization, interwar policy inadvertently reinforced preexisting institutional rigidities.

The Underdevelopment of Industrial Research

State policy initiatives in the area of research and development originated at the onset of World War I with concern over the inability of British industry to supply technologically sophisticated materials of strategic military importance. Major policy initiatives included the establishment of a state-owned corporation (British Dyestuffs) and state-subsidized industrial research associations for the promotion of cooperative research and development by firms in the private sector. British Dyestuffs, however, was handicapped by a lack of trained chemists in top management positions and a reliance on chairs in universities for research efforts.

Government promotion of industrial research associations reflected a concern that few firms in Britain were large enough to undertake their own in-house research and development programs. As many as 24 Research Associations were established in industries ranging from woolen textiles to laundering. But firms often lacked the in-house technical expertise required to evaluate and employ the results of extramural research. As a result, Research Associations failed to gather the anticipated financial support from the private sector, and their impact on innovative performance was modest. Government-sponsored cooperative research proved to be an inadequate replacement for the in-house research capabilities of modern corporations.[24]

The Ruin of the Regions

Industrial decline in the interwar period created severe problems of regional unemployment and decaying infrastructure because of the high degree of local concentration of the staple industries. Interwar regional policies were, however, a limited and ad hoc response to diverse political pressures for regional aid, rather than a coherent attempt to deal with the social costs and benefits of relocation of economic activity. The most consistent element in regional policy was the reluctance of the government to become directly involved in industrial development. Instead, the state sought to alleviate regional disparities by policies directed towards improving the operation of labor and capital markets.

The effectiveness of these policies was constrained by macroeconomic conditions, the limited size of the programs, and the underlying assumption that facilitating the operation of market mechanisms would suffice to combat regional problems. Initially, the government promoted labor transference by providing assistance for individual workers or

[24] Mowery, "British and American Industrial Research."

households to move to more prosperous regions. But the unemployed workers in the depressed regions were mainly adult males, who were heavily unionized, whereas many of the expanding industries sought primarily new entrants to the labor force, particularly women and juveniles.

By 1937 the emphasis had shifted to moving jobs to unemployed workers by providing businesses with special sources of finance and subsidized factory rentals. Provision of capital to firms in the depressed areas, however, could not overcome the limits on investment demand posed by depressed regional markets. Nor could it overcome the inability of the single-industry family firms that predominated in interwar Britain to manage diversified industrial and regional operations. Expanding industries, which had already begun to develop in the South prior to the stagnation of the 1920s, continued to grow in these more prosperous areas during the interwar period.[25]

The Protection of the Pound

Following the lead of Keynes, a long line of economists have argued that interwar macroeconomic policies had seriously adverse effects on the British economy. A contrast is often drawn between the industrial depression of the 1920s, when restrictive policies preceded the 1925 resumption of the gold standard at the prewar parity, and the relatively strong performance of the economy in the 1930s, when devaluation and protectionism were forced upon the government. Yet if the deflationary impact of the macroeconomic policies of the 1920s seems beyond dispute, there has been a lively debate about its significance for the trend in growth of output per head. Detailed examination of the staple industries, which were the most seriously affected by the 1920s depression, indicates that slack domestic demand, intensified international competitive pressure, and high interest rates *exacerbated* rather than caused problems of excess capacity, shrinking profit margins, and a heavy debt burden. The problems of the staple industries were structural and long-term in character, and if dramatized during the low waters of recession, were also an increasingly evident undertow during the high tides of prosperity before and after the interwar period.

THE LEGACY OF HISTORY

The British economy of the post-World War II period inherited a legacy of major industries too troubled to survive the renewed onslaught of international competition that began in the 1950s. As competitive pressure mounted, the state began to nationalize industries such as coal,

---

[25] Carol Heim, "Regional Development and National Decline: The Evolution of Regional Policy in Interwar Britain," in *The Decline of the British Economy*.

steel, and automobiles that were deemed of strategic importance to the nation, and (with the exception of steel in 1951) that were in imminent danger of collapse. But nationalization, however necessary, was by no means a sufficient response to Britain's long-run economic decline. Public ownership overcame the problem of horizontally fragmented private ownership, but not inherited problems of enterprise productive structure, managerial organization, and union job control. Nationalized enterprises still had to confront these problems while attempting to overcome the technological leads already established by competitors.

Although the British government was called upon willy-nilly to play an increased role in industrial affairs, the basic theoretical and ideological framework guiding public policy has remained that of the self-regulating market economy. The rise of Keynesianism has led to widespread acceptance of interventionist fiscal and monetary policies, but for the most part has left unchallenged the neoclassical belief in the inherent dynamism of unfettered market competition.

The monetarist policies of the Thatcher government have taken the neoclassical perspective to its extreme. Invoking laissez faire ideology, Thatcher has attacked the power of the unions and sought revival through the severity of market discipline. But the supposition that there are forces latent in Britain's "free market" economy that will return the nation to prosperity finds little confirmation in historical experience. The only foundation for the free-market perspective appears to be the tradition of orthodox economic theory itself.

There is considerable irony in the neoclassical focus on free market competition as the engine of economic dynamism. The focus derives from the fundamental assumption of neoclassical theory that firms are subordinate to markets. History suggests, however, that successful development in the twentieth century has been achieved by markets being made subordinate to firms. The main thrust of the perspective presented here is that the British economy failed to make a successful transition to corporate capitalism in the twentieth century precisely because of the very highly developed market organization of the economy that had evolved when it was the first and foremost industrial nation.

By now, Britain's relative economic decline has persisted through enough ups and downs in the business cycle to indicate that its roots lie deeper than inappropriate macroeconomic policies. If contemporary economic discussion nonetheless is usually preoccupied with obtaining the right monetary and fiscal policies, it is because there has been comparatively little criticism of the microfoundations of neoclassical theory and related versions of laissez faire ideology. Despite the prominence of mass production methods in corporate economies, conventional economic theory has failed to analyze the associated developmental process of productivity growth and technological change.

If existing institutional arrangements seriously constrained the actions of individual British industrialists and rendered impotent intervention by the state, the example of late-developing nations suggests that a purposive national program can enjoy considerable success in adapting institutions to meet growth objectives. The task for political economy is to identify those elements of the prevailing institutional structure that will promote and those that will hinder alternative strategies of socioeconomic development. The argument presented here contends that planning at the levels of the enterprise, financial institutions, and the state has become increasingly important for international competitiveness and economic growth, even within the so-called market economies. To elaborate and modify this perspective will require historical studies of the interaction of planning and market forces in economic activity and the resultant impact on performance. Thus far we have only begun to research this perspective, and to test the various hypotheses generated by it. But we view the synthesis presented here, as well as the research upon which it is based, as important foundations for understanding modern economic development.

[2]

FACTOR COSTS AND THE DIFFUSION OF RING SPINNING IN BRITAIN PRIOR TO WORLD WAR I*

WILLIAM LAZONICK

A key contribution to the attempt by "new" economic historians to absolve the British economy of the charge of technological conservatism in the late nineteenth century is Lars Sandberg's analysis of the choice of technique between ring spinning and mule spinning. In this article I demonstrate that Sandberg's analysis has serious problems and that a careful reexamination of the rings versus mules question is in order. While I point out some of the methodological problems of the neoclassical approach to choice of technique, the major focus of this paper is on the empirical shortcomings of Sandberg's analysis. My primary empirical conclusions are that the extent of the diffusion of ring spinning prior to World War I was much less than Sandberg's analysis would indicate and that it was the vertically specialized structure of the industry which imposed the major factor-cost constraint on its more rapid introduction.

I. INTRODUCTION

The cotton industry was central to both Britain's rise to world economic supremacy in the nineteenth century and its decline to a secondary industrial power in the twentieth century. In the decades before World War II, it was unable to meet the economic competition of Japan and India and in the decades after, that of many West European countries and the U. S. A. as the cotton industry became capital-intensive [Vitkovitch, 1955; OECD, 1965]. Right into the 1960s, the British cotton industry continued to rely on technologies that other cotton industries, and particularly that of the U. S. A., had long since discarded [Robson, 1957, 355–56]. Britain retained the mule for the spinning of yarn and the power-loom for the weaving of cloth, both of these machines having been fundamentally developed by the mid-nineteenth century, while other industries moved almost entirely to the ring-frame for spinning and automatic loom for weaving. In 1954, with 59 percent of its spindles still on mules, Britain possessed

* Stephen Marglin, Thomas Brush, Lou Ferleger, and William Mass contributed helpful comments on earlier drafts of this paper. Donald McCloskey made some useful suggestions on related issues; Thomas Brush and Gary Mathias provided valuable research assistance; and Laurence Gross of the Merrimack Valley Textile Museum provided some important information. In addition, Lars Sandberg generously responded to a number of queries concerning the calculations underlying his own work on the issues with which this paper deals. Two anonymous referees provided very useful editorial suggestions.

This paper is based upon research supported by the National Science Foundation under Grant No. SOC 78-25671, and by a grant-in-aid from the Merrimack Valley Textile Museum.

The Quarterly Journal of Economics, February 1981   0033-5533/81/0096-0089$02.10

84 percent of all mule spindles, but less than 10 percent of all ring spindles, in world operation. In 1955, when 88 percent of its looms were non-automatic, Britain possessed 12 percent of the power-looms but only 4 percent of the automatic looms in world operation. By the 1950s, both the mule and the power-loom had vanished completely from the U. S. cotton industry [Robson, 1957, pp. 355–56].

The origins of Britain's technological lag can be located clearly in the three decades prior to World War I. The ring-frame, which had been invented in 1828, had been improved greatly in the 1870s and 1880s; and by 1913, 87 percent of all spindles in the United States, but only 19 percent in Britain were rings [Lazonick, 1980a, pp. 25–26]. The automatic (also known as the Northrop or Draper) loom had been invented in 1894; and by 1914 automatics constituted 40 percent of all looms in the United States as compared with between 1 percent and 2 percent in Britain [Mass, 1980].

The lag in the introduction of ring spinning into the cotton industry in Britain compared with the United States prior to World War I is now a well-known fact, among economic historians at least, largely due to an article that appeared in this *Journal* just over a decade ago [Sandberg, 1969]. As part of the development of the "new" economic history, Lars Sandberg performed a direct quantitative test of the economic rationality of British cotton spinning managers in their choice of spinning technique between the two spinning alternatives, the ring-frame and the mule. The article was subsequently included in two collections of essays on economic history, and, in somewhat expanded form but with empirical contents unchanged, in Sandberg's book, *Lancashire in Decline* [1974]. Moreover, this article became Sandberg's contribution to the attempt by a group of the "new" economic historians to refute the hypothesis that entrepreneurial failure was a prime determinant of Britain's long-run relative decline as an economic power in the late nineteenth and early twentieth centuries [McCloskey and Sandberg, 1971; McCloskey, 1971; and Harley, 1974].

Elsewhere I have criticized the approach of these economic historians to the question of entrepreneurial failure on the grounds that the neoclassical "optimization subject to given constraints" methodology imposes a much too narrow definition on the role of management in running the enterprise, failing to recognize that managers from time to time (as innovating entrepreneurs) overcome "given" constraints and on a more regular basis (as supervisors of the enterprise) alter "given" constraints. [Lazonick, 1980a, 1980b]. Indeed, the neoclassical approach is inadequate to deal with issues of economic development in general.[1] The central issues of economic development require explanations of how the constraints facing those who manage the processes of production and distribution are determined in the first place and how, to what extent, and by whom these constraints can be changed. Managers as individuals may very well be optimizing subject to the constraints that they face, that is, acting rationally in the neoclassical sense, while their own regional or national industry loses out to competing regional or national industries due to the existence of different institutional structures that determine different sets of constraints, including unit factor-costs, for the various competitors. As Schumpeter demonstrated long ago, one cannot analyze the *development* of an economy or industry simply by analyzing decision-making by managers who take constraints as given, however optimal their choices may be [Schumpeter, 1934 and 1939]. Rather one needs to analyze the development of the institutional structures that largely determine interregional and international differences in, among other things, factor prices and productivity as well as the role of interested individuals and groups, including managers, in accepting, modifying, or drastically altering these constraints over time.

Nevertheless, within the constraints of its own theoretical vision, the neoclassical approach to the analysis of managerial activity does have a role to play. First, by taking factor and product prices as well as the quality of available inputs, and market opportunities, as given, it permits a systematic investigation of the absolute and relative magnitudes of the constraints involved in choosing between two or more readily accessible alternatives. Thus, in analyzing the issue of choice of technique, for example, we can derive quantitative indicators of what factor-cost constraints would have to be changed in order to make it rational (in the neoclassical sense) to introduce a particular technology, such as the ring-frame, at a faster pace. The analysis of how and why the constraints do or do not change over time, however, requires a much broader theoretical framework.

Second, by facilitating an evaluation of the economic costs and benefits of those choices actually made compared with those choices rejected, the neoclassical approach provides an important indicator as to whether other, as yet unidentified, "extra-economic" factors such as union pressure, lack of relevant knowledge, sentimental attachment to an old technology (such as the mule), etc. might be influencing

1. Notwithstanding the, in my view unsuccessful, attempts by Douglass North to transform neoclassical theory into a grand theory of institutional change. See North and Thomas [1973] and North [1978]. For a critique of neoclassical "institutional" economics, see Field [1979].

managerial decisions. Such a finding would, or at least should, then direct us back to the broader investigation of institutional change if the relevant "extra-economic" factors are to be identified and their quantitative impact assessed.

While Sandberg's analysis of the rings versus mules question does not (despite his own claims) deal with the larger issues of "entrepreneurial failure" or economic development in general, it does represent, within the theoretical limits of the neoclassical approach, an important empirical attempt to assess the relative costs and benefits of two alternative, readily available, technologies. Unfortunately, the empirical content of Sandberg's effort is faulty, leaving us with erroneous notions of investment in rings and mules in Britain prior to World War I as well as the magnitudes of the relative factor costs that were dictating rational choices. In light of these errors, the purposes of this paper are, first, to correct the historical record of investment in ring spinning and the relative factor costs constraining its introduction in Lancashire prior to World War I and, second, in so doing, to retest Sandberg's hypothesis of economic rationality in the choice of technique.

First, I shall summarize Sandberg's evidence and conclusions. Then while pointing out key errors in his estimates of the amount of investment in rings and mules and the relative factor costs involved in the choice of technique, I shall develop a new set of estimates. Finally, I shall discuss some of the implications of my estimates for understanding the economic history of the Lancashire cotton industry.

II. The Choice of Technique

Sandberg's argument for the economic rationality of British cotton-spinning managers in their choice between rings and mules can be summarized as follows. He estimates that the number of "mule equivalent spindles" (m.e.s) spinning yarn under the count of 40 in 1907 was 35 percent of all m.e.s. in Britain.[2] Then, assuming a spindle replacement rate of 2.5 percent per year, he argues that the estimated increase of 2.8 million m.e.s. on ring-frames between 1907 and 1913 was more than sufficient to replace the number of mule spindles that

2. The count of yarn is a measure of the fineness of the yarn, being the number of 840 yarn lengths (hanks) of yarn in one pound weight. Hence the finer the yarn, the higher the count. A "mule equivalent spindle" represents the production equivalent of one mule spindle, the production of one ring spindle prior to World War I being equivalent to 1.3 to 1.7 times the production of a mule spindle depending on the count being spun (see Appendix 1).

wore out during the period. From these calculations and a minimal amount of corroborative evidence, Sandberg's conclusions on what he calls "observed investment behavior" are that most spindles installed for counts up to 40 were rings and that virtually no rings were installed at counts above the low 40s [Sandberg, 1969, pp. 28–29].

He then goes on to argue that a comparison of factor costs per pound of yarn on rings and mules at various counts supports the hypothesis that this investment behavior was rational. His method is to estimate the labor, capital, power, and shipping cost differentials per pound between ring yarn and mule yarn at the count of 40, and then, using 40 yarn as a benchmark, to estimate changes (if any) in . this differential on higher counts. Then against these "other"-cost differentials he weighs the cotton-cost savings per pound of mule yarn over ring yarn for various counts. If "other"-cost savings are greater than cotton-cost savings, it is economically rational to introduce rings and, when the reverse is the case, mules [1969, pp. 29–41].[3]

The major advantage of rings over mules, according to Sandberg, is that they save on unit labor costs. Rings used relatively low-paid female labor and mules used relatively high-paid male labor. He estimates that in Britain the weekly labor cost on ring-frames spinning 40 yarn was about $0.50 per hundred m.e.s., while for mule-spinning it was about $1.65 per hundred m.e.s., so that per pound of 40 yarn the labor cost of ring yarn was about $0.016 lower than that of mule yarn. Then, using 1949 labor productivity figures on rings and mules, he estimates this cost differential for every tenth count from 50 to 120.

Sandberg argues that "mule and ring spinning appear to have been of almost exactly the same capital intensity per unit of output in the production of yarns of a count around 40" [1969, p. 30], and he uses this zero capital-cost differential per pound on higher counts. In his article and book, the estimates of capital-cost and labor-cost differentials per pound are not presented separately (see Table I, column 2), but it is clear that the labor-cost differential dominates the combined estimate on all counts.[4]

Sandberg argues that fuel and lubricant (i.e., power) costs per pound of 40 yarn appear to be almost the same on rings and mules,

3. Sandberg also claims to be analyzing the issue of choice of technique in the U. S. cotton industry despite the fact that virtually all his productivity data refer to British conditions. As I have shown elsewhere, such a procedure leads not only to erroneous quantitative factor-cost estimates for the United States but also to the neglect of key institutional differences between the United States and Britain that result in different unit factor-costs for the same count of yarn [Lazonick, 1980a, pp. 31–33].
4. Personal communication from Lars Sandberg.

TABLE I

SANDBERG'S COST-SAVINGS PER POUND OF RING YARN OVER MULE YARN

(EXCLUDING COTTON) NOS. 40–120

(1) Count	(2) Labor & capital	(3) Warp total	(4) Weft total
40	$0.016	$0.015	$0.012
50	.017	.016	.013
60	.018	.017	.014
70	.018	.017	.014
80	.018	.017	.014
90	.016	.015	.012
100	.015	.014	.011
110	.012	.011	.008
120	.008	.007	.004

Source. Sandberg [1969, pp. 41–42].

and he ultimately assigns a power-cost savings of $0.001 for mules over rings on all counts of warp and weft yarn. However, the next cost item—transportation costs—is quite significant in determining the cost differential of all counts of *weft* yarn spun on rings and mules. Mule yarn was wound into packages on the bare spindle or on lightweight paper tubes while ring yarn had to be wound into packages on wooden bobbins that were costly to transport. Since spinning and weaving in Lancashire were carried out largely in separate firms and in distinct areas, and since about 13 percent of Lancashire yarn was exported [Robson, 1957, p. 345], the possibility of considerable differences in transportation cost per unit of output had to be taken into account in choosing between rings and mules. Twist (warp) yarn from either machine had to be rewound in any case in preparation for warping, and hence the fact that ring twist was spun on bobbins was inconsequential, provided that the ring spinning mill did its own warping. Weft yarn, however, was used in the weaving process in the form of the package into which it had been spun, and therefore the extra cost of transporting the ring bobbin was a factor to be considered in choosing between rings and mules. Sandberg's estimate is that the extra cost per pound of shipping ring weft as opposed to mule weft in Lancashire was $0.003.

Taking all these "other"-cost factors into account yields Sandberg's results in Table I against which must be weighed the cotton-cost savings per pound of mule warp and mule weft yarn over ring warp and ring weft yarn, respectively. The fact that on the mule

the spinning and winding of the yarn were done in two separate motions, whereas on the ring-frame they were done simultaneously meant
the former subjected the cotton to less strain, and hence for any given
count, the mule could use cotton inferior (shorter staple and less free
of impurities) to what the ring-frame could use. Also, warp yarn
produced by either machine had to be stronger than weft yarn, and
therefore required superior cotton for any given count. Drawing on
British data on cotton staple requirements as a function of counts for
mule twist, mule weft, and ring twist, as well as prices per pound of
certain staple lengths, Sandberg comes to the following tentative
conclusions:

First, the differential in cotton costs between rings and mules for warp yarn probably
starts to appear at a count around 28 and then increases to a peak somewhat below three
cents per pound, probably in the vicinity of 45 or 50. In all probability, the difference
reaches two cents in the low 40s. Secondly, the cost differential does not drop significantly below two cents again, at least not [up to the low 80s]. As for weft, the cost differential starts around a count of 35 and rises to more than two cents in the 50s. It
probably reaches two cents in the upper 40s. The differential then stays at least as high
as one and one-half cents for higher counts [1969, p. 38].

Weighing the cotton-cost savings per pound of mule yarn against
the "other"-cost savings per pound of ring yarn for the same counts,
Sandberg concludes that it was rational for British spinners to prefer
rings "for warp production up to a count perhaps a little below 40,
while for weft they were probably to be preferred even for counts in
the low 40s" [1969, p. 42]. His reasoning is that at the low 40s twist and
upper 40s weft a gradually increasing cotton-cost savings of mule yarn
reaches $0.02 and, therefore, must have surpassed a gradually in-
creasing "other"-cost savings of ring yarn in the vicinity of the high
30s and low 40s, respectively. "When these results are compared with
the actual behavior of British manufacturers," Sandberg concludes,
"they appear to have behaved in a rational manner" [1969, p. 43].

The problem with this analysis is that both Sandberg's depiction
of investment behavior in pre-World War I British spinning and his
analysis of relative costs on rings and mules are inaccurate. First, let
us consider what in his book he calls "actual observed investment
behavior" [1974, p. 26]. His contentions—crucial to his overall argument—that most new sub-40 spindles installed in Lancashire during
the period 1907–1913 were rings and that virtually all new rings spun
sub-40 counts rest on two rather weak pieces of evidence: (1) his calculation that the aggregate increase in mule equivalent ring spindles
between 1907 and 1913 was at least enough to replace the number of

sub-40 mule spindles that had to be retired during this period; and (2) the fact that on the Universal Wage List for Ring Spinning adopted in Lancashire in 1912 "accommodation is made for counts up to and including 43, but then stops abruptly" [Sandberg, 1969, pp. 28–29].[5]

The first piece of evidence tells us very little about investment behavior, and in particular the circumstances under which rings were being installed. Given the growth of the industry over the period, it is conceivable that all the rings were going into new mills, while new mules were replacing old mules even on sub-40 counts. Between 1907 and 1913, the number of ring spindles increased by 3.1 million (4.1 million m.e.s.) and the number of mule spindles by 4.2 million.[6] The fact is that a large proportion (perhaps as much as one-half) of this increase in ring spindles consisted of ring-frames installed in new mills or extensions of old mills, and hence did not replace retired mules. A compilation of data from the *Cotton Factory Times* for the years 1907 through 1912 reveals just over one million ring spindles (i.e., over 1.3 million m.e.s.) introduced into old mill extensions and new mills. This figure excludes many items that read, e.g., "new mill, 60,000 spindles" with no indication whether rings or mules were involved. A detailed study of investment in mule and ring spindles between 1896 and 1914 in the Oldham district (potentially ideal breeding ground for the ring-frame with its "standard" count of 32 and its large limited liability companies) shows that the increase in the number of ring spindles was just over 1.4 million (rising from 350,000 in 1896 to over 800,000 in 1905 to 1.8 million in 1914) of which 67 percent were installed in new mills and 33 percent either replaced old mules *or* added to existing capacity. Over the same period the number of mule spindles in the Oldham district increased by 6.4 million from 10.7 million in 1896 to 17.1 million in 1914. Over 6.5 million mule spindles were installed in new mills during this period which means that the number of mule spindles replaced by ring spindles was 100,000 plus the

5. In fact, Sandberg's statement is misleading, since the list provides weekly wages per hundred spindles for nine ranges of counts from "8 to 9" to "43 and upwards." See Jewkes and Gray [1935, p. 121].

6. These estimates differ substantially from those presented by Sandberg [1969, p. 29], primarily because the 1913 spindle totals, taken from Robson [1957, p. 355], are clearly understated when compared with the spindle totals reported by Worrall [1913, p. 358]. The Worrall data were adjusted to remove doubling spindles and to reflect spindle capacity in Great Britain rather than just in Lancashire. On the other hand, spindle estimates derived from Worrrall's 1907 figures are virtually identical to the estimates that Sandberg derived from the 1907 Census of Production [Great Britain, 1912a, pp. 293–94]. Compared to Sandberg's estimate, my estimates yield an additional increase of 2.7 million mule spindles and 1.0 million ring spindles between 1907 and 1913.

equivalent of an unknown number of mule spindles installed in extensions of old mills [Jones, 1959]. Of considerably less importance is the probability that about 0.2 million ring spindles were being put into space occupied by the like number of throstle spindles (an antiquated ancestor of the ring spindle) that existed in 1907.

It should also be noted that Sandberg underestimates the number of sub-40 mule spindles that, on the assumption of a 2.5 percent annual replacement rate, would have been scrapped in the period 1907 to 1913. Using 1924 data on the distribution of yarn output over four broad ranges of counts, Sandberg estimates that in 1907, 35 percent of all m.e.s. in Britain are spinning sub-40 counts. This figure is much too low, and hence leads us to underestimate the actual importance of sub-40 counts in the Lancashire cotton spinning industry prior to World War I. A much more direct estimate of the proportion of sub-40 spindles in Lancashire in 1907 can be derived from a Board of Trade report in 1906, which contains data on the different ranges of counts spun by about 45 percent of all mule spinners in the United Kingdom. The returns show 5,058 mule spinners on counts below 40, 4,017 on counts from 40 to 80, and 1,282 on counts above 80 [Great Britain, 1909, pp. 59–61]. If we assume that in all ranges spinners on average operated the same number of spindles, then the proportion of sub-40 spindles is 48.8 percent. However, since the spindles per mule spinner in the main fine spinning area of Bolton (which contained 32 percent of all 40-plus mule spinners enumerated) are known to have been about 10 percent less than the spindles per mule spinner in the main coarse spinning of Oldham (which contained 39 percent of all sub-40 mule spinners enumerated), the proportion of sub-40 spindles was undoubtedly somewhat higher than 49 percent [Jewkes and Gray, 1935, p. 205].[7]

The second piece of evidence, derived from the Ring Spinning List, certainly would support the factually correct proposition that *insofar as rings were used* in Britain, they were used primarily on sub-40 counts. But it certainly tells us nothing about the extent to which rings actually were used on these counts. The Jones [1959] study of Oldham reveals that of the ring spindles installed in new mills, about 60 percent were installed in mills spinning *wholly* 44 yarns and

7. Sandberg's 1924 data source can be reconciled with my estimate that at least 50 percent of all 1907 m.e.s. were sub-40 spindles if we recognize that there was a marked shift to finer counts between 1907 and 1924, and that the "American" section of the industry (that is, firms using American cotton and spinning sub-50 counts) was, due to the loss of the Indian and Chinese markets, operating inefficiently relative to the "Egyptian" section (counts of 50 and over) in 1924, whereas such was not the case in 1907. See Daniels and Jewkes [1928].

under, and probably 85–90 percent of the entire increase in ring spindles in old and new mills were spinning these counts. However, some rings were used for spinning up to 80, and indeed one new fine spinning mill used its 90,768 mule spindles to spin 70 to 120 weft and its 33,000 ring spindles to spin 50 to 80 twist. On the other hand, one-third of the mule spindles installed in new mills were spinning wholly 44 yarns and under, amounting to roughly three times the number of ring m.e.s. that were installed in new mills spinning these counts, and another 16 percent of the mule spindles installed in new mills were spinning 12 to 54 yarns. In all, almost 50 percent of mule spindles installed in new mills were for spinning 44 yarns and under, and these represented 70–75 percent of all m.e.s., ring and mule, which were installed in new mills to spin sub-45 yarns between 1896 and 1914.

Hence, contrary to Sandberg, investment in rings for these counts was by no means the rule, at least not in Oldham, which not only specialized in spinning those counts (20 to 50) in which, as we shall see, rings attained their peak in economic feasibility, but which also was by far the largest spinning center in Lancashire and indeed in the world. Three percent of all Oldham's spindles were on ring-frames in 1896, 6 percent in 1905, and 9 percent in 1914. By way of contrast, Fall River, Massachusetts, which spun the same range of counts as Oldham and which was the primary mule spinning center in the United States in the last half of the nineteenth century, had about 25 percent of its spindles on rings in 1880, 61 percent in 1894, 81 percent in 1904, and 91 percent in 1913 [Lazonick, 1980a, p. 26].

The fact is that prior to World War I ring-frames were rarely used for spinning weft yarns in non-integrated spinning mills (i.e., those that did not also weave) in Lancashire; new mules typically replaced old mules for the spinning of lower as well as higher counts of weft. And non-integrated mills accounted for over 75 percent of all spindles in the Lancashire industry [Jewkes and Jewkes, 1966, p. 118; Copeland, 1912, p. 321]. Ring spindles were installed disproportionately in integrated mills, 46 percent of all ring spindles being in these mills in 1913. Moreover, a detailed examination of the types of spinning equipment in Lancashire cotton mills in 1913 reveals only 2,100 ring spindles that can positively be identified as spinning weft in the non-integrated mills [Worrall, 1913].

What then is an accurate characterization of aggregate investment in rings and mules in this period? The evidence presented earlier suggests that about 85 percent of ring spindles existing in 1907 and installed over the next six years were spinning sub-40 counts. Assuming that 50 percent of all m.e.s. in 1907 were sub-40 and that the mule depreciation rate was 2.5 percent per year, then about 2.7 million mule spindles would have been scrapped over the six-year period. The increase of sub-40 ring m.e.s. would have been 3.5 million of which about 1.6 million would have gone into new mills, or extensions, or have been used to replace throstles, leaving 1.9 million sub-40 ring m.e.s. to replace an equal number of sub-40 mule spindles. Therefore, 0.8 million sub-40 mule spindles would have been replaced by other mule spindles primarily for spinning sub-40 weft yarns, although many of the new mules could have been used for spinning fine counts of warp and weft instead of the lower counts previously spun. In addition, another 4.2 million mule spindles were added on all counts due to growth of the industry, and we can assume that these too were used primarily for spinning supra-40 counts of warp and all counts of weft.

How does this corrected picture of investment behavior, particularly the almost universal installation of mules to spin sub-40 weft yarn (and hence roughly half of the total sub-40 yarn output), affect Sandberg's argument that British managers were acting rationally? As we shall see, his argument, but not his quantitative estimates, can still be saved, since his overestimation of the investment in rings on sub-40 counts is balanced by an overestimation of the relative factor-cost advantages of rings on these counts.

Sandberg's most fundamental mistake is in his estimate of unit labor costs on mules spinning 40 yarn. Although his calculations for ring spinning are plausible, his estimates of labor costs per hundred mule spindles are about twice their actual magnitude, primarily because Sandberg did not realize that in Lancashire (and indeed almost everywhere in the world) a mule spinner along with any assistants (piecers) he might have operated a *pair* of mules and not one mule as Sandberg assumes in his calculations. Hence his estimates of the labor-cost savings per pound of ring yarn in each country are about twice what a correct use of his data would yield. Since he uses the count of 40 as a benchmark, his calculations of this cost saving for higher counts also yield results that seriously overestimate the labor-cost advantages of rings (not to mention his use in estimating these higher count differentials of *1949* labor productivity figures on rings and mules).

There is no problem with Sandberg's estimates of capital and power (fuel and lubricants) cost differentials per pound, both of which turn out to be insignificant factors on all ranges of counts. However, it should be noted that his estimates of the various factor-cost differentials are all derived from different sources, some of which refer to conditions in the industry some four decades after the period under analysis. Fortunately, it is unnecessary to use such scattered pieces of information, since drawing upon one source that Sandberg himself uses extensively, we can compute labor-cost, capital-cost, and power-cost differentials over a range of counts from 16 to 100 as shown in Table II. Winterbottom derived the data underlying the calculations in Table II from medium-count mills in Southeast Lancashire around 1907, and he presented them as generalizable estimates to guide cotton-spinning managers throughout the industry [Winterbottom, 1907, p. 231].[8]

An extremely important factor to be considered is the extra cost of shipping ring weft from spinning mills to weaving sheds. For reasons mentioned earlier, mule weft could be shipped in packages ("cops") made up completely of yarn, whereas ring yarn had to be shipped in packages of yarn wound on relatively heavy wooden bobbins. An American visitor observed that there was a saying in Lancashire that "a mule cop is like a good soldier always ready to go anywhere" [Whittam, 1907, p. 207]. Sandberg's figure for the extra cost per pound of shipping ring weft is too low. The calculation is based on the figures in Table III except for the cost of returning the wooden bobbins, which would have to be $0.03 instead of $0.30 to yield his results of $0.003 per pound of weft yarn. But information on freight charges indicates that it cost as much to return the bobbins as to send them [Railway and Shipping, 1928, pp. 114, 155; Great Britain, 1912b, pp. 31–32]. Using the figures in Table III, the extra cost per pound of shipping ring-weft yarn on the bobbin is $0.0054. In addition, however, there was always the possibility that some or all of the bobbins would be lost or broken [*Textile Manufacturer,* 1893; Nasmith, 1896, p. 532; and Robinson, 1918–1919]. At a cost per bobbin of $0.02 and with roughly 1,100 bobbins per shipment of 112 pounds of yarn, a probability of loss of 2 percent of the bobbins per shipment would add $0.004 to the cost of shipping ring yarn on the bobbin and a probability of 5 percent would add $0.010, raising the actual cost per pound of shipping to

8. In utilizing the formulae in Appendix 2 to derive the Table II estimates, I am assuming that Winterbottom's factor-cost per spindle data are applicable to all counts of yarn, the variations in the cost differentials over counts being determined solely by the conversion factor and output per m.e.s. In effect these formulae will yield realistic estimates if (1) Winterbottom's data are in fact indicative of "good practice" costs per spindle in pre-World War I Lancashire; and (2) insofar as these costs per spindle do vary over counts, the variations in cost *differentials* per m.e.s. between rings and mules are small.

TABLE II

FACTOR-COST SAVINGS PER POUND OF RING YARN OVER MULE YARN, NOS. 16–100, EXCLUDING COTTON COSTS

(1) Count	(2) Type of cotton	(3) Labor	(4) Capital	(5) Power	(6) Warp total	(7) Weft total*
16	American	$0.0027	$0.0006	$0.0000	$0.0033	$−0.0021
18	American	.0032	.0008	.0001	.0041	−.0013
20	American	.0035	.0008	.0000	.0043	−.0011
22	American	.0038	.0008	.0000	.0046	−.0008
24	American	.0039	.0007	−.0002	.0044	−.0010
26	American	.0045	.0010	.0000	.0055	.0001
28	American	.0047	.0009	−.0001	.0055	.0001
30	American	.0048	.0008	−.0003	.0053	−.0001
32	American	.0050	.0007	−.0004	.0053	−.0001
34	American	.0055	.0008	−.0004	.0059	.0005
36	American	.0058	.0008	−.0005	.0063	.0009
38	American	.0061	.0008	−.0007	.0062	.0008
40	American	.0066	.0008	−.0007	.0067	.0013
40	Egyptian	.0083	.0018	.0001	.0102	.0048
50	Egyptian	.0106	.0019	−.0004	.0121	.0067
60	Egyptian	.0137	.0024	−.0007	.0154	.0100
70	Egyptian	.0160	.0020	−.0017	.0163	.0109
80	Egyptian	.0204	.0032	−.0015	.0221	.0167
90	Egyptian	.0237	.0028	−.0028	.0237	.0183
100	Egyptian	.0268	.0025	−.0039	.0254	.0200

* Weft total = warp total − extra transportation cost of ring weft ($0.0054), not including estimate for loss and breakage of bobbins.
Sources. See Appendices 1 and 2.

TABLE III

THE AVERAGE COST OF SHIPPING WEFT YARN WITHIN LANCASHIRE

	Ring weft	Mule weft
Shipping 112 lbs. of yarn, 30 miles	$0.15	$0.15
Shipping wooden bobbins*	.30	——
Returning wooden bobbins*	.30	——
Returning basket	.02	.02
	$0.77	$0.17

* 200 percent of cost of shipping yarn; does not include cost of lost and broken bobbins.
Sources. Sandberg [1969], p. 32; Whittam [1907], p. 32; Great Britain [1912b], pp. 31–32; and Railway and Shipping [1928], pp. 114, 115.

$0.0094 and $0.0154, respectively [Winterbottom, 1921, p. 274; Howard & Bullough, 1917; and Copeland, 1912, p. 19].

An alternative to shipping the yarn on the bobbin was to rewind it, a practice that became quite common by the middle of the twentieth century after a number of innovations that greatly speeded up the winding process [Robson, 1957, p. 106]. But prior to World War I, the labor cost per pound of winding No. 20 yarn was between $0.0036 and $0.0062 [Winterbottom, 1921, pp. 273–274; Thornley, 1923b, p. 39] so that the extra cost per pound incurred by rewinding ring yarn at the spinning mill would have posed roughly the same constraint for marketing of ring weft by non-integrated mills as did the extra freight charges of the alternative of shipping on the bobbin. Moreover, once the rewound yarn had reached the weaving mill, it would have had to be rewound onto special shuttle bobbins.

The net results of "other"-cost savings of ring yarn over mule yarn (see Table II, columns 6 and 7) can be compared with the very different results reported by Sandberg (Table I, columns 3 and 4). Since in the use of cotton—the final factor to be considered in this cost comparison—the mule had the economic advantage on all counts, it remains to be seen at what counts, if any, the cotton-cost savings per pound of mule warp and mule weft outweighed the "other"-cost savings per pound of ring warp and ring weft, respectively.

Sandberg's own conclusions on cotton-cost differentials are very imprecise and tentative, and rightly so, since within limits, different combinations of grades and staples of cotton could be used on any given count. Moreover, the amount of waste per pound of cotton used was a very important expense in the spinning of yarn and varied inversely with the grade of cotton used [Winterbottom, 1921, pp.

242–43]. Since the cost of cotton constituted about 80 percent of total costs on 16 yarn declining to about 60 percent on 60 yarn and 45 percent on 100 yarn [Winterbottom, 1921, pp. 259–60], a major managerial function was to ensure that the grades and staples of cotton used were such as to minimize total unit costs for a desired quality of yarn. The mule, in fact, gave the manager more leeway in his choice of cotton quality, since for any given count the mule was adaptable to *wider ranges* of cotton grades and staples than the ring-frame, primarily due to the lesser amount of stress that the mule put on the cotton as it was being spun and wound. Since, in the Lancashire spinning industry, cotton was purchased by spinners from week to week as orders were placed, a manager with mules could take greater advantage of changes in relative cotton prices than a manager with rings spinning the same count.

Indeed, from the late 1880s, the use of inferior cotton—a condition known to the operatives as bad spinning because it greatly intensified their work—became endemic in Lancashire as a means of cutting costs and meeting competition. As I have explained elsewhere, the relative immobility of labor and the structure of industrial relations in Lancashire actually encouraged the use of lower quality cotton despite the habitual conflicts over bad spinning; and hence the greater technological flexibility of the mule over the ring-frame in the use of lower quality, lower cost, cotton helped to maintain the dominant position of the former machine in Britain. In contrast, managers in the United States had to use much better cotton on their mules for any given count than was the case in Lancashire in order to attract good mule spinners and to ensure that the operative did not have the opportunity to slow the pace of work; and hence, due to the nature of the labor supply, the use of lower quality cotton on the mules could not be fully exploited in the United States industry [Lazonick, 1980a, pp. 10–25].

This variability in cotton quality in Lancashire makes it very difficult to specify precisely cotton-cost differentials on various counts. Hence the question we must pose is whether, given our "other"-cost savings figures, one could reasonably expect cotton-cost savings that would have made it economically rational to use rings instead of mules. From Winterbottom's data (used by Sandberg), we can assume that a plausible range of the cotton-cost differential at the counts of 30 to 35 was \$0.01 ± \$0.005, and that the differential was generally higher on higher counts (up to a maximum of about \$0.03) and lower on lower counts (but probably never falling to zero)

[Sandberg, 1969, pp. 36–39; Winterbottom, 1921, pp. 234–35].[9] Now looking at my "other"-cost savings calculations, it is clear that British spinning managers would have been economically irrational if they had invested in any ring weft spindles on *any* counts, and cotton-cost savings of only $0.005 to $0.007 would have made it irrational to invest in ring twist spindles in the 20 to 40 count range. Hence it is plausible to argue that the general investment behavior that prevailed in Lancashire prior to World War I—namely, mules for all counts of weft and for most warp over 44, and rings for most counts of warp under 44—reflected rational decisions on the part of managers subject to the constraints they faced. In any case, there is no evidence here of gross or pervasive managerial irrationality in the Lancashire industry.

III. ECONOMIC RATIONALITY AND ECONOMIC HISTORY

Hence the hypothesis that Sandberg set out to test—that British cotton spinners acted in an economically rational manner—may be accepted despite the numerous problems with his quantitative estimates. But, as stated at the outset, this test of managerial performance covers only a narrowly defined subset of managerial activities. Allocative activity in the choice of technique constitutes only a part of managerial activity, and rational allocation might coexist with inept supervision and inability to innovate on the part of the same managers.[10] The passive acceptance of "given" constraints by managers over the "long run" would indicate technical and organizational conservatism even if they were continuously optimizing within those constraints. Hence the assessment of British managerial performance must be carried out within a broader theoretical and historical framework that integrates the study of the allocative, supervisory,

9. Note that there is no basis for Sandberg's assumption that the cotton-cost differentials are zero at 28 twist and below and at 35 weft and below. Apparently, just because Winterbottom did not report cotton *prices* for staples below one inch, Sandberg assumed that the differential was zero on counts using staples of less than one inch. But Winterbottom himself recognized the use of staples as short as 0.70 inches on 10 mule twist and 0.76 inches on 10 ring twist. Moreover, as we have seen, when the lower limits of staple length had been reached for a particular count, further cost-cutting by shifting to inferior grades of cotton could be done more readily on the mule than the ring. See Winterbottom [1921, p. 235], and also Morris and Wilkinson [1897, pp. 24–25] and Peake [1926, p. 26].

10. I might point out that by the 1890s, and certainly by the 1900s, the introduction of rings into a spinning mill was not in any sense an "innovation"; the factor costs and productivity potential of the ring-frame were widely known and readily available, and the mule spinners' union did not present a labor-relations constraint that had to be overcome in order to introduce the machine. On this last point, see Lazonick [1979].

and entrepreneurial activities of management; that is, a framework that analyzes managerial attempts to modify and overcome constraints over time as well as to optimize within constraints at a "point" in time.

Such an assessment will not be attempted here (but see Lazonick [1980b]). What is important to stress for present purposes is that, whatever the conclusion on allocative rationality, the facts that are marshalled to support the conclusion do have significance as historical data. Sandberg's underestimation of the proportion of spindles spinning sub-40 counts in Lancashire gives a misleading impression of the product structure of the British cotton textile industry before World War I. Given the fact that it was the "American" (sub-50) section of the industry that was hardest hit by the irreversible loss of markets during World War I and in the 1920s, an estimate of the proportion of spindles in this section prior to the war is of some importance for understanding the impact and rapidity of Lancashire's subsequent decline. Moreover, the fact that ring spinning did not dominate these counts before the war, as Sandberg's analysis would lead us to believe, becomes important as part of a larger story of the inability of Lancashire to rationalize and reequip its industry in the 1920s and 1930s, especially since (as Sandberg himself notes) [1969, p. 26] ring spinning was the wave of the future. As for factor-cost differentials, my results give primacy to very different economic constraints on the choice of rings or mules than do those of Sandberg. The failure of Sandberg to make himself familiar with basic facts about the mule spinning production process—particularly that each mule spinner tended two mules and not one—leads him to seriously overestimate the labor-cost advantage of rings in Lancashire. At the same time, by making unsupported assumptions about the cost of returning empty ring bobbins and by neglecting to consider the problems of the loss and breakage of bobbins, Sandberg seriously underestimates the magnitude of the constraint that vertical specialization placed on the adoption of the ring-frame. In contrast, my quantitative estimates indicate that it was vertical specialization that ruled out the introduction of ring weft spindles on any counts for the vast majority of spinning mills in Lancashire.

Indeed, the constraining influence of vertical specialization on the diffusion of ring spinning emanated not only from the supply side. Specialization also created problems in the generation of demand for ring yarn that was needed to motivate spinning mills to invest in the new technology at a more rapid pace. It was not just the fact that the demand for ring yarn depended on the economic rationality of the weaving managers.[11] Economically rational decision-making was required in integrated mills as well. The primary problem was that due to technical interrelatedness the rational choice between using mule yarn or ring yarn could be very different in an integrated context where market exchange had been superseded than in a specialized context where the extent of the demand for and supply of ring yarn was uncertain to the spinner and weaver, respectively.[12] Aside from the prohibitive cost of shipping ring weft on the bobbin or winding it into "cheeses" for shipping, the use of weft yarn by the weaver required investment in special shuttles on looms to hold the ring bobbins and, if ring weft was received in the form of cheeses, winding machinery to rewind the yarn onto shuttle bobbins. The large-scale use of ring twist, on the other hand, required a shift of the warping process from the weaving mill where it was customarily performed when mule twist was used to the spinning mill in order to avoid shipping on the bobbins, and hence the demand for ring twist depended partly on the willingness of weavers to let their warping machines sit idle or their confidence in dispensing with the process altogether [Political and Economic Planning, 1934, p. 95; Great Britain, 1932, p. 133]. Hence, while in terms of relative factor costs, it may have been rational for spinners to choose rings, the uncertainty of demand for ring yarn may have led them to choose mules; and while it may have also been economically rational for weavers to introduce (or get rid of) equipment to accommodate rings, the uncertainty of supplies of ring yarn may have led them to continue to demand mule yarn. Thus, in the specialized industrial structure uncertainty on both sides may have led to a situation where ring yarn was neither supplied nor demanded, although with coordinated decision-making as would be the case in vertically integrated mills, rings would have been used.

The fact is that from 1850 to 1950 the Lancashire cotton textile industry became increasingly specialized, a development that may

---

11. One manufacturer claimed that weaving with 8 yarn, the cost per pound of winding ring weft was more than outweighed by the extra cost per pound due to a higher rate of waste in using mule weft. In arguing for the rationality of using ring weft, he assumed that the delivered price of both types of yarn was the same. Whether or not this assumption was valid, it is clear that the demand for ring yarn depended not only on economically rational decision-making on the part of the spinner, but also on the part of the weaver [Cook, 1911–12, p. 176]. Many weavers also claimed that ring yarn did not give cloth the soft feel of mule yarn, although in the years just prior to World War I there was disagreement on this issue. See e.g., Taylor [1909–10, pp. 77–78]. There was, however, general agreement that mule warp held size better than ring warp (due to less twists per inch in the former yarn), so a weaver would have to take into account the issue of how much size he wanted in his cloth in making his choice of yarn.

12. Frankel, [1955]. It is perhaps not a coincidence that Frankel chose the Lancashire cotton textile industry as one of his examples in this article (although his specific reference was to the slow introduction of the automatic loom).

have been quite rational from the point of view of individual spinning and weaving capitalists who took advantage of the manifold external economies that Lancashire offered. But there is ample evidence that it was not rational from the point of view of the industry as a whole [Lazonick, 1980b]. Excessive competition and vertical disintegration from cotton suppliers to cloth merchants deprived capitalists in the industry of the possibility of developing, individually or collectively, a strategy to reshape the technical structure of production and to control markets in order to meet the challenge of the new corporate structures developed in countries such as Japan and the United States. The British cotton textile industry was unable to make the transition from nineteenth-century competitive capitalism to twentieth-century corporate capitalism. Neoclassical economics seems to have had much the same problem. For how else can one explain the joy of neoclassical economic historians in contemplating that Britain's twentieth-century managers went right on optimizing subject to nineteenth-century constraints?

APPENDIX 1:

POUNDS PER HUNDRED SPINDLES PER WEEK (56 1/2 HOURS)

	Mules		Rings		Rings/mules	
Counts	American cotton	Egyptian cotton	American cotton	Egyptian cotton	American cotton	Egyptian cotton
16	196.5		306.9		1.56	
18	174.8		292.5		1.67	
20	156.0		250.3		1.60	
22	142.1		219.8		1.55	
24	130.4		190.4		1.46	
26	120.4		188.7		1.57	
28	111.6		167.6		1.50	
30	106.0	104.3	151.5		1.43	
32	98.2	90.5	135.4		1.38	
34	89.9	83.3	126.0		1.40	
36	84.4	76.6	116.0		1.38	
38	78.3	70.5	106.0		1.35	
40	73.3	66.0	98.8	106.0	1.35	1.60
50	53.8	48.8		71.6		1.47
60	40.0	37.2		53.8		1.45
70		30.0		40.5		1.35
80		24.4		34.4		1.41
90		20.0		26.6		1.33
100		17.2		22.2		1.29

Source. Taggart [1923], pp. 202–03.

APPENDIX 2

Formulae for calculating factor-cost savings per pound of ring yarn over mule yarn as functions of counts (derived from Winterbottom [1921], pp. 272–73):[13]

$$\text{Labor-cost savings per lb.} = \frac{\$0.900 - \$0.566/cf}{\text{lb. per 100 m.e.s.}}$$

$$\text{Capital-cost savings per lb.} = \frac{\$0.450 - \$0.525/cf}{\text{lb. per 100 m.e.s.}}$$

$$\text{Power-cost savings per lb.} = \frac{\$0.312 - \$0.490/cf}{\text{lb. per 100 m.e.s.}}$$

where, for any given count,
m.e.s. = production equivalent per unit of time of one mule spindle
and cf = ratio of production per ring spindle to production per mule spindle per unit of time.

HARVARD UNIVERSITY

REFERENCES

Cook, C., "Economics in a Weaving Mill," *Journal of the British Association of Managers of Textile Works* (Lancashire Section), III (1911–1912).
Copeland, M., *The Cotton Manufacturing Industry of the United States* (Cambridge: Harvard University Press, 1912).
Daniels, G., and J. Jewkes, "The Post-War Depression in the Lancashire Cotton Industry," *Journal of the Royal Statistical Society*, XCI (1928), 153–206.
Field, A., "What's Wrong with Neoclassical Economics: A Critique with Special Reference to the North/Thomas Model of pre-1500 Europe," *Explorations in Economic History* (April 1981).
Frankel, M., "Obsolescence and Technological Change in a Maturing Economy," *American Economic Review*, XLV, No. 3 (June 1955), 296–319.
Great Britain, Board of Trade, *Enquiry into the Earnings and Hours of Labour: Textile Trades in 1906* (London: HMSO, 1909).
——, *An Industrial Survey of the Lancashire Area* (London: HMSO, 1932).
Great Britain Census of Production, *Final Report on the First Census of Production of the United Kingdom 1907* (London: HMSO, 1912a).
Great Britain, Railway and Canal Traffic Act, 1888, *An Analysis of the Railway Rates and Charges Order Confirmation Acts, 1891 and 1892* (London: HMSO, 1912b).
Harley, C., "Skilled Labour and the Choice of Technique in Edwardian Industry," *Explorations in Economic History*, XI, No. 4 (Summer 1974), 391–414.
Howard & Bullough records, DDPSL/3 Lancashire Record Office, Production Notebook 13, 1917.

13. The formulae in Appendix 2, from which the Table II estimates are derived, embody the assumption that, for any given count, roving cost per pound on rings is 25 percent more than on mules [Winterbottom, 1921, p. 261]. It is also assumed that there are 0.15 roving spindles per ring spindle [Thornley, 1923a, p. 579]. Data used to make the calculations in Table II were derived from Taggart's "good average" production figures presented in Appendix 1. I have used Taggart's 1923 data for the conversion factor (cf) and output per spindle because it covers a wider range of counts than similar data presented by Winterbottom [1921, p. 204] and Thornley [1923a, p. 376]. The Winterbottom [1921, p. 204] and Thornley [1923a, p. 376]. The Winterbottom data were reprinted unchanged from the 1907 edition of his book. Comparisons of these three sets of data show that they are all consistent with one another.

Jewkes, J., and E. Gray, *Wages and Labour in the Lancashire Cotton Spinning Industry* (Manchester: Manchester University Press, 1935).
Jewkes, J., and S. Jewkes, "A Hundred Years of Change in the Structure of the Cotton Industry," *Journal of Law and Economics,* IX (Oct. 1966), 115–34.
Jones, F., "The Cotton Spinning Industry in the Oldham District from 1896 to 1914," M.A. thesis, University of Manchester, 1959.
Lazonick, W., "Industrial Relations and Technical Change: The Case of the Self-Acting Mule," *Cambridge Journal of Economics,* III, No. 3 (Sept. 1979), 231–62.
——, "Industrial Relations, Work Organization, and Technological Change: U. S. and British Cotton Spinning," Harvard Institute of Economic Research Discussion Paper No. 774, July 1980a.
——, "Industrial Organization and Technological Change: The Decline of the British Cotton Industry," Harvard Institute of Economic Research Paper No. 794, October 1980b.
Mass, W., "The Adoption of the Automatic Loom," xerox, Harvard University, April 1980.
McCloskey, D., ed., *Essays on a Mature Economy: Britain After 1840* (London: Methuen, 1971).
——, and L. Sandberg, "From Damnation to Redemption: Judgments on the Late Victorian Entrepreneur," *Explorations in Economic History,* IX, No. 1 (Fall 1971), 89–108.
Morris, J., and F. Wilkinson, *The Elements of Cotton Spinning* (London: Longmans, Green, 1897).
Nasmith, J., *The Student's Cotton Spinning* (Manchester: Heywood, 1896).
North, D., "Structure and Performance: The Task of Economic History," *Journal of Economic Literature,* XVI, No. 3 (Sept. 1978), 963–78.
——, and R. Thomas, *The Rise of the Western World* (Cambridge: Cambridge University Press, 1973).
OECD, *Modern Cotton Industry: A Capital Intensive Industry* (Paris: OECD, 1965).
Political and Economic Planning, Industries Group, *Report on the British Cotton Industry* (London: HMSO, 1934).
Railway and Shipping Publishing Co., *The Manchester ABC Railway Rates Book of Distances and Standard Charges* (Birmingham, 1928).
Peake, R., *Cotton: From the Raw Material to the Finished Product* (London: Pitman, 1926), rev. ed.
Robinson, B., "Business Methods in the Cotton Trade," *Journal of the British Association of Managers of Textile Works* (Lancashire Section), IX (1918–1919), 95–99.
Robson, R., *The Cotton Industry in Britain* (London: Macmillan, 1957).
Sandberg, L., "American Rings and English Mules: The Role of Economic Rationality," this *Journal,* LXXXIII, No. 1 (Feb. 1969), 25–43; reprinted in S. Saul, ed., *Technological Change* (London: Methuen, 1970), and in R. Floud, ed., *Essays in Quantitative History* (Oxford: Clarendon, 1974).
——, *Lancashire in Decline* (Columbus: Ohio State University Press, 1974), Ch. 2.
Schumpeter, J., *Business Cycles* (New York: McGraw-Hill, 1939), Chs. II and III.
——, *The Theory of Economic Development* (New York: Oxford University Press, 1934), Chs. I and II.
Taggart, W., *Cotton Mill Management* (London: Macmillan, 1923).
Taylor, H., "The Development of Ring Spinning," *Journal of the British Association of Managers of Textile Works* (Lancashire Section), I (1909–1910).
Textile Manufacturer, April 8, 1893, p. 262.
Thornley, T., *Advanced Cotton Spinning* (London: Scott, Greenwood, 1923), 3rd ed.
Vitkovitch, B., "The U. K. Cotton Industry, 1937–54," *Journal of Industrial Economics,* III, No. 3 (July 1955), 241–65.
Whittam, W., *Report on England's Cotton Industry* (Washington: GPO, 1907).
Winterbottom, J., *Cotton Spinning Calculations and Yarn Costs* (London: Longmans, Green, 1907, 1921), 1st ed., 2nd ed.
Worrall, J., *The Cotton Spinners' and Manufacturer's Directory for Lancashire* (Oldham: Worrall, 1913).

[3]

By *William Lazonick*
ASSOCIATE PROFESSOR OF ECONOMICS
HARVARD UNIVERSITY

Industrial Organization and Technological Change: The Decline of the British Cotton Industry*

¶*In this important study Professor Lazonick provides an astute reappraisal of why Britain's once dominant economy has failed to meet the challenges of international competition in the twentieth century. The vehicle for his discussion is cotton manufacture, the industry which, through the technological and commercial innovations of the late eighteenth and early nineteenth centuries, made Britain the leading industrial power. Among Dr. Lazonick's questions are why did Britain's preeminence in this industry come to an end? Why did technological innovation yield to stagnation? Why did inefficient modes of economic organization persist in the face of manifest inadequacy? And what does the history of this industry have to teach us about recent economic theory?*

Only twice in the history of industrial capitalism has a national economy that dominated international economic affairs entered into a relative decline in the face of foreign competition. The first nation to undergo this experience was Britain after achieving its peak of supremacy in the third quarter of the nineteenth century. The second was, or rather is, the United States after its turn at the top in the quarter century following World War II. Where the relative decline of the United States will leave it in the world economy remains to be seen. But for once powerful Britain all the returns are essentially in. Not surprisingly, for a number of decades economic historians have been busy trying to understand why and how it happened. Preferred explanations include Britain's "early start," the problem of "technical interrelatedness," a disease known as "entrepreneurial failure," and, when all other explanations are happily rejected, "conditions outside its control."[1]

Business History Review, Vol. LVII (Summer 1983). Copyright © The President and Fellows of Harvard College.

*A summary of this paper appeared under the title, "Competition, Specialization, and Industrial Decline" in the *Journal of Economic History*, Vol. XLI, No. 1, March 1981. The analysis presented here has benefitted greatly from collaborative work with Stephen Marglin on the history and theory of the firm and with William Mass on the historical development of the cotton textile industry in Britain and the United States. An anonymous referee pointed out some important omissions in an earlier draft of this paper which I have attempted to rectify. Thomas Brush offered useful comments and very important research assistance. Additional research assistance was provided by Todd Hennis and Martha Smith. This paper is based upon research supported by the National Science Foundation under Grant No. SES 78-25671, and by a grant-in-aid from the Merrimack Valley Textile Museum.

[1]See e.g. the bibliographical survey in D.H. Aldcroft and H.W. Richardson, *The British Economy 1870–1939* (London, 1969, pp. 305–313; see also D. McCloskey and L. Sandberg, "From Damnation to Redemption: Judgements on the late Victorian Entrepreneur," *Explorations in Economic History*, Ser. 2, Vol. 9, No. 1, (Fall 1971) pp. 89–108.

195

The academic debate over the explanation of Britain's relative decline is far from settled. A prime purpose of this article is to ensure that the debate goes on. The historical experience of British industrial capitalism has intellectual significance far beyond its obvious importance as a case study of the fall of a once powerful economy. It is this particular historical experience, variously interpreted, that exerts to this day the preponderant influence on how neoclassical, neokeynesian, and neomarxist economists conceptualize the process of capitalist development.[2] Hence, our own understanding of British economic history since the late nineteenth century provides a basis for assessing the descriptive and predictive relevance of alternative theoretical perspectives that have purported to comprehend that experience. It is only with such insight into the relation between theory and history that we can *begin* to develop a theoretical analysis that captures the essence of the dynamics of capitalist development as it is occurring today.

This article on the British cotton industry's decline is an attempt to understand the relation between history and theory. As such it is both critical and constructive. It is critical in demonstrating that when a certain set of facts are crammed into typical neoclassical baggage, the latter bursts apart at the seams. Either the facts are too weighty or the baggage too flimsy, or both. It is constructive in suggesting an alternative, and hopefully sturdier, explanation of the British decline, based on the nature of the cotton industry's organizational structure and the influence of this structure on changes in technology.

The British cotton industry played a central role in its country's nineteenth-century development. On the eve of World War I, it remained Britain's largest manufacturing employer, contributed almost one-quarter of all the nation's exports, and was still expanding its capacity.[3] There is no question that, in order to cope with growing international competition and tariff walls in the first four decades of the twentieth century, the British cotton industry would have had to contract in size significantly no matter how it might have reorganized and re-equipped itself internally. It is significant, however, that the need for such a long-run contraction was not perceived and acted upon at all until the late 1920s. The issues we shall address are 1) why the industry had such great difficulty accomplishing the necessary contraction, and 2) why, even when it had become much smaller, it was unable to modernize organizationally and technologically that capacity that remained as was being done for example in the cotton industries of the United States and many Western European countries. The main argument of the article is

---

[2]For a systematic theoretical analysis of how these three views of the economy fundamentally differ, see S. Marglin, *Growth, Distribution and Prices* (Cambridge, Mass., 1984).

[3]P. Deane and W. Cole, *British Economic Growth 1688–1959* (Cambridge, England, 1964), p. 32; G. Jones, *Increasing Return* (Cambridge, England, 1933), p. 277.

Courtesy Baker Library, Harvard University.

Bobbin and Drawing Frames.

Courtesy Baker Library, Harvard University.

Weaving.

Idealized scenes in an Early Nineteenth Century Textile Mill.

THE DECLINE OF THE BRITISH COTTON INDUSTRY   197

that the failure of the British cotton industry to re-equip its production processes on the basis of advanced technologies in the first half of the twentieth century was due to the structure of industrial organization that it had inherited from the heyday of nineteenth-century competitive capitalism.[4]

Right into the 1960s, the British cotton industry continued to rely on technologies, such as the spinning mule and the Lancashire loom, that almost all other cotton industries has long since discarded (see Table 1). The ring-frame had been greatly improved in the 1870s and 1880s. In 1913, 87 percent of all spindles in the U.S. but only 19 percent in Britain were rings, despite the fact that British textile machinery firms were manufacturing the ring-frame on a large scale to be shipped to industries around the world. In 1954, with 59 percent of its spindles still on mules, Britain possessed 84 percent of all mule spindles, but less than 10 percent of all ring spindles, in world operation. By this time, the mule spinning machine had vanished completely from the U.S. cotton industry. With the help of a government scheme in the late 1950s, large numbers of mules were finally scrapped, and by the early 1970s the machine had become a virtually extinct breed in the land of its birth.[5]

In the adoption of the automatic loom Britain was even slower, hanging on to the less automated Lancashire loom. The automatic, or Northrop, loom was invented in the U.S. in 1894. In 1914 automatics constituted 40 percent of all cotton looms in the U.S. as compared to between one and two percent in Britain. In 1936, 68 percent of U.S. looms but only three percent of British looms were automatic; in 1955, these figures were 100 percent and 12 percent respectively.[6]

Britain also lagged far behind in the adoption of all the new cotton manufacturing processes of the first decades of this century. After World War II, single-process openers, high-draft spinning, high-speed winders, and high-speed warping machines were among the processes that were widely used in the U.S. and other major cotton industries, but still rare in the British industry. The equipment Britain did have was not only obsolete by world standards but also extremely old, while the workloads and modes of work organization utilized on these machines dated back to the mid-nineteenth century if not before.

In what follows, I shall outline the nature of industrial organization in the British cotton industry in the first half of the twentieth century. Then I shall demonstrate how this structure of industrial organization

---

[4]Elsewhere, I analyze the influences of both the structure of industrial relations and the structure of foreign demand on productivity on the traditional machines. See W. Lazonick and W. Mass, "The Performance of the British Cotton Industry, 1870–1913," *Research in Economic History*, Vol. 9, (1984).

[5]R. Robson, *The Cotton Industry in Britain* (London, 1957), p. 355; A. Ormerod, "The Prospects of the British Cotton Industry," *Yorkshire Bulletin of Economic and Social Research*, Vol. 15, No. 1, (May 1963), p. 6.

[6]W. Mass, "The Adoption of the Automatic Loom," paper presented to the Cliometrics Conference, Chicago, May 1980, Table 1; Robson, *Cotton Industry*, p. 356. See also United Textile Factory Workers' Association, *Plan for Cotton* (Ashton, 1957), p. 15.

impeded the introduction of more advanced technologies — particularly the ring frame in spinning and the automatic loom in weaving — during this period. Next I shall inquire why so little progress was made in the organizational restructuring of the industry so as to facilitate the adoption of modern production methods. Finally I shall consider the implications of my interpretation of the British cotton industry's decline for the broader analysis of the relative decline of the British economy in the twentieth century.

COMPETITION AND SPECIALIZATION

In the early decades of the industrial revolution, vertical integration of marketing with various levels of production (including in many cases machine-making) had been a necessity if pioneering cotton textile firms were to ensure themselves adequate supplies of inputs for their factories as well as sufficient outlets for their products. But from the beginning of the nineteenth century as the industry grew in and around Manchester, there developed what Alfred Marshall was later to call "external economies" in the form of financial services, market exchanges, transportation networks, and readily available supplies of cotton, machinery, and industrial workers.[7] The development of this geographically-concentrated economic infrastructure made it increasingly possible for small-scale production units to enter the industry. Moreover, as far-flung foreign markets became of ever-increasing importance to the industry, the capital and managerial requirements of a concern that integrated production and distribution were beyond the capacities of the vast majority of family firms seeking to produce yarn and cloth. Except for a few large enterprises, marketing and manufacturing had become almost completely vertically specialized in the British cotton industry by the mid-nineteenth century.[8]

From the 1820s to the 1840s, however, the combined spinning and weaving firm apparently grew in importance in the British cotton industry as large numbers of spinning firms (many if not most of which had been directly involved in the putting out of yarn to hand-loom weavers)

[7]A. Marshall, *The Principles of Economics* (London, 1925), eighth edition, ch. VIII–XIII.

[8]M. Edwards, *The Growth of the British Cotton Trade 1780–1815* (Manchester, 1967); A.J. Taylor, "Concentration and Specialization in the Lancashire Cotton Industry, 1825–1850," *Economic History Review*, 2nd ser., Vol. I, No. 2 and 3, (1949), pp. 114–122; V.A.C. Gatrell, "Labour, Power, and the Size of Firms in Lancashire Cotton in the Second Quarter of the Nineteenth Century," *Economic History Review*, 2nd series, Vol. XXX, No. 1, (February 1977), pp. 95–139; R. Lloyd-Jones and A.A. LeRoux, "The Size of Firms in the Cotton Industry: Manchester 1815–1841" *Economic History Review*, 2nd ser. Vol. XXXIII, No. 1, (February 1980), pp. 72–82; S.D. Chapman, "British Marketing Enterprise: The Changing Role of Merchants, Manufacturers, and Financiers, 1700–1860," *Business History Review*, Vol. LIII, No. 2, (Summer 1979), pp. 205–233; S.D. Chapman, "Financial Restraints on the Growth of Firms in the Cotton Industry, 1790–1850," *Economic History Review*, 2nd ser. Vol. XXXIII, No. 1, (February 1980), pp. 50–69; J. Jewkes and S. Jewkes, "A Hundred Years of Change in the Structure of the Cotton Industry," *Journal of Law and Economics*, Vol. IX, (October 1966) pp. 115–134; D.A. Farnie, *The English Cotton Industry and the World Market 1815–1896*, (Oxford, 1979).

added power-loom weaving sheds to their production facilities.[9] But from the 1830s the rapid growth of foreign trade in yarn to serve the weaving industries of the Continent, India, and China meant that there was an increasing role for specialized spinning firms in the British industry. These firms, once in place, stood ready as well to supply yarn to specialized weaving firms within the home market. During the 1850s, the spinning capacity of specialized mills surpassed that of combined mills, and over the next century vertically-specialized spinning and weaving firms became increasingly dominant in the industry (see Table 2).[10] For most firms spinning and weaving represented two separate industries linked by the Manchester Exchange, with the spinning industry becoming increasingly localized in south Lancashire towns such as Oldham and Bolton (which in turn tended to specialize in different types of yarn) and the weaving industry becoming increasingly localized in northwest Lancashire towns such as Blackburn and Burnley.[11]

Accompanying this high degree of vertical specialization was a high degree of horizontal competition. Over time these two structural characteristics of the industry were mutually reinforcing. As the external economies linking the vertical structure eased entry into the horizontal levels of spinning, weaving, and marketing, the specialized skills required of managers as well as the large number of suppliers and buyers at each of these levels discouraged the development of the internal organizational structures necessary for effective forward or backward integration.[12]

Of these three levels, the minimal capital requirements were greatest in spinning. From the 1860s, however, new spinning firms were able to tap large sources of capital from local residents who not only bought equity in the mills but also opened savings accounts at the mills, receiving almost twice the rate of interest offered by regular savings banks.[13] The development of these limited liability spinning mills went furthest in Oldham which, by the 1870s, had become by far the largest cotton spinning center in the world. Between 1884 and 1914, the average annual rate of entry of firms into the Lancashire spinning industry was 3.6 percent while the average annual rate of exit was 3.3 percent.[14]

In weaving, entry was even easier than in spinning, requiring, in the late nineteenth century, an investment of £20–50 per employee as com-

[9]Taylor, "Concentration," p. 119; J. Jewkes, "The Localisation of the Cotton Industry," *Economic History*, Vol. II, No. 5, (January 1930), pp. 92–93; D. Bythell, *The Handloom Weavers* (Cambridge, England, 1969), pp. 89–92.
[10]Taylor, "Concentration,"; Jewkes, "Localisation"; J.R.T. Hughes, *Fluctuations in Trade, Industry and Finance, 1850–1860* (Oxford, 1960), pp. 97–99; Farnie, *English Cotton*, pp. 86–90.
[11]Jewkes, "Localisation."
[12]In what follows I shall ignore the finishing (bleaching, dyeing, and printing) level of the industry since its firms were neither buyers nor sellers of intermediate products but rather served as sub-contractors for the merchant-convertors who bought gray cloth and determined its final color and design.
[13]Farnie, *English Cotton*, p. 256.
[14]T. Ashton, "The Growth of Textile Businesses in the Oldham District 1884–1924," *Journal of the Royal Statistical Society*, Vol. LXXXIX, (1926), p. 573. See also Farnie, *English Cotton*, ch. 6–7.

pared to £250–300 per employee in spinning.[15] Entry was facilitated particularly by the widespread adoption of the room-and-power system from the last decades of the nineteenth century in newly expanding weaving areas such as Burnley. On this system, a firm rented space, power, and at times even looms from the proprietor of a large weaving shed, an average of four firms being housed under one roof.[16] Moreover, looms were built to last in Lancashire, and new entrants to the industry could often obtain used ones at low prices from those who had recently exited (or at least from their creditors). In an industry prone to recurrent overproduction due to intense competition, the bankruptcies were usually the products of a conjuncture of high yarn prices and low cloth prices, whereas the "newcomers" (who had often been weaving capitalists before) rushed in when yarn prices fell.[17]

The marketing of yarn and cloth was carried out by a plethora of shippers, home trade houses, and merchant convertors, the firms altogether numbering at least 2,000 even in the post-World War II period at a time when the marketing of U.S. production had become highly concentrated in 50–60 New York selling agencies closely allied or integrated with particular manufacturing concerns.[18] Many of these Lancashire firms were substantial export houses, and a portion of the home market was served by fully integrated firms. Still there was plenty of room for small merchants to set up by making use of the readily available finishing, packing, and shipping facilities in Manchester and by specializing in a particular type of yarn or cloth to be sold in a particular market.[19]

Linking these various highly competitive layers of the industry was a neoclassical economist's dream of a hierarchy of extremely well-developed markets — indeed in 1919 Alfred Marshall referred to the Lancashire cotton industry as "perhaps the best present instance of concentrated organization mainly automatic."[20] The raw cotton market was centered in Liverpool and the yarn and cloth markets in Manchester. An Oldham spinning mill manager might ride the train to Liverpool on Mondays to purchase cotton sufficient to fulfill yarn orders already received (very little being produced in anticipation of demand) and then visit Manchester on Tuesdays and Fridays to seek out new orders on the

[15]Farnie, *English Cotton*, p. 219.
[16]*Ibid.*, ch. 8.
[17]*Ibid.*, pp. 287–295; *Cotton Factory Times*, *(CFT)* 20 Nov. 1885.
[18]R. Robson, "Structure of the Cotton Industry: A Study in Specialization and Integration" (Ph.D. Thesis, University of London, 1950), p. 190; Robson, *Cotton Industry*, p. 87–88; S. Barkin, "The Regional Significance of the Integration Movement in the Southern Textile Industry," *Southern Economic Journal*, Vol. XV, No. 4, (April 1949) pp. 395–411; Fabian Research Group, *Cotton–A Working Policy* (London, 1945), p. 3; Committee on Industry and Trade, *Survey of the Textile Industries*, (London, 1928), pp. 20–22; Henry Clay, *Report on the Position of the English Cotton Industry*, Confidential Report for Securities Management Trust, Ltd. October 20, 1931, pp. 30–39; Economic Advisory Council, Committee on the Cotton Industry, *Report*, pp. 13–14, in *Parliamentary Papers*, 1929–30, XII; Great Britain, Board of Trade *Working Party Reports: Cotton* (London, 1946), p. 46, Association of Cotton Textile Merchants of New York, *Twenty-five years* (New York, 1944).
[19]M. Copeland, *The Cotton Manufacturing Industry of the United States* (Cambridge, Mass., 1912), pp. 365–70; Robson, *Cotton Industry*, p. 149.
[20]A. Marshall, *Industry and Trade* (London, 1919), pp. 600–601.

TABLE 1

MACHINERY IN THE BRITISH COTTON INDUSTRY, 1907–1979

(INSTALLED CAPACITY)

| | Spinning spindles (millions) | | | Weaving looms (thousands) | | |
	Mules	Rings			Lancashire	Automatic
1907	43.7	8.3	1911	763.0		5.4
1913	47.9	11.4	1924*		792.0	
1927	43.8	13.5	1930*		700.0	
1937	28.0	10.8	1936	489.5		15.2
1947	19.9	9.8	1948	358.0		26.0
1951	17.7	10.6	1955	294.7		39.2
1955	14.5	10.9	1961	117.0		47.0
1959	8.7	9.5	1964	56.6		41.3
1963	1.6	5.6	1967*		57.8	
1967	0.4	3.9	1973*		49.4	
1971	0.2	3.3	1975	27.0		22.1
1975	—	2.7	1977	21.6		22.4
1979	—	2.1	1979*		35.4	

* = Total Number of Looms

Sources: W. Lazonick, "Factor Costs and the Diffusion of Ring Spinning in Britain prior to World War I," *Quarterly Journal of Economics*, Vol. 96, No. 1, (February 1981), p. 96; R. Robson, *The Cotton Industry in Britain* (London, 1957), pp. 339, 340, 342, 344, 355–356; U.S. House of Representatives, *Cotton Manufactures*. Report of the Tariff Board, Vol. 2 (Washington, 1912), p. 494; B. Mitchell and H. Jones, *Second Abstract of British Historical Statistics* (Cambridge, England, 1971), p. 42; A. Ormerod, "The prospects of the British cotton industry," *Yorkshire Bulletin of Economic and Social Research*, Vol. 15, No. 1, (May 1963), p. 19; Amalgamated Textile Workers' Union, *Fifth Annual Report* for the Period January 1 to December 31, 1979 (Rochdale, 1980), p. 31. Organization for Economic Cooperation and Development, *Textile Industry in O.E.C.D. Countries* (O.E.C.D.: Paris) 1973–74, pp. 121, 124, 1976–77, pp. 40–41.

floor of the Royal Exchange. In many cases, alternatively, spinners and weavers would transact their purchases and sales through cotton, yarn, and cloth agents who added even more layers to the vertical structure.

Vertical specialization increased in Lancashire from the mid-nineteenth century until after World War II. Between 1884 and 1911, the number of firms combining spinning and weaving fell by 37 percent while the number of spinning firms increased by 4 percent and the number of weaving firms by 28 percent (see Table 2). In 1930 only twenty-six of the more than 2,000 cotton yarn and cloth producers in Britain had their own marketing facilities, and only nineteen of these combined spinning and weaving as well. These twenty-six firms controlled about 7 percent of the spindles and 10 percent of the looms in the industry.[21] They generally had their origins in the nineteenth century, many in the early phases of the industrial revolution when some form of integration of production and distribution was a requirement of doing business.[22]

[21]Clay, *Report*, pp. 26A, 26B.

[22]E. Hopwood, *The Lancashire Weavers' Story* (Manchester, 1969), p. 15; Clay, *Report*, p. 26A. W. Mills, *Sir Charles W. Macara, Bart.* (Manchester, 1917) p. 50; A. Muir, *The Kenyon Tradition* (Cambridge, England, 1964); B. Ellinger and H. Ellinger, "Japanese Competition in the Cotton Trade, *Journal of the Royal Statistical Society*, Vol XCIII, pt. II, (1930) p. 209.

TABLE 2
VERTICAL SPECIALIZATION OF FIRMS IN THE BRITISH COTTON INDUSTRY
1884–1965

| Year | Spinning only | | Weaving only | | Weaving and spinning combined | | |
	percent of firms	percent of spindles	percent of firms	percent of looms	percent of firms	percent of spindles	percent of looms
1884*	40.5	59.8	33.0	42.6	26.5	40.2	57.4
1911*	38.6	77.4	46.3	64.6	15.1	22.6	35.4
1924	35.4	n.a.	52.1	n.a.	12.5	n.a.	n.a.
1931	29.0	n.a.	57.0	n.a.	14.0	n.a.	n.a.
1939**	22.0	76.8	67.0	76.4	11.0	23.2	23.6
1946	22.1	84.1	67.6	75.6	10.3	15.9	24.4
1955	21.8	72.1	65.7	64.5	12.5	27.9	35.5
1959	22.6	42.4	63.2	64.4	14.2	57.6	35.6
1965	25.1	32.7	58.1	57.8	16.8	67.3	42.2

n.a. = not available
* = The statistics for these years apply to Lancashire only
** = The data on firms are for 1940, on spindles and looms for 1939.
Sources: J. Jewkes and S. Jewkes "A hundred years of change in the structure of the cotton industry," *Journal of Law and Economics*, Vol. IX, (October 1966), p. 120; H. Clay, *Report on the Position of the English Cotton Industry*, Confidential report for Securities Management Trust Ltd., October 20, 1931, p. 2; United Textile Factory Workers' Association, *Report on the Legislative Council on Ways and Means of Improving the Economic Stability of the Cotton Textile Industry* (Ashton, 1943), p. 156; R. Robson, *The Cotton Industry in Britain*, (London, 1957), p. 122; Great Britain, Board of Trade, *Working Party Reports: Cotton* (London, 1946), p. 37.

No doubt this specialized vertical structure as well as the ease of entry into its various levels attracted much in the way of individual initiative into the industry and promoted the expansion of capacity prior to World War I. So long as the industry's markets were growing absolutely, as was generally the case up to 1914, the specialized and competitive structure fostered the economic growth of production to meet this demand. With expanding markets, the development of production came about by the re-equipment of existing firms and perhaps even more by the entry into the industry of new, usually larger, firms in booms and the exit of the inefficient firms in slumps, thus up-dating and enlarging the capital stock.

With generally contracting markets after World War I, however, very few existing firms re-equipped and very few new firms entered the industry. In the 1920s many inefficient firms that might have been forced to exit had there been technical development and enlargement of the more efficient firms, found that they could hang on despite the dramatic decline in demand, living, so to speak, off their capital. Throughout the 1920s, both spinning and weaving capacity varied little from its pre-World War I levels. Many "American" spinning and weaving firms remained in business in the early 1920s by shifting some of their capacity, machinery permitting, into the production of finer goods, thereby overcrowding the "Egyptian" section of the industry by the late 1920s and creating inefficiency through less standardized production within mills.[23]

The problem of excess capacity in the coarser goods section of the spinning industry in the 1920s was exacerbated by what turned out to be an enormous overcapitalization of spinning mills in the brief post-war boom of 1919–1920. High profits led to the buying up and recapitalization of existing mills at about three times their pre-war value per spindle and with an increase of loan capital of approximately 50 percent per spindle. Involved in this financial reconstitution were 46 percent of the spindles in the industry and 14 percent of the looms, the latter belonging mainly to combined firms. When the slump hit the industry beginning in the mid-1920s, the firms were forced to throw their yarn on the market at any price to meet fixed interest charges. The resultant low yarn prices were probably a prime reason for the survival of many coarse weaving firms in the depressed 1920s.[24] The financial condition of all the spinning mills was made even more unstable by the fact that shareholders in the Lancashire spinning industry were generally required to have only half of their share capital paid-up with the other half on call for emergencies. When this unpaid share capital was called in during the 1920s, local residents, who were preponderant among the stockholders, often had to withdraw their savings deposits from the mills in order to retain their equity, thus deepening the market crisis and the further dependence of the recapitalized mills on banks to whom they were already deeply indebted for working capital.[25]

The extreme competition for a declining market at all horizontal levels of the British cotton industry was neither propitious for re-equipment by existing firms nor for the up-dating of plant and machinery by the entry of new firms. In a survey undertaken in 1930, 96 percent of the mules and 87 percent of the rings in 200 mills had been installed prior to 1920, and 77 percent of the mules and 67 percent of the rings prior to 1910.[26] Horizontal competition in a contracting market stifled *any* type of re-equipment. Vertical specialization, however, constrained the adoption of modern capital-intensive technologies not only in the depressed periods of the 1920s and early 1930s but even in the much stronger

---

[23]Political and Economic Planning, Industries Group, *Report on the British Cotton Industry* (London, 1934), p. 21; M. Kirby, "The Lancashire cotton industry in the inter-war years: a study in organizational change," *Business History*, Vol. XVI, No. 2, (July 1974), pp. 145–159; Committee on Industry and Trade, *Survey*, pp. 33–34; J. Pennington, "Competition and specialisation in the cotton trade," *Journal of the National Federation of Textile Works Managers' Associations* Vol. VI, (1926–1927), p. 216.

[24]Committee on Industry and Trade, *Survey*, p. 37; G. Daniels and J. Jewkes, "The Post-war Depression in the Lancashire Cotton Industry," *Journal of the Royal Statistical Society* Vol. XCI, (1928) pp. 169–177; see also United Textile Factory Workers Association, *Inquiry into the Cotton Industry* (Blackburn, 1923), p. 15; O. Jones, "The Agitation for Control of the Lancashire Cotton Industry," *Harvard Business Review*, Vol. 2, No. 4, (July 1924) pp. 447–452.

[25]Committee on Industry and Trade, *Survey*, pp. 36–38.

[26]J. Ryan, "Machinery Replacement in the Cotton Trade," *Economic Journal*, Vol. 40, (December 1930) p. 7; Political and Economic Planning, *Report*, p. 54.

market conditions of the two decades or so prior to World War I, the late 1930s, and the years after World War II. Specifically, vertical specialization greatly impeded, among other technological advances, the introduction of ring spinning (which in turn restricted the introduction of the high-draft preparatory process which was not well suited to mule spinning), the automatic loom, as well as high-speed winding and warping machines.

The primary constraint on the introduction of ring spinning in Lancashire was the cost of shipping ring yarn. Mule yarn was spun into packages (called "cops") on the bare spindle or on lightweight paper tubes while ring yarn had to be spun into packages on wooden bobbins. If the yarn was shipped on these relatively heavy bobbins the cost of transport was increased significantly since freight on the bobbins had to be paid not only to the weaving mill but also back to the spinning mill.[27] Moreover the bobbins themselves were relatively expensive — one mill manager claimed that they were "one of the costliest of mill stores for a ring spinning mill to keep up."[28] Shipping on the bobbin for the export trade was therefore simply out of the question. But even when shipping within Lancashire, the spinner had no assurance that the bobbins would be returned promptly, in usable condition, or at all. As late as the interwar period, there were no arrangements in the Lancashire cotton industry whereby the spinning mill could charge the weaving mill for the skips, cases, and warping beams that the latter was constantly receiving along with the yarn and then credit the weaver when these items were returned. Competition among spinners undoubtedly impeded their ability to institute such practices on an individual basis. That the problem was recognized is evident from the following complaint by a spinning mill manager in 1919:

> The present system leads to a state of "no value" or "nobody's property" after it leaves the mill. There is no responsibility for returning [skips, cases, beams, etc.], and at present prices — 60s. for skips, 32s. for cases, etc. — it becomes a very serious item. The number used for receptables in warehouses, fencing gardens, and poultry farms are legion. The number used by doublers, dyers, etc. to send their own products to their customers is the same. Users of yarn take unto themselves the right to use the spinners' property for any purpose they may desire. It is not what is called a "square deal". It is time the spinner "woke up" and make a charge, and credit it on return.[29]

[27]See W. Lazonick, "Factor Costs and the Diffusion of Ring-spinning in Britain prior to World War I," *Quarterly Journal of Economics*, Vol. XCVI, No. 1, (February 1981).

[28]J. Kershaw, "Uses of Paper-tubes in the Textile Trade," *Journal of the British Association of Managers of Textile Works* (Lancashire Section), Vol. IV, (1912–1913), p. 86.

[29]B. Robinson, "Business Methods in the Cotton Trade," *Journal of the British Association of Managers of Textile Works* (Lancashire Section), Vol. IX, (1918–1919) p. 96. There had been a court decision in 1895 absolving a weaver of responsibility for a spinning mill's skips burnt while in his possession, a decision that was upheld when appealed by the FMCSA. *Textile Mercury*, August 10, 1895. As for bobbins, they were commonly used as grips for skipping ropes — today such items, complete with old Lancashire skipping rhymes, can be purchased any Saturday in Portobello Road.

As a result of these costs, ring yarn was virtually never shipped on the bobbin in Lancashire. One alternative would have been to develop a ring-frame to spin on the bare spindle, an endeavor which in fact absorbed much time and energy on the part of Lancashire's expert machine makers, but with no commercial success.[30] A second alternative for weft yarn was to rewind it into large packages at the spinning mill and then rewind it onto shuttle pirns at the weaving mill. On the winding machines in use in Lancashire (which even before World War I were far from being the most advanced technology), such rewinding of ring weft posed a cost constraint of roughly the same, and equally as prohibitive, magnitude as shipping on the bobbin. As a result ring spindles were virtually *never* used to spin weft in the disintegrated Lancashire spinning mills.[31] These cost-constraints imposed by vertical specialization in transferring ring weft from the spinning mill to the weaving mill were the major cause of the slow rate of adoption of the ring-frame in Lancashire from the 1870s on.[32]

On the other hand, twist (or warp) yarn, whether ring or mule, had to be put onto warping beams in any case; so with either technology some winding costs would be incurred. When mule yarn was used, the warping process was usually carried out at the weaving mill where it could be supervised by the management since faulty warping could result in costly stoppages and waste in the subsequent sizing and weaving processes.[33] However, in order to save the costs of shipping on the bobbin (or, before World War I, on the even larger warping spools then in use) or alternatively to avoid performing an extra stage of winding, it became the practice to do the winding and warping of ring twist at the spinning mill.[34] Hence the demand for ring twist, and the rate of diffusion of the ring-frame, depended partly on the willingness of weaving managers to forego supervision of the winding and warping processes as well as on their perceptions of the added costs of letting their own winding and warping machines sit idle or their confidence in dispensing with the processes altogether.[35]

Insofar as the warping processes were shifted to the spinning mills, the introduction of high-speed warping machinery (which by the late 1920s ran almost four times as fast as the ordinary machinery) was

[30]*Textile Manufacturer*, June 15, 1979, p. 179; December 15, 1889, p. 567, March 15, 1980, pp. 88–89; November 15, 1908, p. 361; J. Nasmith, *The Student's Cotton Spinning* (Manchester, 1896) 3rd ed., p. 532; W. Walsh, "Fifty-years' Progress in Ring-spinning Machines," *Textile Manufacturer*, Dec. 1925, p. 96.

[31]Copeland, *Cotton Manufacturing*, p. 74; Lazonick, "Factor costs," p. 14.

[32]*Ibid.*, pp. 13–16.

[33]Copeland, *Cotton Manufacturing*, p. 72n; T. Thornley, *The Middle Processes of Cotton Mills* (London, 1923), p. 127.

[34]Thornley, *Middle Processes*, p. 110; R. Peake, *Cotton: From the Raw Material to the Finished Product* (London, 1926), pp. 79–80; Great Britain, Board of Trade, *An Industrial Survey of the Lancashire Area* (London, 1932), p. 135; E. Gray, *The Weaver's Wage* (Manchester, 1937), p. 63.

[35]Peake, *Cotton*, pp. 79–80; Political and Economic Planning, *Report*, p. 95; E. Snowden, "Cotton Yarn Preparation Developments," in Cotton Board, *Cotton and Rayon Machinery and Processing Development* (Manchester, 1945), p. 92.

The United Mill at Chadderton shortly after its Construction in 1874.

impeded. The maximum feasible speed of a warping machine was dependent on the diameter of its warping beam, the larger the diameter, all other things being equal, the faster the machine could be run. But the larger diameter of the beam also meant that it weighed more, and as a speaker to the National Federation of Textile Managers' Associations warned, "this type of beam is only suitable for the manufacturer [i.e., the weaver] who does his own warping, and is not suitable for spinners who have to transport their own beams."[36] It might also be noted that in the 1930s, ring spinning mills came to a minimum price agreement on warped yarn, an agreement which prompted some weaving firms to bring previously idle winding and warping equipment into use again, and, perhaps, to shift back to using mule twist yarn.[37] Facing all these uncertainties and constraints, it is not surprising that in 1913 nonintegrated spinning firms had only 50 to 55 percent of the ring spindles in the industry even though they possessed about 80 percent of all spindles, and that in 1946 they possessed 65 percent of ring spindles but 92 percent of mule spindles and 84 percent of all spindles.[38]

The method of buying cotton in Britain also favored the retention of mule spinning over ring spinning. In the United States most of the cotton needed for the upcoming year was bought just after the cotton har-

---

[36]F. Holt, "High-speed Winding and Warping," *Journal of the National Federation of Textile Managers' Associations*, Vol. IX, (1929–1930) pp. 104–105.
[37]Gray, *Weaver's*, p. 62.
[38]J. Worrall, *The Cotton Spinners' and Manufacturers' Directory for Lancashire* (Oldham, 1913); Great Britain, Board of Trade, *Working Party*, p. 37.

vest to ensure that, for a given staple length, the yarn would be of the high quality and consistency required for standardized, low end-breakage production.[39] In effect such advance purchasing and warehousing of cotton was a form of vertical integration — over the course of the year it ensured a regular and consistent supply of the firm's crucial raw material. In Britain, however, the structure of industrial relations meant that consistently low-breakage yarn was neither required by the spinning manager nor demanded by the weaving manager.[40] Hence, such large-scale buying and warehousing of cotton was rarely done.[41] Instead, the spinning manager would buy his cotton in Liverpool (or increasingly in Manchester) essentially from week to week, never knowing exactly what quality cotton would be available and always keeping his eyes open for feasible mixes of cotton that would enable him to cut costs. Due to its intermittent (rather than continuous) spinning motion, the mule put much less strain on the yarn being spun than the ring-frame. As a result, the mule was much more adaptable to not only inferior cotton but also a *wider range* of cotton quality than was the ring-frame. Hence the mule provided the Lancashire cotton buyer with more week-to-week flexibility in the quality of cotton he could feasibly purchase.

Due to the differences in spinning motions on rings and mules, ring yarn was harder twisted than mule yarn for any given count spun at normal production levels per spindle. Ring yarn was therefore stronger, more uniform, and more break-resistant than mule yarn and tended to have a relative advantage where weaving managers put a high priority on low end-breakage rates. Given the structure of industrial relations in Britain which fixed piece-rates regardless of output and which limited the number of looms per weaver, weaving managers with Lancashire looms did not try to minimize end breakages but rather sought out the lowest quality yarn that their operatives, and buyers, would stand. In addition, quite apart from the industrial relations structure, end breakages, and resultant down-time, were less costly on the Lancashire looms than on the much more expensive automatic looms. Moreover, the use of high quality yarn could permit a significant increase in looms per weaver on the automatic loom since the primary work of the operative was repairing warp breaks. But on the Lancashire loom use of such yarn might not permit any increase in looms per weaver since on this machine the primary work of the operative was changing shuttles. Hence, the use of low quality yarn on the automatic loom would greatly reduce its labor-cost saving potential.

The choice of technique between Lancashire looms and automatic looms was, therefore, greatly dependent on the ability of the weaving

[39]C. Brooks, *Cotton* (New York, 1898), pp. 282–284; Copeland, *Cotton Manufacturing*, pp. 180–184.
[40]See Lazonick and Mass, "Performance."
[41]Brooks, *Cotton*, p. 209.

manager to obtain low-breakage yarn on a regular basis. But in the Lancashire industry, where the Lancashire loom dominated, where spinning mills sought to cut costs by using inferior cotton and by "indifferent" yarn preparation (as one manager put it), and where even ring yarn was of a much lower twist than in the United States, the manager of a specialized weaving mill had no assurance whatsoever that he could obtain the necessary supplies on the market.[42] As the 1944 Platt Mission to the U.S. stated in its report:

> The [economically] optimum twist . . . for spinning does not always coincide with that for weaving. Under American conditions, where spinning is standardized and subordinated to weaving, it is possible to determine this optimum twist, and equally important, maintain it.[43]

In 1913, almost all Britain's automatic looms were in firms that combined spinning and weaving. In 1957 combined firms, which then controlled 33 percent of all looms, possessed 67 percent of the automatic looms in the industry.[44]

High quality yarn had always been important in the United States as a labor-saving measure.[45] It became all the more important with the advent of high-speed ring spindles from the 1870s, the Northrop loom from the 1890s, and high-speed winding and warping processes from the first decades of the twentieth century. By the interwar years quality control not only of the cotton but also of the yarn at each process up to the loom had become the key to achieving high productivity on the new machines. There could be no interest in the spinning department of an integrated mill, as was often the case in a specialized spinning mill, in passing the breakage problems on to the weaving room where they were particularly costly.[46] A crucial stage of quality control was the winding of all yarn, twist and weft (or "warp" and "filling" in the U.S.), after it came off the spinning frame so that it could be "cleaned and cleared," that is, so that the chance of further breakage could be minimized. Such rewinding of ring weft also permitted the spinning of larger packages on the ring-frames (since they did not have to be ready for the shuttle) which cut down on time lost in doffing, while the cost of winding itself was greatly reduced by a number of important improvements from the beginning of the century.[47] By the 1930s almost all yarn in the U.S. was

[42]Ormerod, "Prospects," p. 12; W. Lazonick "Production Relations, Labor Productivity and Choice of Technique, U.S. and British Cotton Spinning," *Journal of Economic History*, Vol. 41, No. 3, (September, 1981,) pp. 491–516; United States Productivity Team Report, *The British Cotton Industry* (British Productivity Council: London, 1952), p. 12.

[43]Great Britain, Ministry of Production, *Report of the Cotton Textile Mission to the U.S.A.* (London, 1944), p. 26.

[44]Ormerod, "Prospects," p. 12.

[45]It saved labor in more than one way; the better work conditions not only permitted more output per worker, but also helped to keep good workers from seeking jobs elsewhere. See Lazonick, "Production Relations."

[46]*Textile Manufacturer*, 15 March 1903, p. 89; Ormerod, "Prospects," pp. 12–13.

[47]Copeland, *Cotton Manufacturing*, p. 74; W. Turner, "Universal Winding," *Journal of the British Association of Managers of Textile Works* (Lancashire Section) Vol. II, (1910–1911), pp. 122–132; Robson, *Cotton Industry*, p. xvii.

rewound on these machines whereas in Britain the new winding technology was, like the automatic loom, barely adopted even by the 1940s. The break-prone yarn used in Britain could not stand the high speeds of these machines while quality control was not a great concern to British cotton managers in any case.[48]

The integration of spinning and weaving was a necessary condition for the adoption of more automatic and high-speed machinery in the British cotton industry. But it was by no means a sufficient condition. As Alfred Chandler has demonstrated, it is the integration of distribution with production which gives managers the incentive to mass produce while it is their coordinated control over the interrelated production processes and the assurance of regular supplies of inputs all along the line which enable them to do so.[49] The separation of marketing from production in Lancashire and the large number of firms at each level meant that weavers could never be sure of long runs and that both spinners and weavers rarely produced for stock.[50] In the weaving sector, at least, vertical specialization meant anything but product specialization and standardization, especially when the market contracted at which time even spinning firms were forced to pick up small orders and widen their range of counts. In spinning, a change in the cotton mixings meant a day or two of work stoppage, although within certain limits the flexibility of the mule meant it could spin different counts from the same mixing with only a much less costly alteration of the machinery gearing. The Lancashire loom could be fitted with attachments for plain or fancy work, and hence was well-adapted to non-standardized production. It was not unusual for a weaving operative to be tending looms weaving different types of cloth.[51] In 1963, the Managing Director of Ashton Brothers accused his industry of having "clung tenaciously to the two most flexible machines ever known in any industry — the Lancashire loom and the mule."

> [T]he Lancashire manufacturer expects to use the same equipment to manufacture a heterogeneous range and type of goods, with little in common except width! This sets the pattern for equipment. Not only is he unwilling to "through manufacture" a product; he cannot become really efficient in his selected horizontal tier.[52]

---

[48]L. Tippett, *A Portrait of the Lancashire Textile Industry* (London, 1969), pp. 66–67; Productivity Team Report, *Cotton Weaving* (London, 1950), p. 12; U.S. Productivity Team Report, *British Cotton* (London, 1950), p. 17.

[49]A. Chandler, *The Visible Hand* (Cambridge, Mass., 1977). Gray, *Weaver's*, p. 30.

[50]W. Reekie, "The Marketing of Cotton Goods Abroad," *Journal of the National Federation of Textile Works Managers' Associations*, Vol. VI, (1926–1927) pp. 174–175; Great Britain, Ministry of Production, *Report*, pp. 30–31.

[51]Ormerod, "Prospects," pp. 11–12.

[52]J. Jewkes, "Is British Industry Inefficient?" *Manchester School*, XIV (January 1946), 1–16.

Workers at Mule Frames in the Dee Mill, part of the Courtaulds Group, 1956.

ATTEMPTS AT STRUCTURAL CHANGE

Ashton Brothers itself was a fully integrated concern, and as the first to introduce Northrop looms into the British industry stands out as an innovator as well as profit-maximizer. The key difference between Ashton Brothers and the vast majority of firms in the Lancashire industry was that its well-established market position as a plain-cloth producer gave it the power both to experiment and to play a part in *defining* the constraints it would ultimately (but not necessarily irrevocably) face. The profits that a firm like Ashton Brothers maximized were the result of the profitable opportunities which the firm itself had a hand in creating, not simply ones that the market presented to it. When it introduced its first automatic looms in 1903, Ashton Brothers used them with mule cops because that was the type of spinning equipment it had at the time. The firm fought a short battle with the weavers' union, and settled on ten looms per weaver. By 1908 it had scrapped over half its 160,000 mule spindles and had installed 90,000 ring spindles as well as about 1,000 Northrop looms designed for ring bobbins. It engaged the union in a thirteen-week contest and this time achieved twenty looms per weaver.[53] Clearly a firm like Ashton Brothers (and there were few like it in Lancashire) faced many constraints it could not control — for example, operating in highly-unionized territory and employing half the people in the town, it could not just ignore the unions. But by virtue of its power as a large integrated firm which could introduce new interrelated technologies and take on the unions alone, it (and a few others) did not face the same constraints as did the rest of the firms in the industry. Specialized spinning managers and specialized weaving managers may very well have been acting rationally by optimizing within the constraints *they* faced as they retained the mule and Lancashire loom. But it was the specific nature of the organizational structure in which market forces were imbedded that largely defined these constraints and consequently the technologies they chose. The issue of the technological backwardness of the British cotton industry from the late nineteenth century cannot be understood by merely analyzing the individual managerial decision subject to constraints. One must analyze why the constraints developed the way they did, or, what is the same thing, why these particular constraints could not be overcome. Let us, then, address this issue.

To be sure, there were intelligent observers of the industry who denied there were any constraints worth overcoming. In 1919, Alfred Marshall (no great authority on the cotton industry but influential nonetheless) wrote:

> It is generally recognized that the chief economy in production, as distinguished from marketing, that can be effected by a cartel or other association of producers, is that of so parcelling out the demand for various sorts of the same class of product that each business can specialize its plant on a narrow range of work, and yet keep it running with but little interruption. This specialization is however thoroughly effected without conscious effort in the Lancashire cotton industry; and especially in those branches of it, which are mainly in the hands of a multitude of independent businesses of moderate size. As is well known, fine spinning, coarse spinning and weaving are localized separately. Individual firms frequently specialize on a narrow range of counts for spinning. Blackburn, Preston, Nelson, and Oldham are centres of four different classes of staple cloths, and so on.[54]

In 1946, John Jewkes (who was an eminent authority on the cotton industry) argued that the flexible structure of the British cotton industry gave it a comparative advantage in the production of specialized products. He went on to claim that vertical integration would rob the industry of this advantage. "Vertical integration may be a form of industrial

[53]A. Fowler, "Trade Unions and Technical Change: The Automatic Loom Strike, 1908," *Bulletin of the North West Labour History, Society,* 1980; W. Mass, "Technological Change and Industrial Relations in the Cotton Textile Industry: The Diffusion of Automatic Weaving in Britain and the United States" (Ph.D. dissertation, Boston College, 1983).
[54]Marshall, *Industry and Trade,* p. 601.

organization associated with relative immaturity," he conjectured, and went on to assert that the "case against British industry as a whole is very thin."[55]

The problem with Jewkes's argument is that over the next decade, as the British cotton industry retained its fragmented structure, it lost not only the lowest quality markets to India, Japan, and Hong Kong, as had been the case before the war, but also higher quality markets to Western Europe and the U.S.A. (see Table 3).[56] Between 1956 and 1961, the U.K. experienced a 10 percent increase in labor productivity mainly due to the attrition of inefficient firms, while labor productivity increases in Belgium, France, and Italy were 15 percent, 28 percent and 52 percent respectively. In 1960, output per worker in spinning was from 30 to 60 percent higher in France, Germany, and Holland than in Britain despite the fact that the average count spun was higher (and therefore, other things equal, the output per spindle-hour lower) in these countries.[57]

The post-World War II period thus extended the long-term decline of the British cotton industry in a world economy extremely favorable to growth. The roots of this long-term decline, as I have argued, must be located in the institutional structure which developed in the "laissez-faire" period of the nineteenth century when serious competitors had not yet arisen and the British industry dominated the markets of the world. Yet despite the inapplicability of its fragmented structure to twentieth century competition, by the 1950s a restructuring of the industry had barely occurred.

In the decades prior to World War I, structural change was rare in the British cotton industry. Besides the formation of two oligopolistic (and multinational) firms in the manufacture and sale of sewing thread (J.P. Coats in 1896 and, in response, the English Sewing Cotton Co. in 1897), there were apparently only two important amalgamations in the cotton industry prior to World War I — Horrockses, Crewdson (1887), a large enterprise that integrated spinning, weaving, and marketing, and the Fine Cotton Spinners' and Doublers' Association (1898), a holding company of some thirty firms spinning very fine yarns, each firm retaining a high degree of operational autonomy.[58]

Rare, as well, were the advocates of structural change. In 1904 Frederick Merttens, President of the Manchester Statistical Society, argued

---

[55] J. Jewkes, "Is British Industry Inefficient?" *Manchester School*, Vol. XIV. No. 1, (January 1946) pp. 1–16. The Association of Vertical Specialization with Economic Progress is Made in George Stigler, "Division of Labor is Limited by the Extent of the Market," *Journal of Political Economy*, Vol. 59, No. 3, (January 1951); reprinted in Stigler, *The Organization of Industry* (Homewood, 1968).

[56] For a comprehensive analysis see B. Vitkovitch, "The U.K. Cotton Industry, 1937–54," *Journal of Industrial Economics*, Vol. III, No. 3, (July 1955), pp. 241–265.

[57] S. Pollard, *The Development of the British Economy 1914–1967* (London, 1969) 2nd ed., p. 422; Ormerod, "Prospects," p. 6.

[58] H.W. Macrosty, *The Trust Movement in British Industry* (London, 1907), pp. 124–141; G. Carter, *The Tendency Towards Industrial Combination* (London, 1913), pp. 309–315.

in a very general way that horizontal combination and vertical integration were necessary prerequisites to the cheapening of production and meeting of foreign competition. In 1905 W.H. Guthrie, in an article entitled "The Cotton Mill of the Future," outlined the advantages of integration from spinning through marketing, optimistically predicting that the introduction of advanced technologies would result in the re-emergence of the integrated firm in the British industry. "There is no doubt," he argued, "that the greatest hindrance to the more general adoption of the ring frame in this country is the decentralisation of spinning and weaving plants. With the advent of the automatic loom (which is at its best when using weft spun on a bobbin) these conditions will be changed, and our mills, will again become cotton-manufacturing concerns."[59] Unfortunately for Guthrie's prediction, it was structure which determined technology and not vice versa, and over the next decade as the number of firms in Lancashire increased by 14 percent, the number of spindles by 30 percent and the number of looms by 24 percent, the industry became more horizontally competitive and more vertically specialized than ever.[60] In such generally prosperous times, those within the industry had little inducement to undertake institutional innovation and those outside the industry were hardly in a position to be critical.

But as the slump in the coarser goods section of the cotton industry in the early 1920s failed to disappear within the "normal" one or two years, first the spinning capitalists and then the banks began to take action to control competition. In order to keep up yarn prices, the Federation of Master Cotton Spinners' Associations organized short-time work between 1921 and 1926, which, insofar as it was adhered to, created conditions more favorable for the survival of the less efficient firms. In 1923 some spinning capitalists (including Charles Macara, who had been President of the FMCSA from 1894 to 1916) advocated a scheme to permit more efficient mills to run while compensating the workers and owners of less efficient firms to cease production, but the FMCSA rejected the plan.[61] In the same year, the FMCSA instituted a scheme of minimum prices, and the following year, in order to enforce it on "disloyal" spinners, sought to have it legalized by Parliament. Unfortunately for the spinners, the weaving industry successfully opposed such an attempt to raise the price of one of its basic inputs. In 1927, the FMCSA attempted once again to assert its own authority, setting up a cartel called the American Cotton Yarn Association to set prices and limit

[59] F. Merttens, "Productivity, Protection and Integration of Industry," *Transactions of the Manchester Statistical Society*, 1903–1904; W.H. Guthrie, "The Cotton Mill of the Future," *Textile Manufacturer*, 15 August 1905, p. 255.

[60] Jones, *Increasing Return*, p. 277.

[61] P. Fitzgerald, *Industrial Combination in England*, (London, 1927), pp. 9–10; Committee on Industry and Trade, *Survey*, p. 34; G. Daniels and H. Campion, "The Cotton Industry and Trade," in British Association, *Britain in Depression* (London, 1935), p. 340; C. Macara, *The New Industrial Era* (Manchester, 1923), p. 90; Jones, "Agitation," p. 450.

production. Within ten months the cartel had been eroded by competitive forces.[62] Meanwhile the banks, still expecting a recovery, continued to extend credit to (or agree to moratoria for) the deeply indebted spinning mills, the financial position of which was being further weakened by the general deflation of the 1920s.[63]

Now it was the banking sector that required some leadership to extract its members from a difficult situation. Encouraged by the general movement towards "rationalization" of industry in the late 1920s, the Bank of England sought to effect a large-scale amalgamation of spinning capacity that, by providing a highly concentrated entity under centralized control with the financial ability to re-equip, could set the tone for the industry and force inefficient producers out. The idea was to set up a firm — the Lancashire Cotton Corporation — which expected to merge as many as two hundred mills and twenty million spindles in the American section of the spinning industry, wiping out all fixed interest charges in the process by issuing preference shares to ordinary creditors and debenture holders and new common shares to old shareholders.[64]

By all accounts the directors and managers of the Lancashire cotton mills resisted attempts at merger on the grounds — quite rational from the individual point of view — that any such amalgamation would involve their loss of individual control over their enterprises.[65] As Keynes put the problem in 1928:

> There [is] probably no hall in Manchester large enough to hold all the directors of cotton companies; they [run] into thousands. One of the first things should be to dismiss the vast majority of these people, but the persons to whom this proposal would have to be made would be precisely those directors.[66]

Or as John Ryan, Managing Director of the Lancashire Cotton Corporation (and himself a relative newcomer to the cotton industry brought in by the banks) argued:

> I do not think we can leave it to the individuals. Vested interests will always resist a movement which tends to remove them, and vested interests can very

[62]Committee on Industry and Trade, *Survey*, pp. 35–36; Daniels and Campion, "Cotton industry," p. 341.

[63]M. Kirby, "Lancashire Cotton," p. 148; H. Clay, *The Problem of Industrial Relations* (London, 1929), pp. 138–139; H. Clay, *The Post-War Unemployment Problem* (London, 1929), p. 163; Committee on Industry and Trade, *Final Report* (London, 1929), p. 46; A. Lucas, "The Bankers' Industrial Development Company," *Harvard Business Review*, Vol. XI, No. 3, (April 1933), pp. 272–273. For a case of prolonged optimism see Fitzgerald, *Industrial Combination*, p. 8; "The cotton trade is one of the few sections of industry in which English firms have little to fear from foreign competition."

[64]Clay, *Post-War Unemployment*, p. 49; Economic Advisory Council, *Report*, p. 20; R. Streat, "The Cotton Industry in Contraction: Problems and Policies of the Inter-war Years," *District Bank Review*, No. 127, September 1958, p. 7; A. Lucas, *Industrial Reconstruction and the Control of Competition: The British Experiments* (London, 1937), p. 155; J. Wisselink, "The Present Condition of the English Cotton Industry," *Harvard Business Review*, Vol. VIII, No. 2 (Janaury 1930) p. 158. On the rationalization movement in general, see L. Hannah, *The Rise of the Corporate Economy: The British Experience* (Baltimore, 1976), ch. 3.

[65]Streat, "Cotton Industry," p. 7; "Combinations in the Cotton Trade," *Journal of the National Federation of Textile Works' Managers' Associations*, Vol. XII (1932–1933) pp. 5–9; D. Macgregor, J. Ryan *et. al.*, "Problems of Rationalisation: a Discussion," *Economic Journal*, Vol. XL, (September 1930), pp. 360–361; see also A. Chandler, "The Growth of the Transnational Industrial Firm in the United States and the United Kingdom: a Comparative Analysis," *Economic History Review*, 2nd series Vol. XXXIII, No. 3, (August, 1980); Hannah, *Rise*, pp. 147–148.

[66]In discussion of paper by Daniels and Jewkes, "Post-war depression," p. 200.

easily hold a position which is acceptable to themselves but yet is acting as a parasite on an industry and slowly driving it to death. . . .[67]

By 1930, the Lancashire Cotton Corporation had coerced 96 firms and 9.3 million spindles (almost one-fifth of the Lancashire total) into the fold, as the bankers threatened the reluctant directors of these firms with termination of credit.[68] Another group of indebted directors sought to create a corporation of "spinners of American cotton for the benefit of the spinners," but were (as Wisselink put it) "loath to give up their functions," and the banks refused to lend their support.[69] The Lancashire Cotton Corporation, however, which did not have centralized control, was unable to develop an effective managerial structure, and in 1932 its chief executives resigned when the board of directors decided that the mill managers, who had been displaying a lack of initiative, should be given more autonomy.[70]

The problems of the Lancashire Cotton Corporation ultimately benefitted the rest of the spinning industry by ridding it of a significant amount of excess capacity. By 1939 it had scrapped about 4.5 million spindles which it had brought under its control.[71] As the world-wide depression hit an already stagnant British cotton industry in the early 1930s, it became apparent that a more coordinated and explicit scrapping policy was required to eliminate machinery and firms. By 1934, British yarn production had declined by 40 percent and cloth production by 55 percent from their 1912 levels while the number of spindles in the industry had contracted by only about 20 percent and the number of looms by about 25 percent.[72] In approving a scheme for eliminating spindles in 1934, the FMCSA stated that the problem of surplus capacity had been with the industry for nearly fifteen years, and that the "ordinary processes of economic law" had not so far solved it. "The Surplus Spindles Bill," they argued, "may be regarded as an insurance against a price war between the combines and the smaller independent firms, which, however it ended, could only be a disaster for Lancashire."[73] The scheme, which called for a compulsory per spindle levy on all operating firms to be used to buy up and scrap the capacity of spinning firms

[67]Macgregor, Ryan et. al., "Problems," p. 361
[68]Hannah, *Rise*, p. 84; Kirby, "Lancashire Cotton," pp. 149–151.
[69]Wisselink, "Present Condition," p. 159.
[70]*Economist*, October 8, 1932, p. 635; Hannah, *Rise*, pp. 84–85; Lucas, *Industrial*, pp. 156–159; Kirby, "Lancashire Cotton," p. 152.
[71]Pollard, *Development*, p. 122. The *purpose* of the Lancashire Cotton Corporation was not to reduce surplus capacity in the cotton industry as some have argued. See e.g. G.W. Furness, "The Cotton and Rayon Textile Industry," in D. Burn (ed.), *The Structure of British Industry* (Cambridge, England, 1958), pp. 187–188; and Kirby, "Lancashire Cotton," p. 151. Rather its purpose was to salvage the financial investments of the bankers which inevitably involved some scrapping of the least serviceable machinery in the plant acquired. That the founders of the L.C.C. *intended* in 1929 to scrap about half of the Corporation's spindleage capacity over the next decade is by no means evident.
[72]Federation of Master Cotton Spinners' Associations, *Cotton Spinning Industry Bill (1935): The Industry's Case for the Bill* (Manchester, 1935), p. 2.
[73]*Ibid.*, pp. 11–13.

willing to be compensated for going out of business, became law under the Spindles Act of 1936. By World War II, the Spindles Board set up under the Act had acquired and scrapped 6.2 million spindles, reducing capacity to two-thirds the pre-World War I level.[74]

In 1929, when the Lancashire Cotton Corporation was in the process of formation, John Ryan, its first Managing Director, declared to the cotton textile Managers Association: "The horizontal amalgamation is no use to Lancashire; it must be vertical . . ."[75] Yet in the inter-war years vertical integration was rarely discussed, never mind attempted. The Lancashire Cotton Corporation, which had initially intended to integrate vertically, had enough difficulty managing its horizontal operations, and simply scrapped the 20,000 looms which had been in the mills that it had acquired.[76]

Nor was there any significant vertical integration or technical change in the context of the more favorable market conditions after World War II. From 1946 to 1951, the British cotton industry experienced a dramatic boom, with yarn production increasing by 50 percent and cloth production by 56 percent (see Table 4). Mills that had been closed during the war, and whose plant and equipment had long since been written off, were able to enjoy profits on the basis of traditional production methods. There were no labor productivity gains in spinning and only slight gains in weaving during this period. In 1951, only 8 percent of spinning capacity and 6 percent of weaving capacity was post-World War II vintage.[77]

That Lancashire cotton managers complained of labor shortage during these boom years was due to their continued reliance on labor-intensive methods of production which prevented them from matching the wages and work conditions of more modern industries that were developing in the Lancashire area. In 1948 the government intervened to try to solve this problem both by recruiting labor for the industry and by passing the Cotton Spinning Industry (Re-equipment Subsidy) Act. Under the Act, firms having at least three mills and a minimum number of spindles were eligible to receive a 25 percent re-equipment subsidy to be used to modernize some of the mills and close down the remainder. But the Act provided no incentive to integrate spinning and weaving as part of the re-equipment process, let alone to integrate production and distribution. Government intervention in effect took the vertical structure of

[74]Robson, *Cotton Industry*, pp. 229, 230, 340.
[75]J. Ryan, "Combination in the Cotton Trade," *Journal of the National Federation of Textile Works Managers' Associations*, Vol. VIII, (1928–1929) p. 24. See also H.A. Marquand, *The Dynamics of Industrial Combinations* (London, 1931), pp. 108–110.
[76]Robson, *Cotton Industry*, pp. 120–121.
[77]C. Miles, *Lancashire Textiles: A Case Study of Industrial Change* (Cambridge, England, 1968), pp. 38–39. See also D.C. Shaw, "Productivity in the Cotton Spinning Industry," *The Manchester School*, Vol. XVIII, No. 1, (June 1950).

the industry as given. Not surprisingly, the Act of 1948 had only a minimal impact on re-equipment.[78] The ossification of the British cotton industry into its horizontal layers, and the attendant problems for technical change, were well summed up in 1950 by the British Productivity Team on Cotton Weaving. Reporting on their recent visit to U.S. mills, the Productivity Team stressed the multi-fold advantages of vertical integration, but went on to warn:

> To attempt to change the horizontal structure would affect operatives, managements, shareholders, spinners, merchants, merchant-convertors and many others. New buildings would be needed in addition to new machinery. Clearly such a proposal is out of the question.[79]

The boom ended in 1951 with cloth output for the home market somewhat larger than it had been in 1937, but with exports down some 50 percent and imports up by close to 700 percent (see Table 4). In 1937 imports had represented only 3.1 percent of domestic consumption whereas by 1951 they had grown to 16.1 percent, coming in mainly from Hong Kong, Pakistan, and India which enjoyed duty-free access under the 1932 Ottawa agreements that had been designed to secure Commonwealth markets for British cotton goods. To attribute the stagnation of the British cotton industry that ensued after 1951 to cheap imports, however, would be an oversimplification. In fact, between 1951 and 1958, import penetration was slight.[80] The fundamental problem was an industry mired in its own highly competitive and vertically specialized structure, lacking any internal forces to set in motion structural transformation. In 1958, there were almost 1500 firms undertaking converting activities in the Lancashire cotton industry, and over three-quarters had no formal marketing or financial links with any particular weaving firms.[81] As this mass of marketing firms fed small orders to firms in the vertically disintegrated production structure, production runs grew shorter while delivery times grew longer, further worsening Lancashire's competitive position in the world's markets.[82]

The weaving sector itself continued to consist of small family firms in the 1950s. Indeed between 1940 and 1959 the average number of looms per firm actually decreased from 470 to 403. Even though the number of firms declined by over 40 percent during this period, there were still 567 specialized weaving enterprises remaining in the industry in 1959. And despite major governmental intervention in the early 1960s to rid

---

[78]Miles, *Lancashire*, pp. 26–27, 40; Robson, *Cotton Industry*, p. 219. See also Ormerod, "Prospects," pp. 8–9.

[79]Productivity Team Report, *Cotton Weaving*, p. 16.

[80]Miles, *Lancashire*, p. 26.

[81]*Ibid.*, p. 68.

[82]Lucas, *Industrial Reconstruction*, p. 159; Clay, *Report*, p. 68; Vitkovitch, "U.K. Cotton," p. 262; Ormerod, "Prospects," p. 14; UTFWA, *Plan*, p. 16. See also, F. Vibert, "Economic Problems of the Cotton Industry," *Oxford Economic Papers*, N.S., Vol. 18, No. 3, (Nov. 1966).

the Lancashire cotton industry of excess and antiquated capacity, 322 specialized weaving firms still remained in the industry in 1965.[83] On the basis of her first-hand investigations of about one hundred family firms in the industry in the 1960s, Caroline Miles presented the following profile:

> . . . old equipment, largely if not entirely written off; an aging, immobile labour force, possessing skills not readily transferable to modern plant; aging management with no successors in view; and stagnant or declining markets. With low fixed costs and an available labour reserve (since the aging workers were not able to get permanent jobs elsewhere), such a firm was able to disrupt prices, under-cutting firms with relatively high fixed costs when demand was rising and withdrawing again when trade was slack.[84]

Most of the spinning firms were joint-stock companies, although even in these businesses family control and management were often exercised.[85] From 1940 to 1959 the spindle capacity of the average spinning firm increased by about 23 percent, largely due to horizontal amalgamation (some of which was stimulated by the Act of 1948 that only applied to firms with at least three mills). In 1940 there were 280 firms carrying out spinning in the British cotton industry; in 1959, 141.[86] The largest of these firms, the Lancashire Cotton Corporation, had long since abandoned the notion of vertical integration. Other large amalgamations such as the Fine Spinners and Doublers and the Combined English Mills were loosely organized federations of largely autonomous units. With persistent over-capacity at the weaving level and with their own lack of internal organization, even the largest spinning firms were content to take the horizontal structure of the industry as given during the post-World War II decades. They provided no leadership whatsoever in structural change.

By 1959, the British cotton industry was struggling to survive in a highly competitive international environment in which success was based on a degree of tariff protection combined with high capital-intensity and high throughput production. Once again the British government intervened, this time on a much more massive scale than ever before, in an effort to improve Lancashire's productive base (a strategy it pursued in lieu of the imposition of strict import controls on goods from Commonwealth countries). The 1959 Cotton Industry Act sought to rid both the spinning and weaving sections (as well as the finishing section) of excess capacity while providing financial assistance for the re-equipment of the plant that remained. Firms were paid for scrapping

---

[83]Miles, *Lancashire*, pp. 44, 73, 120–121.

[84]C. Miles, "Protection of the British Cotton Industry," in W. Corden and G. Fels, *Public Assistance to Industry* (Boulder, 1976), pp. 203–204.

[85]G. Bennett, "The Present Position of the Cotton Industry in Great Britain," (unpublished M.A. thesis, University of Manchester, 1933), ch. III.

[86]Miles, *Lancashire*, p. 44.

TABLE 3

U.K. COTTON INDUSTRY: DECLINE IN VOLUME OF PIECE-GOOD EXPORTS
1910–1953

| Period | Lower total imports | Per cent change in piece goods exports due to: | |
		Competition from Japan, India, Hong Kong	Competition from other countries
1910–13 to 1927–29	−25.8	−54.7	−17.0
1927–29 to 1935–37	−34.3	−60.2	3.9
1935–37 to 1949–53	−30.5	− 2.8	−67.3

Source: B. Vitkovitch, "The U.K. Cotton Industry 1937–54," *Journal of Industrial Economics*, Vol. III, No. 3, (July 1955), pp. 254, 255, 257.

some or all of their equipment with a premium being paid to those firms that went out of business. Operatives were also compensated for lost jobs. Under the Act, 48 percent of all spinning spindles, 27 percent of all doubling spindles, and 38 percent of all looms in the industry were scrapped. Forty-four percent of specialized spinning firms and 22 percent of specialized weaving firms left the industry altogether. Integrated firms tended to stay in business, and hence the industry became more verticalized by the process of attrition. By 1963, 80 firms integrating spinning and weaving controlled 70 percent of spinning capacity and 40 percent of weaving capacity. But the Act itself had done nothing to promote vertical integration of production in the remaining firms nor did it deal in any way with the highly fragmented marketing sector.[87]

The 1959 Act, by providing a 25 percent subsidy for re-equipment, did result in some modernization of Lancashire's stock of machinery. Of the total machinery in place as of October 1965, 13 percent of the spindles and nine percent of the looms had been purchased with re-equipment grants. Scrapping and re-equipment under the 1959 Act apparently resulted in significant productivity increases in both spinning and weaving compared to the low rates of productivity increase in the decades before.[88] But the industry as a whole still retained managerial and marketing structures that impeded the introduction of mass production methods.

From 1964, however, the structure of the British cotton industry experienced a dramatic transformation by a vertically-related, but heretofore, external force, namely the producers of man-made fibres. Begin-

[87]*Ibid.*, pp. 50–57, 60, F. Fishwick and R. Cornu, *A Study of the Evolution of Concentration in the United Kingdom Textile Industry* (Commission of European Communities, October 1975), pp. 27–29; Tippett, *Portrait*, p. 161.
[88]Miles, *Lancashire*, pp. 65, 85, 87.

TABLE 4

UNITED KINGDOM — PRODUCTION, EXPORTS, AND IMPORTS OF COTTON
AND MAN-MADE FIBRE PIECE-GOODS, 1912–1973

(MILLION SQUARE YARDS)

	Production	Exports	Imports
1912*	8050	6913	98
1924	6074	4444	36
1930	3500	2472	123
1937	4532	2022	71
1946	2390	665	18
1951	3550	1078	473
1958	2350	468	434
1965	1900	300	676
1973	1421	348	1018

* = linear yards

Sources: R. Robson, *The Cotton Industry in Britain* (London, 1957), p. 345; C. Miles, *Lancashire Textiles: A Case Study of Industrial Change* (Cambridge, England, 1968), p. 26; R. Shaw and C. Sutton, *Industry and Competition* (London, 1976), p. 157.

ning in the mid-1930s, cellulose fibres, and in particular rayon, had been processed into yarn and cloth using cotton spinning and/or weaving equipment. In 1936, rayon had made up only one percent of total spinning output, but by 1951, ten percent. Although the absolute amount of man-made fibre used in spinning and weaving remained more or less constant from the early 1950s to the mid-1960s, it became an ever-increasing proportion of the total output of the Lancashire "cotton" industry as the output of both cotton yarn and cloth steadily declined. In 1966, cotton entered into less than 60 percent by weight of Lancashire weaving, man-made fibres (now both cellulosics and synthetics) making up the rest.[89]

The dominant firm in the transformation of the industry was Courtaulds, a U.K.-based multinational corporation that had a virtual monopoly in the supply of rayon to the British market. But with the development of synthetic fibres by chemical giants such as I.C.I. in Britain and Dupont in the U.S., the demand for Courtaulds' most important product, rayon, began to decline. During the 1950s, Courtaulds attempted to diversify its products, but was not overly successful. After fighting off a takeover bid by I.C.I. in 1962, the directors of Courtaulds staked the future of their company on the vertical integration and revitalization of their most important single product market — the Lancashire "cotton" industry. The original plan, drawn up in 1962, was to gain control over five large firms in the spinning industry — the Lancashire Cotton Corporation, Fine Spinners and Doublers, English Sewing Cotton, Tootals,

[89]Robson, *Cotton Industry*, p. 345; Miles, *Lancashire*, pp. 13, 85.

and Combined English Mills — as a basis for rationalizing the structure of the industry as well as to exert pressure on the government to protect the home market and thereby provide incentives for the capital-intensive investments that were needed to make the cotton and man-made fibres industry viable. By 1964 Courtaulds had acquired the Lancashire Cotton Corporation and Fine Spinners and Doublers (one-third of the industry's spinning capacity), and in 1968 it added Ashton Brothers. Meanwhile it built completely new facilities to weave its fibres, finding nothing that was worth taking over in the traditional Lancashire weaving industry.[90]

At the same time, I.C.I. was securing its own man-made fibres markets by financing acquisitions and plant modernization by other firms with an interest in the Lancashire industry. Viyella International, an outsider to the Lancashire cotton industry which acquired Combined English Mills, was backed by I.C.I., while the English Sewing Company (which acquired Tootals) was financed by both I.C.I. and Courtaulds.

In 1968, the five-firm concentration ratio in the spinning of cotton and man-made fibres was 50 percent, up from 37 percent in 1963 and 32 percent in 1958. These firms controlled over one-third of weaving sales in 1968, more than double the market share of the top five firms a decade before. The five largest firms in 1968 were fully integrated concerns, Courtaulds being the most dominant by far followed by two other firms that had been financed by the corporate giants of the British chemical industry.[91] Between 1963 and 1974 employment in the British "cotton" industry was halved and output remained constant but productivity rose by 86 percent, or about 8 percent per annum.[92] Since 1974, these new giants in the textile industry, like all othe British industrial enterprises, have had to cope with a sagging national economy and an unstable international environment as well as the ever-present danger of bureaucratic ossification. But they have certainly overcome the problem of a fragmented structure of industrial organization and the technological stagnation that had ensued from it since the late nineteenth century. Now, ironically enough, the problem facing British industry is a political perspective that draws upon neoclassical orthodoxy to argue that the free market system is an engine of economic prosperity.[93]

---

[90]D.C. Coleman, "Courtaulds and the Beginning of Rayon," in B. Supple (ed.), *Essays in British Business Experience* (London, 1974); Coleman, *Courtaulds*; Knight, *Private Enterprise and Public Intervention: The Courtaulds*, Volume III (Oxford, 1980), espec. pp. 270–281; Miles, *Lancashire*, pp. 91–93; Fishwick and Cornu, *Evolution of Concentration*, pp. 37–39, 76, 78–79, 188–191.

[91]Fishwick and Cornu, *Evolution of Concentration*, pp. 30, 37–39, 179–220; W. Reader, *Imperial Chemical Industries: Volume II* (Oxford, 1975); D. Channon, *The Strategy and Structure of British Enterprise* (Boston, 1973), pp. 173–178; Textile Council, *Cotton and Allied Textiles* (Manchester, 1969), Vol. I, ch. 2; United Kingdom, Board of Trade, *Census of Production*, Summary Tables (London, 1970), p. 131/109.

[92]Fishwick and Cornu, *Evolution of Concentration*, p. 21.

[93]For an elaboration of this theme, see B. Elbaum and W. Lazonick, "The Decline of the British Economy: An Institutional Perspective," Harvard Institute of Economic Research Discussion Paper No. 878, January, 1982.

UNDERSTANDING STRUCTURAL CHANGE

Why did it take so long for the internal organization of the British cotton industry to be restructured in response to the new international environment of the twentieth century? Why, for example, could the British Productivity Team on Cotton Weaving argue in 1949, apparently with good reason, that a strategy of vertical integration was "out of the question"? In a freely competitive industry, what prevented the emergence of a number of fully integrated, technologically progressive firms that could force the specialized manufacturing and marketing firms to adapt or get out?

Orthodox economic theory with its analytical focus on managerial choices subject to *given* market and technical constraints does not take us very far in understanding issues of structural change. In his influential article on "the nature of the firm" (published in Britain in the late 1930s), Ronald Coase portrays the decision to whether or not to integrate as a matter of "substitution at the margin," thus bringing the theory of vertical integration within the limits of the theoretical imagination of the neoclassical economist.[94] Operating within factor-price constraints as set by market forces the manager of the firm will decide to use the market to supply an input or sell a particular output when the cost of doing so is less than the cost of superseding the market by organizing the particular vertically-related process under his own management, and vice versa when the cost of doing so is more. As a proposition subordinating the choice of enterprise form to the decision to maximize profits subject to given constraints, Coase's theorem is a perfectly logical extension of neoclassical analysis. But as a fundamental proposition for analysing the nature and development of the modern capitalist enterprise, Coase's approach is highly misleading for three basic reasons.

First, the modern enterprise, if it is to reap the benefits of mass production, cannot shift its mode of operation with every change in relative factor prices, but rather must engage in long-term investment planning

---

[94]R. Coase, "The Nature of the Firm," *Economica*, N.S. Vol. IV, (November 1937); reprinted in G. Stigler and K. Boulding (eds.), *Readings in Price Theory* (Chicago, 1952). Over three decades later, Coase argued quite correctly that "modern economists writing on industrial organization have taken a very narrow view of their subject," and he specifically criticizes the work of Joe Bain, Richard Caves, and George Stigler for treating the study of industrial organization as simply applied price theory. R. Coase, "Industrial Organization: A Proposal for Research," in V. Fuchs (ed.), *Economic Research: Retrospect and Prospect* (New York, 1972), Vol. III. "What one would expect to learn from a study of industrial organization," Coase argues, "would be how industry is organized now, and how this differs from what it was in earlier periods; what forces were operative in bringing about this organization of industry, and how these forces have been changing over time; what the effects would be of proposals to change, through legal actions of various kinds, the forms of industrial organization." *Ibid.*, p. 603. Indeed, Coase claims that such issues had been his prime concern when he wrote "The Nature of the Firm" in the 1930s. Coase's latter-day critique of the neoclassical approach is well-taken, but he seems oblivious to his own important role in bringing the study of "the nature of the firm" into the ahistorical neoclassical perspective of constrained optimization. After all, the central analytical point of Coase's 1937 article was the notion that "substitution at the margin" can explain both horizontal combination and vertical integration. "A firm can expand in either or both of these ways," he argued there. "The whole of the 'structure of competitive industry' becomes tractable by the ordinary technique of economic analysis." Coase, "Nature", p. 398.

which includes a firm commitment of capital to producing certain products by certain interrelated technical processes. Indeed, in the post-World War II Lancashire cotton industry we find spinning and weaving firms or weaving and merchant firms combining and then separating for the sake of short-term supply and demand advantages without in the least altering their organizational or technical methods of production. Such actions constituted precisely Coasian managerial decision-making. But ironically these actions *exemplified the failure to develop the modern corporate enterprise* as illustrated in the following remarks by the Managing Director of Ashton Brothers to Section F of the British Association for the Advancement of Science in 1962:

> In 1946, 22.5% of installed looms were owned by combined operations — I have avoided the term "verticals". By 1959 this figure had risen to 33% . . . Most of the "combined operations" were not vertical in the strictest sense. The vertical operation converts fibre into the final fabric, merchandising the goods through appropriate trade channels. The three horizontal tiers — spinning, weaving and finishing — are, of course, included as are yarn processing and stitching operations if appropriate. The mere ownership of facilities in all sections does not necessarily satisfy this definition. Financial control is not integration. Unless fused commercially, administratively and technically such units can be mutually inhibiting, and the combined activities weaker than the horizontal constituents. The history of post-war organizational changes confirms this. In the late 1940s, weavers frequently acquired converting facilities to obtain a more secure marketing basis; convertors acquired weaving facilities to obtain assured supplies. These associations were frequently short-lived. Of 264 weaving units closed down in the four years before the 1959 Act, 109 were also convertors. A further 62 were members of groups which covered converting.
>
> Under the Yarn Spinners' Association and with fixed prices, spinners tended to integrate forward to secure weaving facilities and so obtain indirect yarn business, being content to weave at cost and obtain the constituent yarn profit. Today, the reverse is occurring, and we have supposedly-vertical organizations closing spinning units because it is claimed either that yarn can be imported cheaper than it can be spun in the U.K. or that capital can be conserved. One essential requirement for vertical integration is stability. This is incompatible with such an opportunist approach to organization.[95]

In short, the manager who integrates and disintegrates according to the ebb and flow of the market situation does so in lieu of the long-term planning of the organizationally-interconnected and technically-interrelated production and distribution processes that characterize the modern corporation.

Second, the Coasian approach ignores the role of concentrated product market power in the development of modern enterprise. No firm will produce a product unless it has a reasonable chance of selling it.

[95]Ormerod, "Prospects," pp. 10–11. See also U.S. Productivity Team, *British Cotton*, p. 6; Miles, *Lancashire*, p. 56; Furness, "Cotton," pp. 214–217.

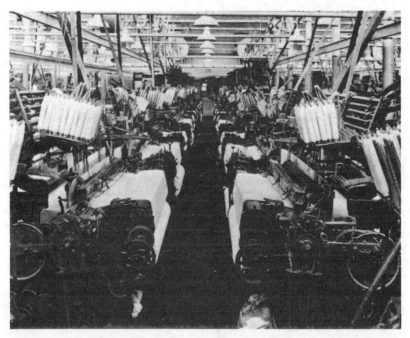

A Weaving Shed with Non-Automatic Looms Driven by Belts from Overhead Shafting.

A Weaving Shed Built in 1966 with Automatic Looms.

THE DECLINE OF THE BRITISH COTTON INDUSTRY   225

And no firm will *mass* produce a product unless it has reasonable prospects for mass sales. Moreover, since mass production requires long-term planning, reasonable sales prospects must be long-term as well. It is for this reason that the development of the firm's ability to mass distribute is a necessary condition for the development of its incentive to mass produce. Hence a firm's control over mass markets must precede, or at least emerge simultaneously with, the development of large-scale, standardized production.[96] In this sense, the development of the British textile industries in the 16th to 18th centuries was in large measure induced by the development of national supremacy over world markets. In the eighteenth and nineteenth centuries, this national control created the opportunites for numerous merchants to enter the cotton industry, thus creating for the British industry as a whole a structure of mass distribution characterized by numerous competitors and specialization along product lines. This structure of marketing still worked admirably in the decades prior to World War I during which world trade was expanding, the Japanese economy was still in the process of commercial development, and British control over India, by far its largest cotton goods market, remained supreme.

But it was a structure of marketing which, when challenged during and after World War I, was incapable of unified and concerted response. For example, Burnett-Hurst describes how, when World War I broke out, disrupting Lancashire production and distribution facilities

> [the two largest] Japanese mercantile houses . . . opened branches in Bombay and a large number of agencies and subagencies throughout India. These firms also acquired and operated ginneries and presses. The Yokohama Specie Bank and other Japanese banks extended the fullest facilities for financing the trade with India, while Japanese shipping lines established regular and direct services between India and Japan. There is no doubt that the immediate success achieved by Japan in the Indian market was due largely to the rapidity with which she secured her position by the effective co-operation of her various commercial interests.[97]

Between 1914 and 1932, Britain's share of Indian piece-good imports declined from 97 percent to 50 percent while Japan's share rose from .1 percent to 45 percent.[98] In the latter year the British Trade Commissioner in India warned:

> It should be realized that unless steps are taken very quickly to re-establish the competitive power of United Kingdom goods we shall lose the valuable co-operation of many efficient distributing organizations upon which we have relied for more than half a century. Meanwhile Manchester merchants appear to be losing that close touch with the Indian situation which has been so valuable

[96]Chandler, *The Visible Hand*, Parts II–IV.
[97]A. Burnett-Hurst, "Lancashire and the Indian Market," *Journal of the Royal Statistical Society*, Vol. XCV, Part III, (1932), pp. 399–400.
[98]*Ibid.*, p. 422.

in the past. Travellers no longer visit India, correspondence falls off in these difficult times, and, to an observer on the spot, it sometimes appears as if the greatest single export trade in the world is gradually being allowed to "peter out," no active measures being taken to deal with the situation.[99]

In 1929 one united attempt — the Eastern Textile Association Ltd. — actually had been made to mass distribute in China, but its quick failure was "the death-knell of all attempts to unite in promoting new developments from the selling angle."[100] Instead there remained over a thousand merchants in the Lancashire export trade and many hundreds more in the home trade from the 1920s into the 1950s.[101] A precondition for any significant structural and technical reorganization of production was a concentrated marketing sector that would create the incentive for production firms to mass produce and perhaps integrate forwards and that could itself integrate backwards. Such a reorganization of the cotton industry along corporate lines had taken place in the United States by the 1950s, bringing to dominance a small number of giant, fully-integrated cotton corporations.[102] Neither the development of American enterprises such as Burlington Industries and J.P. Stevens nor the massive forward integration by Courtaulds in Britain in the 1960s can be understood as "substitution at the margin" by optimizing managers taking market forces as given. Rather, such structural change was the result of entrepreneurial strategies to attain or maintain concentrated market power. Up to the 1960s such power was lacking in Lancashire precisely because "perfect" competition, and the dominance of marginal decision-making by spinning, weaving, and marketing managers to which it gave rise, made the exercise of such coordination impossible.

Third, Coase's approach ignores the problem of *managerial structure,* the implicit assumption being that this structure does not change qualitatively with changes in vertical or horizontal organization but only perhaps quantitatively in terms of the number of managers who are incorporated into the existing mode of management. As Alfred Chandler has shown, the key to the successful development and stability of the large corporation in the United States has been the development of new hierarchical structures of managerial control.[103] The development of such

---

[99]Quoted in *Ibid.*, p. 424; see also Pennington, "Competition," pp. 213–228.

[100]Streat, "Cotton industry," p. 14; see also Robson, *Cotton Industry*, pp. 215–216; Daniels and Campion, "Cotton Industry," p. 342.

[101]See note 18; Miles, *Lancashire*, p. 68. In 1965 there were still 1000 merchant-convertors in the industry. A.M. Alfred, "U.K. Textiles — A Growth Industry," *Transactions of the Manchester Statistical Society*, 1965–66, p. 9.

[102]Barkin, "Regional Significance"; J. Markham, "Integration in the Textile Industry," *Harvard Business Review*, Vol. 28, No., 1, (1950); W. Kessler, "Chapters in Business History," and W. Crook, "Corporate Concentration in the Textile Industry," both in *Textiles — A Dynamic Industry* (Colgate University Textile Study Project, 1951); U.S. House of Representatives, Committee of the Judiciary, *The Merger Movement in the Textile Industry* (Washington, 1955); W. Simpson, *Some Aspects of America's Textile Industry* (Columbia, South Carolina, 1966), ch. 6; Alfred, "U.K. Textiles," p. 21; According to Arthur Knight, who became Chairman of Courtaulds in the 1970s, U.S. corporations such as Burlington Industries and J.P. Stevens provided models of vertical integration that his company could emulate as it integrated forward in the 1960s. Knight, *Private Enterprise*, p. 46.

[103]A. Chandler, *Strategy and Structure* (Cambridge, Mass., 1962); Chandler, *Visible Hand*, Part V.

a managerial structure in the transformation of a number of smaller firms into a large corporate entity entails a coming to power of some managers and a loss of power of others as the structure of decision-making and authority is qualitatively altered.

Horizontal amalgamation in itself does not necessarily mean, however, an end to managerial autonomy for the heads of the participating firms. The case of the Lancashire Cotton Corporation, in which local mill managers refused to abide by and eventually overturned centralized control, is a case in point. In British industry in general the development of hierarchical managerial structures did not follow large-scale amalgamations, primarily because the directors of the constituent firms insisted on maintaining family control and almost complete operational autonomy even within the new amalgamated setting.[104]

In the British cotton industry, the implications of the failure to develop coordinated control of an amalgamation are well illustrated by the case of Combined English Mills (C.E.M.), a combination of fourteen largely autonomous spinning mills that had been formed in the late 1920s in an attempt to support yarn prices and that produced five percent of the total yarn output of the British cotton industry in the early 1960s. C.E.M. had taken advantage of re-equipment subsidies under the 1959 Act, and by the end of 1963 produced all its output on modern machinery. Even though output per spindle rose by 38 percent and labor productivity by 25 percent between 1960 and 1964, C.E.M. was experiencing losses. In 1964 the amalgamation was taken over by Viyella International which then proceded to rationalize C.E.M.'s spinning operations and integrate them with other textile activities. Within two years under corporate management, half the mills had been closed, and the remaining mills were producing for 120 relatively large customers rather than for the 735 relatively small customers that had previously been serviced. As a result, inventories were dramatically reduced, output per customer was increased by about 550 percent, output per spindle rose by 60 percent while labor productivity rose by 50 percent. The profitability of C.E.M. was restored.[105]

As a general rule the directors of family firms in the British cotton industry insisted on retaining managerial control over their enterprises, even though to hand over the reins of power to a centralized source may have been in their long-term interests as shareholders. Raymond Streat, a prominent figure in Lancashire cotton affairs in the interwar years, recalled that "[e]ven some spinners who joined passionately in the de-

[104]Chandler, "Growth of the Transnational"; see also L. Hannah, "Managerial Innovation and the Rise of the Large-scale Company in Interwar Britain," *Economic History Review*, Vol XXVII, No. 2, (May 1974), pp. 252–270; P. Mathias, "Conflicts of Function in the Rise of Big Business: The British Experience," in H. Williamson (ed.), *Evolution of International Management Structures* (Newark, Delaware, 1975).
[105]Miles, *Lancashire*, pp. 22–23, 91.

bates [on amalgamation in the 1920s and 1930s] never really contemplated that their own mill should be amalgamated though they may scarcely have realized themselves that they were so built that their sole and personal authority was something they would never part with voluntarily."[106] The prolonged persistence of excess capacity in the industry, which absorbed all the attention of government programs from the 1930s into the 1960s, was due in part at least to the persistence of family firms. Very much in the tradition of the handloom weavers a century before, the owners of these firms hung on to their businesses at extremely low profits in order to maintain their relatively independent status.[107] In view of the large numbers of small, technologically-backward firms that remained in the cotton industry in the mid-1960s, Miles contended that higher prices for scrapped machinery under the 1959 Cotton Industry Act would not have enticed more firms to leave the industry:

> . . . . the main barrier to movement has been and still is the lack of "mobile" management skills. For the owners of most small firms the choice lay between retirement and continuing in the same business, however small its return.[108]

By the same token, those owners-managers that did remain in business had little interest or ability to participate in vertical integration. The owner-manager of a Lancashire spinning firm, for example, typically knew nothing about weaving, never mind marketing.[109] He was a specialist in his trade, with, particular expertise in the buying of cotton.[110] Indeed, as one spinning manager opposed to combinations argued in the early 1930s, "every practical cotton spinner, who understands spinning thoroughly, but has only a slight working knowledge of weaving, is anti-vertical combine."[111]

The vast majority of businessmen in the British cotton industry, therefore, had neither the incentive to participate nor the ability to lead in the internal transformation of their industry. The competitive and specialized organization of the industry had developed a breed of managers with specialized skills and individualistic attitudes who were not only ill-suited for involvement in a transition from competitive to corporate capitalism but also by their very presence obstructed such a transition. The

[106]Streat, "Cotton industry," p. 7.
[107]Fabian Research Group, *Cotton*, p. 13n.
[108]Miles, *Lancashire*, p. 74.
[109]See e.g. E. Helm, "The Middleman in Commerce," *Transactions of the Manchester Statistical Society*, 1900–1901, p. 57; W. Whittam, *Report on England's Cotton Industry* (Washington, 1907), p. 13; "Problems between spinners and manufacturers," *Journal of the British Association of Managers of Textile Works* (Lancashire Section) Vol. III, (1911–1912), pp. 127–136; "The Most Essential Improvement Required in the Cotton Trade," *Journal of the National Federation of Textile Works Managers' Associations*, Vol. V, (1925–1926) pp. 94–96; Bolton and District Managers and Over-lookers' Association, *Report of Delegates on American Tour* (Bolton, 1920), p. 39; Streat, "Cotton industry," p. 3.
[110]F. Jones, "The Cotton Spinning Industry in the Oldham District from 1896 to 1914," (unpublished M.A. Thesis, University of Manchester, 1959).
[111]"Combinations," *Journal of the National Federation of Textile Works Managers' Associations*, Vol. XII; 1932–1933, p. 9.

modern capitalist corporation is not a logical outgrowth of competitive market conditions. In the British cotton industry corporate organization failed to emerge on any significant scale until the 1960s precisely because competitive market conditions were so deeply entrenched. The result was prolonged technological backwardness and industrial decline.

EXPLANATIONS OF BRITAIN'S DECLINE

This study of the British cotton industry suggests that a fundamental cause of Britain's relative decline from the late nineteenth century was the inability of its capitalists, divided as they were by competition and markets, to adapt Britain's nineteenth-century economic structure to the conditions of twentieth-century international competition. While the cotton industry represented only one of Britain's staple industries, there is evidence that similar problems faced Britain's other staple industries — coal, iron and steel, and shipbuilding — as well.[112] The structure of industrial organization which arose in the context of Britain's unchallenged domination of world markets in the mid-nineteenth century left the subsequent generations of capitalists powerless, both individually and collectively, to supersede the market so as to develop the coordinated managerial structures and introduce the high throughput production processes that characterize the modern capitalist enterprise.

What light does this analysis shed on some previous attempts to explain Britain's relative decline? In what follows I shall consider the hypotheses of technical interrelatedness and entrepreneurial failure, stressing the importance of the correct specification of the type of managerial activity with which a particular explanation is concerned.

The hypothesis of technical interrelatedness, which can claim Thorstein Veblen as its most distinguished proponent, is essentially an argument that Britain was handicapped by its early start.[113] Marvin Frankel, in his attempt at systematic formulation of the hypothesis, identifies the problem of technical interrelatedness with the effects of sunk costs, and distinguishes this cause of technological backwardness from those which derive from institutional rigidities on the one hand and resource inadequacies on the other.[114] He attempts to demonstrate that, even in the absence of institutional and resource constraints, an old industry will

---

[112]See e.g. B. Elbaum and F. Wilkinson, "Industrial Relations and Uneven Development: A Comparative Study of the British and American Steel Industries," *Cambridge Journal of Economics*, Vol. 3, No. 3, (September 1979) pp. 275–303; M. Kirby, *The British Coalmining Industry* (Hamden, 1977); S. Pollard and P. Robertson, *The British Shipbuilding Industry 1870–1914* (Cambridge, Mass., 1979).

[113]See T. Veblen, *Imperial Germany and the Industrial Revolution* (Ann Arbor, 1968), Ch. IV. For discussions of early start hypotheses, see C. Kindleberger, "Obsolescence and Technical Change," *Bulletin of the Oxford Institute of Statistics*, August 1961, pp. 281–297; E. Ames and N. Rosenberg, "Changing Technological Leadership and Industrial Growth," in N. Rosenberg (ed.), *The Economics of Technological Change* (Harmondsworth, 1971), pp. 413–439; A. Levine, *Industrial Retardation in Britain, 1880–1914* (London, 1967), ch. 6.

[114]M. Frankel, "Obsolescence and Technological Change in a Maturing Economy," *American Economic Review*, Vol. XLV, No. 3, (June 1955), pp. 296–297.

have greater difficulty adopting a new technology than a new industry. As he puts it:

> As an industry (or industrial economy) grows and adapts to changing and increasingly complex production methods, interconnections, more or less rigid, develop among its technological components — among machines, plant, transport network and raw material supplies — that make increasingly difficult the introduction into the system of new, cost-saving changes. It may then happen that the entire system becomes obsolete because, as Veblen has observed, "An adequate remedy by detail innovation is not always practicable; indeed, in the more serious conjunctures of the kind it is virtually impossible, in that new items of equipment are necessarily required to conform to the specifications already governing the old." Unable to utilize the new production methods, the industry continues with its old ones. As a result, its costs are higher and labor productivity lower than they would be in a less "mature" industry. The old industry finds itself penalized for having taken the lead and shown the way to its young competitors in other regions.[115]

The crux of the problem is that not all the technically-interrelated components of a production process can be expected to wear out at the same time, so that the introduction of a new technology will generally require the scrapping of a great deal of existing plant and equipment that still has useful service to render. Thus, generally speaking, the greater the degree of technical interrelatedness, the more likely it will be that a manager, optimizing subject to given constraints at a point in time, will continue to invest in new *components* of the old technology, thus locking himself into the utilization of the old technology over the longer run.

This argument has obvious merit as one possible explanation of technological backwardness — it would be interesting to see it applied to the U.S. automobile and steel industries of the present day. As for Frankel, he in fact refers to the British cotton industry, and in particular to the failure to adopt the automatic loom, as a prime empirical application of the hypothesis of technical interrelatedness. But despite his careful categorization of the sources of technological backwardness into institutional rigidities, resource inadequacies, and the effects of sunk costs, his own account of the constraints on the adoption of the automatic loom emphasizes institutional rigidities rather than the effects of sunk costs although it is the latter hypothesis that he is purportedly attempting to demonstrate. For what Frankel emphasizes is the problem of vertical specialization and the consequent lack of coordinated decision-making *across* technically-interrelated industrial units as opposed to the timing of the component obsolescence of technically-interrelated processes *within* a decision-making unit.[116] The problem of sunk costs, reflecting the long-run pitfalls of short-run maximizing behavior (and in this sense

[115]*Ibid.*, p. 297.
[116]*Ibid.*, pp. 313–314.

reflecting the constraint of highly competitive conditions on managerial decision-making), undoubtedly played a role in the technological backwardness of the British cotton industry.[117] But in the decade prior to World War I, during which the number of spindles and looms installed in Lancashire grew by 31 percent and 23 percent respectively, there was plenty of opportunity for "new starts" unencumbered by the component problem of technical-interrelatedness within spinning, weaving, or combined firms.[118] Yet it was during this period that Britain was falling far behind the U.S. in the adoption of modern methods of production. The larger problem was the inability of managers to develop modern corporate production structures even in the context of these "new starts." Britain was indeed handicapped by its early start — its nineteenth century mode of development permitted highly competitive and highly specialized managers to dominate the industrial structure, managers who were then unable to transform their organizational environment as a precondition for responding to the production and distribution methods of twentieth century international competition.

In attempting to explain the technological backwardness of an industry (or an economy), it is of utmost importance to identify carefully the constraints on managerial decision-making that are inherent in one's explanation if one is actually to test the particular hypothesis under consideration. The debate over the hypothesis of entrepreneurial failure is plagued by just such problems in the specification of the type of managerial activity under scrutiny.

It was, of course, Joseph Schumpeter who accorded the entrepreneur a central role in the process of economic development. For him, the understanding of the process of economic development went beyond the theoretical boundaries of what is today called neoclassical economics, and he argued that "changes in technique and productive organization require special analysis" and "non-recognition of this is the most important single reason for what appears unsatisfactory to us in economic theory."[119] In order to rectify this shortcoming, Schumpeter's theory of economic development was based on a clear distinction between the manager of neoclassical theory who, to use modern language, optimizes subject to "given" constraints and the entrepreneur who alters these constraints, thus creating new profitable opportunities. One need not accept Schumpeter's theory of economic development as complete nor subscribe to all his conclusions in order to recognize the relevance of the

---

[117]See e.g. *CFT*, 16 January 1885 for a specific example.

[118]Frankel also argues that the Lancashire weaving industry had little opportunity for modernization because the industry grew little after 1900. But see the data in Jones, *Increasing Return*, p. 277.

[119]J. Schumpeter, *The Theory of Economic Development* (New York, 1961), p. 60n. On these issues, Schumpeter finds himself drawn to Marx's theory of capitalist development, but, as he humbly notes, "my structure covers only a small part of his ground." *Ibid.*

analytical distinction between working within constraints and changing them. Indeed if Schumpeter's conceptual distinction between managerial activity and entrepreneurial activity is accepted as valid, it can readily be seen that the presence of successful "neoclassical" managers who optimize subject to the constraints they face in no way precludes the failure of some person or groups of people to fulfill the entrepreneurial role of altering those constraints. Managerial activity may well pass the test of constrained optimization while the firm, industry, or economy fails to engage in entrepreneurial activity and hence fails to generate a *new* array of optimal decisions within a *new* array of "given" constraints.

In contrast to the Schumpeterian distinction, the general practice of neoclassical economists has been to use the labels "manager" and "entrepreneur" interchangeably, in all cases signifying a businessman who, in his decision-making role, takes prices and productivity as given by the market and technology respectively. It is therefore not surprising to find that some "new" economic historians, who pride themselves on their rigorous application of neoclassical theory to economic history, fail to notice any significant distinction between the entrepreneur and manager in their attack on the hypothesis of entrepreneurial failure.

The attack began in the late 1960s, and the initial efforts were summarized in an article published in 1971 by Donald McCloskey and Lars Sandberg in which they emphasize the theoretical and quantitative precision of the "new" economic history in testing the hypothesis of British entrepreneurial failure in the late nineteenth and early twentieth centuries.[120] McCloskey and Sandberg are highly critical of not only the conclusions but also the methodology of the "heirs of Veblen and Schumpeter" (by whom they apparently mean David Landes and Derek Aldcroft) who "taking a sociological view of the matter," attach great importance to the failure of entrepreneurship in the explanation of Britain's decline. At the same time, they point out the limitations in the analyses of those "old" economic historians who have cast doubt on the entrepreneurial failure hypothesis, categorizing the detractors into those such as Charles Kindleberger who argue theoretically with a minimum of facts and those such as S.B. Saul who argue empirically with a minimum of theory. The "new" economic historians claim to have united the best of both these intellectual approaches, the combination of neoclassical economic theory and quantitative methods providing them with the analytical tools to test rigorously the hypothesis of entrepreneurial failure.[121]

---

[120]See McCloskey and Sandberg, "From Damnation." See also the collection of essays in D. McCloskey (ed.), *Essays on a Mature Economy: Britain after 1840* (London, 1971) and C. Harley, "Skilled Labour and the Choice of Technique in Edwardian Industry," *Explorations in Economic History*, Vol. II, No. 4, (Summer 1974), pp. 391–414. In what follows, I shall be concerned only with the theoretical merits of the work of the "new" economic historians. For a critique of Sandberg's quantitative efforts, see Lazonick, "Factor Costs."
[121]McCloskey and Sandberg, "From Damnation," pp. 91–94.

The result of these tests, as McCloskey and Sandberg see it, is a clear rejection of the hypothesis. "[T]he late Victorian entrepreneur," they conclude, "who started his historiographic career in damnation is well on his way to redemption."[122]

My concern here is not with the empirical content of the "new" economic historians' test of the hypothesis of entrepreneurial failure, but rather with the nature of the test itself. For while McCloskey and Sandberg argue that the "range of our ignorance of the influence of entrepreneurship has been greatly narrowed by its intensive study,"[123] I shall argue on the contrary that what they have "greatly narrowed" is the *definition* of entrepreneurship itself and along with it our comprehension of the processes of economic development. The "new" economic historians bring the study of entrepreneurship within the scope of neoclassical economic theory by defining the entrepreneur as a neoclassical manager. Hence the test of entrepreneurial performance is the extent to which managers can be shown to have minimized costs subject to given constraints. For example, in one neoclassical contribution to the debate, entitled "Yardsticks for Victorian Entrepreneurs," Lindert and Trace argue that "the cardinal rule [for judging the calibre of entrepreneurship] is that the comparison must reflect the conditions faced by the individuals or firms whose performance is being judged. It will not do, for example, to fault Victorian manufacturers for not having adopted techniques that were preferable under American or German, but not British price relationships."[124] In order to test the quality of "entrepreneurship" they propose the neoclassical test of allocative rationality, namely "a straightforward cost-benefit calculation to measure the private profits foregone by a non-optimal choice of technique," taking price relationships, and presumably productivity potential, as given to the firm and industry.[125]

In their joint article, McCloskey and Sandberg use the terms "entrepreneur" and "manager" interchangeably, making absolutely no attempt to justify the implicit conceptual assumption. In his own work on the British iron and steel industry, however, McCloskey is quite explicit on this issue: "I use the word "entrepreneur" throughout in the general sense of a businessman or manager rather than in the restricted sense of a *good* businessman or manager, that is, an innovating Schumpeterian

[122]*Ibid.*, p. 108. This view has begun to gain acceptance in the textbooks. See e.g. P. Payne, *British Entrepreneurship in the Nineteenth Century* (London, 1974), pp. 48–51; A. Musson, *The Growth of British Industry* (New York, 1978), p. 163. For a critique, see C. Kindleberger, *Economic Response* (Cambridge, Mass., 1978), ch. 7.
[123]McCloskey and Sandberg, "From damnation," p. 108.
[124]In McCloskey (ed.), *Essays*, p. 241.
[125]*Ibid.*, p. 243. This approach is explicit in Sandberg, *Lancashire*, ch. 2–4, and implicit in Harley, "Skilled Labour," and D. McCloskey, *Economic Maturity and Entrepreneurial Decline: British Iron and Steel 1870–1913* (Cambridge, Mass., 1973). For a much earlier statement of the neoclassical approach, see F. Jervis, "The Handicap of Britain's Early Start," *Manchester School*, Vol. XV, No. 1, (January, 1947), p. 212: "It is a commonplace of economic theory that the entrepreneur combines his factors in the optimum manner under the circumstances applicable to him."

entrepreneur."[126] Thus, McCloskey, while recognizing that his own analysis does not deal with Schumpeter's distinction between entrepreneurship and management, minimizes the importance of that distinction by characterizing it as a difference in degree rather than in kind. Hence the Schumpeterian notion of the entrepreneur is reduced to an (unspecified) "special case" of the (presumably) "broader" neoclassical notion of the manager.

It should be noted that neither David Landes nor Derek Aldcroft — the proponents of the hypothesis of entrepreneurial failure whom McCloskey and Sandberg criticize explicitly — highlight the distinction between entrepreneurs and managers. Landes, however, was a collaborator at Harvard's Research Center in Entrepreneurial History in the 1950s, and his approach is clearly influenced by the Schumpeterian tradition.[127] Aldcroft, on the other hand, was apparently untouched by Schumpeterian influence. Indeed, he subsequently indicated that he did not see any problem with the neoclassical definition of entrepreneurship.[128]

Yet there is in existence an extensive literature on the nature of the Schumpeterian notions of entrepreneurship and management, as well as some excellent empirical work (most notably that of Alfred Chandler) that explicitly utilizes the distinction.[129] One might expect, therefore that neoclassical economic historians would at least make some attempt to justify empirically and theoretically their rejection of Schumpeter's insights into economic development as well as to defend the superiority of their own approach as a prelude to testing their own definitions of "entrepreneurial failure." Instead of confronting the issues of economic development raised by the Schumpeterian approach, they simply define them away, proceeding, in a manner not uncommon among contemporary orthodox economists, *as if* all fundamental theoretical questions

[126]McCloskey, *Economic Maturity*, pp. vii–viii; see also the following statement in a piece extolling the recent work of "new" economic historians: "[F]ew economists outside of agricultural economics and economic history have given serious attention to measuring (as distinct from theorizing about) managerial ability or, in more elaborate language, entrepreneurship," D. McCloskey, "Does the past have useful economics?" *Journal of Economic Literature*, Vol. XIV, No. 2, (June 1976), p. 452.

[127]See D. Landes, *The Unbound Prometheus* (Cambridge, England, 1967), p. 354; D. Landes, "Factor Costs and Demand: Determinants of Economic Growth," *Business History*, Vol. II, (January 1965), p. 26.

[128]In McCloskey (ed.), *Essays*, pp. 272–277.

[129]Chandler, *Strategy*; Chandler, *Visible Hand*. See also E. Dahmèn, *Entrepreneurial Activity and the Development of Swedish Industry 1913–1934* (Homewood, 1970). On the conceptual distinction, see J. Schumpeter, "The Analysis of Economic Change," *Review of Economic Statistics*, Vol. XVII, No. 4, (May 1935), pp. 2–10, and "The Creative Response in Economic History," *Journal of Economic History*, Vol. 7, No. 2 (November, 1947), pp. 149–159, both reprinted in R. Clemence (ed.), *Essays of J.A. Schumpeter* (Cambridge, Mass., 1951), pp. 1–19 and 216–226; G. Evans, "The Entrepreneur and Economic Theory: A Historical and Analytical Approach," *American Economic Review*, Vol. XXXIX, No. 3, (May 1949), pp. 336–355; G. Evans, "Business Entrepreneurs: Their Major Functions and Related Tenets," *Journal of Economic History*, Vol. XIX, No. 2 (June 1959), pp. 250–270; A. Cole, *Business Enterprise in its Social Setting* (Cambridge, Mass., 1971); A. Chandler and F. Redlich, "Recent Developments in American Business Administration and Their Conceptualization," *Weltwirtschaftliches Archiv*, No. 86, (1961), pp. 103–130; H. Hartmann, "Managers and Entrepreneurs: A Useful Distinction?" *Administrative Science Quarterly*, Vol. 3, (1958–59), pp. 429–451; W. Baumol, "Entrepreneur in Economic Theory," *American Economic Review*, Vol. LVIII, No. 2, (May 1968), pp. 64–71; J. Soltow, "The Entrepreneur in Economic History," *American Economic Review*, Vol. LVIII, No. 2. (May 1968), pp. 84–92.

concerning the functioning of the capitalist economy have been resolved so that matters can be settled by an appeal to the "facts."[130]

The facts as I see them are that British businessmen performed admirably as neoclassical managers — they took the conditions facing them as given and tried to do the best they could, subject to these constraints. As entrepreneurs, however, they failed precisely because as individualistic managers in highly competitive and vertically-specialized industries they were powerless to alter the organizational constraints that determined feasible technological choices and profitable opportunities. As a result, they barely even tried, individually or collectively, to transform their industrial environment. Certainly in the decades prior to World War I, when the German, American, and Japanese economies were developing on the basis of modern corporate structures, British capitalists were oblivious to the need to make these institutional changes if Britain was to maintain its position in the world economy in the long-run. It is true that in the long-run, to paraphrase Keynes, all these British capitalists were dead. Their economy, however, lives on, as does neoclassical economics. To this day, neoclassical economists continue to extoll as the ideal form of economic existence the short-sighted capitalist and the competitive capitalism in which he was enmeshed. Certainly, the neoclassical notion that high levels of capital mobility, and hence allocative efficiency, are associated with high levels of competition is hardly borne out by the 20th century experience of the British cotton industry. In dealing with the real world, neoclassical economists remain every bit as trapped by their theoretical vision of economic activity in which firms are subordinate to markets as were the British cotton capitalists for whom such subordination was a reality. The era of competitive capitalism has long since past. It is time that orthodox economists began to learn some lessons from history. Perhaps then they could begin to illuminate rather than obscure our understanding of the dynamics of the corporate capitalist economy that exists today.

[130]In some quarters, however, there is genuine confusion concerning the theoretical issues involved. For example, Peter Payne, in his recent contribution to the *Cambridge Economic History of Europe*, is careful to make a distinction between entrepreneurs who make strategic decisions and managers who keep the concern running. Yet after discussing the empirical contributions of the "new" economic historians he concludes that the hypothesis of entrepreneurial failure has taken "quite a beating." P. Payne, "Industrial Entrepreneurship and management in Great Britain," in P. Mathias and M. Postan (eds.), *The Cambridge Economic History of Europe*, Vol. VII, Part I, (Cambridge, England, 1978). pp. 180–181, 208–209. Similarly, Nathaniel Leff notes that "in recent years the term entrepreneurship has sometimes been used as a synonym for the firm, or for management in general, with little regard for special 'entrepreneurial' qualities," but he then goes on to accept the McCloskey-Sandberg argument that entrepreneurial performance was not an important problem in the relative decline of the British economy. N. Leff, "Entrepreneurship and Economic Development: The Problem Revisited," *Journal of Economic Literature*, Vol. XVII, (March 1979), pp. 47, 50–51. A recent discussion of British entrepreneurial activity that well reflects this confusion can be found in the opening chapter of M.W. Kirby, *The Decline of British Economic Power since 1870* (London, 1981).

THE BRITISH COTTON INDUSTRY AND INTERNATIONAL COMPETITIVE ADVANTAGE: THE STATE OF THE DEBATES

By WILLIAM MASS and WILLIAM LAZONICK

The case of the cotton industry has figured prominently in recent debates over Britain's loss of industrial leadership in the twentieth century.[1] As participants in these debates, our purposes here are to clarify our own arguments concerning the sources of British dominance and decline in international competition for cotton textile markets, and to consider how other perspectives on the determinants of economic performance in this industry differ from ours. In doing so, we want to show the importance of dynamic theories of competitive advantage and economic development for analysing the process of economic change.

Our approach focuses on the relation between nation-specific institutional structures and shifts in international competitive advantage over the past century. We stress the impacts of institutional structures in different national economies on the abilities and incentives of economic actors to *develop and utilise* the productive resources that they control. We then seek to explain why the development and utilisation of productive resources gave a particular national economy sustained competitive advantages over its international rivals in one era and why, in a later era under altered conditions, these competitive advantages could not be be sustained. In cotton textiles, the outstanding cases of sustained competitive advantage in international competition are Britain up to World War I and Japan in the inter-war period.

We do not have the space here to elaborate the theories of competitive advantage and economic development that we apply to the analysis of international competition in cotton textiles.[2] But some key conceptual definitions that enter into our analysis are in order. The development of productive resources – both human and physical – occurs when a given amount of useful output can be produced with a smaller quantity of human effort than was previously possible. Hence we define economic development in terms of the relation between necessary labour and the useful goods and services that labour produces. We view this effort-saving impact of the development process as the distinctive way in which technological change makes possible higher standards of living. With effort-saving technological change, a given amount of human effort produces more goods and services of a given quality.

The development of productive resources does not, however, result in higher standards of living unless these resources are utilised. Indeed, when productive resources that have been developed go unutilised, living standards may be lowered (because resources have been wasted) rather than raised. Conversely, the more the productive resources that have been developed are utilised, the more the enhanced productive potential of these developed resources are realised, and the more possible it becomes to sell the resultant outputs on competitive markets without a deterioration in living standards.

In focusing our analyses of international competitive advantage on the development and utilisation of productive resources, we do not deny that factor prices and government policy (in particular tariff protection) can have impacts on competition for markets. Low wages and protected markets have often been critical conditions for the entry of new competitors into international competition. In our view, however, the development and utilisation of productive resources enable a national economy to become a *major* competitor on international markets – to experience *sustained* competitive advantage.

In the case of the evolution of international competition in cotton textiles, we ask how particular modes of developing and utilising productive resources permitted a national industry that emerged as dominant to cut unit costs for a given quality of useful product in ways that were unavailable to its rivals. More specifically: (1) How during the nineteenth century did the British cotton industry develop and utilise its productive resources in ways that gave it sustained competitive advantages over the cotton industries of other national economies? (2) How did the British cotton industry manage to dominate international markets until the eve of World War I? (3) How during the inter-war period did Japan gain sustained competitive advantage over the once-dominant British producers? (4) Why did the British cotton industry experience such great difficulty in responding to the Japanese challenge?

I

Sources of Britain's Competitive Advantage

Britain's nineteenth-century competitive advantages derived from the concentration of the industry in Lancashire and from the modes of labour management within the industry's constituent firms. We discuss the sources of Britain's competitive advantages under the following five headings: (1) labour costs, (2) fixed capital costs, (3) materials costs, (4) marketing costs, and (5) administrative costs. In each case, we point to the unique capabilities of the British cotton industry for developing and utilising its productive resources. As much as possible, we indicate how these sources of competitive advantage were dynamically interrelated, the realisation of one source of competitive advantage making possible the realisation of another source. For, as we shall make clear in this essay, we view sustained competitive advantage as a cumulative and continuous process in which the development and utilisation of a number of key productive factors reinforce each other.

(1) *Labour costs*

During the nineteenth century, the development and utilisation of labour resources provided the British cotton industry with its unique sources of competitive advantage. The major machine technologies of the nineteenth century required complementary applications of experienced human labour to keep them in motion. Experience gave workers not only specific cognitive skills (of which a process such as mule spinning was much more demanding than a process such as plain weaving), but also (and more important over the long run) the general capability to work long hours at a steady pace without damaging the quality of the product, the materials, or the machines.

These general capabilities manifested themselves as an 'habituation to factory work' on the part of the labour force of Lancashire, where over the course of the nineteenth century the cotton industry became increasingly concentrated. Yet the accumulation of experience did not in and of itself ensure that workers would supply the high levels of effort that ensured high levels of utilisation of both their own labour and the employer's plant and equipment. A major problem in the British Industrial Revolution was the creation of a disciplined factory labour force.[3]

During the first half of the nineteenth century the British cotton factory benefited from the accumulation of experienced workers in domestic industry. Early in the century mule spinners came into the factory from domestic industry and craft pursuits with considerable industrial skills. They were willing to take up factory employment because of the relatively high wages offered as well as the considerable control they retained in the factory setting over the organisation of work and the recruitment, training, and supervision of other workers. Older handloom weavers may have resisted entry into the factory, but younger workers from the seats of domestic industry in northwest Lancashire brought their already acquired skills into the weaving mills in the middle decades of the nineteenth century.[4]

Besides the general habituation to factory work that came from growing up in factory communities and entering the mills at a young age, cotton workers developed specialised skills in spinning particular types of yarn and weaving particular types of cloth. The growth of abundant, locally concentrated supplies of experienced factory labour with specialised skills led to a growing localisation of industry – coarser yarns in Oldham, finer yarns in Bolton, coarser cloths in Burnley and Blackburn, finer cloths in Nelson and Colne. Once the process of localisation began it was reinforced by the tendency for specialised workers to remain in the spinning and weaving centres that demanded their particular skills. Localisation was also reinforced by the emergence of supplies of skilled mechanics, their engineering capabilities geared particularly toward servicing the needs of the specialised machinery that dominated the locality.[5] By the second half of the nineteenth century, employers who chose to locate outside the main centres of specialised production either had to develop the requisite supplies of specialised labour themselves (with the distinct possibility that these specialised workers would ultimately migrate to the manufacturing centres in which their skills were in most demand) or forgo the productivity advantages of having ready at hand a large supply of experienced and specialised labour. Increasingly, employers who located in the specialised centres within Lancashire had distinct competitive advantages over those British employers who did not.

During the generally prosperous conditions of the third quarter of the nineteenth century, the reliance of cotton firms on experienced and specialised workers, concentrated in certain localities and attached to their communities, provided foundations for the emergence of strong and enduring trade unions in both spinning and weaving. The unions helped workers to keep up wages in the face of generally abundant labour supplies. But relatively high wages in the main spinning and weaving centres were offset by the productive benefits that employers derived from making use of this more experienced and more specialised labour. Trade union influence in the determination of conditions of work and pay gave workers the confidence to expend high levels of effort without the fear that employers would be able to cut piece rates as earnings increased. Those employers who adhered to union wage-lists found that they had industrial peace and co-operative workers, especially during the booms when there were profits to be made. During slumps the unions helped to enforce organised short-time working, which dampened the decline in the price of a textile centre's specialised product and alleviated the pressure on employers to cut wages.

The industrial relations structures encouraged the technical improvement of the machine technologies. During the last half of the nineteenth century, the most dynamic cotton centres – Oldham and Bolton in spinning, Burnley and Nelson in weaving – were districts where the distribution of value gains inherent in the collective agreements gave workers an interest in working harder for the sake of more pay and employers an interest in making improvements to their plant and equipment for the sake of higher returns. The results were investments in improved spinning mules and power-looms that permitted higher levels of capital per unit of labour and higher levels of output per unit of capital without *necessarily* requiring workers to expend more effort.

Yet as the potential productivity of the machines increased during the last half of the nineteenth century, workers often responded by supplying more effort, thereby achieving even higher levels of labour productivity. Senior workers (minders on the self-acting mules and weavers on the power-looms) had incentives to work harder because their union power ensured that more effort would result in more earnings. Moreover, because of their habituation to factory work, they had (up to a point) the ability to work harder without an offsetting deterioration in product quality. At the same time, the senior workers were often able to drive their junior workers (piecers in spinning and tenters in weaving) to exert more effort because these assistants were dependent on the senior workers for continued employment. Over time, moreover, the exertion of more *effort* by the cotton workers generated a new *skill* – the endurance that permitted the higher level of productivity without necessarily experiencing it as a higher level of effort.[6]

With workers trained at a young age and at low pay on the job, and with the acceptance of factory work permeating the communities in which they grew up, the development of this highly productive work force occurred in Lancashire at a very low cost to employers or the industry as a whole. Moreover, the habituation to factory work combined with the union-protected assurance of rewards for harder work meant that once junior workers had became senior workers the costs of supervising and disciplining them were low. Where and when it was needed, an abundant supply of supervisory labour could be drawn from the ranks of those workers who had over the years demonstrated the ability to lead on the shop floor and a willingness to co-operate with management. Shop-floor supervision was made all the more effective and all the less costly by industrial relations structures that permitted workers to redress grievances by calling in the district secretary rather than by engaging in continuous shop-floor conflict.

By the 1870s cotton industries around the world could readily purchase British plant and equipment and even British engineering expertise. But no other cotton industry in the world could readily acquire Britain's highly productive labour force; no other industry in the world had gone through the century-long developmental process that had produced the experienced, specialised, and co-operative labour force that Britain possessed.[7]

(2) *Fixed capital costs*

The growth of the British cotton industry generated vertically related industries, also concentrated in Lancashire, for the building of cotton mills and machinery. The growth of these capital goods industries meant that the initial development of mill and machine design was geared toward the technological requirements of Lancashire, particularly the complementary capabilities of its labour supplies and Lancashire's peculiar advantages in cotton utilisation. Because the industry was so entrenched in Lancashire, because Lancashire was so dominant in the world economy, and because local labour supplies with specialised skills were so abundant, Lancashire spinning and weaving firms were willing to buy machines that were built to last. As a result, equipment could be used for decades on end, with the engineering industry developing improvements to be used on existing machines with existing labour supplies.

Nevertheless, the engineering industry was responsive to the need for technical change, whether the demand came from within Lancashire or from abroad. During the American Civil War, the engineering industry rapidly adapted mule spinning technology to permit the Lancashire cotton industry to shift (temporarily as it turned out) from scarce, longer staple American cotton to the more abundant, shorter staple Indian cotton. In the 1880s, the textile engineering industry was also quick to take up the manufacture of ring spinning – an American innovation – and almost immediately dominated in exporting these machines around the world.[8]

The cost of transporting machines (along with the men to build the mills and set up the equipment) around the world gave the Lancashire cotton industry a one-shot cost advantage over purchasers abroad. More important in giving Britain a continuing competitive advantage was the ready availability in Lancashire of skilled mechanics and parts to keep the machines in motion on a day-to-day basis as well as to prolong the useful life of the equipment. Indeed to a certain extent the requisite mechanical ability was readily available within each cotton firm on the shop floor because the long-term attachment of workers to the industry, and indeed to particular machines in particular firms, gave many skilled workers the practical expertise to minimise the downtime caused by malfunctioning equipment that went unserviced. The results were high levels of utilisation of the productive capabilities of both labour and installed plant and equipment.

(3) *Materials costs*

As the most expensive input in the production of yarn and cloth, the cost of raw cotton could be of critical importance as a determinant of competitive advantage. The Lancashire industry's peculiar advantage in the cost of cotton derived from its ready access to Liverpool. During the nineteenth century, in response to the growth of the British cotton industry, Liverpool evolved into the world's leading and most highly concentrated cotton exchange, not only supplying cotton to Lancashire but also re-exporting some of it to Europe, Africa, and the Middle East. Compared with those foreign cotton industries that found it less expensive to secure their cotton from Liverpool rather than directly from the source (as for example the Germans began to do with Indian cotton from the 1880s), Lancashire spinners had a cost advantage.[9]

After the building of the Manchester–Liverpool railway in 1830, Lancashire's spinning firms were able to secure cotton from Liverpool as it was needed. Over the middle decades of the century access of spinning managers to Liverpool was further enhanced by the building of railway connections between Manchester and the major cotton towns (an infrastructural investment that further reinforced the specialised localisation of the industry). The growth of the spinning industry spread out the costs of the communications infrastructure for buying and shipping cotton within Lancashire, thus reducing the unit costs incurred by individual Lancashire firms in securing their required cotton.

The ready availability of cotton on the Liverpool market meant that spinning firms avoided the warehousing of large stocks of cotton, as was the case in most other countries. But, except for possible economies of scale inherent in having the cotton warehoused with the broker rather than with each firm, the cost of warehousing the cotton still had to be incurred somewhere between harvest and usage, and ultimately had to be paid for by the spinning firm.

Rather, the main advantages that the Liverpool market conferred on Lancashire lay in the flexibility that it provided to spinning firms in keeping their plant, equipment, and labour utilised by accepting orders requiring the use of different grades and staples of cotton. Lancashire firms adjusted, within limits, and often with considerable cotton cost savings, the grade and staple of cotton utilised to produce a particular yarn in response to changes in the relative prices of grades and staples of the raw cotton. The ability to take advantage of this flexibility in cotton utilisation depended on the skills of the Lancashire labour force. A prime skill of a spinning mill manager (or his agent), whose function it was to purchase cotton in Liverpool on a week-to-week basis, was his ability to buy the grades and staples of cotton that would minimise the cost of yarn production, given the productive capabilities of his machinery and his labour force. In turn, a prime skill of his shop-floor labour force – both overseers and minders – was to reset the spinning machinery to make use of different qualities of cotton without yarn breakages becoming excessive. Indeed, from the 1880s, when ring spinning became a viable technology, a major advantage of the mule spinning technology was its flexibility in using cotton of lower grade and shorter staple to produce a given count of yarn. So too, when in the mid-1890s the automatic loom became a viable technology, a major advantage of the Lancashire power-loom was its flexibility in using inferior yarn – that is, break-prone yarn made from cotton of lower grade and shorter staple.

The flexibility of the mule and power-loom in using inferior cotton inputs, along with the accumulated experience of the workforce in adapting to the use of these inputs, meant that the Lancashire industry had a unique technological capability for producing for virtually any market in the world. Indeed, through the use of inferior cotton, the industry had, within limits, the capability of adjusting the cost of production to the income constraints of buyers, thus permitting the British industry to increase its extent of the market in low-income areas of the world.[10]

(4) *Marketing costs*

In the mid-nineteenth century, cotton yarn and cloth accounted for about 40 per cent of all UK exports. In 1900 the British cotton industry still accounted for 26 per cent of UK exports, this share declining by only two per cent over the next decade. Over the last half of the nineteenth century, as the weight of cotton consumed in the UK almost tripled, the cotton industry became increasingly export-oriented, with exports making up about 60 per cent of the value of the industry's product at mid-century and just under 80 per cent at the end of the century.[11]

The British cotton industry was exporting cloth to all parts of the world, with India as its largest market. The goods did not sell themselves. Besides the transportation infrastructure needed to move yarn and cloth from the various specialised cotton towns to destinations in all corners of the globe, the industry required information concerning the types of yarns and cloths that buyers in the various markets around the world desired and could afford. The early 1870s saw the completion of a worldwide network of cables emanating from Manchester, and the early 1880s saw this communications network augmented by the telephone. Unique to Lancashire was its position as the hub of not only a worldwide transportation system but also a worldwide information system.[12]

Like the Liverpool cotton market, this worldwide marketing structure developed during the nineteenth century with the growth of Lancashire as the world's centre for the spinning of yarn and the weaving of cloth. Foreign merchants, desirous of profiting from the trade in Lancashire textiles, set up offices and warehouses in Manchester, while British merchants gravitated to Manchester and sent commission agents abroad. In Manchester the merchant would receive information from the particular foreign market that he served concerning the quality and price of yarn and cloth demanded in those markets. This information had to be updated on a regular basis because of changes in fashion and disposable income in the particular foreign market.

On receipt of an order, the merchant would purchase cloth from weavers or yarn from spinners, and, if required, have it finished (or 'converted') according to the specifications of the order. Alternatively, in the case of the more standard products, he might buy the desired finished goods from other merchant-converters or directly from finishers. Increasingly from 1809 these transactions, along with the sale of yarn from spinners to weavers, were conducted twice weekly on the Manchester Royal Exchange, with an internal transportation system evolving to carry spinning and weaving managers from the cotton towns to Manchester to receive orders and then yarn and cloth to Manchester when the orders had been completed. Servicing the merchant-converters was a capital-intensive and increasingly concentrated finishing industry, vertically specialised from the manufacturing of yarn and cloth as well as the marketing of the finished goods.[13]

With this marketing structure in place in the last half of the nineteenth century, no other country could match the ready access of the Lancashire cotton industry to (save for the impediment of tariff barriers) the full extent of the world market. The Lancashire industry had the capability to deliver relatively quickly whatever type of product the customer demanded. The practice of production to order combined with rapid delivery of products to distant markets meant low inventory costs. Moreover, the very extent of the market that became accessible to Lancashire through the development of this marketing infrastructure made the workshop of the world all the more capable of generating the products customers demanded at prices they could afford. For once this transportation and communications infrastructure was in place, every increase in the extent of the market helped to spread out the fixed costs of the infrastructure over more output, thereby driving down unit costs. These were the scale economies, largely external to the spinning and weaving firms but more internal to the more capital-intensive finishing firms, that were central to Alfred Marshall's understanding of nineteenth-century British economic development.[14] When demand was strong, moreover, the very size of the market enabled spinning and weaving firms to accept orders (even if from a number of merchants) for a restricted range of yarns and cloths that gave the producers the benefit of long runs and augmented their internal economies of scale.

These economies of scale could be, and through competitive pressures were, passed on to the consumers of yarn and cloth in the form of lower product prices, thus dynamically increasing the extent of Lancashire's markets and lowering further unit costs. Within Lancashire, meanwhile, supply-side responses to the growth of the market ensured that, as industry output grew, economies of scale would not be transformed into diseconomies of scale. The very prosperity of Lancashire combined with its concentration of engineering capability meant that new capacity could be and (particularly with the advent of limited liability in the late 1850s) was put in place to respond to the rapid growth of demand.[15] The increased demand for spinning and weaving labour was met by the employment of an abundant supply of 'apprenticed' young men and (especially in weaving) women who in turn expanded the corps of operatives charged with recruiting and training the next generation of workers. And when cotton was in short supply, Lancashire was least affected, not only because it harboured the cotton market of the world, but because its experienced workers and flexible machine technologies enabled its spinning and weaving firms to make use of inferior cotton.

(5) *Administrative costs*

As the British cotton industry became more export-oriented and as overseas marketing became a highly specialised function, the production processes became more vertically specialised as well. Up to the mid-nineteenth century, the tendency had been for firms to combine both spinning and weaving. Even before the widespread diffusion of the power-loom in the 1830s and 1840s, many spinning firms operated their own putting-out operations. The steady expansion of yarn exports from the 1820s meant not only that combined firms turned to producing some yarn for sale but also that increasingly it became a viable proposition to set up a specialised spinning firm. A growing supply of marketed yarn in turn encouraged investment in specialised weaving firms, a tendency that was reinforced by the localisation of the cotton industry, fostered as it was by the development of specialised weaving labour supplies in the old hand-loom centres of northwest Lancashire and the completion of the internal transportation network that linked the north-west power-loom centres with the south-east spinning centres. As a proportion of employees and capacity, the combined firms declined in relative importance over the course of the last half of the nineteenth century and indeed throughout the first half of the twentieth century.[16]

As the British cotton industry became more vertically specialised, it also became more horizontally fragmented, because the well developed input and output markets reduced the amount of financial resources and the array of managerial skills required to participate in the industry. Compared to the more vertically integrated enterprise structures in cotton industries abroad – industries that lacked Lancashire's unique institutions for the buying and selling of raw materials and intermediate products – the Lancashire industry economised on administrative expenses. The low cost of internal enterprise organisation in Lancashire was reinforced by the institutions of industrial relations (already discussed) that generated a self-disciplined operative labour force requiring relatively little direct supervision.

With little in the way of managerial organisation internal to individual enterprises, and (the other side of the same coin) with the industry highly reliant on markets to co-ordinate the transformation of purchased raw materials into sold outputs, the economies of scale that Lancashire cotton textiles achieved through capturing a large extent of the market in the last half of the nineteenth century were external rather than internal to its constituent spinning and weaving firms. For those who believe that market co-ordination and successful capitalist development go hand in hand, no better example can be found than the British cotton industry of the late nineteenth century. Indeed, in 1919, Alfred Marshall described the Lancashire cotton industry as 'perhaps the best present instance of concentrated organisation mainly automatic'.[17] Unfortunately, as we shall see, as Marshall committed these words to print, the automatic market mechanism was breaking down in the face of planned co-ordination of the specialised division of labour abroad – and particularly in Japan – that would over the following decades eliminate the competitive advantages that the market co-ordinated Lancashire industry had inherited from its nineteenth-century era of international dominance.

II

Alternative Perspectives on British Dominance

The summary of our perspective on the sources of Britain's competitive advantage is consistent with the accounts of historians of the British cotton industry. Of particular value is the work of D.A. Farnie, whose historical argument is cast in an explicitly developmental perspective, with a concern for identifying the sources of Lancashire's unique competitive advantages in the late nineteenth century.[18] Over the past 25 years, however, not all the contributors to the analysis of the performance of the British cotton industry have approached the issue in dynamic, developmental terms. The 'new' economic historians, their academic roots more in economics than in history, have made the issue of British economic performance in the decades before World War I a centrepiece of their attack on the theoretical and empirical imprecision of an older-style economic history that had its roots more in history than in economics.

Trained as economists ourselves, we applaud the new economic historians' concern with the integration of theory and history and their attempts to derive quantitative estimates of the relative impacts of the phenomena under study. But, for us, a coherent perspective of the dynamic interaction of institutions and technology in generating economic outcomes is of more fundamental importance for economic analysis. It is just such a perspective that Anglo-American economists who choose to do economic history generally lack. The problem with the new economic history is that, insofar as the statistical arguments possess any theoretical structure at all, it is *neo-classical* economic history. Trained in the static methodology of neoclassical economics, the new economic historians have sought to analyse the process of historical change without any well-defined conception of the dynamics of economic development.

The new economic historian who has researched the British cotton industry in most detail is Lars Sandberg. But his 1974 book, *Lancashire in Decline*, contains only a two-page statistical overview of the growth of the industry in the nineteenth century.[19] Sandberg did not raise the issue of why the British industry rose to international economic dominance. Rather he began his analysis with the issue of choice of technology and alleged entrepreneurial failure after 1880, a debate that we shall take up later.

Gary Saxonhouse and Gavin Wright have used data on Britain's textile machinery exports of ring-frames and mules in an attempt to examine 'the global experience of the cotton textile industry' from 1870 to 1920.[20] They did not ask why Britain was so dominant in the industry at the starting date, and indeed focused their own research on the logic of technological choice rather than on the sources of competitive advantage. But they did cite as important two sources of Britain's competitive advantage – the utilisation of cotton inputs and the industry's marketing structure – that are prominent in our account.[21] We shall return to the implications of the persistence of these competitive advantages in Britain before World War I for the longer run competitive position of the British industry as well as for the ongoing debate over these issues between Lazonick and Mass on the one hand and Saxonhouse and Wright on the other.

More recently, Gregory Clark, a newer 'new' economic historian, has used the case of cotton textiles to ask the ambitious question, 'Why Isn't the Whole World Developed?', with his search for some answers focused on the relative productivity and factor costs in cotton textile industries around the world circa 1910. Pointing to 50 per cent increases in both the number of looms per weaver and the speed per loom in British cloth manufacture between 1850 and 1906, as well as to a 145 per cent increase in spindles per spinning operative and a more than 100 per cent increase in the speed per spindle on mules, Clark's only attempt to explain the international dominance of the British industry during the nineteenth century was to argue that 'labor intensification could . . . be an important source of productivity increases'.[22] We shall also return to a consideration of Clark's focus on labour intensity as the source of Britain's competitive advantage just prior to World War I.

The case of the British cotton industry has been used as a rhetorical example in a more general neoclassical explanation of British nineteenth-century economic success. In a survey of 'econometric history', Donald McCloskey took issue with 'the common argument that rising output of, say, the British cotton textile industry from 1815 to 1860 "spread fixed costs over a larger output and therefore reduced costs per unit"'. McCloskey went on to argue that the problem with the economies of scale argument is that 'it takes as given and unalterable the institutional fact of the number of cotton textile firms', but that 'growing output causes in the normal course of events a growing number of firms'. In an industry with a high degree of horizontal competition as was the case with British cotton textiles in the nineteenth century, existing firms can sell all that they can produce – 'the size of the market was not a constraint on an individual firm'.[23]

McCloskey did, however, recognise the plausibility of the argument that 'the cotton textile industry did in fact exhibit "economies of industry scale", as it is put' – what Alfred Marshall called external economies of scale. These economies of industry scale, McCloskey posited, 'would be cheapenings of production arising from better training of the workforce or more specialised production of machines – arguments consistent with rationality, if not necessarily important in this particular case'.[24]

In his choice of examples of economies of industry scale, McCloskey confounded the development of productive resources – 'better training of the workforce or more specialised production of machine' – with the more complete utilisation of these superior resources. Because of the fixed costs incurred in the development process, unless the productive resources that have been developed are sufficiently utilised, they result in higher, not lower, unit costs. In the last half of the nineteenth century, it was the export-led expansion of the British cotton industry, that created the incentive for Lancashire's economic actors – both workers and capitalists – to make further investments in human and physical resources. In addition, by permitting a high level of utilisation of the expanded industry capacity, this export-led expansion was a critical condition for enabling these actors to realise returns on their investments.

Moreover, as we have argued, because these actors were willing and able to make these investments that expanded the supply of industry inputs, the British industry did not succumb to *diseconomies* of scale as it serviced an ever-growing market.

Perhaps McCloskey was arguing that those (mainly the workforce itself) who undertook to invest in the better training of labour and those (mainly Britain's textile machinery producers) who undertook to produce more specialised machinery could rationally expect that the growth of the industry would ensure that these investments would be sufficiently utilised to achieve 'economies of industry scale'. If so, we are in agreement. Yet in an earlier piece written with C. Knick Harley, McCloskey argued (with reference to the cotton industry as the most prominent example) that foreign trade was unimportant to British economic performance in the nineteenth century.[25]

They derive this conclusion from a static framework of economic analysis. 'Foreign trade', said Harley and McCloskey, 'can be viewed as an industry producing imports, say wheat, in exchange for sacrifices of exports, say cotton cloth'.

> The 'productivity' of this industry is the rate at which quarters of wheat exchange for yards of cloth, i.e. the 'terms of trade' . . . This matter of concept settled, the remaining question is the counterfactual one of how much in fact the terms of trade would have moved had Britain insisted on growing all its own wheat, and by the same token consuming all its own cloth.

Based on a simple arithmetic calculation, they argued that 'self-sufficiency in 1860 . . . would have cost Britain only . . . 6 per cent of national income'.[26]

'This matter of concept' of the role of foreign trade in national economic performance may be settled among the disciples of neo-classical trade theory because their static methodology permits (and indeed compels) them to take comparative advantage as given. But 'this matter of concept' is not settled among those of us who want to explain shifts in international competitive advantage. In deriving their estimate of 6 per cent of national income, Harley and McCloskey make the implicit assumption that the extent of the market does not affect the supply-side responses that determine the development and utilisation of productive resources. In dynamic perspective, as we have just argued, this assumption is untenable. By creating incentives for making investments and conditions for utilising these investments, the expansion of the market, whether through domestic or foreign sales, can and generally does affect the development and utilisation of productive resources, and hence economic outcomes.

We have not invented this dynamic argument. In Britain itself, it resonates with a well known proposition put forth by Adam Smith in the late eighteenth century, a perspective on British economic development elaborated by Alfred Marshall in the late nineteenth century, and, more recently, the increasing-returns arguments of Nicholas Kaldor.[27] Smith, Marshall, and Kaldor all proposed theories of economic development based on a dynamic interaction of demand and supply: the growth in the market creates incentives to invest in productive capabilities (even if only because market expansion increases opportunities for learning by doing), and also ensures a high level of utilisation of the investments that are made.

What did Harley and McCloskey have to say about the sources of Britain's competitive advantage in cotton textiles? Drawing on an earlier article by Harley, they argued that 'when British industries were compared with their German and American counterparts it was clear that Britain's competitive position was strongest in certain old industries – textiles, shipbuilding, heavy engineering, and even some branches of ferrous metal production. This advantage appears to have been based on the skills that the labour force had developed over a century of industrial experience'.[28] Again we agree. But why was Britain unique in this accumulation of 'skills . . . developed over a century of industrial experience'? Harley and McCloskey attributed Britain's competitive advantage before 1860 to the nation's 'own ingenuity in making exported cotton cloth cheaper'.[29] These arguments are not wrong. But they are arguments in search of a perspective on economic development that the static theorising of neoclassical economics does not, and cannot, provide.

III

The Extension of British Competitive Advantage

By the late nineteenth century, the British cotton industry had developed an experienced labour force which worked with process technologies – the self-acting mule and the power-loom – that, after well over a half century of widespread use, were reaching the limits of mechanical perfection. The Lancashire industry continued to rely overwhelmingly on mules through the 1940s and on power-looms through the 1950s, even as cotton textile industries around the world were shifting almost exclusively to ring spinning as well as to much higher proportions of automatic looms than was the case in Britain.

Invented in 1828, ring-spinning technology was dramatically improved and made commercially viable in New England during the 1870s and early 1880s in the wake of the rapid post-Civil War growth of mule spinning in Fall River and a series of strikes staged there by mule operatives of Lancashire origin. The ring-frame required the use of higher quality (longer staple and higher grade) cotton than the mule to spin a given count of yarn, but permitted the use of inexperienced labour and, by virtue of using higher quality cotton, produced a stronger yarn. Although perfected by the machinists of New England, ring spinning was the technological breakthrough that permitted the rapid expansion of the cotton textile industry of the American South from the 1880s – a regional industry that increasingly outcompeted the older industry of the North.[30]

The first commercially successful automatic loom – the Draper Company's Northrop loom – was also a New England invention. It made its appearance in 1894 as the result of what may have been up to that date the largest research and development expenditure on a single technology in the United States. By automating the previously labour-intensive process of reloading the weft yarn, the automatic loom permitted one operative to tend 20 to 30 looms prior to World War I, compared to the machine-worker ratio of eight that prevailed on power-looms in the United States. In Britain, where the yarn used in ·power-loom weaving was more subject to breakages than in the United States and where collective bargaining determined the number of looms per weaver, the machine-worker ratio on power-looms was only four. The few British firms that invested in automatic looms before World War I achieved machine-worker ratios of 14 to 20.[31]

The fixed cost of an automatic loom was about three times that of a power-loom. With the exception of Britain, the automatic loom was most quickly adopted in the high-wage countries of the world. As late as 1936 only 12 per cent of the cotton looms in Japan were automatic, higher than Britain's 3 per cent, but much lower than the United States's 68 per cent or Italy's 23 per cent.[32] Given its high fixed cost, the automatic loom required high machine-worker ratios to achieve low unit costs. To achieve high machine-worker ratios in turn required the use of strong, break-resistant yarn. The fully integrated firm of Ashton Brothers, the first firm to install automatic looms in Britain, experimented with using its existing mules to supply yarn to its new weaving machinery. But, in keeping with the practice around the world, even this British firm quickly installed rings to supply the break-resistant yarn that could realise the high-throughput potential of the automatic loom.[33]

Just as the advent of a viable ring-spinning technology permitted the US South to use less experienced labour and challenge the predominance of New England within the protected American market, so too did the diffusion of ring spinning enable some low-wage countries in Asia (particularly India, China, and Japan) and Latin America (particularly Brazil and Mexico) to challenge Britain in the markets of the less developed economies. Of these countries, Japan would eventually – in the decades between the two world wars – usurp Britain's position as the leading exporter of cotton goods. But before World War I, in direct competition with these low-wage countries and ring spinning technology, the British cotton industry maintained competitive advantage in all but the coarsest goods. Between 1889 and 1913, the British cotton industry expanded the total value of piece-goods exports by 92 per cent, with the value to India increasing by 89 per cent, to China by 54 per cent, to Hong Kong by 109 per cent, to Argentina by 138 per cent, and to Egypt by 205 per cent. In 1889 India and China together accounted for 46 per cent of the value of British piece-goods exports, and in 1913 still 43 per cent.

Before World War I perhaps as much as two-thirds of the value of British piece-goods exports were absorbed by the less developed areas of the world.[34] To meet the continued growth of its markets, both foreign and domestic, the industry expanded its capacity dramatically prior to World War I. In 1914 the industry had 14 per cent more spinning and weaving firms than a decade earlier, and these firms contained 24 per cent more spindles and 23 per cent more looms.[35]

Over the past two decades, economic historians have debated the question of how the British cotton industry accomplished its phenomenal expansion from the late nineteenth century to World War I despite its marked lag in introducing the new spinning and weaving technologies and its need to pay wages to its workers that were many times those paid by cotton textile firms in the expanding low-wage industries of Asia and Latin America. The focus on the case of the British cotton industry has been part of a larger debate on British economic performance in the decades preceding World War I – a larger debate that was set in motion in the late 1960s and early 1970s by the new economic historians' attack on the hypothesis of 'entrepreneurial failure', with McCloskey and Sandberg in the vanguard. They were highly critical of traditional economic historians such as David Landes and Derek Aldcroft who, taking a 'sociological view of the matter', had argued that British entrepreneurs 'failed' without providing any *economic* evidence that a failure had in fact occurred. As a result of a number of industry case studies by new economic historians, McCloskey and Sandberg claimed that 'the late Victorian entrepreneur who started his historiographic career in damnation is well on his way to redemption'.[36]

Central to the case-study evidence was Sandberg's pioneering analysis, first published in 1969, of the choice of spinning technology in Britain prior to World War I. In his subsequent book, that included this case study, Sandberg described his test of the entrepreneurial failure hypothesis as 'an attempt to see whether in fact British cotton textile firms were irrational and "technologically backwards" in the period after 1880'.[37] Sandberg argued that neither the relatively slow diffusion of ring spinning in Britain in the twentieth century nor the sharp decline in the British cotton industry after World War I 'in any way proves that the British made a mistake, or were irrational, in not introducing more ring spindles before World War I'.[38]

Comparing the relative factor costs inherent in using rings and mules in Britain prior to World War I for spinning different counts of yarn, Sandberg concluded that it was rational for British spinners to invest in rings for spinning twist (warp) yarns that were a little below counts of 40 and weft yarns even for counts in the low 40s. The major factor costs favouring the mule were its use of a lower, and hence less expensive, quality of cotton for spinning a given count and, in the case of weft yarn, the extra transportation costs of shipping ring weft to specialised weaving mills because ring yarn was spun on wooden bobbins whereas mule yarn was spun on the bare spindle. The major factor cost favouring rings derived from the use of cheaper female labour.[39] Based on his estimates of Lancashire's actual aggregate investment in rings and mules for spinning yarns below and above no.40 in the period 1907–1913, Sandberg concluded that 'British manufacturers . . . appear to have behaved in a rational manner. At the very least these results should throw the burden of proof onto those who maintain that the British were irrational in their choice between rings and mules'.[40]

Over a decade after the original publication of this rings and mules analysis, William Lazonick saw fit to subject Sandberg's exercise to an empirical critique. He found that Sandberg had overestimated the factor-cost advantages of rings because his calculations assumed one-half too few mule spindles per worker and did not take into account the cost of shipping wooden bobbins (stripped of ring weft) back to the spinning mill. Lazonick also found that Sandberg had overestimated the amount of investment in rings in 1907–1913. The combination of Sandberg's error in estimating investment in rings with his errors in estimating factor costs made investments in rings look more attractive than they really were.[41]

Lazonick's own empirical findings did not upset Sandberg's managerial rationality hypothesis. On the contrary, Lazonick argued that the corrections showed that, given the relative factor costs that they faced, cost-minimising Lancashire managers had even more of an incentive to invest in mules than Sandberg had thought, and that they indeed did invest in more mules than Sandberg had calculated! Lazonick, therefore, agreed with Sandberg that the managerial rationality hypothesis was appropriate for describing managerial choice of spinning technology in the pre-World War I period. But Lazonick contended that the corrections to the estimates of investments in rings and mules were important because they emphasised the extent to which, even on lower counts and particularly in the spinning of weft yarn, the British cotton industry was still, quite rationally from the perspective of the individual firm, not only relying on but also making *new investments* in the traditional mule-spinning technology prior to World War I.

Lazonick also argued that the corrected estimates of relative factor costs were important because they provided evidence of the particular cost constraints that encouraged the use of the traditional technologies in Lancashire, and hence focused the economic historian's attention on those constraints that would have had to be changed to permit a more rapid diffusion of ring spinning technology. Indeed, the fundamental problem with Sandberg's analysis, and with the attack on entrepreneurial failure to which it contributed, was not empirical but theoretical. In defining the issue of British economic performance in terms of managerial rationality, Sandberg along with McCloskey had adopted the point of view of the individual manager for the purposes of assessing the pre-World War I performance of selected British industries as well as the British economy as a whole.[42]

The McCloskey–Sandberg problematic is appropriate if one wants to see whether managers were optimising subject to certain hypothesised constraints and indeed if one wants to use (as Lazonick suggested that economic historians should) the constrained-optimisation methodology to explore systematically the nature of the constraints on managerial decision-making existing at selected points in time. But, relying as it does on a static (or at best a comparative static) methodology, the constrained-optimisation approach does not permit an analysis of the processes of technological and organisational innovation that are central to sustained productivity growth and shifts in competitive advantage.

As Joseph Schumpeter argued before World War I, the neo-classical problematic of adaptations to 'the circular flow of economic life' cannot explain the process of economic development. In *The Theory of Economic Development*, Schumpeter in effect distinguished between adaptive managers who optimise subject to given constraints and innovative entrepreneurs who take actions to overcome these constraints.[43] As Lazonick argued, McCloskey and Sandberg failed to take cognizance of the Schumpeterian distinction between entrepreneurs and managers, despite the existence of a large literature on the interpretation and usefulness of the Schumpeterian distinction.[44]

McCloskey and Sandberg could justifiably reply that the proponents of the entrepreneurial failure hypothesis did *not* make the Schumpeterian distinction between entrepreneurs and managers central to their own analyses, and hence did not explicitly differentiate their perspective from the neoclassical conception of managerial activity. But then neither Landes nor Aldcroft actually posited that British businessmen were acting *irrationally* in their technological choices, as McCloskey and Sandberg implied.[45] In *The Unbound Prometheus*, Landes argued: 'Even when the British entrepreneur was rational, his calculations were distorted by the shortness of his time horizon, and his estimates were on the conservative side'.[46] In the introduction to his edited book, *The Development of British Industry and Foreign Competition, 1875–1914*, Aldcroft argued:

> The fact that some industrialists were slow to adopt new techniques does not necessarily mean that they were inefficient or lacked enterprise. One might, for example, criticize cotton manufacturers on the grounds that they ignored the ring spindle and automatic loom. But this was not due to conservatism on their part but rather to the fact that the new machinery was not really suitable to English conditions of manufacture.[47]

Indeed, in *Lancashire in Decline*, Sandberg cited both the page on which this statement appears and R.E. Tyson's contribution on the British cotton industry to the Aldcroft book as reflecting agreement with the managerial rationality hypothesis.[48]

The real issue, therefore, was not whether British cotton managers were rational (all participants in the debate assumed they were) but the relation between *rational* managerial decision-making and the competitive performance of the British cotton industry. After positing the test for managerial irrationality as his primary purpose in *Lancashire in Decline*, Sandberg stated that 'a secondary question is the extent to which any mistakes [British cotton firms] may have made concerning the new technology could have affected Lancashire's competitive position'.[49] Three amendments to this version of the problematic are in order. First, because managerial irrationality is not at issue, we need no longer label managerial technological choices as 'mistakes' (for as we shall see, the tendency of some later participants in the debate to do so has merely confused the issues). Second, the impact on Lancashire's competitive position of its continued reliance on the traditional technologies becomes the primary, not secondary, question. Third, because the British cotton industry put in place so much new fixed capital – much of it taking the form of the traditional spinning and weaving technologies – in the decade before World War I, the problematic should include a consideration of whether there was any systematic relation between the strong competitive position of the British cotton industry before the war and its dramatically weakened position in the 1920s (and beyond).

The first detailed contribution to the modern debate on the sources of British competitiveness prior to World War I was made in 1968 by R.E. Tyson in his chapter in Aldcroft's edited volume on British industry and foreign competition. Tyson began his essay: 'The British cotton industry in 1913 has been described [by Charles Kindleberger] as "highly developed, technologically stagnant, competitively fragile"'.[50] Tyson succinctly summarised the essential characteristics of demand and supply that affected Britain's competitive position prior to the war. Two-thirds of his article documents the industry's export-oriented expansion in the decades prior to World War I, with the emphasis on the continuing importance of markets in the low-income countries of the world. The last nine pages draw on the (then) standard industry sources to describe more or less correctly the organisational characteristics of the industry and the productive and cost characteristics of the mule and power-loom that enabled the British cotton industry to sustain its competitive advantages in the face of the rise of both low-wage and high-technology competitors.

Tyson did not, however, provide an explanation for why this competitive advantage was lost so dramatically after 1913. Was there something about the pre-war expansion that contributed to the rapidity and extent of the post-war loss of markets, or were the extended rise of the industry and its precipitous fall two largely unrelated phenomena? That even before the war the continued reliance on traditional technologies might have pressed the limits of the industry's accumulated competitive advantages finds statistical support in estimates made by G.T. Jones in the 1930s of prewar trends in 'real costs' – the inverse of what later came to be known as total factor productivity. Jones's general conclusion was that there was 'little, if any, net change in the efficiency of the British cotton [industry] during the period

1885–1910 . . . [as] the real cost of manufacturing began to increase about 1900 and continued to rise until the outbreak of war in 1914'.[51]

Jones himself found his findings paradoxical, indicating as they did 'a progressive fall in efficiency' after 1900, accompanied by a 'great expansion' in plant and equipment.[52] Sandberg, however, raised doubts about the existence of a paradox. His calculations showed a 40 per cent increase in labour productivity between 1885 and 1913, with no apparent slowdown in the rate of productivity growth after 1900. Indeed, by making a number of adjustments to Jones's real cost index, Sandberg estimated 'a reduction of real cost by 9 per cent to 10 per cent between 1885 and 1910 and of 11 to 12 per cent between 1885 and 1914.' 'What is more', Sandberg went on to argue, 'after my corrections have been made, this improvement is spread fairly evenly over the [1885–1914] period. The peculiar deterioration Jones recorded for the post-1900 period has vanished. It has, roughly speaking, been replaced by a continuation of the trend he noted for the 1890s'.[53]

Hence in Sandberg's view, managerial rationality in the choice of technology and progressive reduction in real costs went hand in hand. In 'The Performance of the British Cotton Industry, 1870–1913', the present authors have challenged Sandberg's productivity and real cost calculations. We found a general stagnation in the growth of labour productivity from 1890 to 1913, with negative productivity growth in the spinning sector after the turn of the century. We attributed this stagnation in productivity not only to the continued reliance on technologies that had reached the limits of technical development but more importantly to the way in which these technologies were utilised in the period of more intense competition from the 1890s. We stressed in particular the tendency of spinning and weaving firms to cut costs by the use of inferior – lower grade and shorter staple – cotton for the spinning of given counts of yarn and the weaving of given types of cloth.[54]

The existence of the Liverpool cotton market made it possible to shift to inferior cotton whenever changes in the relative prices of grades and staples warranted it and the going price of yarn necessitated it. In addition, the traditional technologies and modes of work organisation encouraged this use of inferior cotton inputs. On the one hand, compared with the high-throughput ring-frame and automatic loom which required the use of break-resistant yarn made from longer staple and higher grade cotton, the mule and power-loom were more adaptable to inferior cotton inputs. On the other hand, Lancashire's industrial relations systems gave workers an incentive to supply more effort to maintain productivity and earnings in the face of what the workers called 'bad spinning' or 'bad weaving' – increased yarn breakages that arose from the use of inferior cotton inputs. At the same time, these systems prevented managers from using superior cotton as a labour-displacing investment. Even some improvements in the traditional technologies that could have been effort-saving ended up serving as opportunities for managers to use inferior cotton inputs rather than permit workers to achieve higher levels of output with the same amount of effort.[55]

Jones's real cost index did not capture the movement to inferior cotton inputs, nor the impact of this movement on labour productivity. But through the use of inferior cotton it was possible to cut costs and expand markets even while the growth in output per worker-hour was stagnating. When combined with the manifold external economies of scale that Britain still possessed in the early part of the century, the use of inferior cotton inputs as a supply-side response to increased international competition was, moreover, compatible with the capture of markets in the low-income areas of the world. Constrained by low incomes, consumers in these markets were willing to accept cloth that was less durable (because it was made from inferior cotton and, as was generally the case with lower priced British cloth, was heavily sized) as a trade-off for cloth that was less expensive.

This production strategy of the degradation of product quality was particularly viable for cloth to be worn in warmer climates and also opened up new possibilities for the types of goods that could be made affordable to low-income but fashion-conscious customers. As A.J. Marrison has shown for Latin America, income-constrained consumers sacrificed cloth quality in order to be able to afford more highly finished goods, a dimension of product quality that the Lancashire printing and dyeing sectors were able to meet at relatively low cost.[56] The unique capability of Lancashire's spinning and weaving firms to adjust their costs to the low-income constraints in these mass markets furthered the extent to which all vertical levels of the British cotton industry benefited from external economies of scale.

The Lazonick–Mass arguments concerning the way in which the British cotton industry extended its competitive advantage before the war have been criticised by Saxonhouse and Wright in a reply to Lazonick's critique of their earlier work on the diffusion of rings and mules around the world in the late nineteenth and early twentieth centuries.[57] In the earlier work, 'New Evidence on the Stubborn English Mule and the Cotton Industry, 1878–1920', Saxonhouse and Wright propounded the argument that reliance on mule spinning and vertical specialisation was consistent with the expansion and profitability of the British cotton industry in the pre-World War I decades – an argument that Lazonick and Mass had also made.[58] In their response to Lazonick, Saxonhouse and Wright took cognizance of the Lazonick-Mass argument of how the British cotton industry captured the markets of the underdeveloped world before the war but did not find it persuasive. As they argued:

> The combined share of British cotton piece goods exports to the four largest low-income markets (Bombay, Bengal, Turkey and China) was in fact no larger in 1913 than it had been in 1889. The inverse relationship between product quality and market expansion was far more striking during the sixty years *prior* to 1890 than it was

during 1890–1913, the period when Lazonick believes the British made their most fateful mistakes. Lazonick and Mass emphasize the effort to cut costs by use of inferior cotton inputs, but more than 95 per cent of British cotton imports were from Egypt or the United States (i.e., the longer-staple, higher-quality varieties), far higher than any other country, and there was no hint of a decline in this percentage before World War I. Our machinery data show no trend toward production of lower-count yarns, and the best Lazonick and Mass are able to do is to suggest that the quality decline may have taken other forms which they are as yet unable to document. This is, to put it mildly, a weak base on which to erect an ambitious historical superstructure of industrial rise and fall.[59]

The fact that Britain's share of the low-income markets remained constant in the decades prior to the war is irrelevant to the issue at hand. What is important is that these markets continued to take some 45 per cent of the value of Lancashire's exports, despite the rise of low-wage Asiatic competition. As for the rest of their rebuttal, it also has nothing to do with the Lazonick–Mass argument. We did not argue that reliance on the low-income markets meant a shift to lower counts of yarn and coarser cloth. The problem for Lancashire firms from the 1880s was precisely the opposite; they had to contend with the rise of low-wage competitors using ring spinning to capture the coarse goods markets. It was the very existence of these competitors that made Lancashire's ability to maintain its share of the low-income markets all the more remarkable. Nor did we argue that Lancashire maintained its competitive advantage by shifting away from the American cotton that was used for producing the Oldham yarns destined for India and other low-income markets. Rather, as we have already indicated, our 'inferior cotton' argument is that Lancashire spinners cut costs by using shorter staple and lower grade *American* cotton, and that the organisational structures and technologies that characterised the Lancashire industry gave them both the ability and incentive to pursue such a strategy.

Saxonhouse and Wright asserted that Lazonick and Mass were unable to document the 'other forms' that the quality decline might have taken (this despite their own recognition elsewhere of the flexibility of the mule in using lower staple and lower grade cotton).[60] We gave examples of the cost-cutting possibilities:

> In spinning No.32 yarn, cotton costs constituted almost 90 per cent of total costs, and a shift from middling 1 1/16-inch cotton to fair low middling 1-inch cotton would have saved 5 per cent of total spinning costs in 1907, and a shift from the same cotton to good ordinary 1-inch staple would have saved 7.5 per cent. A more dramatic shift from good middling 1 1/8-inch cotton to good ordinary 1-inch cotton would have saved 22.5 per cent.[61]

We lamented the absence of 'data on the utilization of cotton inputs during this period even for one firm in the industry, much less the industry as a whole'.[62] But our recognition that such data were unavailable was not an admission that we lacked evidence on the pervasiveness of the use of inferior cotton as a cost-cutting measure in Britain before the war. We cited the record of mounting industrial conflict over bad spinning and bad weaving from the 1890s to World War I. The collectively bargained compensation paid to spinning and weaving operatives because of bad spinning and bad weaving suggested productivity losses attributable to the use of inferior cotton that were 5 to 10 per cent of normal production. In addition, we re-evaluated Sandberg's index of movements in the quality of cotton goods exports in terms of the use of inferior cotton for producing given counts of yarn as well as heavy sizing for producing given types of cloth.[63]

Further, it should be understood that our focus on Lancashire's use of inferior cotton was not the 'base' upon which we sought to build a 'superstructure' of Lancashire's rise and decline. Our purpose in analysing the causes and consequences of this particular cost-cutting strategy was to show how the record of Lancashire's remarkable prewar expansion could be reconciled with a record of stagnating labour productivity. We argued that the managers of spinning and weaving concerns were motivated to use this strategy because it gave them an *additional competitive edge* in markets where demand was constrained by low incomes.

Our argument was *not* that such cotton cost-cutting was the only, or even the major, source of Lancashire's competitive advantage before the war. The British cotton industry could continue to compete on the basis of its experienced, hard-working labour force and the industry-wide economies of scale (outlined at the beginning of this essay) that came from the high levels of utilisation of the productive resources that had been put in place in Lancashire during the nineteenth century. Our point in focusing on the use of inferior cotton – and on the labour conflicts it engendered because it required operatives to expend more effort for the same pay – was that, given its prior competitive advantages, the British cotton industry sought successfully to gain a competitive edge in the low-income markets through the more intensive utilisation of its traditional productive resources, and not by the further development of effort-saving technologies.

If Saxonhouse and Wright misinterpreted our arguments concerning the pre-war competitive position of the British cotton industry, Gregory Clark has simply ignored them. In an article entitled, 'Why Isn't the Whole World Developed?', Clark has summarised his version of the debate on prewar economic performance:

> Recently scholars have excoriated managers of the British textile industry for their alleged failure to choose the correct techniques in spinning and weaving in the late nineteenth and early twentieth

centuries. The decline of the British industry from the 1920s onwards is attributed to these managerial failures.[64]

Which scholars made such arguments? Clark cited two pieces by Lazonick: his critique of Sandberg's analysis of choice of spinning technology and a summary statement on the relation between industrial organization and technological change in the twentieth-century decline of the British cotton industry.[65] But contrary to Clark (and as we have already summarised), these two contributions by Lazonick *confirmed the validity* of the managerial rationality hypothesis. At the same time, this work stressed the inability of the managerial rationality hypothesis to explain why cost-minimisation subject to given constraints resulted in competitive advantage before the war and competitive disadvantage after the war, and why, after it experienced dramatic losses of world markets in the 1920s, the British cotton industry experienced such difficulty in moving from its traditional, low-throughput mules and power-looms to the newer, high-throughput rings and automatic looms.

Using Lazonick as a foil for his own argument that to focus on 'management failings seems to me misguided', Clark went on to contend that 'given the labor cost [he means wage cost] advantages of Britain's competitors, what really requires explanation is not the ultimate demise of the industry but why British textiles continued to thrive so long'.[66] Yet Clark made no reference to the Lazonick–Mass article, published some three years previous to his own piece, in which we asked precisely this question and offered some answers. Clark himself attempted to explain 'why British textiles continued to thrive so long' by means of a static presentation of relative factor costs in cotton industries around the world circa 1910.

Indeed, in keeping with his static methodology, Clark focused his critical attention on Lazonick's empirical correction of Sandberg's static analysis of relative factor costs in the choice of spinning technology within Britain. 'One of the major mistakes attributed to British managers', Clark asserted, 'was a failure to switch from mule spinning to ring spinning. William Lazonick has argued that this failure stemmed from the more fundamental error of retaining the horizontal [*sic*] specialization of the spinning and weaving factories'.[67] Clark went on to argue that the transport cost savings of not having to ship wooden bobbins that came from retaining the mules was only a small fraction of the unit labour cost disadvantage of the British industry compared with the Indian industry.

Clark has confused the issues. Although the transportation cost savings inherent in the continued use of mules under British conditions did enter into the debate over the choice of technique in Britain, the measure of the transportation cost constraint had little to do with the Lazonick–Mass analysis of how the British industry remained competitive – how the industry reduced costs subject to (among many other factors) such a transportation cost constraint – prior to World War I. 'The correct question', Clark immediately went on to say, 'is not why bad choice of technique doomed the British industry, but why an industry apparently so burdened by high costs for its major input [labour] could remain so long successful, competing against a host of low-wage competitors'.[68]

Although the Lazonick–Mass contribution did not adopt Clark's methodology of comparing factor costs around the world just prior to World War I, we did ask the 'correct question' of how the British cotton industry was able to expand its exports to these countries, and particularly to India, from the 1890s to World War I. In answering this question, we showed that, by adapting on the basis of the traditional technologies and organisational structures that had characterised the rise of the British cotton industry to international dominance, British managers were able to remain competitive against the emerging low-wage industries in the low-income areas of the world. Contrary to Clark's misrepresentation of Lazonick's work, we have never argued that, given the constraints that they faced as individual decision-makers, British managers made mistakes in pursuing, or were mistaken to pursue, this adaptive strategy. Our argument is that, given the organisational and technological contexts within which they made their strategic decisions, British managers of specialised firms were able to continue to cut costs on the traditional technologies but were prevented from obtaining the high-throughput benefits of the new technologies. Quite rationally, they avoided making investments in the new technologies. And generally speaking, their very experience in the industry enhanced their abilities to optimise subject to the constraints they faced – to be good 'neo-classical' managers.

Clark's own answer to the 'correct question' of how Britain maintained competitive advantage before World War I was to show that just before the war the British cotton industry was paying wages that were some 35 per cent higher than in Germany and France, over 50 per cent higher than in Russia and Italy, well over 500 per cent higher than in Japan and India, and over 800 per cent higher than in China. Britain had a marked competitive advantage in the cost of coal over all countries except Japan (whose coal cost, according to Clark, was just nominally higher), and a competitive advantage in the cost of physical capital, except when compared with China, Japan, and Mexico whose mills ran double shifts. Britain's main competitive advantage lay, however, in the greater number of machines that each British worker tended; almost 60 per cent higher than in Germany, about 85 per cent higher than in France and Russia, over 130 per cent higher than in Italy, 285 per cent higher than in Japan, and over 300 per cent higher than in India and China. In the US South (but not the North), a higher machine-worker ratio than in Britain more than offset higher wages. The US South lost out to Britain, according to Clark's figures, because of its higher unit capital and coal costs.[69]

'The only countries', Clark argued, 'which ought to have been able to compete with the British on international markets [in 1910] were India, Japan, and China – the only countries that did in fact compete'. Their source of competitive advantage was extraordinarily low wages, but even then much of this advantage was lost because of the very low efficiency of Asian labour, as reflected in the machine–worker ratios.[70]

Clark provided no discussion of, or data on, the British cotton industry's share of various international markets prior to World War I. But we know that the British industry expanded its exports to China and India in the prewar decades despite its inability to compete against cheap labour on the coarsest goods (and particularly yarns). Clark made no attempt, however, to determine on which types of goods – coarse, medium, or fine; yarns or cloths; grey, bleached, printed, dyed – the low-wage Asian countries had competitive advantage. Indeed, his statement that India, China, and Japan were 'the only countries which did in fact compete' might lead the unsuspecting reader to come to the erroneous conclusion that the cotton industries of these very low-wage countries had pushed British goods out of the Asian markets before the war.

Hence, despite his claim that his essay would address the allegedly previously unanswered question of how the British cotton industry remained competitive before World War I, Clark managed to avoid asking the 'correct question' of how Britain maintained such large shares of these very low-income markets before the war in direct competition with the very low-wage producers of Asia. Indeed, at this point in his argument, wittingly or not, Clark changed his own original 'correct question' *from* how, in the face of low-wage rivals, Britain maintained its competitive advantage in the prewar period *to* why labour in these low-wage countries – and his references are generally to India, China, and Japan taken as a group – was so inefficient as reflected in the low machine-worker ratios.[71]

Clark rejected as plausible explanations for the low machine-worker ratios in the low-wage countries such items as the substitution of labour for capital, inferior capital equipment, inferior cotton, labour force inexperience, and malnourishment and undereducation of the labour force. He pointed out, moreover, that when workers from low-wage countries migrated to high-wage countries, they got paid high wages, presumably because they were now more productive than they had been at home.[72] He concluded, therefore, that the inefficiency of labour in the low-wage countries must 'attach to the local environment, not to the workers themselves'.[73]

Clark devoted two pages of his article to a discussion of these 'local effects' (or what in the abstract to his article he called 'local culture'). He gave the example of the resistance of workers in India to taking on more ring spindles, and of workers in various parts of the world, including Britain, to taking on more looms. He dismissed union power, labor–management relations, or personnel policies as determinants of differences in the number of looms per weaver on the grounds that, across countries, the machine–worker ratios were positively correlated with local wage rates. But this statistical correlation is equally consistent with the argument that the local wage rate was a function of worker productivity – that, given the development and utilisation of productive resources in a particular locality, workers got paid what their local industry could afford to pay them.

Clark was right to focus his attention on the influence of particular social environments on worker productivity.[74] Ultimately, however, the purpose of historical analysis is not to posit some preconceived or favoured explanation for an observed statistical correlation between factor productivities and factor prices. Its purpose is rather to explain the dynamic interaction between the two phenomena in a particular social environment.

A dynamic historical analysis quickly exposes a glaring problem with Clark's 'local effects' argument. His cross-national data on wage rates and machine-worker ratios for the years just prior to World War I led him to lump together the cotton industries of India, China, and Japan as having the lowest wages and (save for the inconsequential case of Greece) the lowest labour efficiency in the world. The problem is that, during World War I and throughout the 1920s, Japan was the rising star of the international cotton industry. During the mid-1930s Japan surpassed Britain as the world's dominant exporter, while the Indian cotton industry, with an earlier start and greater capacity than the Japanese, required tariff protection to keep Japanese goods out. Even with the tariff, India became Japan's largest market for the export of cotton cloth. Between 1914 and 1932, while Britain's share of Indian cloth imports declined from 97 per cent to 50 per cent, Japan's share rose from 0.1 per cent to 45 per cent. In 1937 the Japanese cotton industry accounted for 37 per cent by volume of the world's exports of cotton cloth, whereas Britain accounted for 27 per cent and India only 3 per cent.[75]

Japan's rise to international dominance in cotton textiles had much to do with changes in the efficiency of its labour force. In his report of a visit to India in 1930 (one year after he had visited Japan), Arno S. Pearse, the General Secretary of the Manchester-based International Federation of Master Cotton Spinners' and Manufacturers' Associations (and a source whom Clark cited extensively) presented a double column, point-by-point comparison of the cotton industries of India and Japan.[76] He reported that 'wages per head are 10 to 15 per cent. less in Bombay than in Japan, but output being smaller in India, labour cost is higher per pound of yarn and per yard of cloth produced'.[77] The main reason why India's labour costs were higher was because (as Pearse said later in his report, in a passage that Clark cited) 'the workpeople would not look after more than one side [of a ring-frame]'.[78] By contrast, in Japan, 'operatives work as many machines as can be attended under fair conditions, actually up to three sides of a spinning frame, and 5.5 looms per operative (against one side and less than two looms in India)'.[79]

According to 1932 cotton spinning data for no.20 yarn, compared with Britain, unit labour costs were 58 per cent less in Japan but 8 per cent more in India. Spinning wages were just 6 per cent greater in Japan than in India but the number of spindles per worker 143 per cent greater.[80] By 1932 the number of power-looms per weaver in Japan was more than three times as great as in India. Compare these figures to Clark's data for 1910, when Japan's wages were 3 per cent higher than India's and its machinery–worker ratio only 6 per cent higher.[81] Even if these statistics make it reasonable to characterise both the Japanese and Indian cotton industries as low-wage and low-efficiency producers in 1910, it is a fatal error for understanding why the whole world is not developed – or why some previously poor countries *are* developed – to lump the two national industries together some two decades later.

For how would Clark explain what happened to Japan's 'local environment' that made its labour so inefficient in 1910, but so efficient in 1930? If we take this to be the 'correct question', it is one that cannot be answered with the static, ahistorical methodology that Clark has used. Clark himself has not bothered to raise this question, even when, by virtue of Mira Wilkins' protest that managerial structure and capability might have something to do with the answer, the reality of Japan's success stared him in the face. Clark's response to Wilkins relied on data from 1929–30 on the relative efficiency of Japanese-owned mills in Japan compared with both Japanese-owned and Chinese-owned mills in Shanghai. Compared with the Chinese-owned mills, spindles per worker (holding yarn count constant) were 8 per cent higher in Japanese-owned mills in Shanghai but 92 per cent higher in the mills in Japan.[82]

There is a good reason why Clark had to get such data from the inter-war period rather than from the pre-war period with which his original article had been concerned. In 1910 the Japanese cotton industry, barely 20 years old, had not yet developed the organisational or financial capability to engage in direct investment abroad (even though Japan's exports had already made substantial inroads against the Indians in the Chinese yarn markets and the Americans in the Chinese cloth market). Yet, as Clark himself recognised in his response to Wilkins (and despite his original position that differences in technology do not explain the wealth of nations), 'by the 1920s Japanese cotton mill managers had fully absorbed modern textile technology, had dispensed with the need for foreign managers and technicians, and had developed methods and machines of their own even though the industry was still less than one-tenth the size of the British industry'.[83] Clark took no notice, however, of the contradiction between the data he used to reply to Wilkins and his original answer to his question, 'Why Isn't the Whole World Developed?'. For those social scientists concerned with understanding the wealth and poverty of nations, the 'correct question' is how in the first few decades of the twentieth century did the 'miracle' of the Japanese cotton industry occur. Given what we now know about the longer run technological and economic trajectories of Japan, the answer to this question has potentially momentous implications for understanding the dynamics of economic development today.

IV

The New Competition

We can consider the sources of competitive advantage of the Japanese cotton industry in the inter-war period under the same five cost headings – labour, fixed capital, materials, marketing, administrative – that we used in our earlier discussion of the sources of competitive advantage of the British cotton industry in the late nineteenth century. In the process, we shall contrast the sources of Japanese competitive advantage with those that enabled the British industry to dominate international markets a few decades earlier, and indeed up to World War I. We shall then be in a position to consider the state of the debate over the British response to the Japanese challenge in the inter-war period.

(1) *Labour costs*

The conventional wisdom among economic historians is that low-wage labour was critical to the rise of the Japanese industry. Even Clark, who focused on how inefficient the Japanese were in 1910, argued that low wages had enabled the Japanese to outcompete the British before World War I. Recently John Singleton has put forth the 'cheap labour' argument as a superior alternative to Lazonick's 'structural rigidity thesis' for explaining the decline of the British cotton industry.

> The most successful cotton industries in the present century have been in the developing countries, firstly Japan, and later India, Hong Kong, and Pakistan. Their rise stemmed from low production costs resulting from low labour costs. The product cycle model, in which dominance in a product group passes from the innovating region to areas possessing cheaper labour provides a better explanation of Lancashire's fortunes than the structural rigidity thesis.[84]

In fact, before the war, Japan's main export success was the displacement of India as China's main external source of very coarse yarn. But wages in India were even lower than in Japan; hence low wages could not have been the determining factor. Low wages were important in Japan's successful displacement from the China market of the very high wage but high productivity competition from the US South. From 1902 to 1913, Japan's share of imports of cloth into China rose from under 3 per cent to over 20 per cent. Nevertheless, low wages did not enable Japan to replace the relatively high-wage British, who still supplied over 53 per cent of the cloth imported into China in 1913, just 2 per cent less than their share in 1902. From 1900 to 1930 Japanese wages rose faster than British wages, especially after World War I when Japanese wages quadrupled while British wages only doubled. Therefore, a relative rise in British wages cannot be held responsible for giving Japan competitive advantage after the war.[85]

Moreover, the Japanese measure of expenditures on labour is biased downwards if limited to weekly wage rates. According to the pre-war data presented by Clark, Japan had very high costs of 'plant and machinery' per spindle, ranging from 40 per cent greater than the per spindle costs of India to 93 per cent greater than those of Britain.[86] Only the Swiss cotton industry had greater capital costs per spindle than the Japanese. The high cost of building a spinning mill in Japan (which Clark attributed simply to the cost of plant and equipment) was in part because of expenditures on the construction of dormitories for housing the labour force. In 1929 Pearse found that the cost of dormitories accounted for one-sixth of the cost per spindle for building and equipping a spinning mill. A firm's current expenditures on room and board subsidies, welfare work, pensions, health care, recruitment, and education could generate labour costs equal to about 25–30 per cent of a young woman's wages (including semi-annual bonuses).[87]

The dormitories housed rural farmgirls who entered the mills between the ages of 14 and 17 for periods of two to three years. Female overseers were selected from among these girls and remained in the mills for longer periods of time. Conditions were reportedly very poor even in the best mills until the 1920s, with the propensity for the girls to run away creating high levels of labour turnover. The prosperity of the 1920s and the emergence of ever more dominant companies in the highly productive export sector appear to have improved work conditions and worker morale substantially by the end of the decade.[88]

The relatively short stints of the girls in the mills placed a downward limit on the reduction of turnover rates. But once the girls stopped running away, the turnover became systematic, thus permitting the companies to meet their labour requirements in a planned and co-ordinated way. In his reply to Wilkins, Clark inaccurately stated that the average experience of Chinese in Japanese-owned mills in Shanghai 'was only slightly less than that of mill workers in Japan in 1927'.[89] It was true that 39 per cent of the Chinese workers and 45 per cent of the Japanese workers stayed more than three years. But the figures that Clark cited also reveal that 42 per cent of the Chinese workers but just 18 per cent of the Japanese workers had been in the mill only a year. Among Chinese workers who had less than three years on the job, there was a significantly higher level of unpredictable turnover.

In 1932, an American observer described the Japanese mill hands as 'docile, nimble, and deft', even though they lacked 'the physical strength or size of similar American labour and probably would not continue at our unusual pace on piece work'.[90] During the inter-war period the physical productivity of labour also remained higher in Britain compared with Japan, but the gap was rapidly closing. It was reported that in 1930 British cotton mills had a 30 per cent unit labour cost advantage over Japanese cotton mills. But the British advantage had been 47 per cent as recently as 1926.[91]

In addition to social investments to improve the labour of female operatives, each of the dominant Japanese cotton companies made investments in the technical capabilities of male workers whose services the firm expected to retain over the long term. Some of these human resource investments took the form of in-house training in machine maintenance. Machines running at high speeds virtually around the clock had to be maintained in top condition to avoid costly downtime. Another key technical skill, unique to the Japanese industry and requiring firm-specific knowledge of products and processes, was the blending according to firm-specific formulae of more expensive, longer staple (typically American) cotton with less expensive, shorter staple (typically Indian and Chinese) cotton. These blending techniques permitted a reduction in cotton costs while still producing a yarn that was strong enough to gain the benefits of high-throughput production technologies.[92]

Investment in human resources often meant sending technical and managerial personnel abroad to acquire knowledge of Western technology and business methods.[93] Such training enhanced a company's capability to engage in effective in-house R&D. The firm-specific interaction between scale and training was one reason for the increasing concentration of spinning in the Japanese cotton industry. Dynamically, firms that had attained competitive advantage over other Japanese rivals possessed the internal resources to make these costly and specialised investments in human resources as well as to offer the trained personnel attractive incentives to remain with the firm. The investments in human resources gave the firm access to superior technical capabilities while compelling the firm to attain a large share of the market to transform its high fixed costs into low unit costs.

(2) *Fixed capital costs*

The high fixed costs that the Japanese cotton industry incurred by investing in human resources could help to keep down the costs of physical capital investments. For example, firms tended to repair rather than replace machinery. But when dramatically improved machines, such as the Toyoda automatic loom, came on the market, the leading Japanese companies quickly made substantial investments in the new technology. Over the long run, the development and utilisation of new effort-saving, high-throughput machinery provided the foundation for Japan's sustained competitive advantage. The most important technological advances were in machines designed specifically for utilisation with the blended cotton that the Japanese spinning companies used to cut cotton costs. The development of these technologies depended on sustained investments in the Japanese textile machinery industry.

The first dramatic change in technology occurred in the sector of the Japanese industry oriented toward the domestic market – a sector in which firms were protected by both tariffs and limitations on the access of foreigners to the domestic distribution network. The production of yarn for both both export and domestic consumption became increasingly concentrated in large companies that used imported British ring-frames and preparatory equipment.[94] On the home market, these powerful spinning companies sold yarn to a multitude of small, specialised weaving firms that until the late 1890s produced cloth on handlooms. As late as 1922, 43 per cent of all cotton looms in Japan were still handlooms. By 1938, however, this figure had fallen to 9 per cent as weaving firms adopted domestically produced power-looms.[95]

Central to the development of a power-loom that could replace the handloom were the inventive efforts of Sakichi Toyoda. In 1896 Toyoda developed a wooden power-loom that, unlike the imported iron power-loom, was affordable to the small-scale Japanese weaver and was designed to produce the narrow cloth demanded in the Japanese and contiguous Asian markets. Toyoda's company motto, 'Complete import substitution and then exportation', applied to both the cotton goods and textile machinery industries. In making the transition from the exportation of yarn to the exportation of cloth as well, the 'spinning' companies had integrated forward into weaving. Using primarily imported looms, in 1915 these integrated companies controlled 95 per cent of the Japanese manufacture of wide cloth, virtually all of which was exported. From 1914, however, the dependence on imported looms for the export sector was overcome by the introduction of the Toyoda Model N loom, an all-iron power-loom for weaving wide cloth that was rapidly adopted by the integrated 'spinning' companies and that also diffused more slowly to those specialised weaving mills that sought to take advantage of growing export opportunities during World War I and throughout the inter-war period. By 1920 loom imports into Japan had virtually ceased. At that time 64 per cent of the looms installed in the weaving mills of the integrated companies were imported. Of these imported looms, 94 per cent were British-made power-looms and 6 per cent were Draper automatic (bobbin-changing) looms. Toyoda power-looms represented 92 per cent of the Japanese-made looms in the integrated mills.[96]

Profits from the sale of Toyoda power-looms financed the research and development of a Japanese-made automatic loom – an R&D effort that extended over two decades.[97] To be economically viable, the automatic loom had to work at high speed using yarn made from the relatively short staple, blended cotton produced by the Japanese mills. Based as it was on the principle of injecting a fresh bobbin into the same shuttle, the Draper automatic loom required stronger, more break-resistant yarn, particularly on the first picks after the bobbin was changed. The technological basis for the ultimate success of the Toyoda automatic loom was the perfection of a shuttle-changing weft replenishing device that permitted continuous, high-speed operation even with the less break-resistant Japanese yarn.[98]

When the Toyoda automatic loom came on the market in 1924, it was an immediate success. By 1931 17,000 machines had been installed, and by 1936 40,000 machines. Initially it was the integrated mills of the 'spinning' companies that introduced the automatic looms on a large scale to produce cloth for export. But by the late 1930s some 30 per cent of the industry's automatic looms were in specialised weaving mills that, purchasing standardised yarn from the concentrated 'spinning' companies and selling standardised products through the powerful trading companies, were able to share in the industry's competitive success. When a Toyoda automatic loom replaced a Toyoda power-loom, labour productivity increased by 5 to 19 times, and when a Toyoda automatic loom replaced an imported power-loom, labour productivity increased by 3 to 9 times.[99]

The result was Japanese domination of world cotton textile exports. In the China market, for example, in 1913 Britain had had a 53 per cent share of cotton cloth imports and Japan only 20 per cent. By 1919 Britain's share had fallen to 26 per cent and Japan's had risen to 61 per cent. Britain recovered some of its market share in the early 1920s – in 1921 Britain and Japan each had a 43 per cent share. In 1925, however, Britain had only 24 per cent of the market while Japan's share had climbed to 66 per cent, and in 1930 Britain's share was 13 per cent and Japan's 72 per cent. It was in the last half of the 1920s, after the Japanese 'spinning' companies had introduced the automatic loom, that British competitiveness in the China market collapsed, with loss of competitive advantage following quickly in other markets around the world.[100]

The Japanese capture of large market shares permitted the high fixed costs of the adoption of the Toyoda loom to be transformed into low unit costs. Greatly enhancing the ability of the export-oriented integrated mills to achieve higher levels of utilisation of their plant and equipment than their foreign competitors were their investments in the dormitory system, already described. By giving the mills control over the allocation of workers' time around the clock and by thwarting the development of independent worker organisations, the dormitory system helped to overcome the constraints on shift work that might otherwise have been imposed by worker opposition to the disruption of family life. In Britain the opposition of unions to multiple shifts was a major obstacle to the adoption of automatic looms. In Japan, legislated limits on night work had been on the books from 1911 but were not enforced until 1929, after the cotton industry's international competitive advantage had been established. Even then, the legislation permitted two 8½-hour shifts.[101] Besides lowering the unit costs of plant and equipment, the ability of a Japanese mill to run two shifts offset the high fixed costs of recruiting and housing its labour force.

The spinning processes continued to require imports for the basic technologies, despite attempts by Toyoda to develop a complete line of Japanese machines for transforming raw cotton into yarn. But Japanese textile engineering firms did produce improved parts, such as spindles, rings, and travellers, for the imported machines. As a result, during the 1920s Japanese engineers were able to achieve spindle speeds of up to 11,000 rpm compared with the maximum of 9,000 rpm achieved by foreign competitors. With Toyoda again leading in the development of machine technology suited to Japanese cotton blending practice, during the 1930s the major cotton companies adopted high-draft spinning equipment that raised labour productivity in spinning by 150 per cent.[102]

(3) *Materials costs*

The achievement of the Japanese textile machinery industry was its development of high-throughput technologies that did not require that the producers of yarn and cloth forgo the cost advantages of cotton blending. That the Japanese cotton industry was able to gain unique competitive advantage through the blending of cotton requires an understanding of the unique organisational features of the industry that determined the relation between cotton purchasing and textile production. Contemporary observers of the Japanese cotton industry pointed to the importance of cotton blending for the industry's competitive advantage, but lamented that the blending techniques used by particular firms were closely guarded secrets.[103] The organisational requirements for achieving cost savings on the basis of blended cotton are, however, quite clear.

Three import companies, Toyo Menkwa (a subsidiary of Mitsui Trading Co.), Nippon Menkwa, and Gosho Nippon, dominated the bulk purchasing of cotton for the Japanese spinning industry. These three firms consistently controlled 70–80 per cent of cotton imports. In terms of concentrated buying power – the ability to get favourable prices on bulk shipments – these import companies were without rivals in the US, Indian, and Chinese markets where they purchased most of Japan's cotton supplies. In turn, the concentration of the Japanese spinning sector into a group of dominant integrated companies whose common interests found unified expression in the Japan Cotton Spinners' Association permitted the spinners to secure favourable cotton prices from the cotton importers.[104]

But favourable cotton prices by no means represented the full extent of Japanese competitive advantage in unit cotton costs. Besides enabling the dominant Japanese cotton textile producers to secure lower cotton costs by sharing in the economies of scale of mass cotton buying, the concentration of cotton importing and spinning sectors created the organisational foundations for the success of the cotton cost-cutting strategy based on cotton blending. The task for engineers within Japanese cotton mills was to find ways to use shorter staple, and hence cheaper, cotton without losing the productivity advantages of high-throughput technology. Through blending, the Japanese were able to use a combination of Indian and American (and some Chinese) cotton in spinning counts of yarn for which mills in Britain and the United States would only use American cotton.

The ability and willingness of Japanese cotton importers to make mass purchases in different parts of the world for selected customers enabled the dominant Japanese spinning companies to buy and warehouse four to six months' cotton stock to be sure that each mill had the types of cotton it needed for the mass production of its standard yarn on the basis of its own predetermined cotton blend. In the United States, firms also warehoused large stocks of cotton to ensure the availability of sufficient supplies of the particular staples and grades required for mass production of particular standardised yarns. But, unlike the Japanese firms, US mills used American cotton exclusively, thus (all other things equal) encountering less breaks and downtime in spinning and weaving and thus avoiding the challenges in textile engineering that the Japanese faced.[105] For a given cotton product, the productivity of labour and capital was much higher in the United States than in Japan, but so too were cotton costs.

The Japanese practice of warehousing cotton to mass produce standard yarns departed more dramatically from the practice in Britain, where spinners bought cotton in Liverpool on a weekly basis to produce yarn for orders just received. Whereas Japanese firms sought to cut cotton costs by blending Indian and American cotton, British firms sought to cut cotton costs by altering their weekly selections of cotton on the basis of not only the type of yarn orders in hand but also the short-run price differentials for different grades and staples of American cotton. Whereas the Japanese mills sought to compensate for the use of shorter staple cotton by technological engineering to reduce yarn breakages, the British mills looked to the skills and efforts of operatives to maintain productivity levels in the presence of higher levels of breakage when using inferior cotton.[106]

In Japan, the large-scale purchasing of cotton stocks meant that the firm could not take advantage of short-run changes in cotton price differentials, as was the case in Britain. On the other hand, when Japanese firms perceived pending shortages of cotton before World War I or abnormal downturns in cotton prices in the inter-war period, they bought up large stocks and made windfalls when they eventually sold their yarn.[107] Over the long run, however, the Japanese cotton companies made their profits by the planned co-ordination of the blending of cotton with the engineering of machinery so that the utilisation of inferior cotton would not, as was the case in Britain, obstruct the introduction of effort-saving technology and the achievement of high-throughput production. Ultimately, during the 1920s, the Japanese focus on engineering permitted dramatic increases in spindles and power-looms per worker as well as the rapid diffusion of the automatic loom without sacrificing the cotton-cost saving of blending and apparently without compelling their workers to supply more effort.

(4) *Marketing costs*

Two of the major cotton importers, Mitsui (Toyo Menkwa) and Nippon Menkwa also dominated in exporting Japanese cotton goods. Mitsui alone sold 32 per cent of cotton yarn exports between 1897 and 1912, and 36 per cent of cotton cloth exports between 1906 and 1912. These trading companies secured extensive economies of scope as well as scale in marketing. Indeed, in the China market, their wide-ranging trading activities made them willing to barter Japanese cotton goods for agricultural produce that they could then sell.[108]

Particularly in the large Asian markets, the Japanese trading companies built on the advantages of proximity and greater familiarity with local languages and customs. The fully constructed distribution system was based on trained Japanese staff that, after 1900, increasingly replaced local brokers and eliminated several layers of intermediary commissions and fees before reaching the retailers. As early as 1910, 50 per cent of Mitsui's transactions in cotton goods were carried out directly with Chinese retailers. The presence of on-site sales personnel meant the development of systematic selling methods, the consequent ability to lower risk and prices and lengthen the period of credit, and the maintenance of large stocks in the main trading centres that permitted quicker deliveries, especially in Manchuria where the Japanese controlled banks, railways, and steamship lines.[109]

These dominant trading companies did more than buy cotton and sell yarn and cloth. They financed Japanese mills and the development of new technology. For example, Mitsui provided early financial backing to Toyoda. At the same time, the nine spinning combines that produced 80 per cent of Japanese cotton exports had privileged relations with Mitsui – relations that enabled them to secure large orders that generated the economies of long, standardised runs and favourable marketing terms.[110]

The concentration of the Japanese marketing structure was in stark contrast to the fragmented British marketing system. As Barnard Ellinger, a British export merchant in the 1920s, emphasised after noting the various advantages of Japanese methods: 'On the other hand the present organisation of the industry in Lancashire *prevents* mass production and distribution'.[111] Even more than the higher production costs of shorter runs or the added costs of intermediary payments resulting from the fragmented structure of the British cotton industry, Ellinger focused on the competitive disadvantages of Britain's slower delivery times, which he blamed on the combination of 'production to order' and vertical specialisation, rather than the greater distance to market. Because Japanese exporters required financing for only half as long as British exporters and because (aided by a government subsidy) the Japanese rate of interest was only half as high as the British rate, Ellinger estimated that a 1 per cent change in the bank rate had the equivalent unit cost impact of a 10 per cent change in the wages of weavers in the production of dyed cloth.[112] Indeed, even greater distance to market did not necessarily handicap the Japanese cotton industry. For example, because of Japanese economies of scale and scope in worldwide trading along with government subsidies for the extension of Japanese shipping routes, when in the early 1930s Japan took Turkish market share in cotton goods away from Britain and Italy, the shipping charges from Yokohama to Istanbul were about the same as from Trieste to Istanbul.[113]

(5) Administrative costs

Given their privileged relations to the trading companies, the dominant firms were able to produce a variety of products achieving standardisation and long runs in particular mills. But for a dominant firm to co-ordinate the activities of a growing number of mills required an elaborate managerial structure. To develop the requisite organisational capabilities, the dominant cotton companies made considerable investments in training university-educated engineers to occupy management positions.[114]

With a committed corps of managers and developed administrative procedures, the dominant firms were able not only to increase the number of production units but also to disperse them geographically to take advantage of favourable labour conditions in different regions. The ability to administer geographically dispersed production units enabled the cotton companies to locate new mills in areas where land was less expensive and labour supplies more accessible. After 1910 these firms built spinning mills not only in Japan but also in China to take advantage of cheaper labour in the production of the coarsest counts of yarn.[115]

As their managerial capabilities enabled the emergence of ever more dominant firms in spinning yarn for both home and abroad as well as in weaving cloth for export, these firms enhanced the internal career opportunities for the most promising technologists, thus helping to ensure the long-term retention of their technical and managerial services and providing the firms with greater incentives to invest in the capabilities of these key personnel. Although these investments further increased the already high fixed costs of the dominant Japanese cotton firms, they possessed not only the technological and marketing capability but also the administrative capability to transform these high fixed costs into low unit costs, and gain, as they did during the inter-war period, sustained competitive advantage.

V

Explanations of Japanese Success

This summary of the dynamic evolution of the Japanese cotton industry in the first decades of this century and the emergence of Japanese competitive advantage suggests that Britain's competitive disadvantages in the 1920s cannot be attributed *simply* to low-wage competition and tariff protection abroad, as the new economic historians have claimed.[116] Low wages did contribute to Japan's competitive advantage over Britain. But low wages cannot explain why it was Japan rather than India that rose to international dominance. Tariff barriers did allow the development of the domestic manufacturing sector in Japan. The long-run impact of tariff protection, however, was not simply to keep British goods out of Japan but also to foster the development of technology suitable for Japanese conditions. By the late 1920s the development and utilisation of the new technologies permitted the Japanese cotton industry to dominate in open markets.

This development and utilisation of technology occurred, moreover, within a much more planned and co-ordinated structure of business organisation than that which characterised the British cotton industry. Market co-ordination of the specialised division of labour had enabled the British cotton industry to rise to international dominance in the nineteenth century. But, confirming what we already know from the work of Alfred Chandler about the institutional evolution of more capital-intensive industries in Germany and the United States,[117] the Japanese experience illustrates the growing importance for international dominance in the twentieth century of planned co-ordination, even in a relatively labour-intensive industry such as cotton textiles.

During the inter-war period, the British cotton industry was able to continue to compete for a time in certain markets by reaping the benefits of its prior accumulation of productive resources – basically by living off its invested capital. But the organisational structure of the Japanese industry was in striking contrast to the fragmented and market-co-ordinated structure of industrial organisation that the British cotton industry inherited from its era of international dominance and that would persist into the second half of the twentieth century. On the basis of this market co-ordinated structure, the British industry continued during the inter-war period to use technologies which, by virtue of technological developments abroad, had become low-throughput methods that had long since exhausted their effort-saving potential.

For lack of a perspective on the interaction of organisation and technology in the process of economic development, the new economic historians have had problems recognising the importance of planned co-ordination in the rise to dominance of the Japanese cotton industry, and the implications of the organisational character of the Japanese challenge for the structural difficulties that the market co-ordinated British cotton industry faced in responding to the new competition. Sandberg's 'explanation' of Lancashire's competitive decline is a case in point. He argued:

> The dynamic version of [the] comparative advantage argument
> is that Great Britain slowly lost the relative advantage she had

obtained from her early start in cotton textiles, principally because she began to accumulate capital and develop other industries. The effect of this process was to make labor relatively scarce and relatively expensive. Great Britain's comparative advantage shifted into more and more capital- and skill-intensive industries. Eventually it became possible for a peasant economy like Japan's to expand its comparative advantage from raw silk and other agricultural products to include low-capital and skill-intensive manufacturing. The result was the development of the Japanese cotton textile industry.[118]

The basic problem with the 'scarce and expensive labour' explanation of the decline of the British cotton industry is that high levels of unemployment plagued the British economy in general and the cotton industry in particular during the inter-war period when the industry lost its markets. Indeed, in the face of the new competition, the actual problem that confronted the British cotton industry during this period was not that other more capital-intensive and skill-intensive sectors were draining it of 'scarce' economic resources but, on the contrary, as industry observers such as John Maynard Keynes recognised, that existing productive resources were not leaving the industry quickly enough.[119] Nor does Sandberg's argument tell us why it was during the inter-war period that Britain lost the advantage of its 'early start' when, as evidenced by the experiences of Germany and the United States, the rise of the capital-intensive industries of the second industrial revolution had begun in the last quarter of the nineteenth century.

As for the 'cheap labour' explanation of Japan's 'comparative' advantage, Sandberg himself went on to recognise that 'Japan was certainly not the country with the world's relatively most abundant supply of labor'. In answer to his own question, 'Why was Japan more successful than, for example, India, China, or tropical Africa?', he suggested 'the supply of entrepreneurship and management skill together with the adaptability of the work force to factory conditions'. His answer is consistent with the tendency of economists concerned with estimating differential rates of economic growth to define the 'residual' as everything that commonsense tells them is important but, for lack of a theory of economic development, they can neither measure nor understand. Sandberg did recognise the need to explain the residual when he asked why Japan generated such productive human resources when other low-wage countries did not. But, implicitly admitting to the limits of his static theoretical perspective, he responded that 'to discuss why this is so would be to write a textbook on the problems of economic development'.[120]

From our perspective, the 'textbook' – that is, a generally accepted consensus on the dynamics of economic development – is precisely what modern Anglo-American economics both lacks and needs. It is impossible to understand changes in international competitive advantage, whether in cotton textiles or any other industry, without making the problem of economic development central to economic analysis. For only then can we analyse how, over time and under certain social conditions, Japan developed and utilised its productive resources in ways that firms and industries operating under different social conditions could not.

From a developmental perspective, what stands out in the success of the Japanese cotton industry is the importance of planned co-ordination of economic activity, not only within dominant enterprises but also within the industry as a whole. Within the dominant 'spinning' companies, planned co-ordination occurred through the vertical integration of spinning and weaving. Within the industry as a whole, planned co-ordination occurred under the leadership of the dominant 'spinning' and trading companies. In response to Lazonick's earlier arguments concerning the role of vertical specialisation in the decline of the British cotton industry, Saxonhouse and Wright have argued that the vertical integration of spinning and weaving was not an important organisational characteristic of the Japanese cotton industry in its rise to international dominance. Specifically, they took issue with Lazonick's statement that 'movements toward vertical integration, horizontal concentration, and top–down managerial co-ordination characterized high-throughput producers in the United States and Japan', on the grounds that the statement did not apply to Japan. According to Saxonhouse and Wright:

> in 1911 more than 80 per cent of Japanese yarn was sold rather than woven by the spinning firm, a degree of vertical specialization which seems to have exceeded Lancashire's. Throughout its rapid capture of world markets in the 1920s and 1930s, the Japanese industry never wove more than 30 per cent of its yarn on a vertically integrated basis. It is difficult to see how the British decline can be attributed to industrial structure, when the same industrial structure was featured by her chief international rival.[121]

The discussion of the sources of Japanese competitive advantage has made clear the problem with the Saxonhouse–Wright argument. It fails to recognise the movement to vertical integration in the *export-oriented* sector of the Japanese cotton industry as it passed from the pre-war phase when its main export was yarn to the handloom weavers of India and China to the phase of cloth exports by vertically integrated producers – a phase that had been gathering momentum since the turn of the century but took off during World War I. Most of the vertically integrated export firms had been major specialised spinning companies during the yarn export phase of the industry's growth. These same firms, still generally called 'spinning' companies, later added looms to their mill operations to compete for international cloth markets. The weight of yarn exports peaked in 1915, and during the 1920s fell off dramatically while the volume of cloth exports rose steadily.[122]

In 1897 the ten largest spinning firms had 34 per cent of the industry's spindles. But in 1913 the ten largest had 88 per cent and in 1928 80 per cent. In 1897 only three of the 10 largest cotton spinning firms in the Japanese industry possessed looms, and for all 10 firms the spindle-loom ratio was 289:1. By 1913 seven of the 10 largest firms had looms, and the spindle-loom ratio for all 10 was 108:1. By 1928 all 10 largest were vertically integrated, their looms all of the wide variety designed to produce cloth for foreign markets. Their combined spindle-loom ratio had fallen to 107:1, although the spindle-loom ratio for all spinning companies was only 87:1. In addition to exporting cloth, the largest spinning companies were the main suppliers of yarn to the specialised weavers who, with their narrow looms, produced primarily for the home market and as well as Korean markets (which they had captured even before the war). By 1938 the spindle-loom ratio in the 10 largest spinning companies had risen to 120:1 as spinning mills increased the supply of low-cost, standardised yarn to an expanding specialised weaving sector that had begun to adopt automatic looms and that was able to participate to some extent in the rapid growth of the Japanese cotton industry's export opportunities.[123]

In 1937, when the Japanese cotton industry was at the height of its international dominance, there were 7,668 mills in the independent weaving sector, with an average of 41 looms each, while the 114 mills that integrated spinning and weaving had an average of 877 looms each. The independent weavers accounted for 61 per cent of the industry's total volume of cloth production, while exports of yarn to weavers abroad accounted for just over 3 per cent by weight of the industry's yarn production.[124] Hence Saxonhouse and Wright may not be far off the mark to argue that 'in the 1920s and 1930s, the Japanese industry never wove more than 30 per cent of its yarn on a vertically integrated basis'.[125]

But this statistic tells us little about how the Japanese industry captured world markets. According to Pearse, writing in early 1929, 'spinning-weaving mills, affiliated with the Japan Cotton Spinners' Association, represent roughly 50 per cent of the whole country, and they are responsible for more than 75 per cent of the export trade as it is in these mills that mass-production methods, with specialisation of work, have been introduced'.[126] Moreover, in so far as the specialised weaving sector contributed to Japan's exports, the supply of their yarn was co-ordinated by the highly concentrated spinning companies and the sale of their cloth by the highly concentrated trading companies. As we have seen, the spinning and trading companies, although financially separate entities, had close, long-term dealings with one another, these relations providing the basis for the planned co-ordination of the vertical structure of the industry, even when the specialised weavers were involved.[127] It is impossible, therefore, to consider the organisational and technological character of the effective Japanese challenge to British markets in the inter-war period without disaggregating the Japanese cotton industry into its export-oriented and domestic-oriented sectors, and even when that is done, without recognising the Japanese organisational innovation in planned co-ordination even across legally distinct firms in the vertical chain of production and distribution.

VI

Explanations of the British Response

How did the British cotton industry respond to the new competition? Sandberg argued that the industry's response was constrained by its 'concentration in markets that contracted very rapidly between the World Wars – mainly, India, China, Turkey, and Egypt – and that, particularly during the 1930s, these markets became highly protected.[128] In general, the inter-war period saw a sharp decline in the percentage of yarn and cloth production (measured in terms of the weight of cotton consumption) entering world trade – from 28 per cent in 1910–13 to 23 per cent in 1926–28 to 16 per cent in 1936–38. Sandberg also recognised that, primarily because of Japanese competition, Britain's share of world production fell from 20 per cent in 1910–13 to 12 per cent in 1926–28 to 9 per cent in 1936–38.[129] Even if the British cotton industry had remained competitive with Japan, he argued, it would have had to contract substantially in the face of protectionism and import substitution strategies abroad.

As indicated by our argument concerning the importance of the low-income markets for the pre-war expansion of the British cotton industry, we agree that, even had the industry had the most modern plant and equipment, it could not have maintained its 1913 size in the face of the continuing world-wide expansion of cotton textile capacity. But the ways in which the British cotton industry had expanded its capacity and remained competitive during the pre-war period made it more vulnerable to the loss of markets in the post-war period and made the process of adjustment – the contraction of supply and the modernisation of the remaining industry – all the more difficult. For, as we have seen, the pre-war expansion not only extended the industry's reliance on its traditional technologies but also increased the degree of vertical specialisation of spinning, weaving, and marketing and the number of firms competing with each other at each vertical level. As Lazonick has shown, in the inter-war period and beyond these organisational characteristics of the industry posed institutional impediments to the restructuring of the British cotton industry on a smaller, but technologically dynamic, scale.[130]

Guided by the belief in the economic efficacy of market co-ordination, Sandberg's work did not contemplate that the organisational basis for international competitive advantage in the twentieth century might require movements away from market co-ordination toward planned co-ordination of specialised divisions of labour. Sandberg reasoned that 'a mass installation of automatic looms in Lancashire prior to World War I would probably have resulted in a worse situation than that which actually occurred'.[131] He might have added, as economists often do, 'all other things equal'. For Sandberg's statement implicitly assumes that 'a mass installation of automatic looms' would have occurred on the basis of the British cotton industry's fragmented industrial structure and hence subject to the same organisational constraints on the development and utilisation of high-throughput production methods that affected the vertically specialised firms that relied on the traditional technologies. Yet the evidence from Lancashire is that a firm such as Ashton Brothers – a firm that had originated in the eighteenth century, that integrated spinning, weaving, and marketing, that exported relatively high-quality goods to China, and that introduced half of the automatic looms of the entire British cotton industry up to 1913 – was able to remain technologically dynamic and economically successful between the wars and after World War II.[132]

Sandberg recognised that, in so far as the immobility of the industry's capital stock and its workforce compelled existing manufacturers and workers to take lower returns on their capital and labour, the British cotton industry could remain competitively viable even as it lost competitive advantage.[133] But, beyond the possibility of this adaptive response, Sandberg contended that the rise of low-wage competition and tariff barriers meant that 'Lancashire's decline after World War I was principally due to causes beyond her control'.[134] If by 'Lancashire', Sandberg meant the individual owners and managers of the industry's 2,000 spinning and weaving firms and 1,000 marketing firms acting autonomously, then he was undoubtedly correct to argue that the decline of their industry was beyond their control. But subsequent research has explored the *collective* responses to the decline of the industry, and has sought to analyse why even the collective responses that did occur did not eliminate the horizontal and vertical fragmentation of the industry and create the organisational foundations for the introduction of the high-throughput technologies.

As J.H. Bamberg has recently analysed in detail, the most important collective response was the formation of the Lancashire Cotton Corporation (LCC) by the Bank of England in 1929.[135] At that time, the LCC's first managing director declared that 'the horizontal amalgamation is of no use to Lancashire; it must be vertical'.[136] By 1930 the LCC had amalgamated 96 firms that possessed one-fifth of the spinning capacity in the British cotton industry. The amalgamation centred on the 'American' section of the industry, which was the hardest hit by the rise of the new competition. In the process of formation, spinning managers and owners who did not want to lose control over their individual firms obstructed and raised the costs of horizontal amalgamation. After the amalgamation, those managers and owners whose firms, by virtue of their over-indebtedness to the British banking system, were forced to amalgamate in the LCC, refused to accede to centralised attempts by the LCC to rationalise its capacity to achieve long production runs, as for example the large spinning combines in Japan were able to do. Ultimately by the end of the 1930s, the LCC did manage to shed its most inefficient capacity and become profitable. By that time, however, it had definitively abandoned efforts to become a vertically integrated firm. Instead the LCC chose to sell its yarn to the specialised weavers who proliferated in the industry.

If Saxonhouse and Wright have misunderstood the organisational character of Japan's successful challenge to British competitive advantage in the cotton industry, they have also misconstrued the organisational constraints on the British industry's response. In their own response to Lazonick's criticisms of their arguments that British spinning managers were not constrained by the structure of vertical specialisation to adopt mules rather than rings for the spinning of weft yarn, they claimed that Lazonick failed to use 'the term "constraint" in a consistent or rigorous way', and hence that the apparent clarity of his model of the relation between constrained optimisation and choice of technology 'fades and then vanishes when we pursue the question concretely'.

> Exactly what was it that blocked Lancashire's path to ring spinning? Lazonick's answer is 'vertical specialization', but this only replaces one question with another: what was it that blocked the path to vertical integration? Was this organizational structure a binding 'constraint' on individual firms? The difficulties noted by Lazonick in his present comment relate exclusively to the case of *existing* spinning firms attempting to sell ring-spun weft yarn in the open market. But why could not these firms integrate forward into weaving, or why could not new integrated firms replace the constrained specialized spinners and weavers? These are the economic questions raised by Lazonick's formal analysis, but to date he has not confronted them explicitly.[137]

Saxonhouse and Wright cited Lazonick's 1983 *Business History Review* article on the constraining influences of British cotton's fragmented industrial organisation on the horizontal and vertical reorganisation of the industry that was a precondition for adopting the new high throughput technologies. But the very questions that Saxonhouse and Wright posed are the ones that, in that article, Lazonick asked and answered. Saxonhouse and Wright might disagree with Lazonick's answers to 'the economic questions raised by [his] formal analysis'. But that is a very different position than their unfounded allegation that he had not confronted these questions explicitly.

As for their own perspective, Saxonhouse and Wright formulated the question too narrowly in asking 'what . . . blocked Lancashire's path to ring spinning'. The empirical basis for Lazonick's argument was that with the diffusion of the automatic loom and the subsequent development of high-speed spinning, winding, and warping processes, the effective utilisation of high-throughput production processes to transform high fixed costs into low unit costs required the planned co-ordination of the flow of work from purchased cotton to sold cloth. Perhaps because their own research into cotton textile technology had itself been vertically specialised on the choice of *spinning* technology, Saxonhouse and Wright fundamentally ignored the interconnections between the advances in weaving and spinning as mass production technologies, as well as the need for mass marketing to create the incentive for firms to invest in the more capital intensive, high-throughput technologies. As a result they have neither understood the role of planned and co-ordinated organisation in developing and utilising the new mass-production technologies in Japan nor the constraints that the horizontally fragmented and vertically specialised structure of the British cotton industry imposed on the adoption of these technologies.

Indeed, Saxonhouse and Wright contended that Lazonick was wrong to argue that vertical integration posed a 'constraint' on the decision-making of Lancashire's managers on either the choice of technology or organisation. On the technology question, they argued that the existence before World War I of ring-frames that could spin yarn onto paper tubes instead of wooden bobbins overcame the transportation cost constraints of shipping wooden bobbins from the spinning mill to the weaving mill that vertical specialisation had imposed on the Lancashire industry.[138] As in the case of Clark, however, Saxonhouse and Wright took Sandberg's static framework of the major factor cost constraints on the more rapid adoption of the ring-frame and imposed it on Lazonick's dynamic analysis. As stated earlier, Lazonick corrected Sandberg's factor cost estimates, in part by showing that the cost of transporting the wooden bobbins was greater than Sandberg thought. But at the same time (as even Saxonhouse and Wright at one point recognised), Lazonick argued that, considering the technical interconnection of spinning and weaving technology, even on the traditional technologies that Lancashire used, the major constraint that Lancashire faced in adopting the new high-throughput technologies was organisational. The diffusion of these technologies required interconnected – planned and co-ordinated – decision making on the adoption of spinning methods that produced break-resistant yarn and weaving methods that were only cost effective when using break-resistant yarn. The requisite planned co-ordination could not occur on the basis of the vertical specialisation of spinning and weaving that predominated, and indeed that in the pre-war period became more predominant, in Lancashire.[139]

In their critique of Lazonick, Saxonhouse and Wright have argued that the pre-war expansion of the industry did not significantly increase its vulnerability to post-war collapse because ring spinning only became a 'dominant technology' as the result of technological developments – most notably high-draft spinning – that occurred after 1913. Once ring spinning became clearly dominant in the mid-1920s the British cotton industry did not make any further investments in new mules. Hence, in contrast to the Lazonick–Mass thesis, Saxonhouse and Wright concluded that the prior investments in mules, made when ring spinning was not the 'dominant technology', cannot be held responsible for the loss of British markets in the 1920s.[140]

Aside from noting that Lazonick raised the 'broader problem of co-ordinated decision-making, or "technical interrelatedness" between ring spinning and numerous complementary changes in weaving and winding machinery',[141] Saxonhouse and Wright have ignored the relation between the evolution of spinning and weaving technology. Yet the analyses of Lazonick and Mass have stressed the growing importance of the technological interrelatedness of spinning and weaving in the rise to dominance of the new high-throughput technologies that tranformed raw cotton into cotton cloth.[142]

On its own, the main advantage of the ring-frame over the mule was that it permitted the use of low-wage, unskilled labour in the spinning process. The main disadvantage of ring spinning (again on its own) was the need to use longer staple and superior grade cotton to spin a given count of yarn to achieve the same level of productivity as the mule. The main advantage of ring yarn when used in conjunction with the weaving process was that, because it was stronger than mule yarn of equal cost, it broke less often. For a given amount of labour effort, less breakages yielded higher output per loom. In Lancashire, however, where the weavers' union generally limited the number of power-looms per weaver to four (as compared with eight in the United States) and where weavers were willing to supply their effort to keep the looms in motion and their earnings up, the weaving employer had little interest in purchasing yarn that minimised breakages and simply permitted weavers to achieve the same level of earnings with less effort. Hence the structure of labour–management relations and work organisation in Lancashire weaving mitigated the prime productivity advantage of ring yarn in the weaving process.

Quite apart from the problem (highlighted in the Sandberg–Lazonick exchange) of shipping wooden bobbins from a specialised spinning mill to a specialised weaving mill, the main disadvantage of ring spinning when used in conjunction with the power-loom was the inverse relation between the amount of yarn on a *shuttle-ready* bobbin and the level of ring spinning productivity for a given quality of cotton. Small amounts of yarn on the shuttle-ready bobbin meant the need for the weaver to replenish the loom shuttle more frequently. Weft changing was the most labour-intensive part of the weaver's job, and more frequent weft changes inevitably reduced productivity no matter how hard the weaver worked. The alternative was to rewind the ring weft yarn onto smaller shuttle bobbins that, by virtue of being smaller, held a larger amount of weft yarn. But, when used with the break-prone yarn that British spinning firms (in their efforts to reduce cotton costs) tended to produce, rewinding was prohibitively expensive.[143]

When used in conjunction with *automatic* looms instead of power-looms, however, the relative advantages and disadvantages of ring spinning took on wholly different dimensions. The main advantage was that the need in any case to use higher quality cotton on the ring-frame to maintain productivity meant that ring spinning provided the weaving process with a more break-resistant yarn than mule spinning. And minimising the number of breaks per unit of time was critical to achieving both a high number of machines per worker and a high level of output per machine on the automatic loom. At the same time, with the move from power-looms to automatic looms, the main disadvantage of ring yarn – the small amount of yarn on a shuttle-ready bobbin – disappeared because the innovation of the automatic loom was the automatic replenishment of the shuttle with weft. Indeed, this innovation put an even greater premium on break-resistant yarn because of the high level of tension placed on the yarn during the first pick after the shuttle had been reloaded.[144]

It was not high-draft spinning but the diffusion of the automatic loom that ensured that ring spinning would become the dominant spinning technology. High-draft spinning (which permitted the mill to dispense with some intermediate machines for attenuating and twisting the cotton into rovings that then became the material input on the spinning frame) worked better with stronger yarn. Hence, high-draft spinning gave the greatest advantages not only in transforming raw cotton into yarn but more importantly when ring spinning was being used to prepare break-resistant yarn for automatic looms. Indeed, high-draft spinning was just one of a number of new high-speed technologies, including high-speed winding and high-speed warping, that were developed during the first two decades of the twentieth century that were of the greatest benefit when using the strong ring yarn required for automatic looms. As a result of these improvements, it became the practice to rewind all weft yarn for use in high-speed looms for purposes of quality control; 'cleaning and clearing' weak yarn in the winding process was much less costly than mending it in the weaving process, not least because frequent yarn breakages undermined the enormous labour-displacing possibilities of the automatic loom. In addition, the rewinding of weft yarn saved doffing labour and downtime in the spinning process; the ring-frame did not have to spin shuttle-ready packages, and hence larger yarn packages could be spun.[145]

Hence, where, as was especially the case in both the United States and Japan, ring spinning emerged as an *element* of the new high-throughput textile technology by the 1920s, it was because cotton industries, and indeed cotton firms, had undertaken co-ordinated investments in ring-frames and automatic looms as well as in a series of supplementary high speed processes, all of which required the use of break-resistant yarn. Lancashire's vulnerability in the 1920s was not only that its cotton industry was so highly dependent on markets in the low-income areas of the world, but also that it had maintained its share of these markets in the face of the new competition by means of a cotton cost cutting strategy on its traditional technologies that moved the industry even further *away* from the adoption of high throughput, effort-saving, production methods. Lancashire's competitive problem in the 1920s was not only that it had exhausted the cost-cutting potential of its effort-using strategy but also that it now faced global competition from the Japanese who, during the first two decades of the twentieth century, had been putting their own unique high throughput methods in place.

From the late 1920s, when many observers of the British cotton industry began to recognise that its pre-war markets had been definitively lost, the incompatibility between the fragmented and specialised structure of industrial organisation on the one hand and the diffusion of the high-throughput technologies on the other did constrain the British cotton industry's response to its loss of competitive advantage. What was the social character of this constraint? As evidenced by the title of their rejoinder to Lazonick, Saxonhouse and Wright did not believe that vertical specialisation constrained the diffusion of the new technologies (or at least, from their 'vertically specialised' technological frame of reference, the diffusion of ring spinning).[146] They quoted Lazonick (from his 1984 rejoinder to Sandberg's response) that 'the overriding constraints on vertical integration in the British cotton industry were the lack of managerial skills and the *individualistic attitudes on the part of Lancashire's specialised managers themselves*', noting 'emphasis in original'. They went on to contend that:

> saying that managers are 'constrained' by their own 'attitudes' stretches the meaning of the term beyond reasonable limits and makes the 'institutional rigidity' hypothesis indistinguishable from the more venerable diagnosis of 'entrepreneurial failure'. If, as we argued, Lancashire managers actively believed that the mule was a superior technology and vertical specialisation a superior form of organisation, what does it contribute to argue that their behaviour was 'constrained' by these beliefs?[147]

Saxonhouse and Wright continued by recognising that Lazonick did not argue that these individualistic attitudes impeded the expansion of the industry before World War I or that pre-war Lancashire managers could have or should have forseen the loss of markets in the 1920s. How then did the 'individualistic attitudes' of Lancashire's managers constrain technological change?

In their interpretation of Lazonick's argument, Saxonhouse and Wright made two basic errors, both of which stemmed from a failure to assimilate Lazonick's analysis of the role of organisational structure in the British cotton industry's postwar decline. First, they quoted Lazonick's reference to 'individualistic attitudes' from his exchange with Sandberg, an exchange which was primarily concerned with the empirical question of the choice of spinning technology before the war. But Lazonick's statement about the constraining influence of 'the lack of relevant managerial skills and individualistic attitudes' specifically referred to his analysis of the postwar experience when markets were lost and, as in the case of the Lancashire Cotton Corporation, attempts began to be made to reorganise the industry. Before the war, the same lack of managerial skills and the same individualistic attitudes constrained specialised

Lancashire managers from participating in vertical integration. But because, for the reasons we have outlined, the industry was able to remain competitive on the basis of its traditional organisational structures and technologies, these constraints were non-problematic; Lancashire managers could optimise subject to these constraints and still remain competitive in international markets. After the war they could not remain competitive, and it was then that their very presence in the industry and, specifically, their resistance to giving up control of their individual firms, constrained attempts by others at industrial reorganisation.

Second, even in the sentence that Saxonhouse and Wright quoted, Lazonick did not emphasise the words 'individualistic attitudes', as they claimed. Given their focus on the 'beliefs' of British managers, the error is not incidental. As is clear from the context of the 1983 *Business History Review* article, Lazonick saw the lack of relevant managerial skills and the individualistic attitudes as reinforcing one another.[148] Specialised Lancashire managers lacked the general managerial skills required to participate in the reorganisation of the industry, and hence clung to control of their specialised firms as their means of livelihood. As a result they never did acquire the relevant skills to manage a high-throughput, vertically integrated enterprise.

Especially in the weaving sector, which was much more resistant to horizontal reorganisation than spinning, the individualistic attitudes of managers reflected less a belief that (to use Saxonhouse and Wright's words) 'vertical specialisation [was] a superior form of organisation' (and certainly not the belief that 'the mule was a superior technology') but much more a desire, and because of their limited skills perhaps even a need, to maintain their independent means of support. 'Very much in the tradition of the handloom weavers a century before', Lazonick argued, 'the owners of these firms hung on to their businesses at extremely low profits in order to maintain their relatively independent status'.[149] The persistence of this specialised, and largely written off, capacity into the 1960s reduced the incentive for others who did have the relevant managerial skills to invest in high-throughput technologies on the basis of vertically integrated organisational structures. Hence as late as 1955 only 12 per cent of all looms in Lancashire were automatic.[150] The British industry became less vertically specialised during the 1950s, but only because it became increasingly difficult for its family firms with their outdated machinery to hang on in the face of foreign competition not only from 'low wage' (but more technologically advanced) competitors but also from high wage, high-throughput competitors.

VII

The Analysis of International Competitive Advantage

The analysis of changes in international competitive advantage requires a perspective that can comprehend the dynamic interaction of organisation and technology in transforming high fixed costs into low unit costs. An adherence to the static, ahistorical approach to economic analysis that pervades 'modern' economic thinking renders one ill-equipped to analyse the sources of international competitive advantage and disadvantage. But whatever the grip of neoclassical economics on the new economic history some 20 years ago, we believe that most economic historians now recognise the need for an analytical approach to the development process that can comprehend the processes of organisational and technological change. We would hope that the arguments that we have made here will serve to reinforce such an intellectual tendency.

More than that, we would hope that our analysis of the sources of competitive advantage and disadvantage can serve as a framework for, and impetus to, further research into changes in international leadership in a wide array of industries. From our perspective, the analysis of changing industrial leadership presents a special challenge for business historians because an understanding of the historical evolution and economic impacts of business organisation is at the heart of the analysis of competitive advantage. By its very nature, the study of business organisation as a determinant of international competitive advantage compels an analysis of the microeconomic foundations of macroeconomic outcomes. It is precisely in its comprehension of the inner workings of the business enterprise that mainstream economics has failed so miserably, and that 'business historians' – social scientists who take business history seriously – can make the most profound contributions to economic analysis.

Beyond the methodological issues, our analysis of the decline of the British cotton industry in the face of Japanese competition has implications for economic ideology as well. We have argued that the problem of the British cotton industry after World War I was an outmoded economic individualism in an era that required collective response. The prior success of the individualistic structures of business organisation stood in the way of institutional transformation toward a more collective capitalism. Our outline of the interaction of organisation and technology in the rise to dominance of the Japanese cotton industry emphasises the collective character of the competitive challenge that Britain faced.

In the 1990s Anglo-American economists and historians are beginning to understand the competitive realities of the Japanese version of collective capitalism. The case of the cotton industry suggests that the 'Japanese miracle' did not begin in the 1950s, as is commonly believed. Widely recognised as the sources of Japan's competitive advantage in automobiles and electronics in the post-World War II decades were the major institutions – concentrated organisation in production and distribution in combination with small-scale enterprise where economically feasible, horizontal and vertical co-ordination across legally distinct firms, intensive research and development, the planned co-ordination of personnel to develop and utilise human resources, a developmental state – that contributed to the rapid rise to international dominance of the Japanese cotton industry between the wars. To study the rise of Japan and the decline of Britain in cotton textiles in the inter-war period is to gain valuable insights into the historical foundations of Japanese competitive advantage more generally in the last half of the twentieth century.

University of Lowell
Barnard College of Columbia University

NOTES:

1. The main contributions to the debate have been L. Sandberg, *Lancashire in Decline* (Columbus, 1974); W. Lazonick, 'Competition, Specialisation, and Industrial Decline,' *Journal of Economic History*, Vol.XLI No.1 (1981); idem, 'Factor Costs and the Diffusion of Ring Spinning Prior to World War I,' *Quarterly Journal of Economics*, Vol.XCVI No.1 (1981); idem, 'Industrial Organisation and Technological Change: The Decline of the British Cotton Industry,' *Business History Review*, Vol.LVII No.2 (1983); W. Lazonick and W. Mass, 'The Performance of the British Cotton Industry, 1870–1913', *Research in Economic History*, Vol.IX (1984); L. Sandberg, 'The Remembrance of Things Past: Rings and Mules Revisited,' *Quarterly Journal of Economics*, Vol.XCIX, No.1 (1984); W. Lazonick, 'Rings and Mules in Britain: Reply,' *Quarterly Journal of Economics*, Vol.XCIX No.1 (1984); G. Saxonhouse and G. Wright, 'New Evidence on the Stubborn English Mule and the Cotton Industry, 1878–1920,' *Economic History Review*, second series, Vol.XXXVII No.4 (1984); W. Lazonick, 'The Cotton Industry,' in B. Elbaum and W. Lazonick (eds.), *The Decline of the British Economy* (Oxford, 1986); W. Lazonick, 'Stubborn Mules: Some Comments,' *Economic History Review*, second series, Vol.XL No.1 (1987); G. Saxonhouse and G. Wright, 'Stubborn Mules and Vertical Integration: The Disappearing Constraint?' *Economic History Review*, second series, Vol.XL No.1 (1987); G. Clark, 'Why Isn't the Whole World Developed?: Lessons from the Cotton Mills,' *Journal of Economic History*, Vol.XLVII No.1 (1987); M. Wilkins, 'Efficiency and Management: A Comment on Gregory Clark's "Why Isn't the Whole World Developed?"' *Journal of Economic History*, Vol.XLVII No.4 (1987); G. Clark, 'Can Management Develop the World?: Reply to Wilkins', *Journal of Economic History*, Vol.XLVIII No.1 (1988). See also B. Elbaum, 'Cumulative or Comparative Advantage?: British Competitiveness in the Early Twentieth Century', *World Development*, forthcoming 1990. For an admirable summary of the more general debate on entrepreneurial performance in Britain in the late nineteenth and early twentieth centuries, see P.L. Payne, *British Entrepreneurship in the Nineteenth Century*, (2nd ed. 1988), pp.43–60.

2. For elaborations of our perspective, see W. Lazonick, *Business Organisation and the Myth of the Market Economy* (Cambridge, 1991), Ch.1; W. Mass, 'Mechanical

and Organisational Innovation: The Drapers and the Automatic Loom', *Business History Review*, Vol. LXIII No. 4 (1989); W. Mass, 'Decline of a Technological Leader: Capabilities, Strategy, and Shuttleless Weaving, 1945–1974', *Business and Economic History*, second series, Vol.XIX (1990).

3. S. Pollard, *The Genesis of Modern Management* (Harmondsworth, 1968); W. Lazonick, *Competitive Advantage on the Shop Floor* (Cambridge, Mass., 1990), Ch.1.

4. Lazonick, *Competitive Advantage*, Chs.3–4.

5. See D.A. Farnie, *The English Cotton Industry and the World Market, 1815–96* (Oxford, 1979), Chs.2 and 8. On the nineteenth-century development of the British cotton industry more generally, see the excellent synthesis in S. D. Chapman, *The Cotton Industry in the Industrial Revolution*, (2nd ed., 1987), and the select bibliography therein. For recent research on labour and labour relations in British textiles, see J.A. Jowitt and A.J. McIvor (eds.), *Employers and Labour in the English Textile Industries, 1850–1939* (1988).

6. K. Burgess, *The Origins of British Industrial Relations* (1975), Ch.4; Lazonick, *Competitive Advantage*, Ch.3–5.

7. Only in the United States did another national industry receive and make use of large numbers of British cotton workers. But in the United States, the occupational and geographic mobility of workers with industrial skills and the (consequent) managerial search for skill-displacing machine technologies meant that a specialised labor force did not reproduce itself in particular localities as was the case in Britain. See W. Lazonick, 'Production Relations, Labor Productivity, and Choice of Technique: British and US Cotton Spinning,' *Journal of Economic History*, Vol.XLI No.3 (1981).

8. Saxonhouse and Wright, 'Stubborn Mules'; G. Saxonhouse and G. Wright, 'Rings and Mules Around the World: A Comparative Study in Technological Change', in G. Saxonhouse and G. Wright (eds.), *Technique, Spirit and Form in the Making of Modern Economies* (Greenwich, Conn., 1984); D.A. Farnie, 'The Textile Machine-Making Industry and the World Market, 1870–1960', *Business History*, Vol.XXXII No.4 (1990).

9. Farnie, *English Cotton*, Ch.2; F.E. Hyde, B.B. Parkinson and S. Marriner, 'The Cotton Broker and the Rise of the Liverpool Cotton Market', *Economic History Review*, Vol.VIII (1955–56). See also M.M. Edwards, *The Growth of the British Cotton Trade, 1780–1815* (Manchester, 1967), Chs.5–6.

10. Lazonick and Mass, 'Performance of the British Cotton Industry'.

11. P. Deane and W.A. Cole, *British Economic Growth, 1688–1959* (Cambridge, 2nd ed. 1969), pp.31–32; B.R. Mitchell, *Abstract of British Historical Statistics* (Cambridge, 1962), pp.60, 188, 284, 305.

12. Farnie, *English Cotton*, Ch.3; S.D. Chapman, 'The International Houses: The Continental Contribution to British Commerce 1800–1860,' *Journal of European Economic History*, Vol.VI No.1 (1977); S.D. Chapman, 'British Marketing Enterprise: The Changing Roles of Merchants, Manufacturers, and Financiers, 1700–1860', *Business History Review*, Vol.LIII No.2 (1979). On the early nineteenth-century development of Manchester, see R. Lloyd-Jones and M.J. Lewis, *Manchester and the Age of the Factory* (1988). See also Edwards, *British Cotton Trade*, Chs.3, 4, 7, 8.

13. M.T. Copeland, *The Cotton Manufacturing Industry of the United States* (Cambridge, Mass., 1912), pp.365–70; R. Robson, *The Cotton Industry of Great Britain* (1955), pp.80–91.

14. A. Marshall, *Principles of Economics*, (9th ed. 1961), Chs.9–10.

15. Farnie, *English Cotton*, Ch.6–7.

16. J. Lyons, 'Vertical Integration in the British Cotton Industry, 1825–1850: A Revision', *Journal of Economic History*, Vol.XLV No.2 (1985); Farnie, *English Cotton*, pp.313–17; J. and S. Jewkes, 'A Hundred Years of Change in the Structure of the Cotton Industry', *Journal of Law and Economics*, Vol.IX (1966); Lazonick, 'Industrial Organization', pp.199–203.

17. A. Marshall, *Industry and Trade* (1919), pp.600–1. See more generally, Lazonick, 'Industrial Organization'.
18. Farnie, *English Cotton*, Ch.1.
19. Sandberg, *Lancashire*, pp.4–5.
20. Saxonhouse and Wright, 'Rings and Mules', p.272.
21. Ibid., p.294.
22. Clark, 'Why Isn't', p.171.
23. D.N. McCloskey, *Econometric History* (1987), pp.26–7.
24. Ibid., p.27. If McCloskey had conducted his 'conversation' with not only economists but also historians such as Farnie (whose book is not cited in McCloskey's survey), he might have been more confident in taking a position on the importance of external economies of scale in the rise to dominance of the British cotton industry.
25. C.K. Harley and D.N. McCloskey, 'Foreign Trade: Competition and the Expanding International Economy', in R. Floud and D. McCloskey (eds.), *The Economic History of Britain since 1700*, Vol.II (Cambridge, 1981), pp.53–6.
26. Ibid., p.54.
27. Adam Smith, *An Inquiry into the Nature and Causes of The Wealth of Nations* (New York, 1937), Book I, Ch.3; A. Marshall, *Principles of Economics* (1961), Book IV, Ch.9–11; N. Kaldor, 'Causes of the Slow Rate of Economic Growth in the United Kingdom', and 'The Irrelevance of Equilibrium Economics', in N. Kaldor, *Further Essays on Economic Theory* (New York, 1978), Chs.4 and 8. See Lazonick, *Business Organization*, Ch.8 for an elaboration, including Kaldor's failure to consider the shift in historical importance from external to internal economies of scale in generating economic growth. See also B. Elbaum, 'The Steel Industry before World War I', in Elbaum and Lazonick, *Decline of the British Economy*, for the case of British steel.
28. Harley and McCloskey, 'Foreign Trade', p.68.
29. Ibid., p.55. See also D.N. McCloskey, 'The Industrial Revolution 1780–1860: A Survey', in Floud and McCloskey, *Economic History of Britain*, Vol.I, pp.112ff.
30. On the development of ring spinning, see T. Navin, *The Whitin Works Since 1831* (Cambridge, Mass., 1950), Ch.10; Mass, 'Mechanical'. See also note 8 above.
31. W. Mass, 'Technological Change and Industrial Relations: The Diffusion of Automatic Weaving in the United States and Britain' (unpublished Ph.D. dissertation, Boston College, 1984), especially Ch.5; A. Fowler, 'Trade Unions and Technical Change: The Automatic Loom Strike, 1908', *North West Group for the Study of Labour History*, Bulletin No.6 (1977).
32. Robson, *Cotton Industry*, p.356.
33. Mass, 'Technological Change', Ch.5. See also M.B. Rose, *The Gregs of Quarry Bank Mill* (Cambridge, 1986), Ch.5.
34. Lazonick and Mass, 'Performance of the British Cotton Industry', pp.5–9; R.E. Tyson, 'The Cotton Industry', in Derek H. Aldcroft (ed.), *The Development of British Industry and Foreign Competition* (1968), pp.104–18.
35. Lazonick and Mass, 'Performance of the British Cotton Industry', p.6.
36. D. McCloskey and L. Sandberg, 'From Damnation to Redemption: Judgments on the Late Victorian Entrepreneur', *Explorations in Economic History*, second series, Vol.IX No.1 (1971),, p.108.
37. Sandberg, *Lancashire*, p.10.
38. Ibid., pp.21–2.
39. Ibid., Chs.2–3. Sandberg's analysis of the choice of spinning technique originally appeared as 'American Rings and English Mules: The Role of Economic Rationality', *Quarterly Journal of Economics*, Vol.LXXXIII No.1 (1969).
40. Sandberg, *Lancashire*, pp.46–7.
41. Lazonick, 'Factor Costs'.
42. Ibid., pp.90–1; Lazonick, 'Industrial Organization', pp.232–36; Lazonick, 'Rings and Mules', pp.396–8.
43. J. Schumpeter, *The Theory of Economic Development* (New York, 1934), Chs. 1–2.
44. Lazonick, 'Industrial Organization', p.232–6.

45. For their uses of Schumpeter, see D.H. Aldcroft and H.W. Richardson, *The British Economy, 1870–1939*, (1969), pp.59, 195, 202, 209; D.S. Landes, *The Unbound Prometheus* (Cambridge, 1969), pp.232, 481.
46. Landes, ibid., p.354.
47. Aldcroft, ibid., p.34.
48. Sandberg, *Lancashire*, p.21.
49. Ibid., p.10.
50. Tyson, 'Cotton Industry', p.100.
51. G.T. Jones, *Increasing Return* (Cambridge, 1933), p.55.
52. Ibid., p.53.
53. Sandberg, *Lancashire*, p.96.
54. Lazonick and Mass, 'Performance of the British Cotton Industry'.
55. Ibid. See also Lazonick, 'Production Relations'.
56. A.J. Marrison, 'Great Britain and Her Rivals in the Latin American Cotton Piece Goods Market, 1880–1914', in B. Ratcliffe (ed.), *Great Britain and Her World, 1750–1914* (Manchester, 1975).
57. Saxonhouse and Wright, 'Stubborn Mules', pp.89–90.
58. Saxonhouse and Wright, 'New Evidence', p.518; Lazonick and Mass, 'Performance of the British Cotton Industry', pp.1–5.
59. Saxonhouse and Wright, 'Stubborn Mules', pp.89–90.
60. See Saxonhouse and Wright, 'Rings and Mules', p.294.
61. Lazonick and Mass, 'Performance of the British Cotton Industry', p.33.
62. Ibid.
63. Ibid, pp.28–9; see also Lazonick, 'Production Relations'.
64. Clark, 'Why Isn't', p.143.
65. Lazonick, 'Factor Costs'; Lazonick, 'Production Relations'. Clark also cites M. Frankel, 'Obsolesence and Technological Change in a Maturing Economy', *American Economic Review*, Vol.XLV No.3 (1955). For Lazonick's own critique of Frankel, see 'Industrial Organization', pp.230–2, and 'Stubborn Mules', p.84n.
66. Clark, 'Why Isn't', pp.143–4.
67. Ibid., p.144.
68. Ibid.
69. Ibid., pp.146, 150.
70. Ibid., p.151. Of the countries in Clark's list, only Greece had a lower machine-worker ratio than India, China, and Japan.
71. Ibid., pp.151–2.
72. Ibid., pp.166–7.
73. Ibid., p.168.
74. Clark failed to cite a previous comparative study on the cotton industry that showed how labour productivity could vary across social contexts, even holding the quality of the labour force and the basic machine technology constant. See Lazonick, 'Production Relations'.
75. K. Seki, *The Cotton Industry of Japan* (Tokyo, 1956), p.389. For a thorough analysis of the changes in market shares during the 1910s and 1920s, see F. Utley, *Lancashire and the Far East* (1931).
76. A.S. Pearse, *The Cotton Industry of India* (Manchester, 1930), pp.11–14.
77. Ibid., p.11.
78. Ibid. See also ibid., p.129; Clark, 'Why Isn't', p.172.
79. Pearse, *Cotton Industry of India*, p.11; C.K. Moser, *The Cotton Textile Industry of Far Eastern Countries* (Boston, 1930), pp.13–14.
80. T. Izumi, 'Transformation and Development of Technology in the Japanese Cotton Industry', Project on Technology Transfer, Transformation and Development: The Japanese Experience, The United Nations University, Working Paper HSDRJE-25/UNUP-91 (Tokyo, 1980), p.81. See also Utley, *Lancashire and the Far East*, pp.204–229.
81. Clark, 'Why Isn't', p.152.
82. Clark, 'Can Management', p.144.

83. Ibid., p.146.
84. See Sandberg, *Lancashire*, pp.213–14; Saxonhouse and Wright, 'New Evidence', p.519; Clark, 'Why Isn't', p.151; J. Singleton, 'Planning for Cotton, 1945–1951,' *Economic History Review*, second series, Vol.XLIII No.1 (1990), p.63. In contrast, see the explicit comparison of Japan and India in, K. Otsuka, G. Ranis and G. Saxonhouse, *Comparative Technology Choice in Development: The Indian and Japanese Cotton Textile Industries* (1988), p.204: 'the analytical lessons of economic history . . . illuminate the importance of differences in institutional and organisational environments' in the choice of technology. For a critique of the comparative analysis of Otsuka, Ranis, and Saxonhouse, see the review of their book by M.D. Morris in *Journal of Japanese Studies*, Vol.XV No.1 (1989), pp.186–96.
85. R.M. Odell, *Cotton Goods in China* (Washington, 1916), p.33; K. Chao, *The Development of Cotton Textile Production in China* (Cambridge, Mass., 1977), p.97; B. Ellinger, 'Lancashire's Declining Trade with China,' *Manchester Statistical Society* (1927–28), p.13; Pearse, *Japan and China* p.134.
86. Clark, 'Why Isn't', p.146.
87. A.S. Pearse, *The Cotton Industry of Japan and China* (Manchester, 1929), p.86.
88. See E. Tsurumi, 'Female Textile Workers and the Failure of Early Trade Unionism in Japan', *History Workshop*, No.18 (1984); Y.A. Kidd, 'Women Workers in the Japanese Cotton Mills: 1880–1920', Cornell University East Asia Papers No.20 (1978); G.R. Saxonhouse, 'Country Girls and Communication among Competitors in the Japanese Cotton-Spinning Industry', in H. Patrick (ed.), *Japanese Industrialization and Its Social Consequences* (Berkeley, 1976); Pearse, *Japan and China*, pp.91–112; Utley, *Lancashire and the Far East*, Chs.6–7; Moser, *Textile Industries of Far Eastern Countries*, pp.14–16.
89. Clark, 'Can Management', p.146.
90. Moser, *Textile Industries of Far Eastern Countries*, p.16.
91. Ibid., p.13.
92. See Seki, *Cotton Industry of Japan*, pp.57–59; Izumi, 'Transformation and Development of Technology', p.10; T. Yanagihara, 'Development of Cotton Textile Industry and Textile Machinery in Prewar Japan', photocopy, Institute of Developing Economies (Tokyo, 1979), pp.20–3. See also Otsuka, Ranis, and Saxonhouse, *Comparative Technology Choice*, Ch.3, where the emphasis is on the importance of cotton-mixing to the Japanese adoption of ring spinning over mule spinning.
93. Pearse, *Japan and China*, p.134; Moser, *Textile Industry of Far Eastern Countries*, p.6. More generally, see S. Yonekawa, 'University Graduates in Japanese Enterprises before the Second World War', *Business History*, Vol.XXVI No.2 (1984); H. Morikawa, 'The Increasing Power of Salaried Managers in Japan's Large Corporations', in W.D. Wray (ed.), *Managing Industrial Enterprise: Cases from Japan's Prewar Experience* (Cambridge, Mass., 1989).
94. S. Yonekawa, 'The Growth of Cotton Spinning Firms: A Comparative Study', in A. Okochi and S. Yonekawa (eds.), *The Textile Industry and Its Business Climate* (Tokyo, 1982); D.A. Farnie and S. Yonekawa, 'The Emergence of the Large Firm in the Cotton Spinning Industries of the World, 1883–1938', *Textile History*, Vol.XIX No.2 (1988), pp.194–7, 205–7.
95. R. Minami and F. Makino, 'Conditions for Technological Diffusion: Case of Power Looms', *Hitotsubashi Journal of Economics*, Vol.XXIII No.2 (1983), p.5. See also S. Sugiyama, 'Textile Marketing in East Asia, 1860–1914', *Textile History*, Vol.XIX No.2 (1988).
96. R. Minami and F. Makino, 'Choice of Technology: A Case Study of the Japanese Cotton Weaving Industry, 1902–1938', *Hitotsubashi Journal of Economics*, Vol.XXVII No.2 (1986), pp.114–5; Yanagihara, 'Development of Cotton Textile Industry', pp.25–26, 43; Izumi, 'Transformation and Development of Technology', pp.15–22.
97. Toyota Motor Corporation, *Toyota: A History of the First Fifty Years* (Aichi, 1988), pp.27–35.

98. Izumi, 'Transformation and Development of Technology', p.18ff; Minami and Makino, 'Choice of Technology', p.125; Yanagihara, 'Development of Cotton Textile Industry', p.40ff. See also W. Mass, 'Mechanical'.
99. Izumi, 'Transformation and Development of Technology' p.22; Robson, *Cotton Industry*, p.356; Seki, *Cotton Industry of Japan*, p.385. Yanagihara, 'Development of Cotton Textile Industry', pp.43–45.
100. Chao, *Cotton Textile Production in China*, p.97.
101. Pearse, *Japan and China*, pp.102–111; Minami and Makino, 'Choice of Technology', p.125.
102. Izumi, 'Transformation and Development of Technology', pp.3–14, 23–27; Yanagihara, 'Development of Cotton Textile Industry', pp.18–23; Utley, *Lancashire and the Far East*, pp.201–204.
103. Pearse, *Japan and China*, pp.45–6; Moser, *Textile Industries of Far Eastern Countries*, p.18.
104. Pearse, ibid., pp.43–50; Moser, ibid., pp.35–7; Seki, *Cotton Industry of Japan*, pp.123–7.
105. Copeland, *Cotton Manufacturing Industry of the United States*, pp.180–4.
106. Lazonick, 'Production Relations'; Lazonick and Mass, 'Performance of the British Cotton Industry'.
107. Pearse, *Japan and China*, p.48; Seki, *Cotton Industry of Japan*, p.61.
108. S. Sugiyama, 'Textile Marketing in East Asia, 1860–1914,' p.288.
109. Ibid., pp.287–9, 295; Chao, *Cotton Textile Production in China*, pp.98–102.
110. Toyota, *First Fifty Years*, pp.30–36; Moser, *Textile Industries of Far Eastern Countries*, pp.5–6; T. Kuwahara, 'The Business Strategy of Japanese Cotton Spinners: Overseas Operations 1890 to 1931', in Okochi and Yonekawa, *The Textile Industry*, pp.142–145.
111. Ellinger, 'Lancashires' Declining Trade with China', p.33.
112. Ibid., pp.30–8.
113. H. Shimuzu, 'Rise and Fall of Japan as a Principal Supplier of Cotton Manufactures for Turkey: The Inter-War Period,' *Middle Eastern Studies*, Vol.XXI No.1 (1985), pp.21–2.
114. Yonekawa, 'University Graduates'.
115. Yonekawa, 'Growth', p.22.
116. See note 84 above.
117. A.D. Chandler, Jr., *Scale and Scope: The Dynamics of Industrial Capitalism* (Cambridge, Mass., 1990).
118. Sandberg, *Lancashire*, p.216.
119. J.M. Keynes, 'Industrial Reorganisation: Cotton', in D. Moggridge (ed.), *The Collected Writings of John Maynard Keynes*, Vol.19, Pt.II (Cambridge, 1981).
120. Sandberg, *Lancashire*, p.217.
121. Saxonhouse and Wright, 'Stubborn Mules', p.92; see also Jewkes and Jewkes, 'Hundred Years of Change', p.130n.
122. Seki, *Cotton Industry of Japan* pp.304–7.
123. Ibid., pp.336–9; Yonekawa, 'Growth', pp.6, 8, 13, 15.
124. Seki, *Cotton Industry of Japan*, p.304, 312–3, 338.
125. Saxonhouse and Wright, 'Stubborn Mules', p.92.
126. Pearse, *Japan and China*, p.128.
127. For the technological and economic benefits of this industry-wide planned co-ordination in the Japanese cotton industry of more recent times, see R. Dore, *Flexible Rigidities* (Stanford, 1987), Chs.7–9. More generally, see M. Best, *The New Competition* (Cambridge, 1990), Chs.5–8.
128. Sandberg, *Lancashire*, pp.182–97.
129. Ibid., p.179.
130. Lazonick, 'Industrial Organization; idem, 'The Cotton Industry'.
131. Sandberg, *Lancashire*, p.205. Ironically, in his study of the resistance of Lancashire to a reduction of surplus capacity and organisational change in the interwar period, Kirby cited Sandberg to argue that the British cotton industry had begun the rapid

BRITISH COTTON AND INTERNATIONAL COMPETITIVE ADVANTAGE   65

adoption of ring spinning for the production of coarse counts prior to the war, and hence that the industry was not technologically laggard during the interwar period. M.W. Kirby, *The Decline of British Economic Power Since 1870* (1981). p.11; idem, 'The Lancashire Cotton Industry in the Inter-War Years: A Study on Organisational Change', *Business History*, Vol.XVI No.2 (1974), pp.152–3. But, as we have seen, Sandberg overestimated the diffusion of ring spinning on coarse counts before the war. See Lazonick, 'Factor Costs', pp.96–9. In his article, Kirby provided a useful overview of the difficulty of organisational change in the inter-war period but betrayed any understanding of the relation between vertical integration and technological change. In his limited discussion of the costs and benefits of vertical integration as inherently the result of 'market failure,' Kirby cited the work of John Jewkes, a long-time proponent of the efficacy of market co-ordination in the British cotton industry and in British industry in general. See J. Jewkes, 'Factors in Industrial Integration,' *Quarterly Journal of Economics*, Vol.XLIV (1930); idem, 'Is British Industry Inefficient?', *Manchester School*, Vol.XIV No.1 (1946); Jewkes and Jewkes, 'Hundred Years of Change'.

132. Lazonick, 'Industrial Organization', pp.211–2; A. Ormerod, 'The Prospects of the British Cotton Industry', *Yorkshire Bulletin of Economic and Social Research*, Vol.XV (1963).

133. Sandberg, *Lancashire*, p.211.

134. Ibid., p.206.

135. J.H. Bamberg, 'The Rationalisation of the British Cotton Industry in the Interwar Years', *Textile History*, Vol.XIX No.1 (1988). See also Kirby, 'Lancashire Cotton', pp.149–52.

136. J. Ryan, 'Combination in the Cotton Trade', *Journal of the National Federation of Textile Works Managers' Associations*, Vol.VIII (1928–29), p.24.

137. Saxonhouse and Wright, 'Stubborn Mules', pp.87–8.

138. Saxonhouse and Wright, 'New Evidence', pp.516–7; idem, 'Stubborn Mules', pp.90–2. For the critique of the 'paper tubes' argument, see Lazonick, 'Stubborn Mules', pp.81–3.

139. Lazonick, 'Industrial Organization'.

140. Saxonhouse and Wright, 'New Evidence', p.519.

141. Ibid., p.515.

142. Lazonick, 'Industrial Organization'; Mass, 'Mechanical'; Lazonick and Mass, 'Performance of the British Cotton Industry'. Despite their focus on choice of technology in Japan and their discussion of both spinning and weaving, Otsuka, Ranis, and Saxonhouse '*Comparative Technology Choice*' Ch.3, did not raise the issue of the interrelatedness of the two processes in achieving high-throughput production.

143. Lazonick, 'Factor Costs', p.102.

144. See note 98.

145. Lazonick, 'Industrial Organization', p.209.

146. Saxonhouse and Wright, 'Stubborn Mules'.

147. Ibid., p.89.

148. Lazonick, 'Industrial Organization', p.229.

149. Ibid.

150. Robson, *Cotton Industry*, p.355.

PART II

ORGANIZATION AND TECHNOLOGY IN THE US ECONOMY

[5]

EXPLORATIONS IN ECONOMIC HISTORY **22**, 53–96 (1985)

The "Horndal Effect" in Early U.S. Manufacturing*

WILLIAM LAZONICK

Department of Economics, Harvard University

AND

THOMAS BRUSH

Department of Economics, University of Michigan

I. THE PRODUCTION-RELATIONS HYPOTHESIS

In a Swedish-language book on productivity and profitability, Erik Lundberg (1961, pp. 130, 131) introduced the economics profession to the "Horndal effect":

> During a period of fifteen years beginning in the mid-1930s, one of the steel works (Horndal) of the Fagersta concern was neglected. No new investments were made

---

* Previous drafts of this paper were presented to the Seminar on the Capitalist Enterprise, Harvard University, in February 1982, the Economic History Workshop, Harvard University, in April 1982, and the 23rd Annual Cliometrics Conference, University of Iowa, in May 1982. The final version was presented to the Labor Seminar at Harvard University in February 1984. Research assistance was provided by Mary Deery, Greg Frazier, Linda Gray, Kathy Hanson, Robert Runcie, Wei Wong, and, especially, Eliot Raiken. Diana Dill and Marta Wenger did some of the computer work. Florence Bartoshevsky and the staff of the Baker Library Manuscripts Division of the Harvard Graduate School of Business Administration offered invaluable assistance in directing us to the relevant documents and data sources. Jo Anne Preston supplied us with data on Massachusetts school teachers. Steven Dubnoff offered advice on the use of his data set on the ethnicity of mill workers, and also brought to our attention the data set compiled by the Philadelphia Social History project. We received useful comments and criticisms from Barry Eichengreen, Stanley Engerman, Louis Ferleger, Richard Freeman, Herbert Gintis, Stephen Marglin, William Mass, Joel Mokyr, Gary Solon, Mark Watson, and Robert Zevin, as well as two anonymous referees for *Explorations in Economic History*. Gloria Gerrig of the Harvard Economics Department made sure that our computer accounts remained operative and that our research assistants got paid. The project has been funded by Harvard University, the Merrimack Valley Textile Museum, the National Science Foundation under Grants SES 78-25671 and SES 83-09335, and the Svenska Handelsbanken Foundation for Social Science Research.

0014-4983/85 $3.00

except for a minimum of repairs and broken equipment replacement (without modernization). In spite of this, there was an annual increase in man–hour production of two percent during this period. This compares to a production growth per man–hour of four percent for the whole concern. In other plants of the company significant new investments were made during this time.[1]

Lundberg referred to the "Horndal effect" as "pure productivity," making no attempt to discover the underlying causes. Instead he called for more analysis "to show the importance of all the undefined factors which are covered under [these] all-encompassing and diffuse labels" (Lundberg, 1961, p. 133).

Some U.S. economists, however, have not been at all reticent to cite the Horndal experience (as reported by Lundberg) as evidence to support very specific explanations of productivity growth. In a seminal article on "learning by doing," Kenneth Arrow (1962) argued that the sustained productivity growth at Horndal could "only be imputed to learning from experience". More recently, Paul David (1973, 1975, Chap. 2) has analyzed the "Horndal effect" in Lawrence Mill No. 2, a cotton textile mill that began operations in Lowell, Massachusetts in 1834. According to David, labor productivity at Lawrence Mill No. 2 increased at an average compounded rate of just under 2% per annum from 1835 to 1856 despite the absence of investment in new machinery. He goes on to argue that the case of Lawrence Mill No. 2 "probably represents the earliest well-documented instance of short-run learning effects [making] its story the true precursor to the Swedish steel mill built at Horndal a century later."[2]

Like Arrow, David merely assumes that the productivity growth at Lawrence Mill No. 2 was the result of "learning by doing." Neither considers the possibility that the "Horndal effect" might have been caused by other (to use Lundberg's words) "undefined factors." Little or no evidence is presented in either case—the Swedish steel mill or the American textile mill—to establish that the temporal configuration of the "sustained" productivity growth even took the form of a "learning curve." For the steel mill, the only evidence cited is that productivity grew at an average of 2% per annum for 15 years. For the textile mill, David uses four data points, representing his estimates for peak labor productivity levels over the period 1835–1856, and finds that the "least-squares fit of the 'learning curve' proves most satisfactory indeed." He concludes

---

[1] Translation by S. Herzenberg.

[2] The Horndal mill was not built in the mid-1930s as David claims, but was already a going concern in the early 19th century. Major investments in plant and equipment were made in the 1880s (Söderlund, 1957–1958). These facts in themselves raise serious doubts about the applicability of the learning-by-doing argument to Horndal in the 1930s and 1940s (see Helper and Lazonick, 1984).

> Surely the evidence presented here provides sufficient cause . . . to insist that
> Horndal share with Lowell the honor . . . in giving its name to the productivity
> effect of learning-by-doing in the context of a fixed production facility. (David,
> 1975, p. 184)

A prime purpose of this paper is to test the learning-by-doing hypothesis as an explanation of the productivity growth at Lawrence Mill No. 2 during its first 2 decades of operation. As illustrated in Fig. 1, there certainly was sustained productivity growth at Lawrence Mill No. 2 from 1834 to 1855. Over this period, output (in yards of "type C" cloth per weaver–hour) rose steadily (with greater cyclical fluctuations before 1842) at an average compounded rate of 3.1% per annum.[3]

But can this growth be attributed to learning by doing? The learning-by-doing hypothesis implicitly assumes that the relation between inputs and output is simply technical in nature, and that the productive capabilities of an enterprise will *of necessity* improve with production experience. If this were the case, one might posit a universal explanation—a "technically determined" learning curve—for cases of productivity growth on the basis of fixed production facilities such as occurred a century apart at the U.S. textile mill and the Swedish steel mill.

But if the relation between inputs and output is partially *social* in nature, then historically specific factors that motivate and condition the objectives and work efforts of different participants in the production process must be considered in explaining changes in productivity. The contention that social factors, and in particular the impact of management–worker relations on work intensity, were determinants of the observed productivity growth at Lawrence Mill No. 2, we call the *production-relations* hypothesis (see Lazonick, 1984).

To posit the production-relations hypothesis is not to reject learning by doing as one *possible* explanation of productivity change. The learning-by-doing hypothesis has intuitive appeal. It is reasonable to expect that the performance capability of participants in production will improve with experience. It is also reasonable to expect that such improved capability is "irreversible" (disappearing only with the disappearance of the learning entity) and that productive capability will improve at a

---

[3] It should be noted that David's growth rate differs from ours. He computed output per worker–hour for the whole mill using an indirect method for estimating the number of actual worker–hours. The weaving process, from which our productivity growth rate is derived, was the most important single component of cloth production in terms of direct labor inputs. David also assumed that each of the four peaks in output per worker–hour that he derived represented the same phase (the peak) of the business cycle at each point in time. In fact, in the main weaveroom, highest levels of output per weaver–hour usually occurred in troughs, presumably because inferior weavers were laid off while the slack labor markets meant that the remaining (technically superior) weavers could be compelled to work harder than at other times.

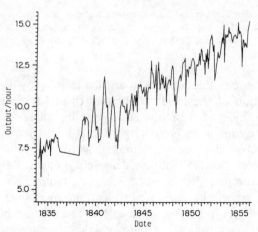

F<small>IG</small>. 1.   Output per weaver–hour, January 1834–November 1855. (Yards of "C" cloth.)
No data available for May 1836 through March 1838. For variable definition, see Appendix.

diminishing rate. These assumptions are embodied in the cumulative
measures of experience that are used in empirical studies of learning by
doing (see David, 1975, Chaps. 2, 3; Fellner, 1969; Rapping, 1965; Sheshinski, 1967; Zevin, 1975).

These assumptions are consistent, moreover, with the basic neoclassical
proposition that the production function is technically determined. An
implicit assumption of the hypothesis is that improved performance *capability* will automatically result in improved *performance*. But if we
recognize that production is a *social process*—that social relations, motivation, and effort influence production outcomes—then we cannot posit
such an automatic translation of changes in input capability into changes
in input performance.

It is worth noting in this regard that Harvey Leibenstein (1966) cited
the Horndal case (again as reported by Lundberg, 1961) as evidence to
support his original formulation of the "X-efficiency" hypothesis—a hypothesis that cannot possibly be equated with learning by doing unless
the latter is turned into a mere tautology. Unfortunately, despite numerous
subsequent books and articles on the subject of "X efficiency," Leibenstein
has never tested or developed the hypothesis by means of empirical
analysis. Hence "X efficiency" has remained a rather vague, and un-
substantiated, concept. In our formulation of the production-relations
hypothesis and its application to the experience of Lawrence Mill No.
2, we hope to reveal something about both the ways in which motivation
and work effort change over time and the extent to which such social
factors affect productivity outcomes.

Our empirical task is to distinguish between the technical determinants
(of which learning by doing is but one) and the social determinants of

productivity growth. The existence of detailed production and payroll records for Lawrence Mill No. 2 has made it possible to construct a relevant microlevel data set. With the exception of 2 years from 1836 to 1838 for which payroll records are missing, we have gathered comprehensive *month-by-month* data on labor productivity, piece rates, earnings, and looms per weaver *for every operative* who worked in the main weaveroom of Mill No. 2 from 1834 to 1855—12,762 observations, of which 12,140 are used in regression analysis. Individual operatives have also been classified by ethnicity and literacy. We have also compiled monthly time series on cotton quality, absenteeism, labor turnover, permanent separations, overseers per operative, and the number of auxiliary workers ("sparehands"). In addition, we have researched a substantial amount of qualitative material including written communications between managers within the Lawrence Company and across Lowell cotton textile firms.[4]

In the next section of the paper, we formulate a production function that distinguishes between the technical and social determinants of productivity change. We also provide some general background on changes in the nature of the labor supply to the Lowell cotton textile mills that is pertinent to the construction of relevant independent variables. In the following section, we present our model for analyzing productivity change at Lawrence Mill No. 2, a model based on our qualitative understanding of the nature of capitalist production, the specific socioeconomic environment in which the textile mill operated, and the types of cross-section and time-series data that we have available. In the next section, we record the statistical results of pooled times-series, cross-section regression analysis of the Lawrence Mill No. 2 data for the period 1834 to 1855. In the concluding section, we discuss the implications of these results for understanding the nature of the production process and the determinants of productivity change in Lawrence Mill No. 2 as well as in capitalist production in general.

II. TECHNICAL AND SOCIAL DETERMINANTS OF PRODUCTIVITY CHANGE

Given the labor-intensive character of cotton textile production in the 19th century, our primary problem is to distinguish between increases in productivity caused by, on the one hand, the application to the production process of *improved* productive capabilities of workers, and, on the other hand, the *more complete* utilization of the *existing* productive capabilities of workers. In other words, we have to account for changes in the quality

---

[4] The Lawrence Manufacturing Company records are to be found in the Baker Library Manuscripts Division at the Harvard Graduate School of Business Administration. A more extensive report on the historical sources is in Brush (1981).

of labor power—the capacity to work—as well as changes in the extent to which this labor power is actually realized in the form of labor services— work effort actually expended in the production process.

In addition, the analysis of productivity change must distinguish between the impacts of changes in the application of labor power to the production process and changes in the capital inputs that enter into production. It is true that over our period there was no *major* investment in the capital equipment at Lawrence Mill No. 2. Nevertheless, there were potentially important modifications and alterations in the quality of the existing capital inputs as well as changes in the quantity of capital inputs per worker that must be taken into account.

Let us therefore formulate the production function as $q = f(t, h, e)$, where q is output *per worker*, t is a measure of the productive capability of the physical capital inputs available to each worker, h is the productive capability of each worker, and e is the work effort actually applied by each worker. For simplicity, h can be viewed as the *quality* of labor services inherent in the worker while e can be viewed as the *quantity* of those services actually expended (although in actuality work effort itself will obviously have a qualitative dimension). If the productivity of physical capital depends on the expenditure of effort by the worker, zero work effort will result in zero output per worker no matter what the quality of t and h that enter the production process.[5] It can be assumed that there will be diminishing returns to increases in work effort per unit of time and that at some point the marginal product of work effort will fall to zero. In this formulation of the production function, increases in t and h are *effort decreasing* in the sense that they permit the worker to produce more *at the same level of work effort.*

If formulated correctly, the learning-by-doing hypothesis as applied to the analysis of the "Horndal effect" posits that increases in q are caused by changes in h which accrue through experience at relevant productive tasks (be they managerial or operative). The production-relations hypothesis posits that increases in q are caused by changes in the level of e, holding t and h constant. Our formulation of the production function, focusing as it does on the quantitative impacts of qualitative phenomena, brings to the fore a host of measurement problems not normally confronted in productivity studies. Our measures of t and h are attempts to capture the quantitative impacts of qualitative changes in productive capability. Moreover, we do not have a direct measure of e, our purely quantitative dimension. Rather we must rely upon our theoretical analysis of the

---

[5] The characteristics of this production function are elaborated in Lazonick (1984). If work effort is viewed as purely quantitative, zero work effort *over a sufficiently long work period* will always result in zero output; if zero work effort resulted in positive output, then the worker would not be necessary to the production process. If work effort is viewed as qualitative, then zero work effort *may* just result in a lower quality product.

social and technical nature of the production process to construct variables that capture changes in work effort.

The analysis of the determinants of work effort (or, as Marx called it, the intensity of labor) is central to understanding the social relations of the capitalist workplace (see Lazonick, 1983a). How hard particular workers work will be manifestations of their individual or collective responses to incentives, both positive and negative, that the enterprise manager holds out. Profit-maximizing managers will attempt to structure incentives to minimize unit costs (over an appropriate time horizon). If we assume (as most economists implicitly do) that workers view work as a disutility— a mere means to an end—then it follows that workers will attempt to get the most remuneration for the least possible expenditure of work effort. Insofar as workers are successful they will undermine managerial attempts to minimize costs. The relation between work effort and rewards will be, therefore, an inherently conflictual issue, with the constraints on cost minimization by capitalists and "on-the-job" utility maximization by workers being determined in part by the relative power of the two sides.

The task of historical analysis is to discover the sources of relative power. One source will be exit. The existence of alternative opportunities permits individuals to protect not only their earnings but also their work conditions. Another source will be collective action—what Hirschman (1970) has called "voice"—either through formal management–union bargaining or informal setting of work norms by the workers themselves. If the response of workers to incentives is individualistic, management can, the labor market permitting, fire workers whose performance is "subpar." If the response of workers to incentives is collective, however, to give all, or even some, of the workers the sack for inadequate performance may be a prohibitively expensive managerial remedy.

In the 1830s and well into the 1840s, workers in the Lowell mills had no formal bargaining power. Strikes staged in 1834 and 1836 over wage cuts were clearly unsuccessful (Brush, 1981; Dublin, 1979, Chap. 6). But these workers did possess considerable power of individual exit. As is well known, the labor force in the Lowell mills of the 1830s was made up primarily of "Yankee farmgirls." To attract the daughters of America's yeomanry into the mills required not just relatively high wages but, more importantly, good working conditions along with the closely supervised structure of life in the Lowell boarding houses. Only then could mill work represent a respectable prelude to womanhood. Attempts by Lowell managers to cut wages or intensify work could, and at times did, lead to an exodus back to the farms and a drying up of new recruits (at least from the regions from which the previous workers had been drawn) (Dublin, 1979, Chap. 3; Ware, 1966, Chap. 8).

By all accounts, from the late 1830s it became increasingly difficult to recruit an adequate supply of farmgirls. On the demand side, in Lowell alone between 1835 and 1847, the number of mills increased by 114%, the number of spindles by 158%, the number of looms by 122%, and the number of female employees by 71% (Eno, 1976, p. 255). On the supply side, the reserves of New England farmgirls were probably declining absolutely by the late 1830s as the economic viability of New England farming was deteriorating (Bidwell and Falconer, 1925, pp. 237ff; Wilson, 1936, Chaps.1–4; Field, 1978).[6] At the same time, the generally well-educated Yankee farmgirls found themselves with an expanding wage-employment alternative to working in the mills. Up until the 1830s, school teaching during the winter months had been a male-dominated occupation, with females—many mill operatives among them—confined largely to summer teaching. From the 1830s, however, women were increasingly employed as winter teachers. As proportions of the winter and summer teaching forces in Massachusetts, females were 33 and 93%, respectively, in 1839–1840, but 50 and 90%, respectively, in 1849–1850. Over this period the number of female winter teachers employed in Massachusetts increased from 1079 to 2142 (Preston, 1982).

As the Yankee farmgirl labor supply dwindled, however, the population of Lowell grew—from 18,010 in 1837 to 33,383 in 1850, an increase of 85%. Increasingly the labor force for the Lowell mills could be drawn

[6] Data from the U.S. Census from 1820, 1840, 1850, 1860, and 1870 show the following trends in agricultural employment in the New England states:

	1820	1840	1850	1860
Massachusetts				
(1)	63,460	87,837	55,699	62,634
(2)	0.58	0.41	0.15	0.14
Maine				
(1)	55,031	101,630	77,016	80,708
(2)	0.82	0.73	0.41	0.39
New Hampshire				
(1)	52,384	77,949	47,408	45,544
(2)	0.84	0.78	0.40	0.39
Vermont				
(1)	50,951	73,150	48,312	52,989
(2)	0.85	0.82	0.43	0.53

(1) = agricultural employment
(2) = proportion of labor force engaged in agriculture

Note. The 1850 Census included only males over 15 in the "total labor force." To adjust the reported labor force figure to include females, the total labor force for each state was estimated by using the ratio of total employment to male employment as stated in the 1870 Census. The 1860 Census includes farmers and farm laborers.

from a pool of local urban residents (Eno, 1976, p. 255).[7] The boarding-house system declined and was replaced by less paternalistic contractual relations between management and labor (Dublin, 1979, p. 166). But, like the Yankee farmgirls, the native-born female residents of Lowell were not in general dependent on factory work for their sustenance. Most of them came from families in which the male head of household was able to earn a family wage, and it was exceptional for an American woman to remain at mill work once she was married (Dublin, 1979, pp. 31, 32, 50–54). Since the minority of workers who *were* dependent on mill work to earn a basic living in the early 1840s were relatively indis-tinguishable parts of a labor force that was not dependent, even they were endowed with substantial power to control their work conditions and earnings.

All this changed with the large-scale influx of Irish into the mills in the late 1840s. As the data from the Mill No. 2 main weaveroom show, output per weaver–hour continued its steady climb from the early 1840s until the end of our period whereas from the late 1840s the previously horizontal trend in real earnings per hour turned sharply downward (see Figs. 1 and 2). Unlike those Yankee workers for whom mill work was not essential to the securing of sustenance, the Irish were in general dependent on mill earnings for their basic livelihoods. As Thernstrom (1964, Chap. 4) has shown, the common laboring jobs available to Irish *men* around 1850 did not provide anywhere near a minimal family wage. Hence the earnings of older children and, in many cases, wives were crucial components of day-to-day subsistence. Lacking the range of al-ternative opportunities open to most American workers and being more dependent on mill earnings to meet their basic needs, the Irish had much less power to resist intensification of labor implemented by means of stretch-outs, speed-ups, and the use of inferior cotton. Moreover, the availability of the Irish posed a serious threat to the ability of the remaining American workers to resist unremunerated intensification of labor. The very presence of the Irish as a reserve army of labor threatened the jobs of the Yankees. Furthermore, the social distance between the two groups on the shop floor probably made it more difficult to enforce the collective setting of output norms in order to protect the relation between work effort and pay.

From the 1830s to the 1850s, therefore, two-stage transformation of the nature of the labor supply took place; first, from one in which Yankee

[7] Data in the Hamilton Manufacturing Company Register Books show that the net change in the number of Hamilton workers who were full-time residents of Lowell as a percentage of the net change in Hamilton workers averaged 5.9% in 1834–1838; 9.8% in 1839–1843; and 9.9% in 1844–1848. Hamilton Manufacturing Company Register Books, Volumes 482–483, 485–490, Manuscripts and Archives Division, Baker Library, Harvard Graduate School of Business Administration.

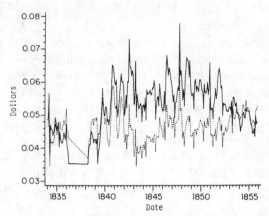

FIG. 2. Average hourly real and nominal wages, January 1834–November 1855. Solid lines represent real wages; dotted lines represent nominal wages. No data available for May 1836 through March 1838. The nominal wage series is the average hourly earnings of weavers in the Lawrence Mill No. 2 main weaveroom. The real wage series is derived by dividing the nominal wages series by the Warren–Pearson Index, Base: 1824–1842, in Arthur H. Cole, *Wholesale Commodity Prices in the United States, 1700–1861* (Harvard UP: Cambridge, 1938), Table 45 (All Commodity Index of Wholesale Prices with Variable Group Weights at New York. Monthly 1797–1861).

farmgirls predominated to one in which permanent Yankee operatives were increasingly prevalent, and then to one characterized by an increasing proportion of Irish workers. Given this transformation, there is reason to believe that the levels of experience on the part of workers and the relative power of management and labor were anything but stable from the mid-1830s to the mid-1850s. In particular, we would expect the importance of learning by doing as a determinant of productivity growth to have been greatest in the 1840s when a presumably more experienced, permanent Yankee labor force was being employed than in either the 1830s or 1850s. In contrast, we would expect the strength of management to effect unremunerated intensification of labor to have been greatest in the last third of our period with the coming of the Irish. It is these specific hypotheses that we wish to test with the data drawn from the main weaveroom of Lawrence Mill No. 2.

III. THE PRODUCTION FUNCTION IN EARLY U.S. TEXTILE MANUFACTURING

Our dependent variable, graphed in Fig. 1, is output per worker–hour (YWH), the observations being average hourly output of each regular weaver ("piecehand") in the main weaveroom of Mill No. 2 for each month from January 1834 through November of 1855 with the exception of the period from May 1836 through March 1838 for which payroll records are missing. (For 9 of these 23 months, however, Mill No. 2 was entirely closed down because of depressed economic conditions.)

Mill No. 2 produced one standard type of cloth throughout the period of analysis, so our productivity measure can be in physical quantities. We shall assume that each unit of this cloth was of constant quality at each point in time as well as over time.

Our independent variables are grouped under three headings: (1) technical variables (t) that reflect changes in technical conditions that are *not* inherently part of a managerial strategy to intensify labor; (2) human capabilities (or physico-cognitive) variables (h) that reflect changes in the performance capability of operatives or management; and (3) work effort variables (e) that reflect changes in the power of management or labor to control the intensity of labor, *given t* and *h*. Since some factors may reflect changes in both t and e (for example, cotton quality) or h and e (for example, overseers per worker), the attribution of factors to particular categories depends crucially upon our identification of the phenomena that the variables are capturing, and hence upon our prior knowledge of the nature of the production process. What follows is a general description of the variables that enter into a production function that relates output per weaver–hour in Lawrence Mill No. 2 to technical conditions, the physico-cognitive abilities of human resources, and the relative power of management and workers to control the levels of work effort. (For the variables listed below, a more complete technical description and discussion is provided in the Appendix.)

Technical Capabilities (t) Variables

(1) D1, D2, . . . D11 are monthly dummy variables (January through November, respectively) that adjust for variations in the technical capability of the Lawrence Mill No. 2 weaveroom because of seasonal factors. Four such factors stand out: increased yarn breakages during the dry winter months; "freshets" or backwaters that typically occurred in April, rendering the power source, and hence production, irregular despite the locks and canal system; shortages of water power in the summer and fall months; and the heat of the summer months (July and August) which may have had a negative impact on the productive capabilities of workers at any given level of work effort. The third factor, however, was not an annual occurrence, and so is treated separately below as WPOW.

(2) DTECH1 is a dummy variable to control for the introduction of a relatively inexpensive, but potentially important, technical change in the main weaveroom in May 1835. What was described in the company records as an "alteration of looms" was probably a device that made the shifting of the pace weight self-acting. The resultant improvement in the let-off motion permitted the production of more consistent and standardized cloth.

(3) DTECH2 is a dummy variable to control for the introduction of a new type of cotton picker into the mills of the Lawrence Manufacturing

Company in August 1844. By permitting the transformation of a given grade and staple of cotton into a higher quality cotton input, the cotton picker would have permitted more output for the same amount of labor effort, holding grade and staple of cotton constant.

(4) DCOTL2 is the cotton quality variable, RCOTL (described below), interacted with DTECH2. This interactive variable allows us to test the hypothesis that the preparation of cotton and its consequent impact on output per worker varies significantly with the quality of raw cotton used.

(5) WPOW is a dummy variable that controls for periods of deficiencies in power supply because of water shortages in the Lowell locks and canals system. During such periods the output of the mill was constrained by lack of power, and hence management had an interest in maximizing output per unit of available water power. To do so management lowered the speed of the looms, reducing both power consumption and yarn breakages. It appears that they then reduced the size of the labor force temporarily, giving the remaining workers more of the slower looms to tend for the duration of the power shortage, but at the piece rate that had previously prevailed. This temporary increase in loom complements is not captured by our looms per weaver variable (LPW below) since it is derived from piece-rate *changes* (see Appendix).

Human Capabilities (*h*) Variables

(6) LNTIME, the logarithm of cumulative months since Lawrence Mill No. 2 opened for operation, is a conventional measure of learning by doing. In fact, Paul David uses this measure in his study of productivity growth in Lawrence Mill No. 2. In early U.S. cotton firms, labor turnover was certainly much higher than managerial turnover, and the very existence of the company records, now at our disposal, demonstrates that the retiring managers did pass on a substantial amount of information and know-how to their successors. We can assume, therefore, that *cumulated learning* in Mill No. 2 resided in management. Hence LNTIME represents the managerial contribution to the productive efficiency of the Mill No. 2 weaveroom.[8]

---

[8] In his study of "learning by doing" in New England textiles, Zevin (1975, p. 5) argues that "the manager alone could be the repository of knowledge acquired from production experience and that this knowledge could be used to make old and new workers and machines more productive." We would argue, however, that the productivity results of many management decisions are determined not so much by accumulated managerial knowledge, but more by changes in the structure of production relations. As one of the authors has shown in another context (Lazonick, 1983b), much managerial knowledge may become irrelevant or even an obstacle to productivity growth as production relations change. Zevin (1975, p. 5) also argues that over time management learns "the most efficient intensity of production." But given the inherent conflict over the intensity of labor, managers and workers may by no means have been in agreement over just what the proper measure

(7) LNEXPADJ, the logarithm of the number of cumulative days worked by each weaver whose name appears on the payroll in any given month, is an attempt to capture the impact of weaving operatives' on-the-job experience as distinct from the experience of the "mill" as a whole. We have incomplete information on the actual relevant experience of individual workers. We have virtually complete information on days spent in the main weaveroom of Mill No. 2, but we do not know how much experience was acquired in other rooms at the Lawrence Manufacturing Company or at other textile mills. The longer the average careers of Lowell mill workers and the shorter the average stay in the Mill No. 2 main weaveroom, the less problematic these truncated job profiles become since in the extreme there would be no reason to assume that, in any given month, those with more experience acquired in the Mill No. 2 weaveroom had any more or less externally acquired experience than those with less internally acquired experience. As explained below, however, we can correct for the bias inherent in truncated job profiles by performing regression analysis on deviations of monthly observations for individuals from the historical (Mill No. 2 main weaveroom) means for those individuals.

(8) CAPUTIL is a measure of capacity utilization in the Mill No. 2 main weaveroom (see Fig. 3). It permits us to take into account variations in output per worker–hour caused by variations in demand. As noted above (note 3), the highest levels of output per worker–hour usually occurred in troughs of the business cycle. During booms, management could sell as much cloth as the fixed machinery capacity could produce, an inducement to maximize output per *loom*. But in slumps, with inventories piling up and productive capacity outstripping demand, management would be more inclined toward maximizing output per *worker*. This objective could be achieved by laying off inferior workers, increasing the number of looms per weaver, and slowing somewhat the speed of each loom. Up until the early 1840s and then less systematically in the early 1850s,

---

of "efficiency" should be. It should also be noted that David specifies a log–log relationship between cumulated time and output per worker–hour, hence positing that each successive increase in elapsed time leads to equivalent percentage increases in output per worker. Given what we know about productivity growth without technical change in capital inputs, however, we have doubts about the appropriateness of this functional relationship. In effect, David is assuming that it is just as easy to obtain equivalent percentage increases in output per worker–hour at higher levels of output as at lower levels of output. We would argue that it becomes more difficult. In order to model this assumption, we specify a linear–log relationship between cumulated time and output per worker–hour, in effect positing that each successive 1% increase in elapsed time results in equivalent absolute increments (and hence declining percent increments) in output per worker–hour. The same arguments apply to our modeling of the relation between individual workers' experience and output per worker–hour, below.

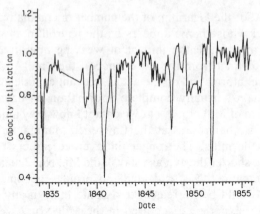

Fig. 3.   Capacity utilization, January 1834–November 1855. (Ratio of looms tended to looms available.) No data available for May 1836 through March 1838. For the reason that capacity utilization is sometimes greater than 1.0, see Appendix.

Mill No. 2 management explicitly made note of high productivity workers in the payroll books, and apparently used this information as a basis for deciding who to retain in slack periods. Also, when water shortages compelled the mill to operate at less than full capacity, weavers tended an extra loom at lower speeds causing labor productivity to rise. It could be argued that the impact of CAPUTIL on labor productivity reflects changes in work effort as well as changes in the quality of physical capital. In slumps, management often temporarily altered the looms per weaver ratio from two to three and less often from three to four, typically slowing the speed of the looms somewhat as the number of looms per weaver increased. In addition, the power of management to intensify the labor of employed workers was undoubtedly greater in a downturn than in an upturn. We believe, however, that we have captured any impacts on work effort directly by means of our "work effort" variables listed below so that changes in CAPUTIL will reflect changes in human capabilities rather than changes in the intensity of labor.

(9) SPARPAUX is the number of "sparehands" doing auxiliary work for each piecehand (regular weaver) in the Mill No. 2 main weaveroom. "Sparehands" (also called "dayhands" since they were on day rates) were employed to learn to weave. Typically, one or two "sparehands" were actually relatively high-paid weavers whose job it was to teach fresh recruits. How was the work of sparehands related to the work of piecehands? We have evidence that sparehands were doing weaving independently of regular weavers. We have found no evidence, however, that sparehands were doing auxiliary tasks such as weft carrying and cleaning that would have had a direct effect on the productivity of weavers. Nevertheless, it is possible that at certain points in our time period

management redivided labor in the weaveroom, utilizing sparehands to perform tasks previously done by regular weavers. For periods following such redivisions of labor (if in fact they did occur), our measure of output per weaver–hour, including as it does only the output and hours of piecehands, would be inflated. SPARPAUX is meant to control (albeit in a rather crude way) for this possibility.

Work Effort (e) Variables

These variables are the most complex in our model. We can divide them into two types: (a) "managerial strategy" variables, reflecting the power of management to get more work effort out of their workers; and (b) "workers' control" variables, reflecting the power of workers to control the relation between the levels of work effort they expend and the rewards they receive.

(a) Managerial Strategy

(10) LPW is the average number of looms tended by each weaver in Mill No. 2 during any given month (see Fig. 4). Management can attempt to intensify work by "stretching-out" (more looms per weaver) and/or by "speeding-up" (more picks per minute per loom). A stretch-out from say two to three looms per weaver does not *necessarily* increase either work effort or output per worker–hour. The looms are always slowed somewhat when stretch-out occurs, but not necessarily to the point where work effort expended per unit of labor–time is at the pre-stretch-out level. Since the slowing of looms per se is effort saving (less yarn breaks per unit of time) while the increase in looms per worker per se is effort increasing (attention must be paid to more looms), the change in the level of work effort required to achieve the same level of output both

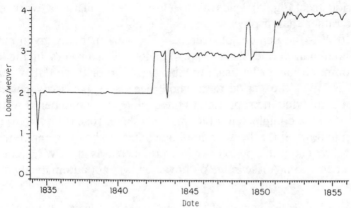

FIG. 4. Average number of looms per weaver, January 1834–November 1855. No data available for May 1836 through March 1838. For variable definition, see Appendix.

before and after the shift to more looms will depend on how these two effects counterbalance one another. If we assume that for any given change in loom complements, the same level of output would require the same level of work effort before and after the change, then a positive relation between LPW and YWH would indicate intensification of labor.

(11) RCOTL is an index of the quality of cotton used by Mill No. 2 (see Fig. 5). An increase in cotton quality (either in terms of longer staple length or cleaner grade) is a form of effort-decreasing technical change: more output per worker–hour can be produced with the same amount of work effort because, *other things equal,* there will be fewer yarn breaks per hour and hence less downtime. A significant *positive* relation between RCOTL and YWH would be consistent with the hypothesis that over time management makes trade-offs based on the relative prices of inputs and outputs between higher unit cotton costs and higher levels of physical productivity. But precisely because higher quality cotton is more expensive, management may very well choose to use lower quality cotton to cut raw material costs even though such a choice of technique will, *other things equal,* result in lower levels of productivity because of more downtime (caused by more yarn breaks per unit of time). Management will find it particularly attractive to use low quality cotton when it can ensure that "other things" will *not* remain equal: when it has the power to compel workers to work harder to repair more yarn breaks per unit of time even though the harder work may not result in either higher levels of output or earnings per hour.[9] A significant *negative* relation between RCOTL and YWH, therefore, would strongly support the hypothesis that management introduced lower quality cotton in periods when it had enhanced power to intensify labor, enabling it to achieve simultaneously lower cotton costs and higher levels of labor productivity. On a priori grounds, the observed deterioration of cotton quality over our period (see Fig. 5) leads us to classify RCOTL as a work effort variable rather than a physical capital variable.

(12) OPW is the number of overseers per worker in any given month. Throughout our period there were one to five overseers in the main weaveroom, although the usual number was two or three. OPW tended to increase over the period as a whole because supervisory personnel were not eliminated in proportion to the decline in the number of weavers employed as the complement of looms per weaver rose from two to three and then to four. Since the amount of machinery to be overseen remained constant throughout this period, we interpret increases in OPW as reflecting closer supervision. A rise in OPW, however, will not automatically result

---

[9] For a more extensive analysis of the interaction of changes in cotton quality with production relations and the resultant impact on productivity and costs, see Lazonick (1981), Lazonick and Mass (1984), and Mass (1984).

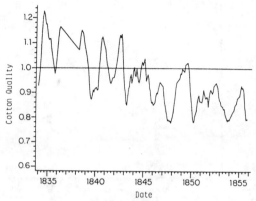

Fig. 5. Cotton quality index by month of use, January 1834–November 1855. (Ratio of mill price to New York price of Uplands cotton.) No data available for May 1836 through March 1838. For variable definition, see Appendix.

in higher levels of labor productivity. Closer supervision will yield productivity results when the collective or individual power of workers to resist intensification of labor is weak.

(b) Workers' Control

(13) ABSENT is a measure of absenteeism for individual weavers; that is, the amount of *voluntary and temporary* labor mobility that Mill No. 2 weavers enjoyed during their employment in the main weaveroom. A human capital theorist might predict a negative relation between ABSENT and YWH on the assumption that individual workers lose job-relevant skills when they experience frequent separations. It is not known, however, what workers did during their temporary absences from the main weaveroom. They may very well have gone to work at other Lowell mills that offered superior work conditions. Our interpretation of ABSENT is that it reflects the power of workers to exit temporarily from unsatisfactory work environments. When ABSENT is high, management efforts to intensify labor are more constrained by the fear of aggravating the problem of high levels of absenteeism. Like the human capital theorist, we would predict a negative relation between ABSENT and YWH, but we would interpret the impact of ABSENT to be on the level of work effort rather than on the level of human capabilities in the production function.

(14) FALLPRES measures the extent to which individual workers were present in Mill No. 2 in the summer and fall months, that is, July–November (see Fig. 6 for annual average FALLPRES). This variable represents an attempt to capture the supposed transition from an impermanent (Yankee farmgirl) to a permanent (urban resident) labor force

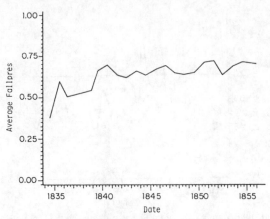

FIG. 6.   Annual average FALLPRES (permanent workforce), January 1834–November 1855. No data available for May 1836 through March 1838. Calculations for 1836 based on average of first 4 months; for 1838, average of last 9 months; and for 1855, average for first 11 months. For variable definition, see Appendix.

in Lowell. We have no direct measure of "farmgirl" status, or lack thereof, among the Lowell operatives. But it has been generally argued that those with agrarian attachments would typically return to the farms during the hot summer months and would help with the harvest and putting up food in the early fall. If we could identify who these people were in the Mill No. 2 sample, we could test the hypothesis that, because of this alternative opportunity, operatives with continuing ties to the agrarian sector were better able to avoid unremunerated intensification of labor during their stints as weavers than those who lacked such ties.

(15) LPQUITD measures the ability of weavers to quit the Mill No. 2 main weaveroom *permanently* (in contrast to ABSENT and FALLPRES which measure temporary separations). We have lagged our measure of permanent quits 1 month to test the hypothesis that the ability of workers to depart definitively from the weaveroom constrained managerial attempts to intensify labor.

(16) TEACH is an index of the availability and relative attractiveness of teaching jobs for "literate" Mill No. 2 weavers. Hence, it is a measure of a very specific alternative opportunity. A significant negative relation between TEACH and YWH would support the hypothesis that the *existence* of an important alternative opportunity undermined the ability of management to intensify labor.

(17) LNPIECER, the logarithm of the average real piece rate times the average loom complement, is a measure of the earnings incentive to which a weaver could respond in any given month. Given current earnings incentives, workers may have *chosen* to work harder in order to achieve higher earnings, although as indicated above we would expect that different

workers had different trade-offs between "on-the-job leisure" and earnings. In contrast to the coercive managerial strategy inherent in OPW, this variable represents an attempt to capture the extent to which workers voluntarily responded in the form of work effort to real piece-rate incentives offered by management. (We do not directly consider here the managerial strategy of *manipulating* the piece-rate incentive in order to minimize costs.)

(18) BEGEND, the total elapsed time since a weaver first entered the Mill No. 2 main weaveroom, is a measure of seniority as distinct from actual shopfloor experience. More days actually worked probably endowed a weaver with more physico-cognitive capacities, whereas those who were around longer (but not necessarily with more accumulated days worked) were less likely to acquiesce in intensified work than those who were relatively new to the weaveroom. Given the development of the Lowell labor supply described above, those with more seniority are likely to have been Yankees who placed a relatively high value on the enjoyment of respectable work conditions, thus limiting the acceptable level of self-imposed work intensity. In addition, a weaver with more seniority probably learned that to drive herself too hard could be self-defeating since it might provide a basis for management to adopt the higher levels of output as new output *norms,* paying lower piece rates to yield the same basic wage. The Irish apparently had little power to resist intensification. Moreover, since being a mill worker undoubtedly represented an *improvement* over previous socioeconomic experiences for the Irish, they probably had less aversion to intense work than did the Yankees. With the coming of the Irish, the traditional Yankee opposition to rate busting must have been severely tested. It is likely that those with long attachments to mill work who remained in the mills despite the advent of "Irish" conditions offered more resistance to intensification of labor than did the newcomers. Hence, controlling for experience, we would expect BEGEND to have a negative impact on YWH throughout our period.

(19) ETHNIC is a variable that specifies the probability that a person is non-Irish or Irish. This variable permits us to test the hypothesis that, holding technology and human resource characteristics constant, the Irish were more susceptible to intensification of labor than were Yankees. A significant positive relation between ETHNIC and YWH would be consistent with our hypothesis that Irish workers, being more dependent on mill work and possessing less social power than Yankee workers, had less power to resist undesired intensification of labor.

(20) ETHNICITY, the proportion of weavers in any given month who are non-Irish (see Fig. 7), measures the extent to which "Irish conditions" pervaded the weaveroom, thus, according to our theoretical framework, subjecting non-Irish as well as Irish to much more oppressive social relations of production than those that prevailed in the "Yankee" era.

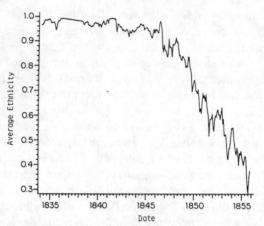

Fɪɢ. 7.   Average ethnicity, January 1834–November 1855. (All Yankee = 1, all Irish = 0.) No data available for May 1836 through March 1838. For variable definition, see Appendix.

IV. EMPIRICAL RESULTS

To test alternative hypotheses concerning the determinants of productivity growth in the Mill No. 2 main weaveroom, we ran pooled time-series cross-section regressions with output per weaver–hour as the dependent variable. In the estimation of two variants of the production function model that are presented below, the data were transformed (as mentioned previously) into deviations of individual observations from the historical means for each individual in the Mill No. 2 main weaveroom.[10] In this way, we avoid the implicit, and unwarranted, assumption that all individuals who worked in the weaveroom started on an equal footing in terms of experience and other related characteristics that might influence individual productivity. In other words, we do not constrain all individuals to have the same intercepts in the functional relationships between their input and output. In the presentation of the empirical results below, the *M* at the end of each variable name indicates that the variable is measured in terms of deviations from the individual's mean for each observation. It should be noted that the use of this method precludes the *direct*

[10]For a mathematical justification of this procedure, see Brush (1983). The difference-from-means OLS estimation used in this paper is similar to that described in Hausman (1978, p. 1261). The deviations from means approach is equivalent to the introduction of separate dummy variables for each individual who appears in the data set. Our model has an unbalanced design because individuals are present in the sample for different lengths of time, and is therefore somewhat different from the standard fixed effects approach. A proof of the equivalence of the covariance transformation estimator with fixed effects and the least-squares dummy estimator (see Hsiao, 1985, Chap. 3; also Wallace and Hussain, 1969, pp. 60, 61), however, is unaffected by the presence or absence of an unbalanced design.

inclusion in our model of variables such as individual ethnicity and literacy directly since the measures of these variables remain constant over time for any given worker, and hence there are no deviations from individual means. "Literacy" (whether or not a weaver signed her name in the payroll book) does, however, enter indirectly in the construction of our TEACH variable (see Appendix) and, as outlined immediately below, ETHNIC is utilized as an interactive variable.

Below we present the regression results of our model with ETHNIC as well as FALLPRES interacted with the human capabilities and work-effort variables listed above. The use of FALLPRES and ETHNIC as interactive variables enables us to discern whether the transformations in the nature of the labor force from impermanent to permanent workers and from Yankee to Irish workers resulted in significant differences in the impacts of the other independent variables on output per weaver—hour, as well as to test the hypothesis that one or both of these trans-formations can be considered as altering the balance of power between management and workers as we have posited.

From the mid-1840s the change in the ethnic composition of the Mill No. 2 main weaveroom is marked (see Fig. 7), whereas from about 1840 there is only a slight upward trend in the relative numbers of "permanent" and "impermanent" workers (see Fig. 6). On the basis of the qualitative evidence presented in Section II, we would have expected a more pro-nounced upward trend in average FALLPRES after the early 1840s. It should be noted, however, that changes in average FALLPRES might give a misleading impression of changes in the underlying cross-sectional data that we actually use for regression analysis. In Fig. 6, for example, increasing permanence among one portion of the labor force could be masked by increasing impermanence among another portion. An ex-amination of the underlying data, however, failed to reveal any persistent movements over time in the distribution of individuals by values of FALLPRES to support such an argument.

Even in the form of cross-sectional data, FALLPRES is, or course, not a direct measure of loss of "farmgirl" status. In our model the existence of agrarian ties serves as an alternative opportunity that permits workers to exert control over work conditions in the mills. But farmgirls who chose to remain in the mills during the summer and fall months would not necessarily relinquish the power that the *threat* of exit afforded them. Yet they would be counted as "permanent" workers. On the other hand, non-farmgirl operatives who taught summer school would be correctly identified as "impermanent" by FALLPRES. Other non-farmgirl operatives may have left Mill No. 2 during the summer and fall months to visit friends (which would have been more difficult during the winter months) or to work in other mills. Moreover, a study by Dubnoff (1976) of Irish mill workers in Lowell has shown higher rates of absence from work by

Irish women than Irish men, and it may be that, for any number of reasons, Irish weavers in Mill No. 2 (all of whom were women) were taking prolonged absences from Mill No. 2 that are captured by FALLPRES. In any case, we do not have clear-cut transitions from "impermanent Yankees" to "permanent Yankees" to "permanent Irish," and must even consider the experiences of "impermanent Irish." In the discussion that follows, the abbreviations MI, MY, PI, and PY refer to impermanent Irish, impermanent Yankee, permanent Irish, and permanent Yankee workers, respectively.

It should also be noted that in Regression 1 below we have not interacted the t variables with ETHNIC and FALLPRES. Our theoretical framework set out in Section III as well as our explicit inclusion of h and e variables in the production function lead us to posit a priori that the impact of these inputs per se on productivity will not differ across groups of workers. Regressions that were run with interactive t variables (excluding the monthly adjustment variables) in conjunction with interactive h and e variables yielded results that were not significantly different from those of Regression 1. Moreover, none of the coefficients of the interactive t variables were statistically significant, supporting our decision not to interact the t variables with ETHNIC and FALLPRES. But in both regressions—with and without interactive t variables—FALLPRES interacted with RCOTL is significant at the 5% level, lending confirmation to our view that cotton quality should be classified as a work-effort variable, not as a technical capabilities variable.

In Regression 1 the unadjusted coefficient of determination is 0.4133 and the adjusted coefficient of determination is 0.3368. Normally in a sample with over 12,000 observations, the degrees of freedom are large enough so that no adjustment to R^2 is required. But because we have

REGRESSION 1
Production Function with ETHNIC and FALLPRES Interacted
Dependent variable: YWHM, SD = 1.6677
N = 12140, R^2 = 0.4133, $\overline{R}^2$ = 0.3368,   SSE = 19809.16

Independent variable	Parameter estimate	SD	T ratio
D1M	−0.409*	0.265	−6.440
D2M	−0.686*	0.269	−10.671
D3M	−0.292*	0.271	−4.394
D4M	−1.524*	0.265	−22.189
D5M	−0.597*	0.268	−8.633
D6M	−0.533*	0.265	−7.519
D7M	−0.152**	0.272	−2.193
D8M	−0.093	0.270˙	−1.269

REGRESSION 1—*Continued*

D9M	0.047	0.268	0.666
D10M	−0.014	0.268	−0.198
D11M	−0.018	0.263	−0.273
DTECH1M	−0.086	0.136	−0.628
DTECH2M	−0.983	0.163	1.711
DTCOT2M	−0.683	0.157	−1.173
WPOWM	0.067	0.301	1.229
LNTIMEM	−0.956	0.210	−0.289
FLNTIMEM	−0.151	1.020	−1.476
ELNTIMEM	0.652	0.208	0.197
LNEXPADJM	0.137	0.703	1.064
FLNEXPADJM	0.602*	1.214	7.793
ELNEXPADJM	0.172	0.618	1.362
CAPUTILM	−1.185	0.086	−1.578
FCAPUTILM	−0.266	0.204	−0.520
ECAPUTILM	−1.550**	0.078	−2.290
SPARPAUXM	0.171	0.049	0.170
FSPARPAUXM	0.425	0.051	0.525
ESPARPAUXM	0.080	0.042	0.092
LPWM	2.379*	0.310	12.673
FLPWM	−0.302**	0.670	−2.157
ELPWM	−0.266	0.280	−1.458
RCOTLM	1.211	0.057	0.927
FRCOTLM	−2.305*	0.203	−3.584
ERCOTLM	−0.156	0.053	−0.135
OPWM	−14.663**	0.008	−2.033
FOPWM	15.781*	0.016	3.461
EOPWM	14.852**	0.008	2.144
ABSENTM	0.921	0.077	1.304
FABSENTM	−1.330*	0.040	−2.647
EABSENTM	−1.045	0.066	−1.394
LPQUITDM	−0.660	0.088	−1.063
FLPQUITDM	0.183	0.074	0.384
ELPQUITD	0.790	0.080	1.465
TEACHM	0.035	0.680	0.942
FTEACHM	0.007	1.824	0.407
ETEACHM	0.046	0.543	0.798
LNPIECERM	−3.125*	0.098	−5.114
FLNPIECERM	−0.289	0.185	−0.743
ELNPIECERM	1.054	0.089	1.822
BEGENDM	−0.011	15.342	−0.594
FBEGENDM	−0.006	13.568	−1.460
EBEGENDM	0.031	14.670	1.675
ETHNICITYM	−6.768*	0.050	−5.201
FETHNICITYM	−0.253	0.183	−0.404
EETHNICITYM	8.505*	0.042	6.479

 * Significant at the 1% level.
 ** Significant at the 5% level.

used a fixed effects model in which all observations are deviations from the historical means of individuals, each individual in the sample has a separate intercept for the regression, adding 1345 implicit variables to those for which we explicitly derive coefficients. Hence the need to calculate an adjusted R^2.

Table 1 shows the impact on YWHM of a standard deviation change in the interacted (h and e) variables for each of the four groups of workers, classified by permanence and ethnicity.[11] If we (rather arbitrarily) describe as high an impact on productivity of over 20%, then the most striking results in Table 1 are that LPWM has a high positive impact on productivity change for *all* four worker classifications, ETHNICITYM has a high negative impact for Irish only, while LNEXPADJM has a high positive impact and RCOTLM a high negative impact for permanent workers only. In addition, LNPIECERM has a medium (10–20%) negative impact for all groups of workers, while BEGENDM had a medium negative impact for Irish and a medium positive impact for Yankees. Note that the impact of LNTIMEM is *negative* for all classifications of workers, not what one would expect if this variable indeed captured the contribution of management to productivity growth.

In Regression 1, the only technical capabilities variables that exhibit significant impacts on productivity are the January through July monthly adjustments. The interpretation of the negative coefficients for all of these variables, D1M through D7M, is that productivity in these months is significantly less than productivity in the excluded month, December. For lack of better information, we might assume that the monthly differences were due to the factors—humidity, backwaters, and July heat—mentioned above.

Of the human capabilities variables in Regression 1, only two, both interactive, are statistically significant. The t ratio for LNEXPADJM indicates that variations in experience among *impermanent Irish* (MI) workers has no significant impact on *their* productivity. The statistical results on the interacted variables reveal, however, that the Mill No. 2 permanent workers (both Irish and Yankee), although not Yankees taken as a group, are significantly different from the MI group in the positive direction in terms of the impact of their experience on productivity. Of all the variable classifications in Table 1, the two largest impacts on

---

[11] To derive the standardized impact, we calculated a standardized coefficient for each h and e variable by multiplying the parameter estimate of each h and e variable in Regression 1 by its standard deviation, and then dividing the standardized coefficient by the standard deviation of the dependent variable, YWHM. If we designate the standardized coefficient of a noninteracted variable as c_1, an associated F-interacted variable as c_2, and an associated E-interacted variable as c_3, the standardized impact for MI workers is c_1, for PI workers is $c_1 + c_2$, for MY workers is $c_1 + c_3$, and for PY workers is $c_1 + c_2 + c_3$.

TABLE 1

Percentage of Standard Deviation Change in YWHM Caused by Standard Deviation
Change in Independent Variable by Permanence and Ethnicity of Worker

	Impermanent Irish	Permanent Irish	Impermanent Yankee	Permanent Yankee
LNTIMEM	− 12.05	− 21.29	− 3.90	− 13.13
LNEXPADJM	5.76	49.59	12.11	55.95
CAPUTILM	− 6.12	− 9.35	− 13.37	− 16.61
SPARPAUXM	0.48	1.80	0.66	1.98
LPWM	44.19	32.08	39.76	27.64
RCOTLM	4.14	− 23.93	3.66	− 24.41
OPWM	− 7.02	8.10	0.12	15.23
ABSENTM	4.26	1.08	0.12	− 3.06
LPQUITDM	− 3.48	− 2.64	0.30	1.14
TEACHM	1.44	2.22	2.94	3.72
LNPIECERM	− 18.35	− 21.53	− 12.71	− 15.89
BEGENDM	− 10.13	− 14.99	17.15	12.29
ETHNICITYM	− 20.27	− 23.03	1.14	− 1.62

productivity change are those of LNEXPADJM for PI and PY workers—
50 and 56%, respectively.

Capacity utilization has a negative sign, indicating that the productivity
of MI workers is higher in cyclical troughs, but the coefficient is not
statistically significant. The impact of declines in capacity utilization on
the productivity of Yankee workers is, however, significantly different
at the 5% level than that for the impermanent Irish, consistent with the
evidence from the payroll books (referred to above) that individual performance was systematically monitored up to the early 1840s when Yankee
workers predominated in the weaveroom. Table 1 shows medium negative
impacts for both classifications of Yankee workers, but low negative
impacts for the Irish.

A number of the work effort coefficients are statistically significant.
LPWM is significant with a positive sign, indicating (under the assumptions
set out in Section III) that the work effort of the MI workers is being
intensified by means of stretch-out. At the 5% level, permanent workers
are significantly different from MI workers, the negative sign of the
coefficient indicating that the labor of permanent workers is more difficult
to intensify than that of MI workers, perhaps because of better shop-
floor cohesion and resistance to intensification by those with more consistent attachments to the workplace. Next to the standardized impact of
LNEXPADJM for PI and PY workers, the impacts of all four classifications of LPWM are the highest in Table 1, all with a positive sign.

RCOTLM, the quality of cotton variable, is not significant for MI
workers. The impact of cotton quality on permanent workers is, however,
significantly different than its impact on MI workers in the direction of

added intensification, suggesting that the fact of being permanent, and the lessened ability to exit from worsening work conditions inherent therein, reduces the ability of permanent workers to avoid the intensification impact of inferior cotton relative to MI workers. Note that, in the presence of permanent workers, the *relatively* successful resistance to increases in looms per weaver may well have led management to resort to the use of inferior cotton in order to cut costs. Permanent workers may well have reacted more adversely to discrete and easily recognizable increases in looms per weaver than to gradual deterioration in the quality of cotton. As can be seen in Table 1, the standardized impacts of RCOTLM for PI and PY workers are of about the same relatively high negative magnitude. Those for MI and MY workers are also of about the same magnitude, but relatively low and positive.

The overseers per worker variable for MI workers is significant at the 5% level with a *negative* sign, indicating that increases in overseers per worker may have been a specific managerial response to particular difficulties in getting high levels of productivity (relative to the prevailing norm) out of MI workers. In Table 1, MI workers are the only group for whom the impact of OPWM on productivity change is negative. An increased ratio of overseers to MI workers may have been needed because impermanent Irish lacked the necessary physico-cognitive capacities to perform factory work—a human capabilities factor. Alternatively, the problem may have been the integration of impermanent Irish into already existing conditions of very high levels of work intensity. In either case, the statistical results clearly indicate a different role of overseers for MI workers than for the other groups: at the 1% level for permanent workers and at the 5% level for Yankee workers the impact of OPWM on YWHM differs significantly from its impact for MI workers, and the coefficients of both interacted variables have positive signs. By the same token, it is possible (although by no means statistically proven) that the main function of overseers for PI, MY, and PY workers was to ensure high levels of work effort, holding human capabilities constant.

The coefficient of the absenteeism variable, ABSENTM, is not significant for MI workers. But the impact of this variable on permanent workers is significantly different than its impact on MI workers with a negative sign, suggesting to us that, for any given level of temporary separations as measured by ABSENTM, permanent workers had less power to control the pace of work than impermanent workers, presumably because of their higher dependence on mill work for earning a living. All of the standardized impacts of ABSENTM in Table 1, however, are relatively low.

The purpose of LNPIECERM is to discern whether workers increased their levels of work effort in response to positive incentives—in this case increases in real income for a given level of output—rather than in response to negative incentives, particularly the threat of job loss. The existence of such noncoerced increases in work effort, leading to higher levels of productivity, would be supported by a positive coefficient on LNPIECERM. The highly significant, but *negative,* coefficient for MI workers rules out this positive incentive as an explanation of their productivity performance. Indeed the negative sign lends support to the contrary hypothesis of unremunerated intensification of labor: as indicated for the period from 1848 through 1855 in Figs. 1 and 2, as productivity went up, real piece rates were cut even to the point where real hourly wages declined. Moreover, permanent workers are not statistically different than MI workers in this regard. Unlike the other two coefficients in the group, however, the coefficient on ELNPIECERM is positive and just shy of being significant at the 5% level, suggesting that Yankee workers responded more positively to income incentives than did MI workers. Nevertheless, in Table 1 all the standardized impacts for this variable have negative signs.

Finally, and of utmost significance given all the other factors that have been held constant, the movement of the ethnic composition of the weaveroom toward more Irish (the inverse of ETHNICITYM) has a highly significant positive impact on the productivity of MI workers. Permanent workers as a group cannot be distinguished from MI workers, but Yankee workers as a group can be. In Table 1, there is a marked difference in the standardized impacts of ETHNICITYM for Irish and Yankee workers, respectively, indicating the ability of Yankees to resist being subjected to "Irish conditions" of stretch-out and speed-up in the early 1850s when the ethnic composition of the weaveroom was shifting heavily to Irish. Similarly, the highly significant positive coefficient of EETHNICITYM can be interpreted to mean that, with movements of ethnic composition toward more Irish, Yankee workers were better able to resist intensification of labor.

F tests on all the ETHNIC interactive variables taken together and all the FALLPRES interactive variables taken together in the regression above show both sets of variables to be significant at the 1% level. For purposes of comparison, however, we think that it is useful to estimate the production function with only ETHNIC as an interactive variable, particularly since we are much more confident that our measure of ETHNIC actually distinguishes between Yankee and Irish workers than that our measure of FALLPRES actually distinguishes between workers with and without *agrarian* ties (or other alternative opportunities such as summer school teaching), the structural distinction that the variable was originally designed to capture.

In Regression 2, the most notable impacts on the *t* variables caused by dropping the FALLPRES interactive variables from Regression 1 are that D7M (July) and D8M (August) are now significant at the 1% level.

REGRESSION 2
Production Function with ETHNIC Interacted
Dependent Variable: YWHM,   SD = 1.6677
N = 12140, R^2 = 0.4049, $\overline{R}^2$ = 0.3270,   SSE = 20093.66

Independent variable	Parameter estimate	SD	T ratio
D1M	−0.387*	0.265	−6.073
D2M	−0.662*	0.269	−10.297
D3M	−0.267*	0.271	−4.031
D4M	−1.502*	0.265	−22.066
D5M	−0.561*	0.268	−8.259
D6M	−0.517*	0.265	−7.539
D7M	−0.265*	0.272	−3.860
D8M	−0.194*	0.270	−2.638
D9M	−0.019	0.268	−0.266
D10M	−0.080	0.268	−1.152
D11M	−0.069	0.263	−1.052
DTECH1M	−0.101	0.136	−0.743
DTECH2M	0.549	0.163	0.957
DTCOT2M	−0.289	0.157	−0.498
WPOWM	0.064	0.301	1.189
LNTIMEM	1.145	0.210	0.347
ELNTIMEM	−1.558	0.208	−0.469
LNEXPADJM	0.485*	0.703	4.171
ELNEXPADJM	0.124	0.618	0.995
CAPUTILM	−1.546**	0.086	−2.516
ECAPUTILM	−1.569**	0.078	−2.320
SPARPAUXM	0.503	0.049	0.651
ESPARPAUXM	−0.079	0.042	−0.091
LPWM	2.205*	0.310	13.656
ELPWM	−0.244	0.280	−1.335
RCOTLM	−1.401	0.057	−1.186
ERCOTLM	0.599	0.053	0.518
OPWM	−1.978	0.008	−0.311
EOPWM	12.740	0.008	1.833
ABSENTM	1.959*	0.077	2.882
EABSENTM	−1.550**	0.066	−2.073
LPQUITDM	−0.494	0.088	−0.988
ELPQUITDM	0.749	0.080	1.382
TEACHM	0.017	0.680	0.467
ETEACHM	0.058	0.543	1.009
LNPIECERM	−3.393*	0.098	−6.528
ELNPIECERM	1.053	0.089	1.820
BEGENDM	−0.018	15.342	−0.974
EBEGENDM	0.037**	14.670	1.967
ETHNICITYM	−7.192*	0.050	−6.189
EETHNICITYM	8.483*	0.042	6.455

  * Significant at the 1% level.
 ** Significant at the 5% level.

The coefficients on D9M, D10M, and D11M (September, October, November) also appear to have been altered more than the coefficients on D1M through D6M (January through June). Since FALLPRES measures differences among workers in regularity of employment during the July–November periods, some of the impact of these differences on productivity may well be captured by the monthly adjustment variables with the exclusion of the FALLPRES interactives.

Table 2 summarizes the standardized impacts of the *h* and *e* variables. For both Irish and Yankees, LNEXPADJM and LPWM have high positive impacts on productivity change. ETHNICITYM has a high negative impact for Irish, while LNPIECERM has a medium negative impact for both groups. BEGENDM has a medium negative impact on both groups, but in opposite directions.

The impact of individual experience is clear-cut in Regression 2. The coefficient of LNEXPADJM refers to Irish workers in general, and is significant at the 1% level with a positive sign. Moreover, Yankee workers are not significantly different than Irish workers, and the sign of ELNEXPADJM is also positive. The positive standardized impacts of LNEXPADJM are both over 20%.

The coefficient of CAPUTILM is now significant at the 5% level with a negative sign, indicating that on average the productivity of Irish workers rose in cyclical troughs. Yankee workers are significantly different from Irish workers at the 5% level, and the negative sign indicates that for these workers the productivity increases in cyclical downturns were even stronger than for Irish workers.

The coefficient of LPWM is significant at the 1% level and positive. As in Regression 1, this finding is consistent with the hypothesis that

TABLE 2
Percentage of Standard Deviation Change in YWHM Caused by Standard Deviation
Change in Independent Variable by Ethnicity of Worker

	Irish	Yankee
LNTIMEM	14.39	−5.04
LNEXPADJM	20.45	25.06
CAPUTILM	−7.98	−15.29
SPARPAUXM	1.50	1.32
LPWM	41.02	36.94
RCOTLM	−4.80	−2.88
OPWM	−0.96	5.16
ABSENTM	9.05	2.94
LPQUITDM	−2.58	1.02
TEACHM	0.72	2.58
LNPIECERM	−19.97	−14.33
BEGENDM	−16.55	16.01
ETHNICITYM	−21.59	−0.24

productivity gains by Irish were the result of the intensification of their labor by means of stretch-out. The coefficient of ELPWM indicates that Yankees as a group were not significantly different from the Irish in terms of the impact of stretch-out on productivity. For both Irish and Yankees, the highest standardized impact is associated with changes in LPWM.

Neither of the coefficients of RCOTLM or ERCOTLM is statistically significant. Comparing these results with the cotton quality findings in Regression 1 suggests that if inferior cotton was used by management in contexts where it had more power to intensify labor, then it was foisted on permanent workers as a group rather than on the Irish as a group or the Yankees as a group. In Regression 1, the overseers per worker variable is significant for impermanent Irish whereas in Regression 2 it is not significant for the Irish as a group, reinforcing the previous interpretation that it was the *impermanence* of the Irish rather than being Irish itself which posed particular productivity problems in the weaveroom.

The impact of the exclusion of the FALLPRES interactives on ABSENTM are particularly interesting. In Regression 1, the coefficient of ABSENTM, referring to the productivity impact of temporary quits for MI workers, is not significant, but in Regression 2 the coefficient referring to the same relationship for Irish workers in general is highly significant. In both cases, the sign of the coefficient is positive, indicating that temporary separations by Irish gave them no power to control the pace of work. But the coefficient of EABSENTM shows that at the 5% level Yankee workers are significantly different than Irish workers, in the *negative* direction: high levels of temporary mobility in and out of the Mill No. 2 main weaveroom apparently gave the Yankee workers relatively more power to control the pace of work than Irish workers. The standardized impacts shown in Table 2 are, however, relatively small for both groups of workers.

As for positive incentives, the coefficient of LNPIECERM in Regression 2 indicates that all Irish were in the same unfortunate position as impermanent Irish as revealed by Regression 1: a highly significant negative relation between real income incentives and productivity. Analogous to Regression 1, Yankee workers cannot be distinguished from Irish workers at the 5% level. For both Irish and Yankees, the standardized impacts of LNPIECERM are negative at a relatively medium (but for Irish bordering on high) level.

Consistent with the findings in Table 1, the impact of BEGENDM is negative for Irish and positive for Yankees, both at a medium level. In Regression 2, BEGENDM is not statistically significant but the ETHNIC interactive is significant at the 5% level. These results suggest that "seniority" led the Yankees to work harder but the Irish to restrict their output, perhaps reflecting the greater ability of employers to inflict *unremunerated* intensification on the foreign-born workers.

Finally, the highly significant negative coefficient of ETHNICITYM shows that, for Irish workers at least, an upward trend of productivity in the Mill No. 2 main weaveroom is highly correlated with the transition from "Yankee" to "Irish" production relations. For Irish workers, the standardized impact of ETHNICITYM is negative, more than offsetting the impact of the individual experience variable, LNEXPADJM. The significant positive coefficient of EETHNICITYM indicates that in this transition, the performance of Yankee workers can be distinguished from that of Irish, the general implication being that the social conditions inherent in "average ethnicity" in a given historical period can have a significant impact on observed productivity performance.

In our view, the regression results lend support to both the "learning-by-doing" and the "production-relations" hypotheses. What can we then say about the relative impacts of technical, human capabilities, and work-effort factors in the determination of productivity change? The inevitable problem of multicollinearity among the independent variables precludes us from giving a definitive answer to this question. We cannot say precisely how much of the variance a particular variable or group of variables explains. But one way to assess the relative impacts of the different variable classifications that takes multicollinearity into account is to calculate the additions to $\bar{R}^2$ when the results of regressions containing different combinations of classifications are compared. For example, if $\bar{R}^2_{q\cdot h}$, $\bar{R}^2_{q\cdot e}$, $\bar{R}^2_{q\cdot th}$, $\bar{R}^2_{q\cdot te}$, and $\bar{R}^2_{q\cdot the}$ are compared, $(\bar{R}^2_{q\cdot the} - \bar{R}^2_{q\cdot th})$ gives us a lower-bound estimate and $\bar{R}^2_{q\cdot e}$ an upper-bound estimate of the independent impact of e variables, while $(\bar{R}^2_{q\cdot the} - \bar{R}^2_{q\cdot te})$ gives us a lower-bound estimate and $\bar{R}^2_{q\cdot h}$ an upper-bound estimate of the independent impact of h variables. Table 3 shows the lower- and upper-bound estimates of percentages of $\bar{R}^2$ explained by variable classifications.

These results suggest that the production-relations hypothesis should be given at least as much attention as the learning-by-doing hypothesis in research into the "Horndal effect." There is more to the process of labor productivity growth than the technical development of inputs. Social influences on productivity growth must be considered as well.

TABLE 3

Lower-Bound and Upper-Bound Estimates of Variance Explained by Variable Classifications (Percent)

Variable classification	Regression 1		Regression 2	
	Lower bound	Upper bound	Lower bound	Upper bound
t	5.19	5.37	5.13	5.89
h	4.69	13.65	4.07	11.18
e	11.04	23.27	10.94	21.76

Despite the extreme microeconomic nature of our data set, we recognize that there is ample room for debate over the measurement and interpretation of all three classifications of variables in our study. Our microeconomic approach, however, at least brings the issue of the socio-technical nature of production into clear view rather than burying the sources of productivity growth within aggregated data, to be barely noticed, nevermind understood. We have constructed variables in particular ways to quantify many technical and social phenomena that are not easily measured and that might be measured in other ways. We have placed specific interpretations on these variables that are suggested by our theory of the production process. Other theories and interpretations are possible. *Given* our general theoretical framework and *given* the ways we have chosen to construct, interpret, and classify our variables, we are satisfied that we have generated meaningful statistical results. The results are meaningful not because of the degree of statistical significance per se, but rather because they support our contention that further research and debate over the theory, measurement, and interpretation of the social and technical determinants of productivity growth are in order.

In particular, it should be recognized that we still do not have a direct measure of the intensity of labor, and probably never will. But measurement problems should not damn the attempt to incorporate the notion of work effort into the production function. On the contrary, by confronting these problems, we can, at a minimum, develop an enlightened skepticism of conclusions drawn from more aggregated analyses, particularly when no attempt has been made to identify or distinguish between the impacts of social and technical factors on productivity.

V. SOME BROADER IMPLICATIONS

The development of theory and the development of empirical work must go hand in hand. For the empirical issues that have been addressed in this paper, neoclassical theory is not much help. A perspective that assumes that the firm simply responds to the dictates of the market while taking technology as given cannot possibly provide us with much insight into the role of social relationships and the exercise of power in an economic system. Over a century ago, Marx argued that the *interaction* of the relations and forces of production was the key to understanding capitalist development. One need not accept Marx's conclusions (Lazonick, 1983a) to agree that this is a proposition worth exploring rather than ignoring. In our view, the present study lends empirical support to the hypothesis that productivity outcomes are significantly affected by *who* has power over whom in the production process and *how* those who possess power choose to utilize it.

In particular, this study supports the proposition that "labor scarcity" puts power in the hands (or more accurately the feet) of workers. As a consequence, labor scarcity will have an impact on the choice of technique, be it the choice of the quality of raw material (e.g., cotton), the choice of number of machines (e.g., looms) per worker, or the introduction of a new technology (i.e., *better* rather than simply more machinery). We would agree that, generally speaking, managers of capitalist firms make rational choices among alternative available techniques. But we would argue that they do not make these choices solely according to relative factor prices.[12] Conditions of labor scarcity endow the relevant workers with the power not only to demand higher wages but also to exercise more control over the pace of work in the production process. We would argue that it is the impact of labor scarcity on productivity, not just its impact on wages, that leads capitalists to look for skill-displacing techniques that will make them less dependent on "scarce" labor.

Alternatively, in conditions of "labor abundance"—as with the coming of the Irish to the vicinity of Lowell—capitalists will not only reap the benefits of lower wages, but will also take advantage of the situation to introduce more effort-intensive production techniques; that is techniques which require *more* work effort (either in the form of more extensive or intensive use of labor power) to achieve the same amount of output. One example is the propensity of capitalists to foist inferior cotton on more dependent workers. Another example is the introduction of more looms per worker without sufficient slowing of the looms to maintain work effort constant.

Lacking a theory of the role of work effort in the production function, economists and economic historians have been led to argue that an increase in the number of looms per worker makes workers more productive because they now have more capital with which to work (see for example, McGouldrick, 1968, pp. 38–40). But such an argument ignores the complementarity of capital and labor inputs in production, and confuses *more* capital with *better* capital. If a certain number of workers are given more looms of the *same* quality, more output can only result from the intensification of their labor, an outcome that is more likely to be achieved in conditions of labor abundance. It is only if these workers are given "better" looms—that is, looms that permit them to produce more output with the same input of work effort—that their labor will be aided by the "choice of technique." And, in contrast to increased capital–labor ratios resulting from stretch-outs, effort-decreasing technical change resulting from the introduction of better machinery is more likely to occur not in periods of labor abundance, but rather in periods of labor scarcity. One implication of our analysis is that economists had best begin to recognize the differences between qualitative and quantitative changes in capital–

---

[12] For debate over choice of technique in early U.S. manufacturing solely in terms of relative factor prices, see, for example, Temin (1966) and Fogel (1967).

labor ratios if they want to understand productivity growth and technological change.

Wages are neither entirely independent nor uniquely related to the intensity of labor. "External" wages function to attract workers into the workplace, but "internal" wages are intended to entice work out of workers once they are there. If, under conditions of labor abundance, an employer seeks to eliminate some or all internal earnings premiums so as to pay workers an amount closer to the external wage, an attempt by the workers to restrict output is the likely result. Alternatively, conditions of labor scarcity will inhibit managerial attempts to eliminate earnings premiums, and hence may lead workers to respond more positively to wage incentives that are tied to output. The intensity of work effort, and with it productivity, will then be determined by the "on-the-job" utility-maximizing preferences of workers, and not by the power of employers to deny any given worker a job. In other words, any observed relation between work effort and pay will depend in part on the structure of social power that characterizes the prevailing social relations of production.

Moreover, given fixed capital, unit capital costs, and hence the return on invested capital, depend to some extent on work effort applied in combination with that capital (Lazonick, 1984). Factor prices are an outcome of the social relations of production as well as a precondition for the choice of technique. To explain not only productivity but also profitability, the interactions of factor prices, technology, and social organization must be analyzed in terms of a dynamic historical process.

The basic argument of this study is that alternative opportunities for attaining a "living" are important determinants of both the productivity of individual workers and the wages they receive. If different groups of workers such as Yankees or Irish—or men or women—face distinctly different alternative opportunities at a point in time or over time, we can expect that the unit labor cost outcomes across these groups of workers will be markedly different. It may be ill-advised, therefore, to impute productivity differences to wage differences of different segments of the labor force, as is done for example by both sides of a recent debate on productivity in the early New England textile industry (David, 1975, Chap. 2; Nickless, 1979). In our study, as the Irish entered the Mill No. 2 main weaveroom, real wages fell while labor productivity rose—if one's measure of "labor quality" is real wages, the Irish were "lower quality" workers than Yankees, but if one's measure of "labor quality" is labor productivity the Irish were "higher quality" workers. The higher levels of productivity achieved with the coming of the Irish were not, moreover, because the Irish had more "human capital" than the Yankees; in all probability they had less. If, on the basis of the productivity criterion, the Irish were "higher quality" workers than the Yankees, it was because employers found it easier to intensify their labor.

Economists have to rethink the whole concept of exploitation. They might start by going back to the distinction, put forth by Marx over a century ago, between the capacity to work and work actually performed, *given* the wage. The neoclassical notion of exploitation as consisting of wages below the value of the marginal product of labor has little to commend it. In the Marxian model, the ability of employers to exploit workers depends upon the existence of a reserve army of labor; that is, a situation where the labor demand curve intersects a perfectly elastic segment of the labor supply curve (Lazonick, 1983a). Given technology and human capabilities, productivity will depend upon the intensity of labor achieved in production. Given the supply price of labor, exploitation will depend on the degree of intensification. Higher degrees of intensification will shift the marginal product of labor curve upwards. *Given* the demand for labor curve (determined in part by the degree of intensification), the fact that profit-maximizing capitalists employ additional units of labor to the point where the market wage just equals the value of the marginal product of labor is incidental to the analysis of exploitation.

Finally, with the intrusion of conflict, power relations, and variations in work effort into the theory of production, the notion of "efficiency" that is so central to neoclassical orthodoxy ceases to be an objective measure of performance capability or welfare. The possibility that productivity may be raised by unremunerated intensification of labor should lead us to ask: efficient for whom? In the production process, the notion of "Pareto-optimal" moves, where nobody is made worse off than before, is only tenable if the structure of relative power is taken as given and remains unchanged. As often as not, references to "efficient" or "Pareto-optimal" outcomes mean only that the economist either views the production function as technically determined or considers a particular structure of production relations as ideal.

APPENDIX: DEFINITION OF VARIABLES

All variables refer to *monthly* observations for individual weavers in the Lawrence Mill No. 2 main weaveroom unless otherwise indicated.

Dependent variable: YWH = Output per weaver–hour of type C cloth.

Independent variables:

(1) $D1, \ldots, D11$ = monthly adjustments for variations in technical capability, where $D1 = 1$ if January, 0 otherwise; $D2 = 1$ if February, 0 otherwise; . . .; $D11 = 1$ if November, 0 otherwise.

Dryer weather exacerbated problems of yarn breakages, holding other factors constant. Mean monthly measures of relative humidity for the Boston area averaged over the years 1886 through 1890 (for which the data are first available) were January, 73.1; February, 72.4; March, 70.8; April, 67.1; May, 74.9; June, 77.1; July, 78.8; August, 79.4; September, 82.9; October, 78.1; November, 74.9; December, 72.7. *Blue Hill Mete-*

orological Observatory, Mudge: Boston, 1886 and Wilson: Cambridge, 1887–1890.

(2) DTECH1 = a dummy variable to control for the introduction of a let-off motion on the looms in May 1835; 0 for every month prior to May 1835, 1 for May 1835 and every month thereafter.

Evidence on the introduction of the let-off motion and details of its mode of operation and function can be found in Lawrence Manufacturing Company records, Baker Library, Manuscripts Division, MAB-1, Letters from William Austin to Henry Hall, March 5, 1835 and May 1, 1835; James Montgomery, *A Practical Detail of the Cotton Manufacture of the U.S.A. Compared with that of Great Britain,* Niven: Glasgow, 1840, 103; Richard Marsden, *Cotton Weaving,* Bell: London, 1895, 72; Amasa Stone versus William and Amasa Sprague, Depositions from the trial, Rhode Island District Court, June Term 1840 at Newport, Rhode Island, located at Archives Branch, Federal Archives and Records Center, National Archives, Waltham, Massachusetts.

(3) DTECH2 = a dummy variable to control for the introduction of a new type of cotton picker into the mills of the Lawrence Manufacturing Company in August 1844; 0 for every month prior to August 1844, 1 for August 1844 and every month thereafter.

Evidence on the introduction of these cotton pickers into the Lawrence mills can be found in Lawrence Mfg. Co., MA-1, Letter from Henry Hall to William Aiken, September 26, 1845; BB-2, Ledgers, August 1844 and August 1845.

(4) DCOT2 = the cotton quality variable, RCOTL (defined below), interacted with DTECH2.

(5) WPOW = a dummy variable to control for known water power shortages for the Lowell mills; 1 for months during which power shortages occurred, 0 for all other months.

The identification of these power shortages is based upon an exhaustive search of the 79-volume collection of bound letters, most of them written to or by James B. Francis, the hydraulic engineer at the Lowell Locks and Canals. Proprietors of Locks and Canals records, Manuscripts Division, A-1 through A-79. The evidence is summarized in Linda Gray, *Water Power at Lowell,* photocopy, Harvard University, August 1983. There is evidence for water power shortages in 1838, 1839, 1840, 1849, and 1852. In addition, we included a known power shortage that occurred in 1846 due to a combination of seasonal shortage and increased demand for power as new mills were opened. Subsequently the supply of water power was expanded to meet this increased demand by the building of the Northern Canal. Where the precise duration of the power shortage was not cited in the Francis letters, a graph of capacity utilization was used to determine how many months on either side of the month cited were likely to have had water shortages. In addition the late summer and fall months of 1841 were so similar to periods of known shortage that occurred in the previous 3 years that we decided to include them as well. September and October of 1845 were also included as power shortage months because capacity utilization during these months exhibited similar characteristics to capacity utilization during the power shortage months of 1846. Power shortage months are 1838(08,09,10), 1839(07,08,09,10,11), 1840(07,08,09,10), 1841(08,09,10,11), 1845(09,10), 1846(08,09,10,11,12), 1847(01), 1849(07,08,09,10), 1852(08,09,10,11).

(6) LNTIME = a measure of learning by doing by Mill No. 2 = logarithm of the cumulative months since Lawrence Mill No. 2 opened for operation in January 1834.

(7) LNEXPADJ = a measure of learning by doing by individual weavers = logarithm of number of cumulative days worked by each weaver whose name appears on the payroll in any given month.

There is a 2-year gap in the payroll records between April 1836 and April 1838. The experience variable is therefore adjusted to add days of experience for those workers who were in the weaveroom during both April 1836 and April 1838. Since the entire mill was shut down for 9 months during the intervening period, we need not adjust for that portion of the gap. We assume also that the average worker under consideration was away from the mill for an additional month before and after the shutdown, leaving 13 months of potential experience that might be ascribed to each worker. Thirteen months (at an average of 27 days per month) are then multiplied by the individual worker's absent rate in April 1838 to yield the days of experience imputed to the payroll-gap period.

(8) CAPUTIL = a measure of capacity utilization during any given month = the proportion of total loom capacity utilized each month = $[(A*B)+(C*B*D)]/(144*E)$, where

A = total days worked by piecehands in a given month,
B = average loom complement of piecehands in that month,
C = total days worked by sparehands in that month,
D = ratio of sparehand productivity to piecehand productivity in that month,
E = Mill No. 2 working days in that month,
and 144 is the number of looms in the Mill No. 2 main weaveroom.

Average daily output per sparehand during any given month is defined as total Mill No. 2 output minus the output of *all* Mill No. 2 weaving piecehands (in both main and auxiliary rooms), divided by the total number of sparehand days worked during the month. Our measure of capacity utilization is rendered inexact by the facts that we know neither the precise number of sparehands nor the precise number of looms tended by sparehands working in the *main* weaveroom. We estimate these values and use them to construct our measure of capacity utilization. The fact that CAPUTIL exceeds 1.0 from time to time (see Fig. 3) despite fixed loom capacity reflects measurement errors in our estimation of these factors. Nevertheless, we believe that CAPUTIL provides a very good index of actual capacity utilization in the Mill No. 2 weaveroom from 1834 through 1855.

(9) SPARPAUX = the number of *auxiliary* sparehands per piecehand in any given month = $[A(1-B)]/C$, where

A = total days worked by sparehands in a given month,

B = ratio of sparehand productivity to piecehand productivity in that month,

C = total days worked by piecehands in that month.

This measure of sparehands per piecehand nets out sparehands who might have been themselves tending looms, and therefore could not have been providing auxiliary services to piecehands.

(10) LPW = average number of looms tended by each weaver in a given month.

We do not in fact have direct evidence on looms per weaver. LPW was derived from information on the piece rates paid at any point in time as well as the trend in *average* number of looms per weaver for the weaveroom. Combining this trend with changes in piece rates over time allows us to distinguish between piece-rate cuts that were wage reductions per se and piece-rate cuts that were due to workers tending more looms. Benchmarks from sources internal to Lowell mills, newspaper accounts, and outside observers at Lowell corroborated our decisions of which piece rates to link to which loom complements. Figure 4 shows the average number of looms per weaver in any given month.

(11) RCOTL = an index of the quality of cotton actually used in main weaveroom production in any given month = the ratio of the price paid per pound of cotton, net of the cost of freight, insurance, and drayage, to the monthly price per pound of *standard quality* Upland cotton in New York.

Upland cotton prices are from Arthur H. Cole, *Wholesale Commodity Prices in the U.S., 1700–1861,* Harvard UP: Cambridge, 1938. The price paid by the mill for cotton, the weight of cotton shipped, as well as freight, insurance, and drayage charges are reported semiannually in Lawrence Mfg. Co. records, HA-2. Hence, the net price that the mill paid for cotton that is derived from these records is an average of the current month and the previous 5 months. The data from the semiannual accounts are interpolated to yield monthly data. The resulting series is lagged 3 months to represent the middle of the biannual reporting period. In order to match this derivation of the price that the mill paid for cotton in any given month as closely as possible to the New York price of standard quality (''middling'') Upland cotton that was in effect when this cotton was purchased (and in the process adjust as well for delivery time from New York, New Orleans, and Charleston to Lowell), we calculated the correlation coefficients of the mill's net price of cotton at time of purchase with the current New York Uplands cotton price, as well as with the New York price lagged 1 month through 5 months.

	Monthly lag in the New York price of cotton					
	0	1	2	3	4	5
Correlation coefficient	0.87747	0.88916	0.89436	0.89434	0.88777	0.87822

These coefficients suggest that a 2- to 3-month lag on the New York cotton price matches the mill's current net cotton price derived from the biannual records. In order to allow for this lag while at the same time making the form of the New York price series similar to the interpolated mill price series, we constructed a New York price series based upon a 6-month running average of the current month and 5 lagged months.

(12) OPW = overseers per worker (piecehands plus sparehands) in any given month.

(13) ABSENT = a measure of temporary separations while employed in the Mill No. 2 main weaveroom for individual weavers present in any given month = the ratio of the total number of workdays absent to the total number of workdays possible for every month in which a weaver worked at least 1 day.

(14) FALLPRES = a measure of the extent to which weavers depart temporarily for the summer and fall months = the number of days present in all prior mid-June through mid-November periods (calendar payroll months July through November) as a proportion of the total workdays possible over all prior mid-June through mid-November periods since that weaver first entered the Mill No. 2 main weaveroom.

Either the same values are entered from December through June of the current stint in the weaveroom, or zero is entered until a weaver has been present for at least 1 day during a July to November period. During July through November the value of FALLPRES is recalculated from month to month if the worker is present in any one of the months.

(15) LPQUITD = the proportion of weavers who quit the Mill No. 2 main weaveroom permanently in any given month = $A - B$, if $B > 0$, and $LPW_{t-1} > LPW_{t-2}$, or $CAPUTIL_{t-1} < CAPUTIL_{t-2}$; otherwise A; where

$$A = \frac{\text{permanent separations in } t - 1}{\text{number of weavers who worked in } t - 1},$$

$$B = \frac{(\text{weaver positions in } t - 2) - (\text{weaver positions in } t - 1)}{\text{weaver positions in } t - 2},$$

t = current month.

The proportion of permanent separations (A) has been adjusted by deducting any decrease in the stock of permanent positions available from the previous month that are clearly the result of underutilization of capacity or increases in loom complements (B), so that $A - B$ reflects only voluntary quits and does not include layoffs. Some of the decreases in the stock of permanent positions may have been due to absolute labor shortages (which, judging from managerial correspondence, did occur at times), and hence should not be counted as permanent layoffs. We have not, therefore, deducted decreases in the stock of permanent positions if *both* capacity utilization was rising and the number of looms per weaver was not increasing. We have been unable to make an adjustment for workers who transferred to other rooms or mills of the Lawrence Manufacturing Company.

(16) TEACH = an index of the remuneration and relative availability of teaching jobs for "literate" weavers = $[LIT*(A \div B)]/C$

  A = number of positions for female teachers in Massachusetts in a given month,

  B = wages of female teachers in Massachusetts in that month,

  C = number of positions for female operatives in Lowell in that month, and ;

  LIT = ·a measure of literacy = 1 if a weaver manifests the ability to sign her name, 0 if otherwise.

Data on numbers of female teachers from 1833–1834 to 1836–1837 and from 1838–1839 through the end of our period, and data on wages of female teachers for 1836–1837 and from 1838–1839 to the end of our period can be found in the *Annual Reports of the Massachusetts Board of Education*. Wage data for 1833–1834 through 1835–1836 were gathered from the manuscript material at the Massachusetts State House Archives. But data for 1837–1838 do not appear to be available in either published or manuscript form, and may never have been collected. Since 1837–1838 was a year for which Lawrence payroll records were also missing, only months from April through August 1838 had missing information. An average of the values for wages and teaching positions in 1836–1837 and 1838–1839 were used for these months. For all other months, annual data were converted to monthly data by assigning the same value for the entire school year starting in September and ending in August.

Data on the number of female workers in Lowell come from the *Annual Statistics of Manufacturing in Lowell*, Vox Populi: Lowell ("Statistics of Lowell Manufacturers"). The yearly figures were assumed to apply to January of that year, and were then converted to monthly data by interpolation.

"Literacy" is determined by whether or not a worker manifested the ability to sign her name in the payroll books. If a worker made a mark in the shape of a cursive L—$\mathscr{L}$—it generally meant that she was present at the mill on payday but could not sign her name. If she was not present, the Mill Agent would write an X or a friend might sign for her. A cursive

L is therefore the most distinctive indication that we possess of "illiteracy" while repeated signatures are the most distinctive indication of "literacy."

(17) LNPIECER = a measure of earnings incentives for weavers in any given month = the logarithm of the average real piece rate times the average loom complement = $\log\{[(A*B) \div C]/D\}$, where

A = average loom complement in a given month,

B = total piece earnings in that month,

C = total yards produced by piecehands in that month, and

D = 0.01 (price index), where the price index used is Arthur Cole's "All Commodity Index of Wholesale Prices," in Cole, *Wholesale Commodity Prices.*

(18) BEGEND = a measure of seniority = in a given month, the total elapsed time since a weaver first entered the Mill No. 2 main weaveroom.

(19) ETHNIC = ethnicity = the probability that a person is non-Irish.

(20) ETHNICITY = a measure of the ethnic composition (that is, "Yankeeness") of the main weaveroom = the proportion of weavers in any given month who are non-Irish.

The ethnicity of workers at Lawrence Manufacturing Company is unknown because register books that may have contained such information (as, for example, Dublin used for the Hamilton mills in *Women at Work*) have not survived. We therefore had to estimate the probability that a given name in our data base is Irish or non-Irish. Virtually all non-Irish workers in our data base were either English, Scottish, or American-born of British ancestry. For the sake of brevity (although not complete descriptive accuracy) we have labeled all these non-Irish as "Yankees."

To estimate these probabilities, we have drawn upon four relevant data sets in which the ethnicity of particular individuals is known.

Data sets used to determine ethnicity

	Set 1[a]	Set 2[b]	Set 3[c]	Set 4[d]	Total
Last names					
Irish	27,746	345	292	405	28,788
Non-Irish	9,525	830	263	10,375	20,993
Unknown				2,895	
Total					49,781
Women's first names					
Irish		291	226		517
Non-Irish		664	199		863
Total					1,380

[a] This data set was supplied by the Philadelphia Social History Project, University of Pennsylvania (funded by the National Institute of Mental Health, National Science Foundation, National Endowment for the Humanities, and the National Institute of Child Health and Human Development). It contains names and ethnicities of Philadelphia region males, 18 years of age and older, from the 1850 census manuscripts. Henry

Williams, Assistant Director of the Project, provided supplementary advice, including the warning that the list of 9525 "non-Irish" names contains a "not insignificant number of second generation Irish." Since the census was made in 1850, any second generation 18+ males would have had to have been born in the United States before 1832, a time at which there were relatively few Irish in the country. Hence we decided to leave the file as is rather than risk even greater distortion of the results by seeking to identify the second-generation Irish.

[b] The Murray Center at Harvard University stores the data files that Thomas Dublin prepared for *Women at Work* (Columbia UP, 1979). The file that was used here includes all workers at the Hamilton Mfg. Co. who were present in August 1850, from which we selected only those individuals with known ethnicity.

[c] This data set was prepared by Steven J. Dubnoff for his dissertation, "The Family and Absence from Work: Irish Workers in a Lowell, Mass. Cotton Mill, 1860," Brandeis University, April 1976. The data file contains the names and ethnicity of workers in Mill A of the Hamilton Mfg. Co. in June 1860.

[d] The Register books of the Hamilton Mfg. Col, Volumes 482, 483, 485, 486, 487, 488, 489, and 490, Manuscripts and Archives Division of Baker Library, were used to supply this list of names and ethnicities. Only the names of individuals who were leaving were used so that names drawn from the register books through March 19, 1849 (Vol. 490) would not overlap with the names in Dublin's file, which includes individuals present in the Hamilton Co. in August 1850.

The first stage of assigning the probability of Irish or non-Irish ethnicity to particular names involved ascertaining the frequency that a given unique last name was Irish or non-Irish from the "population" of last names comprised of the 49,781 surnames of known ethnicity. Since two names could have been the same name phonetically but have been spelled differently by an agent or an illiterate worker, a more liberal phonetic assignment was used on 1730, or 3.5% of the total names (all of which were in the Dublin and Dubnoff samples). Once the frequencies of Irish or non-Irish last names were established, frequencies of women workers' first names were calculated using the Dublin and Dubnoff samples (using the same phonetic rules as for last names). The next step involved pulling out all individuals who, on the basis of surnames, had a 100% probability of being either Irish or non-Irish. The average ethnicity per month of these individuals established a trend rate of ethnicity over the period. The probable ethnicity of individuals who do not have a 100% probability of being Irish or non-Irish depends upon when the individual first arrived in the mill. For example, one might say that a "Catherine Hagar" had a greater probability of being Irish if she arrived in 1855 than if she arrived in 1834. The final step was to use the first and last name probabilities calculated from the four samples to assign an ethnicity probability to each individual in the Lawrence Mill No. 2 sample. The following rules were used: (1) If an individual's surname frequency was 75–100% Irish or non-Irish, then the individual was assigned that probability of being Irish or non-Irish, respectively. (2) If the surname frequency of an individual was between 25 and 75% Irish or non-Irish then the frequency of that individual's first name was also used in the calculation of an equal footing with the surname. (3) If no probability was available for a given surname, then probable ethnicity was assigned by the frequency of first name ethnicity. (4) If no surname or first name frequency was available for an individual, then that individual was assigned the value of the trend in ethnicity for the first month that the individual arrived in Mill No. 2.

REFERENCES

Arrow, K. J. (1962), "The Economic Implications of Learning By Doing." *Review of Economic Studies*, **29**, 155–173.

Bidwell, P., and Falconer, J. (1925), *History of Agriculture in the Northern U.S. 1620–1860*. Washington: Carnegie.

Brush, T. (1981), "The Nature of the Labor Force and Its Relation to Productivity: A Case Study of the Lawrence Mill #2 Upper Weaving Room, 1834–1855," photocopy. Cambridge, Mass.: Harvard University.

Brush, T. (1983), "Transformations and Tests Required to Estimate a Pooled Time-Series Cross-Section Fixed Effects Model," photocopy. Cambridge, Mass.: Harvard University.

David, P. (1973), "The 'Horndal Effect' in Lowell, 1834–1856." *Explorations in Economic History*, **10**, 131–150.

David, P. (1975), *Technical Choice, Innovation and Economic Growth*. Cambridge, England: Cambridge Univ. Press.

Dublin, T. (1979), *Women at Work: The Transformation of Work and Community at Lowell, Massachusetts, 1826–1860*. New York: Columbia Univ. Press.

Dubnoff, S. J. (1976), "The Family and Absence from Work: Irish Workers in a Lowell, Mass. Cotton Mill, 1860." Ph.D. thesis. Waltham, Mass.: Brandeis University.

Eno, A. L. (Ed.) (1976), *Cotton Was King*. Somersworth, N.H.: New Hampshire Publishing Co.

Field, A. J. (1978), "Sectoral Shift in Antebellum Massachusetts: A Reconsideration." *Explorations in Economic History*, **15**, 146–171.

Fellner, W. (1969), "Specific Interpretations of Learning by Doing." *Journal of Economic Theory*, **1**, 119–140.

Fogel, R. (1967), "The Specification Problem in Economic History." *Journal of Economic History*, **37**, 283–308.

Hausman, J. A. (1978), "Specification Tests in Econometrics." *Econometrica*, November, 1251–1271.

Helper, S., and Lazonick, W. (1984), "Learning Curves and Productivity Growth in Institutional Context." Harvard Institute of Economic Research Discussion Paper No. 1066, June.

Hirschman, A. O. (1970), *Exit, Voice, and Loyalty*. Cambridge, Mass.: Harvard Univ. Press.

Hsiao, C. (1985), *An Analysis of Panel Data*. Cambridge, England: Cambridge Univ. Press (forthcoming).

Lazonick, W. (1981), "Production Relations, Labor Productivity, and Choice of Technique: British and U.S. Cotton Spinning." *Journal of Economic History*, **43**, 491–516.

Lazonick, W. (1983a), "Class Relations and the Capitalist Enterprise: A Critical Assessment of the Foundations of Marxian Economic Theory." Harvard Institute of Economic Research Discussion Paper No. 980.

Lazonick, W. (1983b), "Industrial Organization and Technological Change: The Decline of the British Cotton Industry." *Business History Review*, 57, 195–236.

Lazonick, W. (1984), "Work Effort, Pay, and Productivity: Theoretical Implications of Some Historical Research," photocopy. Cambridge, Mass.: Harvard University.

Lazonick, W., and Mass, W. (1984), "The Performance of the British Cotton Industry, 1870–1913." *Research in Economic History*, 9, 1–44.

Leibenstein, H. (1966), "Allocative Efficiency vs. 'X-Efficiency'." *American Economic Review*, 56, 392–415.

Lundberg, E. (1961), *Produktivitet och Räntabilitet*. Stockholm: Norstedt & Söner.

Mass. W. (1984), Technological Change and Industrial Relations: The Diffusion of Automatic Weaving in Britain and the United States, Ph.D. thesis, Boston College.

McGouldrick, P. (1968), *New England Textiles in the Nineteenth Century*. Cambridge, Mass.: Harvard Univ. Press.

Nickless, P. (1979), "A New Look at Productivity in the New England Textile Industry, 1830–1860." *Journal of Economic History*, 39, 889–910.

Preston, J. A. (1982), Feminization of an Occupation: Teaching Women's Work in 19th-Century New England, Ph.D. thesis. Waltham, Mass.: Brandeis University.

Rapping, L. (1965), "Learning and World War II Production Functions." *Review of Economics and Statistics*, 47, 81–86.

Sheshinski, E. (1967), "Tests of the 'Learning by Doing' Hypothesis." *Review of Economics and Statistics*, 49, 568–578.

Söderlund, E. (Ed.) (1957–1958), *Fagerstabrukens Historia*. Uppsala: Almquist Wiksells.

Temin, P. (1966), "Labor Scarcity and the Problem of American Industrial Efficiency in the 1850s." *Journal of Economic History*, 36, 277–297.

Thernstrom, S. (1964), *Poverty and Progress*. Cambridge, Mass.: Harvard Univ. Press.

Wallace, T. D., and Hussain, A. (1969), "The Use of Error Components Models in Combining Cross Section with Time Series Data." *Econometrica*, 37, January, 55–72.

Ware, C. (1966), *The Early New England Cotton Manufacture*. New York: Russell & Russell.

Wilson, H. F. (1936), *The Hill Country of Northern New England*. New York: Columbia Univ. Press.

Zevin, R. B., (1975), *The Growth of Manufacturing in Early Nineteenth Century New England*. New York: Arno.

[6]

THE BREAKING OF THE AMERICAN WORKING CLASS

William Lazonick

David Montgomery. *The Fall of the House of Labor.* New York: Cambridge University Press, 1987. xii + 494 pp. Notes and index. $27.95.

The Fall of the House of Labor supersedes David Montgomery's own *Workers' Control in America* (1979) as the most ambitious attempt to date to document and interpret labor-management conflicts over shop-floor work organization in the late nineteenth and early twentieth centuries. The author delves into the role of "scientific management" in transforming hierarchical and technical divisions of labor in a wide range of industries from coalmining to electrical manufacturing. He also explores the working-class responses, both industrial and political, to scientific management. Leading the opposition, Montgomery argues, were a "militant minority" of working-class activists, aided by sympathetic individuals "from other social strata" who sought to "weld their workmates and neighbors into a self-aware and purposeful working class" (p. 2).

The attempt to link working-class politics to changes in work organization centers upon how management sought to take control of the workplace by taking skills off the shop floor. The historical point of departure is widespread craft control in the 1870s and 1880s. "The manager's brains under the workmen's cap" (ch. 1) contends that craft workers' ability to exercise shop-floor control "drew strength from [their] functional autonomy on the job, from the group ethical code that they developed around their work relations, and from the organizations they created for themselves to protect their interests and values" (p. 13).

Given the nineteenth-century heritage of craft autonomy, *The Fall of the House of Labor* seeks to explain why American workers' "unprecedented quest for power" in the first two decades of this century failed to prevent the degradation of work and build an independent labor party. Not only did managerial control supersede workers' control on the shop floor, but by the 1920s the labor movement had also given up on the possibility of exercising an independent political voice. It would, as a result, be all the more difficult for American workers to regain control over the workplace when militant unionism once again arose out of the debacle of the 1930s.

Most of the book covers the building of a militant labor movement in the first two decades of this century. With the quadrupling of union membership in the United States in the period 1897–1903—years during which, not coincidentally, the Great Merger Movement concentrated the power of business—the American Federation of Labor "for the first time secured its place as the 'House of Labor' " (p. 5). The dominant creed was Gompers's pure and simple unionism. Nevertheless, Montgomery argues that "[b]efore the 1920s the house of labor had many mansions"; the ranks of the AFL "teemed with socialists, Catholic activists, single taxpayers, and philosophical anarchists" (p. 6). Dissident movements, and especially the International Workers of the World, that arose outside the walls of labor's estate at first served to buttress the militancy swelling up within the "legitimate" labor movement. So too did the federal government's alliance with the unions during World War I as part of an effort to encourage high levels of productivity in the face of acute labor shortages.

Three types of workers, differentiated by skill, made up the American working class (see chs. 2–4). Common laborers, their work virtually unchanged from the 1880s to the 1920s, were peripheral to the rise of the militant labor movement. With the exceptions of unskilled dock and building workers, attempts to unionize common laborers appealed primarily to ethnic ties rather than occupational or industrial solidarities. In contrast, the work of both craftsmen and operatives was subject to constant redivisions of labor, both technical and hierarchical, that were key to managerial strategies to end their reliance on craft skills and increase the pace of work.

Basic to traditional craft control had been the "stint"—an accepted norm for the amount of output that represented "a reasonable day's work" (p. 7). By adhering to the stint, craftsmen could protect the quality of their working lives, maintain the quality of the work that they produced, and, for any given level of product demand, control the number of jobs available to their brothers. The possession of skills upon which an employer had to rely gave craftsmen the balance of power in determining what represented "a reasonable day's work."

"White shirts and superior intelligence" (ch. 5), explores how employers turned to scientific management to reduce their reliance on craft skills. As the primary "deskilling" mechanism, Montgomery posits the transformation of key craft jobs into salaried positions:

> Skilled workers in large enterprises did not disappear, but most of them ceased to be production workers. Their tasks became ancillary—setup, troubleshooting, toolmaking, model making—while the actual production was increasingly carried out by specialized operatives. [p. 215]

As late as 1919, Montgomery reveals, rollers at U.S. Steel agonized over whether to join the steel strike because the company's practice of paying them annual salaries made them "part of management."

Yet incorporating skills into the managerial structure did not eliminate resistance on the shop floor. "By the turn of the century," Montgomery argues, "managerial reformers were concerned as much about their operatives' behavior as about that of their craftsmen" (p. 149), especially during booms when tight labor markets meant that workers could resist speed-up and wage cuts by quitting undesirable jobs. The successful open-shop drive of the first decade of the century and the IWW advocacy of shop-floor sabotage as a response to managerial power both served to intensify the shop-floor conflicts.

As Montgomery recounts in " 'Our time . . . believes in change' " (ch. 6), the growth of the Socialist Party between the turn of the century and World War I reflected the radicalization of the American labor movement. Although the Socialist Party "had no formula for coping with scientific management on the job," it did advocate the broad-based political movement for workplace democracy that would be necessary to confront the growing power of the industrial corporations. Around 1907, the Socialists took control of the International Association of Machinists (IAM). But Socialist politics had no appeal in the building trades, in which work organization had remained essentially unchanged from the previous century. In 1912–13 the building workers' support for Gompers prevented the Socialists from taking control of the AFL.

If Socialist politics built upon the breakdown of craft control, revolutionary syndicalism drew support from workers in mass production industries such as autos and electrical manufacturers in which managerial control over work organization had become a *fait accompli*. Unorganized operatives could not build new political organizations to bolster traditional craft prerogatives but rather used whatever sources of "direct action" might gain the attention of the powerful mass producers, as happened for example at Westinghouse in Turtle Creek Valley, Pennsylvania in 1915–16.

Employers' groups did attempt to reach accords with labor during these years of rising militancy. In 1900, under the auspices of the National Civic Federation, the International Association of Machinists and the National Metal Trades Association entered into the Murray Hill·Agreement that sought to promote stable industrial relations by granting workers a shorter workday if they would agree not to interfere with managerial strategies to reorganize shop-floor work. The Agreement quickly broke down; even for the sake of shorter hours (which they could in any case continue to demand through other political means), the workers were unwilling to give up control over output norms, manning ratios, apprenticeship, and modes of payment.

In the aftermath of the 1914 Ludlow massacre, Rockefeller's representative, William Lyon Mackenzie King, formulated the Colorado Industrial Plan; a new agenda to restore industrial peace that recognized that the United States had a "dual economy." As Montgomery details in chapter 7, King hoped to convince the AFL to accept a nonunion corporate sector with managerial control of work organization and income distribution in exchange for corporate support of the established unions in the competitive sector of the economy, where collective bargaining still prevailed.

Within each of the prosperous corporate oligopolies, King argued, workers' cooperation could be secured by using some of the firm's surplus revenues to improve working conditions and increase wages. To ensure that workers could express their preferences and air their grievances, each corporation should establish an employee-representation plan or company union. The corporate goal was to secure, as King put it, "a maximum of publicity with a minimum of interference in all that pertains to the conditions of employment" (p. 350).

"A maximum of publicity" meant that management would pay attention to workers' needs; "a minimum of interference" that management would have control over shop-floor standards. In " 'This great struggle for democracy' " (ch. 8), Montgomery shows how U.S. entry into World War I quickly expanded the "maximum of publicity" side of the agenda as, with markets tight and militancy on the rise, the government took the lead in structuring institutions to secure the cooperation of labor. Through the National War Labor Board, government intervention sought to ensure workers that they would not suffer discrimination because of union membership and that they could augment the supply of labor effort to the war effort without jeopardizing existing output, employment, and payment standards.

Government wartime involvement empowered social reformers within the Democratic Party—among whom Frank P. Walsh, co-chair of the NWLB, was most prominent—who sought to continue state support of labor in the postwar era in order to create "industrial democracy" in the private sector. In 1919, however, the dismantling of the NWLB and the defeat of labor in the great steel strike went hand in hand. In the 1920s, organized labor's influence over conditions of work and pay in the corporate sector vanished.

In concluding the book, Montgomery shows that corporate managers did not consider "a maximum of publicity with a minimum of interference" (the title of the final chapter) to be two independent agendas. The institutional arrangements through which management responded to workers' needs and grievances would also determine the extent to which management could exercise control over work organization on the shop floor.

The "maximum of publicity" that U.S. corporate employers would contemplate to gain the cooperation of workers depended first and foremost upon eliminating the "interference" of militants in the organized labor movement. The attack on revolutionary activists had already begun during the war; the wartime accord to maintain existing workplace standards was entirely consistent with attacks on those factions in the labor movement that might use emergency conditions to improve labor's position. After the war, the Palmer Raids of 1919–20 and systematic deportations of foreign-born "subversives" during the 1920s helped to finish the job.

In contrast with prewar corporate liberalism, the deradicalization of the labor movement reduced the need for corporate statesmen to forge political links with the more conservative AFL leadership to contain labor activism. Nor, with the postwar dismantling of the NWLB, could workers count upon the Democratic Party to provide even the mainstream of the labor movement with direct influence on American political life. Such influence would have to come from an independent labor party, and such a party would have to be built by the "progressive bloc"—primarily miners, railroad workers, and machinists—in the AFL. But, with union membership declining precipitously in the early 1920s in the wake of a renewed open-shop drive and high unemployment, Gompers's counsels of conservatism defeated the progressives. In the early 1920s the AFL expelled dissidents, and, to quote Montgomery, "AFL officials who had once been vociferous reformers now believed they had to bide their time until a more favorable political climate would allow them to lead a union resurgence" (p. 7).

Labor influence over workplace organization did not completely vanish in the 1920s. An alliance of progressive unionists with Taylor Society veterans (who had learned from experience that effective standards could not be set without the consent of the workers) resulted in union-management cooperation in the repair shops of the Baltimore & Ohio Railroad. The AFL touted this model of industrial democracy to the major industrial corporations, but they showed no interest. As Montgomery's extended case study of General Electric's policies and practices in the 1920s shows, the powerful manufacturing·enterprises were able to solve "the labor problem" with "a minimum of interference"—that is, without union participation in the determination of work organization or pay.

The GE experience was repeated throughout the corporate sector. "By the mid-1920s," Montgomery argues, "the designs of corporate management had clearly prevailed over those of its rivals . . ." (p. 464). During the rest of the 1920s, each worker had to settle for what he or she could get individually. The industrial corporations had succeeded in not only tearing down the house of labor that had sought to protect workers' collective interests based upon shop-floor control, but also replacing it with a structure in which control over the workplace resided within the managerial hierarchy.

Unfortunately, Montgomery fails to provide us with a concluding synthesis of his arguments, let alone a discussion of the implications of his interpretation for alternative perspectives on the evolution of the American labor movement. The eight-page section that ends the last chapter of *The Fall of the House of Labor* bears that title, "Bricks for a new house." But Montgomery analyzes neither the social composition of these "new bricks" nor how the new "house of labor" that would be built in the following decades would be constructed upon the ruins of the old.

The struggle over shop-floor control was, as Montgomery contends, central to the rise and fall of the American labor movement in the first three decades of the century. There is, however, a glaring weakness in his analysis of how management won the struggle, with critical implications for understanding the evolution of American class relations. Montgomery accords virtually no role to technological change in the transformation of the U.S. industrial workplace that culminated in the "fall of the house of labor." Focusing almost exclusively on the intellectual concerns of the "new labor history," Montgomery neglects a large and growing body of research in economic history, business history, and the history of technology that permits us to analyze the dynamic interaction between labor-management relations and technological change in structuring work organization during the rise and consolidation of U.S. managerial capitalism.[1]

The failure to analyze the role of technological change is evident in Montgomery's one-sided treatment of the impact of Taylorism on work organization around the turn of the century. He asserts that in the metalworking industries, where "scientific management" developed, "[n]o continuous-flow processes or mechanical remedies were available to rid employers of their dependence on their craftsmen's skill and initiative" (p. 213). As a result, "Taylor and his disciples had virtually nothing to say about what different machinery might do for efficiency. *Their thinking was riveted on commandeering the craftsmen's knowledge*" (p. 232, my emphasis).

Montgomery neglects both Taylor's own technological inventions and the role of technology in "scientific management." According to W. Paul Strassmann, Taylor is "generally considered the outstanding inventor of machine tools in the last two decades of the [nineteenth] century."[2] Even Montgomery (in a rare statement on the impact of technology) admits that Taylor's experiments in "the art of cutting metals" that resulted in the invention of high-speed tool steel "made possible a new relationship between engineer and machinist" because it "rendered the machinists' traditional knowledge of proper cutting speeds and feeds obsolete" (p. 231).

In the 1880s and 1890s Taylor developed his ideas on shop-floor management and sought to put them into practice in machine shops, such as those at Midvale and Bethlehem, that were among the most modern in the world.

In his role as a shop-floor engineer, Taylor had neither the responsibility nor authority to invest in new technology. But he did have the responsibility and authority to ensure the productive utilization of the investments that his capitalist employers had already made. The challenge that confronted Taylor and his followers was to achieve what Alfred Chandler has called "economies of speed"; that is, to secure the high levels of throughput in the machine shops required to transform the high fixed costs of investments in the state-of-the-art plant and equipment into low unit costs.[3]

Montgomery ignores technological change as a general phenomenon in the late nineteenth century. He argues that "[o]verall . . . the steady increase in manufacturing output [during the Coolidge years] was caused by new production methods, in sharp contrast to the last third of the nineteenth century, when new inputs of labor had been the primary cause of rising output of goods" (pp. 457–58). That is, technological change supposedly only became an important phenomenon in the mid-1920s, when the "house of labor" was already in the throes of collapse.

Yet research on late nineteenth-century technological change such as that of Nathan Rosenberg and David Hounshell (Montgomery makes reference to neither) portrays matters differently. Rosenberg stresses the importance of technological change in the metalworking industries of the late nineteenth century. Hounshell traces the evolution of mass-production technology in the last half of the nineteenth century in the manufacture of sewing machines, agricultural machinery, and bicycles, culminating in Ford's assembly line before World War I.[4] For decades before the 1920s, technological change was critical to the growth of the U.S. economy and its emergence as the world's premier mass producer.

These technological changes were, moreover, central to the transformation of the workplace in the late nineteenth and early twentieth centuries. When combined with managerial organization, technological change provided employers with not only a means for dispensing with skilled labor on the shop floor, but also the productive potential that could be shared with operatives to gain their cooperation in generating economies of speed.

The new machine technologies were not only skill-displacing, but also effort saving—the same amount of output could be produced with less effort on the part of the shop-floor worker, so that generating economies of speed no longer necessarily depended upon the operative actually working harder and longer. If only workers would trust "scientific managers" to set output norms consistent with the effort-saving capabilities on the new technologies and piece rates that would give workers a fair share of the productivity gains, Taylor argued both capital and labor could "together turn their attention toward increasing the size of the surplus until this surplus becomes so large that it is unnecessary to quarrel over how it shall be divided." Montgomery quotes Taylor's statement twice (pp. 253, 258) without recognizing the critical role of technological change in "increasing the size of the surplus" that could make both capital and labor better off.

Taylor recognized that the implementation of his "scientific" standards would require a "great mental revolution" (p. 253), particularly for workers who had depended upon their craft organizations to set output norms and enforce piece rates. The minds of workers were not, however, won over for the simple reason that, for Taylor as for the managers of mass production in general, a basic precondition for the setting of "scientific" standards was to deny the existing craft unions any influence. As Taylor found out, it is rather difficult to secure the trust of those whose power and privileges one is attacking. As Montgomery rightly shows, the reaction of workers to the rise of scientific management was to become even more militant in support of their traditional prerogatives.

Despite the failure of Taylorism, technological change did reduce employers' dependence on shop-floor skills. For Montgomery, however, the hierarchical reallocation of skilled labor was the prime means of removing skills from the shop floor, as selected craftsmen were integrated into the managerial bureaucracy. In the short run, such incorporation of craft labor enabled some skilled workers to attain higher earnings and greater employment security compared to those who continued to toil as operatives on the shop floor. In the long run, however, technological change made the traditional craft skills obsolete and generated new skills that had to be acquired. Industrial management gained control over these new skills by sponsoring and shaping the dramatic transformation of the educational system during the first decades of the century,[5] and by integrating the new skilled workforce into the managerial hierarchy as line and staff personnel.[6]

Between 1900 and 1920 U.S. manufacturing saw not only a more than three-fold increase in the number of foremen (typically drawn from the ranks of craft workers) but also a somewhat greater rate of growth in the number of engineers (typically recruited from institutions of higher education). During the 1920s, moreover, the number of engineers grew by another 60 percent to 217,000 while the number of foremen declined slightly to 293,000.[7] There was also a proliferation of other college-educated managerial personnel above the rank of first-line supervisor. Beyond a passing remark that "[e]ducational credentials came to play an increasingly important role in determining the fate of individual employees" (p. 225), Montgomery accords no significance to the educational and organizational transformations that characterized the rise and consolidation of managerial capitalism. Yet these institutional changes both effected and legitimized the segmentation of salaried management from wage laborers.

Technological change not only provided the impetus to incorporate key segments of the laboring population into the capitalist enterprise; it was also the basis for increasing the size of the surpluses that could be used to do so. Firms that had the organizational capability to utilize effort-saving technology sufficiently to transform high fixed costs into low unit costs could generate surpluses that could be shared out not only with employees in the forms of higher wages and better work conditions but also with consumers in the forms of lower prices and better products. As the firm increased its market share by attracting more customers, it was able to offer key employees some of the benefits of greater economies of scale, including the realistic promise of long-term employment stability, and indeed mobility, within the enterprise. And as the firm thereby secured the adherence of key employees to the goals of the firm, it was better able to utilize its investments and increase its market share.

The determination of which employees were "key" to the success of the enterprise and what prospective benefits the firm should offer them were strategic decisions that upper-level managers had to make. In the industrial oligopolies of the 1920s, the promise of higher pay and greater employment stability was extended not only to salaried personnel integrated into the managerial structure but also to many operatives whose cooperation on the shop-floor was critical to achieving the high levels of throughput required to transform high fixed costs into low unit costs. Citing a 1984 conference paper by Sanford Jacoby (there is no reference to his 1985 book, *Employing Bureaucracy*), Montgomery recognizes the salutary impact of internal rewards on employee turnover in the 1920s. But he does not note that, besides reducing quits, the provision of employment stability and higher pay also helped to overcome restriction of output, thereby augmenting the revenues in which these workers could share. The productive power that the dominant mass producers had put in place made it possible for those who could secure jobs with these firms in the 1920s to improve their living standards and work conditions despite— and indeed perhaps even because of—"the fall of the house of labor."

The massive breakdown of employment security in the 1930s would compel American operatives to question managerial control. By the 1920s, however, the dynamic interaction of organization and technology within particular firms—a process that had been going on for decades—dramatically altered the incentives that the dominant mass producers could offer to their operatives. For a while at least, the system could provide these workers with prospects of decent wages and stable employment. At the same time, repression, both industrial and political, rendered ineffective and even nonexistent collective means for operatives to exercise control over shop-floor work organization.

Why does Montgomery ignore the role of technological change in the transformation of work organization and class relations with the coming of managerial capitalism? The prime reason, it seems to me, is his justified desire to attack proponents of "technological determinism"—the untenable notion that the social ordering of the enterprise into managers and workers is the inevitable outcome of modern technology.[8] Technological determinism permits defenders of the status quo to argue that the degradation of shop-floor work is the unavoidable concomitant of material progress. The critique of technological determinism argues that the way in which human and physical resources are combined in productive activity depends upon the social power of interested parties in using the production process to achieve their respective goals.[9]

The one place in the book where Montgomery explicitly takes on a technological determinist argument, the guilt of the alleged culprit is not at all clear. He argues that, in *Taylorism at Watertown Arsenal* (1960), Hugh Aitken "views Taylorism as fundamentally an adaptation of machine-shop practices to the possibilities offered by high-speed steel," and goes on to assert that "[t]his technological determinism is a misleading aspect of what remains otherwise the best existing study of Taylorism" (p. 231n). My own reading of Aitken's book, however, finds a sophisticated analysis of the interaction of technological change and social organization, including a cogent comparison of why Taylor's methods worked better among machinists who could share some of the benefits of planned and coordinated technological change than among molders in the arsenal's foundry whose work was simply speeded up using traditional techniques.[10]

Technological determinism should be attacked. An effective critique cannot, however, simply ignore technology. Rather we must study the social determinants of technological change. Technology is a social construct, involving administrative as well as technical divisions of labor that a firm's decision-makers choose in an attempt to achieve their particular goals. The type of technology in which a firm chooses to invest represents in part a strategy to avoid becoming reliant upon the skills of those who would use their efforts to undermine rather than support enterprise goals. Hence the importance within the capitalist enterprise of the historical evolution of the locus of control over skills that Montgomery documents.

Once it has undertaken an investment strategy, the firm must create an organizational structure—a division of labor, both administrative and technical—to ensure that the technologies in which it has invested will be developed and utilized to produce saleable products at competitive costs. A firm that retains its existing enterprise structure limits the range of technologies in which it can successfully invest. A firm that transforms its enterprise structure in order to take advantage of new technological opportunities invests not only in technological capabilities—plant, equipment, technical skills—but also in organizational capabilities that permit the planned coordination of the firm's new division of labor to ensure the successful development and utilization of its investments.

The characteristics of the organizational change that can successfully implement a particular technological change depend upon the social environment—including the conflictual or cooperative nature of class and production relations—within which the firm finds itself. Historically the social determinants and social consequences of technological change depend upon the dynamic interaction of the nature of technological opportunities and the social environment in which the firm is attempting to pursue its goals.

In elaborating a shop-floor perspective on working-class politics, *The Fall of the House of Labor* is an important contribution to labor history. In his attempt to rebut technological determinism, however, Montgomery fails to explore the dynamic interaction of organization and technology—or to use the Marxist terms, the relations and forces of production—either within the industrial enterprise or the social formation in which it operates. Instead Montgomery simply ignores technology, as if by neglect the bogey of technological determinism—and perhaps, eventually, the reality of capitalist power—will disappear.

To explain the hold that American capitalism has had on the American worker is not that simple. The combined power of organization and technology, wielded by and through the most powerful capitalist enterprises, helped destroy old class relations while shaping a new, more complex, class structure. In the new social order, called managerial capitalism, substantial numbers of the most educated workforce neither owned capital nor labored on the shop floor. Even many shop-floor operatives viewed attachment to the firm rather than to the trade as their primary institutional relation. For its exploration of the transformation of U.S. class relations in the rise of managerial capitalism, *The Fall of the House of Labor* should not be ignored. On the contrary, to comprehend the evolution of the social structure and relations characteristic of modern American capitalism, the book's scholarly research and intellectual concerns must be integrated into a much more systematic and interdisciplinary analytical framework.

William Lazonick, Department of Economics, Barnard College, Columbia University, is the author of Value Creation on the Shop Floor: Organization and Technology in Capitalist Development *(forthcoming from Harvard University Press).*

I gratefully acknowledge the comments and editorial suggestions of Lou Ferleger.
1. See William Lazonick, *Value Creation on the Shop Floor: Organization and Technology in Capitalist Development* (1990).

2. W. Paul Strassmann, *Risk and Technological Innovation: American Manufacturing Methods during the Nineteenth Century* (1959), p. 23. For a list of Taylor's inventions, see Daniel Nelson, *Frederick W. Taylor and the Rise of Scientific Management* (1980), p. 37.

3. Alfred D. Chandler, Jr., *The Visible Hand: The Managerial Revolution in American Business* (1977); see also William Lazonick, "Technological Change and Control of Work: The Development of Capital-Labor Relations in U.S. Mass Production Industries," in Howard Gospel and Craig Littler, eds., *Managerial Strategies and Industrial Relations* (1983), and Lazonick, *Value Creation . . .*, ch. 6.

4. Nathan Rosenberg, *Perspectives on Technology* (1976), p. 24; David Hounshell, *From the American System to Mass Production, 1800–1932* (1984).

5. David F. Noble, *America by Design: Science, Technology and the Rise of Corporate Capitalism* (1977); Samuel Bowles and Herbert Gintis *Schooling in Capitalist America: Educational Reforms and the Contradictions of Economic Life* (1976).

6. William Lazonick, "Strategy, Structure, and Management Development in the United States and Britain," in Kesaji Kobayashi and Hidemasa Morikawa, eds., *Development of Managerial Enterprise* (1986).

7. United States Bureau of the Census, *Historical Statistics of the United States from Colonial Times to 1970* (1976), pp. 140, 142.

8. David Montgomery, *Workers' Control in America* (1979), pp. 6–7.

9. See, for example, Stephen A. Marglin, "What Do Bosses Do? The Origins and Functions of Hierarchy in Capitalist Production," *Review of Radical Political Economics* 6 (Summer 1974).

10. Hugh G. J. Aitken, *Taylorism at Watertown Arsenal: Scientific Management in Action, 1908–1915* (1960), ch. 4.

[7]

Appendix

The Basic Analytics of Shop-Floor Value Creation

Value-Created

The most basic conception of the employment relation is the exchange of labor-time for a wage. The profit-seeking firm employs an income-seeking worker when the value-created per unit of labor-time is equal to or greater than the wage paid. For a given amount of labor-time, value-created on the shop floor can be derived from the following formula:

$$V = R - F - M,$$

where V is value-created, R is revenues, F is the firm's fixed costs of organization and technology, and M is the firm's nonlabor variable costs.

In the determination of revenues, $R = pQ$, where p is product price and Q is the quantity of product sold. In the determination of fixed costs, $F = rS$, where r is the return to financial capital and S is the total cost of the fixed investments in technology and organization employed alongside wage labor to manufacture and market the product. These costs are fixed because, in a given production period, they are incurred irrespective of the amount of output produced on the shop floor. In the determination of nonlabor variable (or materials) costs, $M = gHQ$, where g is the market price per unit of materials and H is the quantity of materials required to produce a unit of output. As in the revenues term, Q represents the quantity of output sold during the production period. Hence the value-created equation can be rewritten as

$$V = pQ - rS - gHQ.$$

The total quantity of value-created in a production period depends on the levels of prices, p, r, and g, and quantities, Q, S, and H.

The distribution of value-created between management and labor depends on the size of the wage bill required to produce V. The wage bill is equal to wL, where w is the wage per unit of labor-time and L is the number of units of labor-time employed. Because value-created, revenues, and costs are mon-

333

199

etary flows per unit of time (the production period) for which the wage bill is paid, the generation of profits in excess of the cost of capital requires that value-created be greater than the wage bill. I shall call these excess profits the "managerial surplus."

The size of the managerial surplus relative to the wage bill can be calculated by deriving a unit cost equation:

$$n = \frac{rS}{Q} + \frac{wL}{Q} + gH,$$

where n equals unit costs and the rest of the terms have already been defined. Solving for rS and substituting into the second value-created equation presented earlier yields

$$V = (p - n)Q + wL = X + Y.$$

$X = (p - n)Q$ is the managerial surplus, and $Y = wL$ is the wage bill. Therefore, this form of the value-created equation expresses the distribution of value-created between management and labor. Algebraically, the managerial surplus can be expressed simply as revenues (pQ) minus costs (nQ). But substantively, an analysis of the size, sources, and uses of the managerial surplus is central to understanding the process of value creation because it enables one to comprehend the economic impacts of investments in organization and technology on the application of skill and effort on the shop floor.

Strategy and Structure

What determines the prices and quantities that enter into the value-created equation? In the conventional theory of the firm (found in virtually any standard economics textbook), p, r, g, and w are market-determined prices that the firm takes as given. The firm then chooses the level of output, Q, that maximizes profits, as well as that combination of capital and labor inputs from a given array of technological alternatives that minimizes the costs of producing the profit-maximizing level of output. The choice of technology determines the amount of physical capital, K, inherent in S and H combined, as well as the amount of L required to complement K.

The acceptance of this orthodox theory of the firm renders one ill equipped to analyze the process of shop-floor value creation. The theory assumes that p, r, g, and w are given by the market and that Q, K, and L are given by technology. Technology also determines the division of K into fixed and variable inputs. Market forces and technological alternatives, both determined external to the firm, combine to determine economic outcomes. In this conception of the firm, there is no apparent role for either enterprise strategy or organizational structure in the creation of value.

The analysis of the process of value creation requires a conception of the nature of the firm that recognizes that the levels of any or all of the prices and quantities that determine the amount of value that a firm creates may depend on firm-specific investment strategies and organizational structures, as well as on the nation-specific and industry-specific competitive environments in which the firm attempts to create value. A theory of value creation that has historical applicability must at least contemplate the possibility that the relevant prices and quantities are determined by the strategy and structure of the firm in response to its competitive environment.

The contribution to a historically relevant theory of value creation that I shall present focuses on enterprise strategy and structure in determining the organization of work on the shop floor. Work organization can play a critical role in generating the expansion of output per unit of time that results in value creation. The firm's management provides physical resources (buildings, machines, materials) required to produce the product as well as organizational resources (engineers and administrators) required to plan and coordinate the specialized division of shop-floor labor. To finance these investments in technology and organization, management pays financiers returns on their capital in the forms of dividends and interest. In the value-created function, this return to financial capital is represented by r.

Workers provide skill and effort. The combination of machines, materials, and workers' skills constitute the shop-floor technology. A given shop-floor technology is characterized by the productive capability to transform inputs into outputs—a capability that I shall signify by the production coefficient, α. At any point in time, productive capability as captured by α only represents *potential* output. The extent to which the productive capability inherent in α is realized depends on the amount of productive effort (E) that workers expend on the job. For a given technology using L units of labor-time, the firm's production function can be described as

$$Q = \alpha f(E),$$

where increases in E result in increases in Q, but at a diminishing rate up to some maximum physically and mentally sustainable level (E_M in Figure A.1). An increase in the productive capability of a technology from α_1 to α_2, as depicted in Figure A.1, can be termed *effort-saving* because the same level of output can be produced with less expenditure of human effort. The value-creating potential of technological change inheres in its effort-saving impact on the process of transforming inputs into outputs.

Substituting this production function into the value-created equation renders value-created a function of technology (which includes the productive capabilities of skill as well as those of machines and materials), effort, product price, and fixed and variable capital costs:

$$V = (p - gH)\alpha f(E) - F.$$

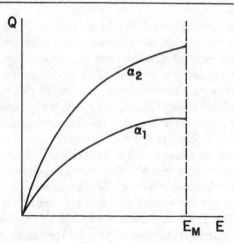

A.1 Effort-saving technological change. E, productive effort; Q, firm's output; α, technological coefficient.

The relation between value-created and effort expended on the shop floor described by this equation is graphed on the right-hand side of Figure A.2. The horizontal axis on the left-hand side of the figure measures the firm's wage bill (Y) that distributes a portion of the value-created to the firm's workers.

Assume that the wage bill is Y_1. As shown in Figure A.2, if workers provide an amount of effort equal to E_A, the value of output produced just covers fixed and variable capital costs, and value-created is zero. If effort rises to E_B, value-created increases to V_1, which equals Y_1. The firm is generating enough value to replace the cost of the fixed capital stock, but workers are capturing all the value-created. Only when value-created on the shop floor is greater than V_1 will there be a managerial surplus—value-created under the control of management over and above the return to financiers, r, and prevailing managerial salaries, which, for the sake of analyzing value creation *on the shop floor*, are included as elements of the fixed capital stock, S. For a managerial surplus to exist, effort must be greater than E_B.

The managerial surplus is central to the achievement of managerial goals over a series of production periods. The managerial surplus can be used for new investments in technology and organization that permit the firm to remain competitive or gain competitive advantage. It can provide management with resources to increase their own compensation, as well as a justification for doing so. It also furnishes management with resources that can be used in economic downturns to pay financiers their expected rate of return and avoid challenges to management control. It can be passed on to

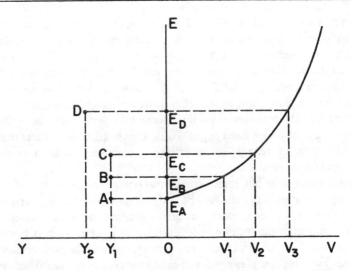

A.2 Effort, value-created, and the managerial surplus. E, productive effort; V, value-created; Y, firm's wage bill.

consumers in the form of price reductions, thus increasing the firm's market share. Or, by providing management with the internal resources to provide employment stability and increased earnings and benefits to their workers, the managerial surplus may form the foundations for cooperative shop-floor relations.

Augmenting the Managerial Surplus

How might the managerial surplus be increased? Recall that the managerial surplus is $(p - n)Q$. Assume that the firm can sell more output without lowering the product price. The most general condition for an increase in the managerial surplus is that an expansion of output, say from Q_1 to Q_2, results in revenues that more than offset the increased costs, $n_2Q_2 - n_1Q_1$, necessary to achieve the output expansion, where n_1 and n_2 are, respectively, unit costs before and after the increase in output.

The challenge facing management is to expand output without an untoward increase in costs. Obviously, if management can increase Q without incurring any additional costs, then more value is created and the managerial surplus expands. Indeed, the managerial surplus increases not only because (assuming that p remains unchanged) the output expansion provides more revenues but also because of the decline in unit costs as fixed costs and the wage bill are spread over more output.

Such costless output expansion can be achieved by eliciting *unremunerated* effort from workers. If workers who are supplying less effort than the maximum that they could physically and mentally sustain would only work up to their productive potential without demanding more wages, more output would be produced without any increase in the firm's costs. The influence of effort on output for a given productive capability is captured in the firm's production function, $Q = \alpha f(E)$. If $\alpha f(E)$ is substituted for Q in the unit cost function above, then it can be seen that the lowering of unit costs, and hence the increase of the managerial surplus, depend on decreases in not only unit labor costs but also unit fixed capital costs. If fixed costs are greater than the wage bill, then an increase in effort lowers unit fixed costs more than it lowers unit labor costs.

For any given wage bill, management may complain that their workers are "shirking," "not pulling their weight," "lying down on the job," and so on. But unless there is an exogenous change in the firm's socioeconomic environment that increases the social power of managers to extract effort from their workers, the level of effort and the managerial surplus will remain unchanged. Two important examples of such changes are increased unemployment that makes workers more fearful of losing their jobs or labor legislation that decreases the bargaining power of unions. In the absence of an exogenous restructuring of social power, management must incur extra costs to elicit more effort from its workers.

A managerial strategy to elicit more effort from workers is closer shop-floor supervision. Supervision costs must then be added to the shop-floor labor costs incurred in the value-creation process. In Figure A.2, supervision costs increase the total wage bill (operative and supervisory) from Y_1 to Y_2. Assume, as shown in Figure A.2, that the resultant closer supervision increases effort from E_C to E_D. The managerial surplus increases if the extra effort achieved through increased supervision results in sufficient value-created to offset the higher shop-floor labor costs. In Figure A.2, the managerial surplus increases because $V_3 - V_2$ is greater than $Y_2 - Y_1$.

The amount of extra effort, and hence value-created per supervisory dollar, depends on the relative social power of management and labor to control the pace of work on the shop floor. Social power in turn depends in part on the technological requirements of production—specifically the dependence of management on the skills of its workers. It also depends in part on the socioeconomic environment in which the firm operates, particularly the opportunities for individual workers to quit undesirable work conditions and the degree of collective organization of shop-floor workers.

Consider the implications for value creation of some of these determinants of social power. Periods of economic boom create opportunities for management to expand output. To take advantage of these demand conditions, the firm must exercise control over the supply of effort. But in periods of economic boom, tight labor markets diminish the costs of job loss to workers because they can easily secure alternative employment, a situation enabling even less skilled workers to resist coercive attempts by supervisors to induce more effort from them. The returns to increased supervision are, therefore, relatively low at precisely those times when, if more effort were forthcoming from workers, the opportunities for increased value-created—for generating value gains—are greatest.

The supervisor *may* (in the absence of workers' organizations that exercise control over hiring, firing, promotion, and remuneration) have the right to dismiss or otherwise penalize workers who do not perform as expected. If, in the attempt to discipline a reluctant labor force, highly skilled workers are replaced with less skilled workers, the decline in α means that more effort will be required to generate a given value-created. If both wages and value-created are directly proportional to skill level, then the managerial surplus will be unaffected by the shift from fewer highly skilled to more less skilled workers. Any increase in value-created and the managerial surplus must come from management's ability to use the hiring (or the threat of hiring) of less skilled workers to depress wages per unit of skill or increase effort per unit of wages.

If workers of different skill levels are not, however, easily substitutable—if the lack of relevant skills results in defective products or damage to plant, equipment, and materials—a deterioration in skill level can both lower revenues and increase costs substantially. Unless management is willing and able to invest in an alternative machine technology that will make the highly skilled workers dispensable (a case that I take up below in the analysis of effort and technological change), it cannot use the availability of less skilled workers to discipline highly skilled workers.

The power inherent in the right to penalize is diminished, therefore, if workers with relevant skills are costly to replace, either because market competition for labor of a given skill level is intense or because the skills that enter into the production coefficient, α, must be developed within the firm. As skill levels rise, labor market conditions have less impact on the supply of effort because the skills of the firm's workers tend to be more "firm specific"—their skills must be developed within the particular firm on the basis of its particular combination of organization and technology. The underdevelopment of these firm-specific skills will result in defective products and damage to the firm's capital stock.

When skills are firm specific, the only way in which the firm can replace reluctant workers is by training new ones, a process that not only requires increased organizational investments (raising F) but also takes time; so there is a lag before the managerial surplus is increased. Moreover, given the firm-specific nature of the skills, the training of newer workers may depend on the cooperation of older workers—a task to which the veterans are not likely to supply much effort if the managerial objective is to generate replacements for them. Furthermore, the firm has no assurance that the new workers will supply any more effort than the old ones.

The effectiveness of supervision and the threat of dismissal as means of

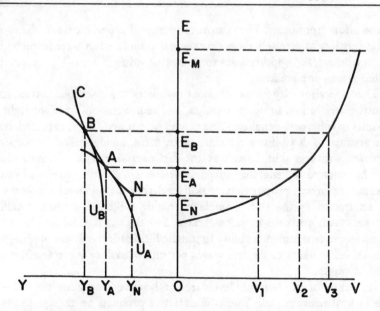

A.3 Workers' preferences, wage incentives, and value-created.
E, productive effort; V, value-created; Y, firm's wage bill.

increasing effort and the managerial surplus may, therefore, be limited by the external economic environment and the internal structure of production. Instead of the stick of job loss, the alternative approach to the problem of effort is the carrot of wage incentives. The amounts of extra effort and output elicited for a given wage incentive depend on the elasticity of the supply of effort in response to wages—an elasticity inherent in workers' utility or preference functions. As illustrated in the left-hand side of Figure A.3, point N connotes the wage bill, Y_N, and effort, E_N, that prevail prior to the introduction of a wage-incentive scheme. The increase in effort and hence output in response to a piece-rate bonus, d, is less for workers with utility functions U_A (which shows the combinations of effort and wages that result in the same level of utility) than for workers with utility functions U_B. The curve CN represents premium earnings as a function of extra effort—in this case, earnings greater than Y_N for effort greater than E_N. The premium earnings function is, therefore,

$$B = d(Q - Q_N) = d\alpha[f(E) - f(E_N)],$$

where B is premium earnings, d is the piece-rate incentive, and Q_N and E_N are the output and effort levels with basic wages, Y_N.

The more willing workers are to supply effort for extra pay, the greater is the augmented output and value-created that can be derived from a wage-incentive scheme. Because fixed costs (F) are held constant as value-created increases in response to a wage-incentive scheme, the additional amount of value-created (or what can more generally be called the value gains) is $(p - gH)(Q - Q_N)$. For any given amount of extra output, the greater the gap between product price and nonwage unit variable costs, the greater are the value gains.

What determines the distribution of the value gains between wages and managerial surplus as workers supply more effort and increase output? The cost to the firm of the wage-incentive scheme is $d(Q - Q_N)$, which represents the workers' share of the value gains. Management's share of the value gains is $(p - gH - d)(Q - Q_N)$. The managerial surplus increases, therefore, if $p - gH$ is greater than d—that is, if the piece-rate incentive is set at less than the excess of price over nonwage variable costs. If this condition is met, then the greater the effort that workers supply in response to the incentive scheme, the greater the output and the greater the managerial surplus.

If, for example, output rises to Q_S, then the wage bill becomes $Y_N + d(Q_S - Q_N)$. The managerial surplus is $(p - n_S)Q_S$, where n_S represents unit costs at Q_S. By using a wage-incentive scheme, management may be able to increase its share of value-created not only because of an increase in revenues as output expands but also by a decrease in unit costs as fixed costs as well as the fixed portion of the wage-bill are spread over more output. With the wage-incentive scheme, the unit cost function is

$$n_S = [F + Y_N + d(Q_S - Q_N)]/Q_S + gH.$$

As output increases, unit costs fall unless the wage incentive, d, is large enough to outweigh the combined cost-reducing effects of the spreading out of the nonincentive wage bill and fixed costs over the greater amount of output. Even if unit costs do rise, however, total managerial surplus will increase as output expands from Q_S to Q_N as long as d is less than $p - gH$.

Limits of Wage Incentives

But what will determine how much extra effort and hence output workers supply in response to a given wage-incentive scheme? Workers will supply more effort up to the point where the marginal disutility of increased effort equals the marginal utility of increased income. Figure A.3 illustrates two such effort-earnings outcomes, A and B, depending on whether workers have U_A or U_B, respectively. If d (inherent in the curve CN) is less than $p - gH$, management would prefer that workers have utility functions U_B rather than U_A. Management, therefore, has an interest in the effort–pay preferences of the workers that it hires, and indeed in the implementation of shop-floor relations that might shape these preferences over time.

Workers may quite rationally refuse to supply any additional effort in response to wage-incentive schemes. Workers may view management's use of wage incentives as simply a speedup or stretchout strategy to reduce the number of workers employed to produce the current level of output (in this case, Q_N) rather than as a market expansion strategy that, by increasing the firm's output, will protect existing jobs. Rather than risk the loss of some of their jobs, workers may attempt to band together, often through informal shop-floor organization and the application of peer pressure, to maintain existing levels of output per worker. Insofar as this collective (even if informal) organization succeeds, the attempt to use wage incentives to increase the managerial surplus is undermined.

When product demand is strong, the supply of more effort may not threaten a reduction in employment because managers can market the expanded output. Nevertheless, workers may believe that a positive response to a wage-incentive scheme might, by increasing generally accepted effort norms, create the conditions for management to extract unremunerated effort. Moreover, with product demand supporting the demand for labor, workers are in a strong position to resist managerial strategies that they believe will eventually result in unremunerated intensification of their labor. Hence, even though their jobs are not at risk, workers may attempt to limit their supply of effort and restrict output.

The earnings and effort levels per unit of time that prevail prior to the introduction of a wage-incentive scheme represent norms that, through shop-floor practice, supervisors had come to expect and workers had come to accept. Compared with effort norms, however, it is easier for shop-floor workers to reach a consensus on what constitutes a normal wage because earnings levels, changes, and variations across workers are easily observable. But because the supply of effort is more difficult to measure than earnings received, workers have more difficulty in exercising a collective voice in the determination and maintenance of effort norms. It is always possible for managers to insist that workers who produce more output per unit of time are doing so because they are more skilled, not because they are exerting more effort. Although one can distinguish between skill and effort conceptually, to do so in practice can be problematic.

Hence the villain in the shop-floor drama is the rate-buster, the worker who demonstrates that it is possible to produce more output per unit of time and thereby justifies management's contention that the other workers are shirking—producing below their productive potential (which, of course, is always the case when E is less than E_M, the maximum effort level physically and mentally sustainable). The manifestation of the rate-busting strategy is a cut in piece-rates that compels workers to supply more effort than E_N to achieve normal earnings, Y_N. If workers view a wage-incentive scheme as a managerial strategy for extracting unremunerated effort rather than as a longer term commitment for sharing value gains, then they will quite rationally refuse the lure of the short-term earnings increases that the scheme offers. In general, if workers view management as engaged in a speedup or stretchout strategy to extract unremunerated effort, they will themselves adopt a "workers' control" strategy (often organized informally on the shop floor) of collective restriction of effort and output in order to influence the determination of effort norms.

To secure the cooperation of workers in the creation of value, therefore, management must manifest its willingness to share out the value-created in terms of both employment stability and wages that workers view as fair (the slogan "a fair day's wage for a fair day's work" extends far back in time). If management manifests both its willingness and ability to provide employment stability and higher wages to workers over a sustained period of time, the aversion of workers to responding to incentive schemes will tend to dissipate. The foundations for cooperative shop-floor relations will have been put in place.

The increase in effort that workers will provide in response to wage incentives has limits, however. Even before workers reach the physical and mental limits of effort expenditure (E_M in Figure A.3), their supply response of effort to wage increases may fall to zero; given workers' preferences, no amount of monetary incentive will induce more effort. Indeed, the effort-supply curve may be backward bending as higher pay per unit of effort induces workers to work less.

Cooperative Shop-Floor Relations

Nevertheless, over time the demonstrated willingness of management to share out value gains not only may induce workers to supply more effort on the basis of given preferences but may even transform workers' underlying utility functions in ways that increase the elasticity of effort in response to wage incentives. Long-term attachment to the firm and cooperative management–labor relations may encourage workers to identify with the goals of the firm, while employment stability and higher wages may induce workers to adopt lifestyles (families, homes, cars, travel, and so on) or aspirations (eventual self-employment, more and better education for their children) that increase the amount of effort they are willing to supply for a given wage.

Cooperative shop-floor relations can affect not only the quantity but also the quality of effort that workers provide for a given wage. Workers may be willing not only to work harder but also to be more careful in the work that they do; they supply not only more effort but also better effort. Even though they were capable of doing more careful work—a capability or skill captured in α—their carelessness, inattentiveness, or even intended destructiveness (commonly termed sabotage) led them to supply a lower quality of effort than their skills would allow. One result of better effort is to reduce the amount of wasted materials or defective products that are considered normal, so fewer materials, H, are required per unit of sold (that is, nondefective) output. As the quality of effort increases, unit costs fall, and value-created rises. Another result of better effort is to reduce machine downtime and repair costs, so less fixed capital, S, is required to maintain a given productive capability, α, in any given time period. In effect, H and S, both of which enter into the value-created function, are themselves functions of the quality of effort.

Over time, the practice of supplying more and better effort results in workers who have more and better skills. Put differently, when shop-floor value creation is considered as an evolutionary process, the assumption implied in the simple production function, $Q = \alpha f(E)$, that the level of effort, E, and the contribution of shop-floor workers to the level of productive capability, α, are independent of one another cannot be sustained. Since Adam Smith it has been a commonplace that repetitive work results in workers who are more skilled in doing that particular work—essentially "learning by doing" on the shop floor. It follows that the greater the quantity of effort workers expend per unit of time, the faster they develop their specialized skills to the peak of their capability. Likewise, it can be argued, the better the quality of effort workers expend per unit of time, the better the quality of the skills they develop over time. In effect, workers who make persistent efforts to do better work learn how to do the work better.

Hence, by encouraging workers to supply more and better effort, cooperative shop-floor relations enable workers to develop more and better skills over a given time period. Moreover, because the development of shop-floor skills occurs by means of learning by doing, the increase in shop-floor productive capability does not require investments that add to the fixed costs of the firm. As both E and α increase over time, and as the growth in one reinforces the growth of the other, value-created on the shop floor will rise *if the firm can retain these specific workers in its employ.* The essence of cooperative shop-floor relations is the willingness and ability of the firm to provide employment stability, higher earnings, and better working conditions to its workers, all of which will help to secure their attachment to the firm, which in turn increases the firm-specific value-created available for managers and workers to share. A dynamic interaction between cooperative shop-floor relations and shop-floor value creation has been set in motion.

Cooperative relations enhance not only management's ability to develop and utilize the skills of shop-floor workers but also its willingness to do so. In the presence of conflictual relations, it cannot be taken for granted that management will want its workers to have more rather than fewer skills, because they may use these skills to exercise control over their jobs and defend themselves against unremunerated intensification of their labor. Indeed, the fear that workers will use their skills to limit rather than increase

value-created may induce management to introduce skill-displacing technologies to rid themselves of truculent workers. In contrast, cooperative
relations render management willing to rely on the skills of workers and
indeed to encourage the development of shop-floor skills in ways that complement the productive capability of the prevailing technology.

The absence of efforts by workers to use their skills to exercise control
over their jobs enhances the ability of management to perform its productive
roles of planning and coordinating the specialized division of labor on the
shop floor. Unobstructed by job control on the shop floor, management can
allocate workers to activities for which their skills are most appropriate and,
indeed, can move particular workers from one activity to another in ways
designed to develop their skills over time. By securing the cooperation of
workers in the supply of effort at the various vertically related stages of the
production process, management can coordinate the flow of work—or
throughput—from one stage of the production process to the next. With
unobstructed managerial coordination, work in progress does not lie idle,
thus reducing the cost of capital tied up in inventories, a cost that would
otherwise increase the firm's fixed capital costs. Moreover, confident that
shop-floor workers will use their skills to create value rather than limit it,
management is willing to rely on, and indeed develop, the skills of workers to
aid in the shop-floor coordination of the flow of work.

Cooperative shop-floor relations, therefore, encourage the development of
skills, often in relatively inexpensive ways, as well as the augmentation of the
supply of effort. Management, however, must be not only willing but also
able to provide workers with the employment stability, earnings increases,
and improved work conditions that are the bases for cooperative relations.
The stability of cooperative relations is vulnerable to those changes in the
economic environment in which the firm operates but over which it can
exercise little or no control.

When cyclical downturns reduce revenues, the managerial surplus shrinks,
and a commitment to relatively high wage levels may make it difficult for
management to meet its commitments to the firm's financiers. The higher the
firm's fixed costs, the more vulnerable it is to the slump. In the absence of
institutional arrangements that encourage managers, workers, and financiers
to moderate their claims on the firm's current revenues, management may be
confronted by challenges from workers and financiers that threaten managerial control. Despite the potential for both managers and workers to benefit
from cooperative relations, therefore, macroeconomic instability as well as
commitments to financiers may render management unable to make the long-
term employment and pay commitments to workers that form the foundations for continued cooperation and the creation of value.

Also destabilizing of cooperative relations between managers and workers
are innovative strategies of the firm's competitors. Faced by competitors

who, through the development and utilization of their productive resources, succeed in selling higher quality products at lower cost, the firm's response can be either adaptive or innovative. At the shop-floor level, the adaptive response is the attempt to induce unremunerated effort from workers, a strategy that may well have the perverse effects on value creation outlined above as workers try to protect effort norms by restricting output.

Alternatively, if the firm can secure the necessary financial resources, it can pursue the innovative response of introducing effort-saving technology. If utilized sufficiently, the investments in technological change can permit a sharing-out of value gains without requiring more effort from workers. As depicted in Figure A.1, the effort-saving impact of technological change is measured by an increase in the production coefficient, α. If the firm introduces a new technology with a production coefficient that is greater than that of the technology it replaces, then more output can potentially be produced with the same effort. But whether or not the new technology will actually yield more value-created will depend both on the level of effort achieved on it and on the costs of introducing it relative to the effort level and costs that prevailed on the old technology.

Effort-Saving Technology

Recall that the value-created equation is $V = (p - gH)\alpha f(E) - F$. Let the production coefficient on the old technology be α_1. The value-created using this technology is described by the curve labeled $E_R G$ in Figure A.4. Now assume that the introduction of a new technology changes α and F but does not change p and gH. If the production coefficient on the new technology is greater than α_1—as will be the case whenever the new technology is effort saving—then the value-created curve using the new technology will be flatter than the curve $E_R G$ that is based on the old technology. Assume that the new technology is effort saving; then, if its fixed costs are less than the fixed costs (F_1) of the old technology, the new value-created curve will cut the effort axis below E_R and will lie wholly below the old value-created curve, $E_R G$. Given its low fixed costs and high production coefficient, for any level of effort, the new technology would yield more value-created than the old.

Assume, however, that the fixed costs of introducing the new, effort-saving technology are greater than F_1; then its value-created curve cuts the effort axis above E_R. The curves $E_S H$ and $E_T J$ in Figure A.4 describe the relation between value-created and effort when the firm adopts technologies with production coefficients α_2 and α_3, respectively. Both α_2 and α_3 are greater than α_1, and hence both the new technologies are effort-saving.

If, as depicted by $E_T J$, the fixed costs of the new technology are sufficiently greater than F_1, then the increased capital costs of the new technology can outweigh its effort-saving impact $(\alpha_3 - \alpha_1)$ on value-created, even at E_M—

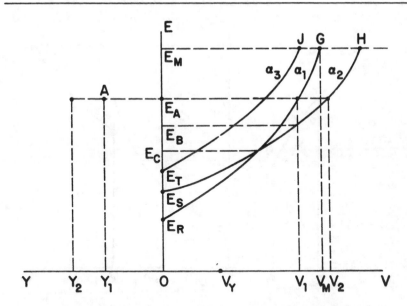

A.4 Effort, fixed costs, and effort-saving technological change.
E, productive effort; V, value-created; Y, firm's wage bill; α,
technological coefficient.

the maximum effort that workers can physically and mentally sustain per
unit of time. In this case, the new value-created curve lies wholly above the
old one. Despite the effort-saving nature of the technology, the high cost of
introducing α_3 into the workplace means that there is no feasible effort level
at which it yields more value-created than the old technology, α_1.

The most interesting, and perhaps most usual, case of technological
change is that described by $E_S H$ in Figure A.4. Although the fixed costs, F_1,
of the new technology are greater than F_1, value-created is greater at E_M
using α_2 rather than α_1. At levels of effort below E_C, the old technology
yields more value-created than the new technology. But at levels of effort
above E_C, the reverse is the case.

Assume, as depicted on the left-hand side of Figure A.4, that workers are
supplying E_A effort for Y_1 wages on the basis of the old technology, the
production coefficient of which is α_1. Given the value-created curve $E_R G$,
value-created is V_1. If $Y_1 = V_Y$, the managerial surplus equals $V_1 - V_Y$. The
maximum value-created attainable on this technology is V_M, at which point
effort is at E_M.

If, after introducing α_2 with its value-created curve $E_S H$, effort remains at
E_A and the wage bill at Y_1, value-created is V_2. The managerial surplus has
been increased by $V_2 - V_1$ without requiring workers to supply more effort

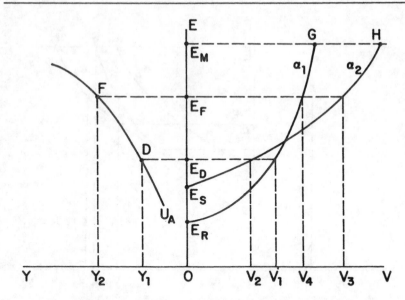

A.5 Customary effort norms and investment in technological change. E, productive effort; V, value-created; Y, firm's wage bill; α, technological coefficient.

or accept lower wages. Indeed, in Figure A.4, effort could fall to E_B or wages could increase to Y_2 (= $V_2 - V_1 + V_Y$) without diminishing the managerial surplus compared with that achieved on the old technology. Given the relation between effort and wages on $α_1$, the effort-saving nature of the new technology and the costs of technological change make it possible to create value that can unequivocally make both management and workers better off. Effort-saving technological change forms the foundations for cooperative shop-floor relations in the value-creation process.

Note, however, that if the effort level had been below E_C on $α_1$, it would not have been worthwhile for management to introduce $α_2$ unless, in utilizing the new technology, it could have been sure of increasing effort or decreasing wages, or some combination of the two. If, using $α_2$, management seeks to restore its surplus by depressing wages, it will not induce value creation but will merely be redividing a smaller amount of value-created. Not only are high levels of effort critical for the creation of value, but adherence to *customary* levels of effort may make it impossible for an effort-saving technology to increase the value shares of both management and workers without requiring workers to supply more effort than they had supplied in the past.

Assume, for example, as depicted in Figure A.5, that the effort level on $α_1$ (the value-created curve of which is E_RG) is E_D, and that the wage bill is Y_1 and the managerial surplus is $V_1 - Y_1$. If, after introducing $α_2$ (which generates the value-created curve, E_SH), the effort level remains at E_D, then value-created will fall to V_2. Unless management can decrease the wage bill—a strategy that is certain to cause a confrontation with labor—the managerial surplus will decrease. If, however, management could convince workers to supply more effort for a higher wage, it is possible that both sides could be made better off. For example, if (as illustrated on the left-hand side of Figure A.5) workers could be convinced to supply E_F for Y_2, they could achieve the same level of utility, U_A, at point F as they did at point D. Value-created on the new technology would be increased to V_3. If $V_3 - Y_2$ is greater than $V_1 - Y_1$, management benefits from the introduction of α_2, and workers are no worse off than before. By paying workers somewhat more or having them supply somewhat less effort, the firm could redistribute some of the increase in the managerial surplus to workers, thereby making both management and workers better off.

Note that on the *old* technology the supply of E_F for Y_2 instead of E_D for Y_1 would have increased value-created from V_1 to V_4. Workers' utility is unchanged at point F compared with point D in Figure A.5. But if $V_4 - Y_2$ is less than $V_1 - Y_1$, then the managerial surplus on the old technology is less at E_F compared with E_D, and the extra value that could have been created by supplying the extra effort, $E_F - E_D$, would not have made both sides better off. Hence, even though the higher level of effort could have created a positive-sum outcome on the *new* technology with production coefficient α_2, workers' effort–earnings preferences would have discouraged management from trying to use wage incentives to elicit this effort on the old technology with its lower productive capability.

Therefore, when the customary effort level on the old technology is low, the problem that management faces in introducing α_2 is to convince workers that they will be better off supplying higher levels of effort in response to wage incentives. If workers do not believe that they will gain by responding to wage incentives subsequent to the technological change, the managerial surplus might be greater using α_1 than α_2. If so, management has no incentive to invest in the new technology, even though α_2 has the potential to make both management and workers better off at higher levels of effort. Customary effort norms, therefore, may be one source of what has been called the productive–technology dilemma.

But why might management have difficulty in securing the cooperation of workers in generating sufficient value-created to make it worthwhile to introduce a technological change that can make both sides better off? The answers are basically the same as those outlined in the previous discussion of effort bargaining on a given technology. Workers may believe that management is engaged in a strategy that will result in job loss or unremunerated effort. They may see the increase of earnings from Y_1 to Y_2 as a means of establishing high effort norms on the new technology that will subsequently remain in place as wages are reduced back toward Y_1. Workers will feel particularly vulnerable to a managerial strategy to extract unremunerated effort if changes in the nature of the skills inherent in the transition from α_1 to α_2 make existing workers more easily replaceable. Indeed, if management expects resistance from shop-floor workers to the implementation of techno-logical change, it might very well choose new technologies that reduce its dependence on workers' skills that are costly to replicate; the choice of technology might represent a strategy to displace skilled workers.

Shop-Floor Control

In an adversarial industrial-relations environment, workers are not without their defenses, even in the absence of unions. When management exercises considerable social power over workers in extracting unremunerated effort, workers can turn to sabotage—the willful infliction of damage to processes and products—as a means to control the relation between effort and pay. Sabotage can result in work stoppages that reduce output, and hence reve-nues, per unit of time. It can also result in greater wastage of materials, in effect increasing H (the quantity of materials per unit of output). Insofar as sabotage causes permanent damage to the productive capabilities of plant and equipment, the firm will have to expend more on fixed costs to possess a given productive capability as captured by the production coefficient, α. The firm will be more vulnerable to shop-floor sabotage the more its productive capabilities are dependent on the skills and efforts of its shop-floor workers. The more expensive the physical technology and the more vulnerable its productive capabilities to sabotage, the greater the threat that such activity poses to value-created and the managerial surplus.

When a new technology is constantly breaking down and damage to equipment and materials is extraordinarily costly, management may suspect sabotage, but it may be difficult to detect. In the utilization of any given technology, it is difficult, if not impossible, for management to distinguish between the relative productive contributions of technology and effort. It is the workers themselves, not management, who are better positioned to judge how hard they are working. The problem of distinguishing between the productive contributions of technology and effort is particularly difficult on new technologies for which production standards have not been established through shop-floor practice. In response to managerial coercion to supply more effort, workers may sabotage the new technology, arguing in their own defense that it is the production engineers' overestimation of its productive potential that is causing breakdowns and damage.

The message to management is that, for the sake of avoiding the destruc-tion of costly capital, supervisors would be well advised to slow the pace of work. In effect, workers are using their power to sabotage as a means of convincing managers that the true production coefficient of the new technology is lower than what the engineers think it is, and that it is useless to try to speed up the pace of work by replacing current workers.

In such a conflictual industrial-relations environment, management may take measures to eliminate its dependence on workers who have sought to use their skills to restrict output. In particular, management might invest in new technologies that deskill the contributions of shop-floor workers to the value-creation process, or it might introduce new hierarchical divisions of labor that vest certain key skills in managerial personnel rather than leaving them on the shop floor in the possession of workers. In adding to the firm's fixed costs, these investments in equipment and personnel may diminish the social power of labor, but they do not solve the economic problem facing the firm. Rather, the augmented fixed costs make the firm all the more dependent on eliciting high levels of effort from their workers. Faced by a deskilled, but alienated, work force, management must try to erect a new structure of cooperation on the shop floor.

In sum, cooperative relations between management and workers promote not only the greater utilization of an existing technology but also effort-saving technological change—a process that is essential for increasing the limits of value creation beyond the constraints posed by the mental and physical capabilities of workers. On the basis of cooperative shop-floor relations, effort-saving technology can potentially make both sides better off. With cooperative relations, moreover, management has an interest in developing shop-floor skills in ways that complement the productive capabilities of physical capital. In the presence of cooperative shop-floor relations, management's ability and incentive to invest in technological change—in both effort-saving machines and workers' skills—depend on the size of the current and expected managerial surpluses. Workers' incentives to supply sufficient effort to maintain or increase value-created on the new technology depend on their expectations concerning the impacts of technological change on the effort they will have to supply and the earnings they will get in return. Cooperative shop-floor relations generate a distribution of value-created that encourages the development and utilization of productive resources that permit the value to be created in the first place. Put another way, shop-floor value creation is the outcome of the dynamic interaction between relations and forces of production, with cooperative arrangements for the sharing-out of value-created providing the critical institutional foundations for generating value.

For workers who want employment stability, improved work conditions, and higher incomes, therefore, the prime industrial-relations issue should not be whether there will be an increase in the managerial surplus at any point in time but what management will do with the value-created under its control over time. Will management, by investing in new technology (including the appropriate retraining of existing workers), use the surplus to protect jobs, increase earnings, and create better work conditions? Or will it devote the surplus primarily to increasing managerial salaries and perquisites or to paying higher than normal rates of returns to financiers (a use of the managerial surplus that interests managers who have substantial shareholdings in the firm)?

Innovation and Adaptation

It is the firm's innovative investment strategy that can create the conditions for cumulative value creation. Just as cumulative value creation can be set in motion by an innovative strategy that gives the firm a competitive advantage, so too can it be brought to a halt by the more successful development and utilization of productive resources by the firm's competitors. As the firm loses market share, value-created is reduced. At the same time, however, the firm needs to devote more resources to finance the new investment strategy. To help augment the managerial surplus in a period of declining value-created, management is tempted to reduce labor's share of value-created while demanding that shop-floor workers supply more effort.

The more that workers perceive that management is actually using its control over the surplus to try to restore the firm's competitive advantage and recreate the conditions for employment stability, earnings increases, and better work conditions, the more likely will they be to continue to cooperate with management in creating value on the basis of a new investment strategy. The willingness of labor to cooperate will be strengthened all the more if management also sacrifices some of its personal share of value-created to help finance the new investments.

Management may, however, decide not to meet the competitive challenge but to live off the productive capability, embodied in the firm's fixed capital stock, that has been accumulated in the past. Rather than reduce its personal claims on value-created, management may attempt to enrich itself by diverting funds from the reinvestment process. At the same time, knowing that the firm is not making the investments that will, over the long run, enable it to compete with its competitors, management may try to increase the managerial surplus by laying off workers, while demanding wage reductions and more effort from those who remain. Once workers perceive that management is pursuing such an adaptive strategy—that it is taking the managerial surplus out of the enterprise rather than putting it back in—and that the firm can no longer offer the employment stability, wage levels, and work conditions that it had in the past, cooperative shop-floor relations will turn into conflict. As both management and workers engage in what Thorstein Veblen called "the conscientious withdrawal of efficiency," a process of cumulative value creation gives way to a process of cumulative value depletion.

[8]

Strategy, Structure, and Management Development in the United States and Britain*

William Lazonick
Harvard University

I. Specialization and Coordination

The dominant institutional feature of twentieth-century capitalist development has been the evolution of the bureaucratic business corporation. Using social organizations rather than impersonal markets to pursue expansionary strategies, corporations based in the United States, Germany, and Japan have brought their economies to the forefront in international competitiveness. In contrast, an important cause of the relative decline of the once-powerful British economy has been the failure of its enterprises to keep pace with international developments in business organization.[1]

There is nothing inevitable about the success of large-scale business organizations. Many corporations that have sought to become too big too fast have stumbled under their own weight, while some once-dominant corporations have found old modes of bureaucratic organization and administration to be formidable obstacles to adaptation to new competitive conditions. The successful implementation of a strategy of corporate expansion requires the development of a managerial structure that permits top management to integrate and coordinate a specialized division of labor to achieve enterprise goals.

Influenced mainly by the persistence of the small family firm in Britain, neoclassical economists have long stressed the limitations that managerial capability places on the growth of the firm.[2] Alternatively, influenced by the ongoing administrative problems of

*Leslie Hannah and the participants at the Fuji International Conference on Business History provided useful comments on an earlier draft of this paper, and Heidi Willmann supplied excellent research assistance.

101

large-scale organizations in the United States, organizational theo-
rists such as Herbert Simon have used the term "bounded rationality" to describe the managerial constraints on enterprise growth.[3]
From either perspective, the limitation on the growth of the firm is
that an individual can only absorb so much knowledge and oversee
the activities of so many people and processes before the marginal
return to his or her managerial capacity becomes negative.

The tremendous expansion of the scale and scope of the enterprise
since the late nineteenth century suggests, however, a considerable
unbounding of organizational rationality that stands in need of
explanation. In his classic work, *The Functions of the Executive*, Chester
Barnard made a valuable theoretical start by emphasizing the
relationship between the collective rationality of the organization
and the individual rationality of the various participants in its
bureaucratic structure.[4] The "functions of the executive" are to
develop sources of information, lines of communication, and structures of authority to render, as far as possible, the goals of individuals consistent with organizational objectives.

How is the collectivization of rationality achieved? At any point
in time, an industrial bureaucracy will be made up of generalists
who coordinate and specialists who carry out detailed technical
(including legal and commercial) tasks. But as a dynamic social
process, the unbounding—or collectivization—of rationality in-
volves a more or less continuous transformation of a proportion of
specialists into generalists. As specialists attain more responsibility
for process and product development within their own functional
areas, they will need a broader understanding of overall enterprise
potential and goals in order to determine what types of information
to supply to coordinators, whose tasks are to make and implement
policy. Similarly, general managers must be capable of evaluating
what types of information to accept from specialists.

As an organizational process in the modern industrial corporation, therefore, successful management development not only trains
competent specialists but also selects the best of these specialists and
turns them into generalists as they climb the corporate hierarchy.
The more complex and far-flung the enterprise, the more must the
process of transformation of specialists into generalists take place

more or less continuously over the careers of upwardly mobile managers. Hence the periodic rotation of promising specialists to new functional areas outside their specialties in order to give them a broader perspective on overall operations. An assumption underlying such firm-level practices is the long-term attachment of particular individuals to particular organizations—attachment that is typically secured by offering vertical mobility within the firm.

Getting desired performance from the specialized division of labor is not, however, simply a technical matter of training, information, and lines of communication. The performance of individuals and groups in a bureaucracy depends not only on their productive capabilities but also on their willingness to exert those capabilities in ways that are consistent with the overall goals of the firm. Conflict and cooperation among interested parties impart a social dimension to the problem of coordination. Specialists will be much more likely to cooperate with generalists if they see successful specialist performance as a means to upward mobility within the firm—mobility to positions where the coordination of specialists and the possession of generalist training and attitudes will be increasingly important.

In a modern industrial bureaucracy, successful management development results in the *bureaucratic integration* of specialists and generalists, making functional specialists amenable to managerial coordination and developing general managers who can effectively coordinate the specialized division of labor. From the point of view of the firm's strategy makers, bureaucratic integration permits the unbounding of rationality by harnessing the individual efforts of managerial personnel to the goals of the enterprise.

In the absence of movement of individuals around and up the corporate organization, *bureaucratic segmentation* will set in. General managers will have to be recruited from outside the firm. By not promoting from within, the firm will forgo the use of a powerful incentive mechanism to elicit work effort from subordinate managerial personnel. Specialists, moreover, will owe no particular loyalty to these outsiders, who may in fact know little about the firm's specialist activities or personalities. With avenues of upward mobility blocked, the best of the specialists will be likely to leave the firm, while the rest will pursue their careers within a narrow specialty, rendering functional departments self-serving entities, impervious to effective coordination from above.

The advantages of the multidivisional form of managerial organization that became increasingly dominant among U.S. corporations in the twentieth century derived less from the flexibility of decentralized management per se, which if not adequately coordinated could lead top management to lose control, than from the scope that this organizational structure provided for bureaucratic integration. What decentralized decision making demanded was the integration of specialist knowledge and generalist capabilities on the part of middle managers. And what helped to ensure that the decisions of competent middle managers would conform to the overall goals of the firm was the promise of promotion within the organization, with the central office as the limit to vertical mobility. Without a process of management development that ensured bureaucratic integration, higher-level management would not have been able to coordinate divisional activities in the interests of long-term enterprise goals.

For the business organization, management development occurs externally, primarily in the system of higher education, as well as internally in accordance with policies of management training and promotion. We can expect a dynamic interaction between these two realms of management development: the demands placed by business organizations on the educational system to supply certain types of management personnel will depend in part on the types of internal policies these organizations seek to pursue, which will in turn depend in part on the types of personnel they find ready at hand. As we shall see, in the first half of this century there occurred in the United States, but not in Britain, a simultaneous transformation of traditional education and traditional structures of bureaucratic organization that brought management development in line with expansionary corporate goals.

In both the United States and Britain, the collectivization of rationality confronted a similar problem of deeply entrenched individualism. If anything the ideal of independent as opposed to corporate employment was stronger in the land of Thomas Jefferson than in the land of Adam Smith. Yet in the United States the confrontation of social organization and individualism resulted in bureaucratic integration, whereas in Britain it resulted in bureaucratic segmentation. The arguments made above suggest that a comparative analysis of the historical evolution of management development in the two countries will provide considerable insight into the relations among bureaucratic integration, organizational form, and business performance.

In the next section of this paper, I outline how management development resulted in bureaucratic integration in the United States in roughly the first half of the twentieth century. To American-style management development I then contrast the mode of management development that generally prevailed in Britain well into the second half of the twentieth century—a mode in which technical specialization and general management were highly segmented in terms of both training and careers, underdeveloping and undermining the ability of general managers to coordinate the specialized division of labor. In the final section, I consider the relationship between management development and the multidivisional enterprise in the light of the U.S.–British comparison.

II. Bureaucratic Integration in the United States

The integration of U.S. higher education with business has provided a model that other capitalist societies have sought to replicate in the post-World War II period. As the foundation of the management development process, the U.S. educational system has provided industrial corporations with large supplies of managerial and technical personnel. Through the liberal-arts orientation of undergraduate education in the United States, potential managers can develop social values, communicative skills, and a general understanding of social process that are basic for cooperative participation and generalist training within the firm. As technical preparation for specialist roles, in which recruits to the bureaucracy must almost always begin their careers, higher education is structured to provide familiarity with basic principles in science, technology, commerce, and human relations. In addition, the professional orientation of graduate as well as some undergraduate

education can equip the potential manager with specialized knowledge in fields as diverse as accounting, marketing, and chemical
engineering.

With this system of higher education in place, corporate employers have been able to take for granted that recruits to the managerial
bureaucracy will possess a level of competency in social and technical skills necessary for effective performance. Within the
corporate structures, management development programs that are
designed to shape social attitudes and cognitive abilities to meet
firm-specific needs can build upon pre-employment educational
foundations.

The fit between the U.S. system of higher education and business
has never been perfect. In the 1950s, for example, there were
complaints that university graduates were too specialized to become
top managers.[5] Besides, as a social institution, higher education
does serve nonbusiness purposes and respond to nonbusiness pressures. Nevertheless, comparative perspective makes it clear that
the U.S. educational system has been very business-oriented since
the turn of the century. As we shall see, the system of higher education had not been brought into the service of business in Britain
even by the 1960s as it had been in the United States some 40 or
50 years earlier. Why was this the case? Why was there a successful
integration of higher education with business in the one country
but not in the other?

In the mid-nineteenth century the form and content of higher
education in the United States and Britain were not markedly
different. Harvard and Yale had been modeled after Oxford and
Cambridge and, along with a few other colleges established in the
colonial period, set the standards for the 261 colleges and universities founded between 1776 and 1865. Until the post-bellum period
(and beyond in many institutions) the basis of the college curric-
ulum was classical—Latin, Greek, mathematics, moral philosophy,
a little Hebrew, and very elementary physics and astronomy—and
reflected Oxbridge tradition in methods of teaching and academic
ritual as well as subject matter.[6]

The early American college ostensibly provided a stepping-stone
to careers in the "learned professions" (law, medicine, and theology)

as well as politics. But a college education was by no means necessary to enter these callings. It was only later in the nineteenth century that the professional schools in law and medicine became part of the system of higher education. Until that time, a college degree had little value as an occupational credential but considerable value as a symbol of elite status.

From the late nineteenth century onward, the American system of higher education—including the most elite colleges, such as Harvard and Yale—underwent a dramatic transformation away from the classical model with its aristocratic creed to a utilitarian model designed to ready large numbers of people for professional and business careers. Two social forces—one ideological and the other practical in nature—were present in the United States that brought about the integration of higher education into economic activity.

First, there was the ideology of equal opportunity that prevailed in the United States, an ideology that flourished in the absence of a traditional aristocratic class on the one hand and the presence of considerable social mobility on the other. In the first half of the nineteenth century the aristocratic pretensions of the existing institutions of higher learning were in conflict with the dominant Jeffersonian ideology, which viewed independent farmers and artisans as the warp and weft of the American social fabric. In the 1820s representatives of these social groups began to argue for the establishment of higher education that would be of relevance to the so-called industrial classes. The outcome of these movements was the passage in 1862 of the Morrill Land Grant College Act, which gave each of the states an endowment for a college that could serve the intellectual needs of the sons and daughters of America's yeomanry.

To some extent the land-grant colleges adapted their curricula and rituals (including the awarding of Bachelor of Arts degrees) to the classical model in an attempt to reap the cultural prestige of the older institutions. But a distinguishing feature of the new colleges was the goal of offering instruction of practical relevance to farmers and artisans. Nevertheless, with the notable exception of Cornell University, the land-grant colleges had difficulty attracting students in the quarter-century after the Civil War, in part because secondary education was not well enough developed in the United States to supply the colleges with qualified students and in part because farmers and artisans simply did not perceive the net benefit to their sons and daughters of a four-year college degree.

It was only in the 1890s, when the U.S. Department of Agriculture and big business began to take an interest in higher education, that the land-grant colleges started to attract large numbers of students. With government funding and private support (mainly from the Rockefeller-endowed General Education Board, banks, large retailers such as Sears, Roebuck, and agricultural machinery manufacturers such as John Deere and International Harvester), the land-grant colleges began to be used for scientific experimentation as well as for the training of agents who could demonstrate new agricultural methods to the farmers. Of more significance for industry was the development of engineering education within the land-grant colleges, most notably at M.I.T., for the purpose of supplying trained personnel to the emerging bureaucratic structures of the large manufacturing corporations.

The integration of the land-grant colleges into the system of corporate production put great pressure on the classical colleges to adapt their curricula, often against the wishes of educators. Particularly after the turn of the century, large sums of money began to flow into higher learning from big business in order to shape the educational system in its own image and to supply its personnel and scientific needs. Bolstered by business support, land-grant colleges such as M.I.T. and Purdue began graduating large numbers of engineers. In 1870 only 100 engineering degrees were conferred in the United States, and these mostly in civil engineering. By 1914 the system of higher education was producing some 4,300 engineering graduates, mainly in industrial, chemical, and electrical engineering, to serve the needs of the new mass-production and science-based industries.

Prior to 1898 there was only one business school—Wharton—in the United States. In 1908 the Graduate School of Business Administration at Harvard University provided the first bona fide graduate education in business, admitting only students with bachelor's degrees. Between 1908 and 1930 more than 100 undergraduate and graduate business schools came into being. By 1952, 173 universities contained business schools, of which ten were exclusively for graduate study.[7]

The U.S. system of higher education underwent significant expansion in all its faculties in the first half of the twentieth century. In 1900 about 2% of 18- to 24-year-olds were enrolled in institutions of higher education; in 1930, over 7%; and in 1950, over 14%. Between 1900 and 1930 the number of bachelor's or first professional degrees per thousand 23-year-olds tripled from 19 to 57, and between 1930 and 1950 more than tripled again. The supply of graduate students also expanded rapidly: in 1900 there were six master's or second professional degrees awarded per 100 bachelor's degrees awarded two years earlier; by 1930 this figure had risen to 15, and by 1950, to 22.[8]

As both cause and effect of this transformation of the system of higher education was a change in attitude toward college graduates that seems to have appeared around the turn of the century. In the nineteenth century Andrew Carnegie argued the case against college education for business:

> In my own experience I can say that I have known few young men intended for business who were not injured by a collegiate education. Had they gone into active work in the years spent in college they would have been better educated in every true sense of the term.

Later Carnegie changed his mind, asserting that "the exceptional graduate should excel the exceptional nongraduate. He has more education, and education will always tell, the other qualities being equal."[9] In 1900 the author of an article entitled "College Education and Business" reiterated the common nineteenth-century view that "the graduate has not the slightest chance, entering [business] at twenty, against the boy who swept the office, or begins as a shipping clerk at fourteen." He went on to argue, however, that as the educational system forsook "culture for its own sake" and sought to bestow "culture for the sake of making the whole man active for the purposes of masterful reaction with an external world of affairs," a college education would become relevant for business.[10]

The rise of the corporate enterprise in the United States created great demands for bureaucratic personnel. The total number of salaried managers and administrators in the United States increased from 352,000 (1.3% of the paid labor force) in 1900 to 1,348,000 (3.0%) in 1930. Over the same period the number of employees with professional degrees rose from 913,000 (3.1% of the paid labor force) to 2,488,000 (5.7%). The number of engineers in the United States grew from 38,000 in 1900 to 217,000 in 1930. The number of chemical, metallurgical, and mining engineers increased from 3,000 to 14,000 over this period, and the number of industrial, mechanical, and electrical engineers rose from 14,000 to 116,000.[11]

Increasingly, the large corporations turned to the system of higher education to find fresh recruits to fill technical and administrative positions in the growing bureaucracies. For example, Procter & Gamble began to recruit technical and sales personnel from college campuses as early as 1918. Similarly, Goodyear began going to the colleges in 1917, and by the 1920s recruitment at engineering and business schools was a basic part of its management development program. In the mid-1920s Goodyear's rival, Firestone, was providing in-house management development to college graduates. By recruiting on the campuses every year, Harvey Firestone, Jr., argued, "we'll have a continuous complement of good men on hand acquiring the experience necessary for filling important posts. Their first jobs will merely be stepping-stones to their future responsibilities."[12]

Prior to 1928 Sears, Roebuck recruited managers for its rapidly growing mail-order and retail-store business from executive placement agencies in New York. In 1928, however, an increase in the number of stores in operation from 25 to 192 strained the limits of outside recruitment. The following year Robert Wood, Sears's chief executive, even considered a merger with J. C. Penney as a means of securing trained store managers. Instead, Sears began recruiting at colleges as a first step in a new policy of training and promoting managers from within (a policy that the company was already pursuing at nonmanagerial levels). By 1934, according to Boris Emmet and John Jeuck, "the company was recruiting from colleges on a systematic basis."[13]

By 1930 well over 90% of the stock of university-educated engineers were employed in technical and managerial positions in industrial firms. Certainly after World War II, if not before, large corporate employers simply assumed that technical and managerial personnel would be recruited from the ranks of college and university graduates. The growing predominance of college graduates in U.S. business is reflected in a number of studies carried out in the 1950s on the changing educational backgrounds of top business executives.[14] Thirty percent had degrees in both 1870 and 1900, but by 1925 the proportion had increased to 40% and by the early 1950s to over 60%. An increasing, but by no means predominant, proportion of these top executives had specialized degrees. In Mabel Newcomer's study, the proportion with engineering degrees rose from under 7% in 1900 to over 13% in 1925 to 20% in 1950, and the proportion with law degrees rose from over 8% in 1900 to 12% in 1925, then fell to slightly under 12% in 1950. In public utilities about 34% of top executives had engineering degrees in 1950, whereas in railroads this proportion was about 20% and in industrials about 16%. In the *Fortune* study of top executives in the early 1950s, 46% had educational backgrounds in science and engineering, 31% in business and economics, 15% in law, and 9% in arts.

The qualitative importance of the reshaping of higher education was that it provided pre-employment foundations for bureaucratic integration within the corporate organization. The relationship between the transformation of U.S. engineering education and the rise of the corporate economy as documented by David Noble is a case in point.[15] In the last decades of the nineteenth century, the prominence of mechanical engineers as owners and managers of growing manufacturing firms led to the professionalization of engineering (the American Society of Mechanical Engineers was formed in 1885) and a clear distinction between the engineer and the mechanic. Although not themselves college graduates, many of the early entrepreneur-engineers began to support the integration of engineering education into the college system as a further move-

ment toward professionalization. Their prime concern was the
development of standards of technical competence and social outlook among potential recruits to the growing bureaucracies. Thus,
by the second decade of the twentieth century, "school culture"
was rapidly replacing "shop culture" in the training of mechanical
engineers. In the new, expanding chemical and electrical industries,
where no strong shop-culture traditions existed, the training of
engineers quickly developed within the system of higher education.

In the professionalization of engineering in the United States, the
expectation was that engineers who demonstrated their technical
worth to the corporation would climb the hierarchy to assume
managerial responsibilities. As the president of the American Institute of Chemical Engineers told the first convention in 1908: "There
must be a body of men supplied in increasing numbers who can
take charge of [the science-based] industries, first as aides and
ultimately as managers of the several works, qualified to continue
the successful administration of the same and able to push them
steadily to fuller development along safe and profitable lines."[16]
From the 1920s onward, the engineering professions made systematic efforts to ensure that engineering education would be adapted
to corporate bureaucratic needs. Management subjects became
increasingly important in engineering curricula (by 1940 a minimum of 20% of the course work had to be in the social sciences,
broadly defined). Many undergraduates with engineering degrees
began to take advantage of the expanding facilities for graduate
studies in business administration.

The influential Wickenden report on engineering education, published in 1930, stressed the social training of engineers to equip
them not only for more immediate technical work but also for
future managerial responsibilities. In the 1930s the Engineers Council for Professional Development, a body that combined engineering
educators and corporate executives, took up the task of imple-
menting the proposals of the Wickenden report. According to Noble,
the efforts of the ECPD meant that "success in the profession now
officially meant education for both subordinate technical employment in and responsible management of corporate industry."[17] In

other words, U.S. engineering education was striving to produce a "bureaucratically integrated" product.

The business schools also sought to provide future managers with a general education while at the same time laying foundations for the development of technical competence in a particular specialty. At midcentury the typical undergraduate program was made up of at least 40% nonbusiness courses, core courses in economics, accounting, statistics, business law, finance, marketing, and management, and specialized courses in one or more of these subjects. At the graduate level, M.B.A. courses sought to provide specialized training in a chosen field, but not at the expense of a general approach to business administration.[18]

For large U.S. corporations, the system of higher education laid the foundations for management development policies designed not only to secure competent specialists but also to transform the best performers among these specialists into general managers. All new recruits were allocated to a specialist department. As Newcomer remarks in her study of big-business executives, "training for general administration [at lower managerial levels] is rare, and the demand for 'general administrators' just out of college is almost unheard of."[19] Engineering graduates went into production, law graduates into legal departments, and those with nonprofessional degrees into purchasing, marketing, finance, or lower-level line positions (where, in effect, specialist experience in human relations could be gained). The new employee then had to demonstrate his or (rarely) her worth to the firm as a specialized cog in the corporate machine if he or she expected career advancement.

By the 1920s, therefore, the system of higher education provided the foundations for bureaucratic integration. But many top executives still viewed the specialization of salaried personnel at earlier stages of their careers as problematic for the development of general managers by promotion from within. In 1936, for example, James O. McKinsey, chairman of the American Management Association, argued, "As activities become more specialized and routinized it becomes more difficult to develop ability in the ranks. . . . It may not be safe for us to rely upon securing a sufficient number from the ranks who will qualify for executive leadership." Or as Barnard put it, "We deliberately and more and more turn out specialists; but we do not develop general executives well by specific efforts, and we know very little about how to do it." Newcomer claims that her search of the management literature revealed a "consensus that the top executive needs broader training than the specialists are apt to get" but that most top executives were in fact being promoted from within the company.[20]

One way to resolve the problem would have been to create an elite group of general managers who would begin their careers as coordinators rather than as parts of the specialized division of labor. In Britain family management and elite education served precisely this role. But the separation of ownership from control in many large U.S. corporations after the turn of the century made it difficult for corporate leadership simply to be passed down from father to son. Nor was there an existing elite in American society whose members, quite apart from property ownership, possessed ascribed status that would have given them legitimacy as candidates for such generalist roles. The growth of the land-grant colleges, moreover, had had a leveling influence on the elite status of the older universities, diminishing greatly the extent to which a Harvard or Yale degree in itself brought its bearer a distinct social standing that could confer a claim to immediate generalist status. Even elite graduate programs in business administration did not create a class of generalist recruits. The route to top-management positions was surer and faster for M.B.A.s, but even they had to begin as specialists and work their way up the corporate hierarchy.[21]

In the early decades of this century the system of higher education was providing the corporations with personnel with a mix of specialist training and generalist outlook. Given the supportive educational environment, the internal promotion of specialists to generalist rank was sound corporate policy. The success of corporate expansionary strategies required the agglomeration of large amounts of specialized knowledge. Specialists were needed in abundance. But in a land of individualism, enterprise, and expectations of social mobility, the corporations had to offer a member of the newly educated elite more than just a job.[22] To retain good specialists and get the desired quantity and quality of work effort out of them, the corporations had to offer the specialist a career.

In 1931 the director of employment and training for the New York Telephone Company asserted that "large companies employ young men and promote to the more responsible places the men who are already in the organization. There usually must be some special reason, which can be stated with justification to those within the organization, when an outsider is brought in and placed in a high-salaried position."[23] To secure the attachment and loyalty of the individual, the corporation had to hold out the prospect of a career unfettered by inherent barriers to upward mobility, such as a rigid segmentation of bureaucratic personnel into lifelong specialists and lifelong generalists. Outstanding performance by lower-level and middle-level bureaucratic personnel would be suitably rewarded by social mobility within the corporation.

Upward mobility on a meritocratic basis also helped counteract tendencies for superiors to stifle the development of subordinates for fear of losing their own jobs. In the interwar period the head of Goodyear, Paul Litchfield (an M.I.T. graduate) was explicit in making dispensability in one's current position a precondition for promotion: "A man is ready for promotion only when he has his department so well organized that it will carry on just as efficiently after he has left it." Given this promotion structure, Litchfield could instruct his middle managers:

> Don't be afraid that the man under you will know more than you do, and so take your job away from you. Give your key men full information. Let them know the reasons for decisions. Put jobs up to them which will compel them to organize their work and make their own decisions—which you can review.

In a similar vein, in 1930 Walter Teagle, president of Standard Oil (New Jersey), warned the company's top operating officers that "no executive can be said to have done his full duty unless and until he has made available for promotion to his position a man or men capable of assuming and administering his office."[24]

Attachment, and presumably loyalty, to the organization could be well rewarded. Newcomer found that only 18% of the 1900 sample had reached higher management levels by working within the company, whereas this proportion was over 37% in 1925 and about 51% in 1950. In the 1950 sample, working from within was particularly important for those who started with high school diplomas (62%) as well as those who had professional and engineering degrees (53% and 54%, respectively), and less marked among those with some college or a college degree (46% and 42%, respectively). The average age of attaining top positions was about 50 years in 1900, 1925, and 1950. The proportion of the 1950 executives who had worked their way up within the company was almost identical in railroad, industrial, and public utility corporations, but increased markedly with the assets of the firm.[25]

Suzanne Keller found that only 10% of the top executives in her 1870 and 1900 samples had worked for only one company, as compared with 27% in the 1950 sample. The careers of 68% of the 1870 sample and 56% of the 1900 sample but only 17% of the 1950 sample were classified as "self-made" or "family-made," with the rest being either "bureaucratically made" or "professionally made." In 1870 only 12% of the business leaders, and in 1900 still only 23%, had spent 20 or more years in their current company before reaching the top. But by 1950, 46% had been with the company for 20 or more years. One-third of the 900 high-ranking executives in the *Fortune* study had spent their whole career with only one company, and another 26% with only one other company.[26]

A standard method for transforming specialists into generalists in large U.S. corporations was to move promising lower-level and middle-level managers around from region to region, department to department, and division to division. By the early 1920s many large industrial corporations gave college graduates a one- or two-year internship, sometimes even before placing them in specialist positions, moving them through the various functional departments of the firm with a view to creating integrated managers. For example, in 1933 Sears began its "reserve-group program" for training personnel who seemed capable of doing more than routine work. By the 1940s Sears was recruiting 200 or more college graduates per year who, through superior performance in initial job assignments, would try to make the reserve group. The basic training technique was four or five years of job rotation. As early as 1913, Goodyear had placed promising technical (and, beginning in 1927, sales) personnel in "flying squadrons," the members of which were moved around within the company in order to gain the broader understanding of operations necessary for the generalist. In developing these training schemes, management did not necessarily take existing job structures as given. As a top executive at Standard Oil (New Jersey) argued in 1949:

> Systematic job rotation is one method used for giving a broader understanding of the business as a whole. Sometimes it is necessary to create assistant or "assistant to" positions to make available some desired experience.[27]

Marshall Dimock contends that the coordination of skilled staff activity at general headquarters with line activity in its divisions was an important factor in the success of administrative decentralization at AT&T from the 1920s onward. "Indeed," he argued, "its staff work, its decentralization policy, and its careful selection of executives constitute what most outside observers consider the three most prominent features of the corporation's management." By the 1930s AT&T was bringing promising recruits from field units to the staff offices in New York, then sending them back to line positions in the field after three or four years. In addition, within its multidivisional structure AT&T elevated top staff positions in its central office to upper-management status. According to Dimock, these transfers between general headquarters and the divisions were used strategically over a person's career:

> At a certain point it may be discovered that a particular individual has an outstanding talent as a central office staff man; he has the necessary temperament plus a certain wisdom and levelheadedness, a philosophical cast of mind and a native diplomacy, that "go down well" with the field. Such a man may be kept in a top staff position for the rest of his official career. But if a man shows any inclination to become stale or to act remote, these being signs of boredom and bureaucracy, he is quickly transferred back to the field because action at that level [that is, on the line] keeps a man alert and discourages complacency and inertia.[28]

The multidivisional form of organization that was becoming more widespread in the corporate sector of U.S. industry from the 1920s onward required bureaucratic integration if it was to be an effective device for administrative decentralization. If middle managers were to be able to make profitable managerial decisions about processes and products, they had to be able to integrate into the decision-making process specialist information concerning market prices, the nature of product markets, the availability of resources, industrial relations, legal constraints on prospective activities, and technological potential. The key to successful bureaucratic integration on the basis of the multidivisional structure was not only the decentralization of line responsibility but also the company-wide coordination of staff activities to ensure that operational decision makers had knowledge of, as well as access to, relevant specialized information.

In 1945 Ralph Cordiner, himself a college graduate who had spent some 20 years climbing up the managerial hierarchy to become a General Electric vice-president (and future president), made the case for bureaucratic integration. He argued that a line type of organization was useful for "the clear definition of responsibility and authority, and ease of securing discipline," but that it would render managers incapable of taking full advantage of specialist knowledge generated by research and development, marketing, and production staffs. The functional form of organization, on the other hand, tended to create confusion in lines of authority and responsibility and "to develop narrowness through specialization." What a diversified company like G.E. needed, he argued, was an integration of line and staff types of organizations to preserve the advantages of each. Besides the decentralization of decision making in manufacturing operations in order to bring general management "as close as possible to the daily problems and daily decisions bearing on the individual transactions and the individual productive efforts," G.E. put into effect "a corresponding integration . . . on a company-wide basis . . . of the functional activities and developments in each technical field."[29]

The training and movement of managerial personnel within the company was critical to the success of the multidivisional structure.

According to Cordiner:

> A distinct line organization cannot properly arrange for the selec-
> tion of technical and prospective executive talent, for the broad
> education of that talent, for the rotation of personnel to provide
> basic experience and determine real aptitude, and for the assuring
> of promotion on a company-wide merit basis, contrasted with a
> restricted department or division basis.

The integrated organizational structure made possible company-
wide coordination of management development, a key component
of which was, in Cordiner's words, "development, through integration, of management ability at an early date." At all levels in
the organization, staff and line executives were accorded equal
hierarchical stature, and the most competent operating executives
were regularly appointed to head the staff functions where they had
some prior expertise.[30]

As we have seen, Barnard, a past president of New Jersey Bell,
did not believe that managerial practice as it existed in the late
1930s contained much knowledge about how to turn specialists into
generalists. Nevertheless, in the interwar years large U.S. corporations were actively confronting the problem of how to implement management development policies that would aid in the
coordination of the specialized division of labor. These efforts were
in sharp contrast to the British situation, documented below. At a
minimum, the transformation of the U.S. system of higher education to provide "organization men" to business created solid
underpinnings for bureaucratic integration within the enterprise in
the first half of this century. As we shall now argue, such a transformation did not occur in Britain, primarily because British
business did not put pressure on the educational system to provide
"integrated" corporate personnel.

III. Bureaucratic Segmentation in Britain

In the late nineteenth and early twentieth centuries, the persist-
ence of a highly fragmented structure of industrial organization in
Britain contrasted sharply with the rise of big business in the United
States. After the turn of the century the largest British firms were

not only much smaller than the largest U.S. firms but also much more under the control of family owners.[31] In many U.S. industries the massive merger movement of the 1890s and 1900s created oligopolistic market power by transferring ownership of existing assets from the entrepreneurial industrialists who had built up the firms to dispersed shareholders. The result was the separation of capital ownership from managerial control. Top managers controlled the long-run destiny of the corporate entity. But as the agents of property owners, they lost any inherent right to pass on that control to their kin as inherited property.

The separation of ownership and control did not render nepotism impossible. In many cases stock ownership of a public company was so widely distributed that top managers could have appointed their successors unchallenged. But given the size of the new oligopolies, the expectations for social mobility prevalent in the United States, and the growing availability of bureaucratic personnel produced by the system of higher education, a nepotistic firm would have been at a competitive disadvantage compared with an enterprise that took up the opportunities for creating an integrated bureaucratic structure. In the American context, therefore, even when the family remained dominant in the firm (as at Dupont and IBM), there were strong pressures for family members to acquire professional credentials and work their way up from specialist to generalist status.

In the British social context, the widespread persistence of the practice of passing on managerial control of the firm to family members from generation to generation had a far-reaching impact on management development (or, more accurately, underdevelopment). For the sake of maintaining control, the family firm often adopted a nonexpansionary strategy in order to avoid becoming dependent upon outside creditors and shareholders or an internal bureaucracy of technical specialists and middle managers. The widespread persistence of the *small* family firm in the early decades of this century meant, therefore, that the industrial demand for managerial and technical personnel was moderate when compared with that in the United States. For many, if not most, British firms a reluctance by owners to share managerial control dictated a low-growth enterprise strategy, which in turn generated little pressure for the creation and expansion of social institutions for the development of professional managerial personnel.

Some British family firms, however, were willing and able to expand in the early twentieth century. In cases such as Pilkington Bros. and Imperial Tobacco, the existence of a large issue of off-spring from whom to recruit top managers meant that the family could pursue an expansionary strategy without facing the danger of losing control over enterprise policy and operations. In other cases, such as Brunner, Mond and Courtaulds, the basis of family-firm expansion was a first-mover advantage secured by control over a key scientific or technological innovation. In still other cases, such as Lever Bros., the source of first-mover advantage was an aggressive entrepreneur who quickly established brand-name recognition for a household product.[32]

Whatever the factors that enabled the growth of the family firm (and, of course, where some succeeded others failed), in the middle of this century family control remained widespread and substantial in the largest British industrial firms, whereas it had already become almost nonexistent in the largest U.S. industrial corporations some four decades earlier. In those large British firms where one family maintained control, the growth of the firm had typically come from internal expansion. During the interwar period, however, an increasingly common route to growth of British firms was amalgamation rather than internal expansion. Competitive firms combined to control product prices rather than to rationalize operations, leaving previous family owners with their managerial autonomy intact within the amalgamated organization.[33]

The persistence of family control meant that at the higher managerial levels recruitment was from within a fairly closed circle. In 1927 Lyndall Urwick, then the organizing secretary for Rowntree, argued:

> Broadly speaking, in ninety-nine hundredths of British industry there is no system of promotion. Family connections, ownership of capital, toadyism, seniority, inertia, or luck decide which men shall be selected to rule their fellows. . . . It is a fact that in the majority of our great enterprises, there is no analysis of the factors which

constitute "fitness" for most of the managerial positions and no
methods of measuring or assessing those factors whatever.[34]

One observer in the 1920s told an industrial conference at Oxford
that the only principle of organization that he had been able to
discover in English industry was "myself, my father, my son, and
my wife's sister's nephew." In the mid-1920s an American visitor,
surveying the then-depressed British industrial scene, wrote that
"a tremendous drawback to effective business organization in
England is the habit of asking who you are, as opposed to the
American inquiry as to what you are."[35] In other words, the
professionalization of British industrial management had not yet
occurred.

The principle of asking "who you are" fit well with notions of
aristocratic privilege that remained entrenched in Britain well into
the twentieth century. British industrialists, however, did not themselves emerge from the ranks of the hereditary aristocracy. In the
nineteenth century their social status was at best middle class. The
upper class, living off parentage rather than achievement, frowned
upon the active pursuit of moneymaking through industry precisely
because it required education (whether formal or informal) in skills
that were not developed through an aristocratic upbringing or
appropriate social connections. Indeed, in nineteenth-century Britain it was skilled workers, even more than middle-class industrialists,
who possessed knowledge of, and control over, technology. The
aristocratic bias against technology was, if anything, strengthened
in the late nineteenth and early twentieth centuries by the fact that
material well-being was becoming ever more dependent on the
application of technical knowledge. Aristocratic antipathy to industry remained strong well into the twentieth century. In 1961, for
example, the deputy secretary of the Ministry of Education recalled
that when he left school (presumably in the 1920s), "trade was not
respectable. The City of London was all right, but manufacturing
industry was not. I believe the picture is changing *slightly and
recently.*"[36]

Rather than confront aristocratic ideology and values, British
industrialists sought to partake of them. Successful British business-

men aspired to use their newly acquired wealth to escape the middle class and become gentlemen.[37] In this goal they were accommodated by the distribution of peerages. If they did not actually put their fortunes into landed estates, they at least sent offspring to the elite public schools and perhaps to Oxford or Cambridge. Data collected in the mid-1950s on a cross section of managers indicate that over the first half of the twentieth century an increasing proportion were recruited from the public schools, and that by midcentury a highly disproportionate number of those from the major public schools had reached top management levels.[38]

Given the aristocratic aversion to industry and technology, therefore, affluent British businessmen who aspired to aristocratic status were loath to exert great pressure on the elite educational system to make it directly useful to business. As early as 1903, a British visitor noted the importance of a university education for rapid promotion within the firm in the United States, not because of the prestige but rather because of the knowledge that it provided. He chided, "In America you cannot waste four years more efficiently than by not going to university. The same is true in England, but for reasons of general culture, not of commercial success."[39] From the point of view of social mobility, the interests of British businessmen lay more in preserving than in transforming existing institutions.

The ultimate impact of the pursuit of aristocratic status by industrialists was to legitimize and reinforce the closed circle of managerial succession by constituting higher management as a social class apart within the enterprise. A powerful mechanism for implanting the existing class structure in the enterprise as well as reproducing it in society as a whole was the evolution of a highly segmented system of higher education. The prestige of the ancient universities, Oxford and Cambridge, could not be challenged by the civic universities that grew up in the early part of this century; and both these institutions stood above the technical colleges that arose out of governmental reform of higher education in the post-World War II period.

At the turn of the century attendance at Oxford or Cambridge was of immense value for achieving high position in the civil service. But there was little flow of these elite graduates to industry. Before

World War I, however, a number of business enterprises began to recruit managerial personnel on a regular basis from Cambridge, on a scale that, according to Michael Sanderson, was "totally new compared with the 1880s and 1890s." Most Oxford and Cambridge graduates who entered industry had arts degrees, a trend that remained true through the interwar period and into the post-World War II era. The study of managerial succession in the mid-1950s by the Acton Society Trust found that in terms of upward mobility in the business world the most advantageous educational background for a British manager was an arts degree from Oxford or Cambridge, and the second most advantageous was attendance at a major public school.[40]

Science graduates from Oxford and Cambridge were not ignored. In the early decades of the century some forward-looking, science-based firms, such as Brunner, Mond, Crosfield's, and British Petroleum, were eager to employ Oxbridge-trained chemists, engineers, and geologists. These companies needed people with scientific knowledge and analytical ability. Elite social credentials were also welcomed, however, as evidenced by Brunner, Mond, where membership in the Winnington Hall Club was "a carefully guarded privilege," and where "the whole structure [of hierarchical status] rested on class distinction." It also helped to become a member of the owning family. A promising Cambridge science graduate hired in 1911 by Pilkington's rose to a high position in the tightly knit family firm, his career aided immeasurably no doubt by marrying into the Pilkington family in 1922.[41]

The loss of potential managerial successors to family-dominated firms in World War I led these firms to approach the Cambridge Appointments Board in the interwar period, seeking Cambridge graduates as suitable substitutes who could rise to the higher levels very quickly.[42] In addition, and undoubtedly of more importance, British firms, constrained in many cases by family size, came to see the products of public schools and Oxbridge as trustworthy family surrogates who would make possible a strategy of growth. These educational institutions continued to stress aristocratic values and social class status, and insofar as British industry recruited from them, the social structure of the firm tended to display the hierarchical social distinctions that were deeply embedded in British society.

The relatively closed ranks at the higher management levels segmented general management from specialists and lower-level line managers (often drawn from the ranks of specialists). As British firms grew in size in the interwar period, bureaucratic segmentation became the norm, and it appears to have remained characteristic of British managerial structures even into the 1960s and 1970s.[43] Again we see a sharp contrast with the United States. Although U.S. managerial personnel were an elite relative to white-collar and blue-collar workers, higher education and internal-promotion policies integrated specialists and lower-level managers into this elite instead of excluding them as was the case in Britain.

The creation of the civic universities in the early decades of this century both reflected and reinforced the bureaucratic segmentation of specialists from generalists. As a practical matter, the main interest of businessmen in the expansion of the system of higher education was the need for technical specialists in the new science-based industries, and particularly in chemicals. Some early science-based firms secured the necessary expertise abroad, typically in Germany. But with the growth of competition for these relatively scarce personnel (who might take trade secrets back with them to Germany), British firms were willing to employ home-grown scientists if they could be found in the slowly growing chemistry departments of British universities.

After the turn of the century some of Britain's wealthier industrialists began to donate large sums for the expansion of higher education through provincial civic universities, such as Manchester, Birmingham, and Bristol. Sanderson suggests that the act of gift giving may have been motivated by unwritten philanthropic prerequisites for knighthood.[44] In any case, the best-off of the new institutions were decently, if not extravagantly, endowed when compared with U.S. land-grant colleges. In 1913 the endowment income of Manchester, the richest of the civic universities, was $112,000, only 15% less than that of M.I.T. But the increasing integration of U.S. higher education into the affairs of a dynamic economy meant that there were sources of income for colleges and universities in the

United States that were not so readily available in Britain. At M.I.T. in 1913 income from students was three times endowment income. Cornell, another land-grant college, had investment income in excess of $450,000 in 1913, and tuition income of about the same amount. In the United States, moreover, the interest of federal and state governments as well as of private foundations and alumni in funding higher education was on the rise. In the late 1930s the total income of the U.S. system of higher education was five times greater per capita than that of the British system, and this ratio may well have been even higher earlier in the century.[45]

To be of practical relevance to industry, the civic universities tended to adopt a more favorable view of instruction in science and technology than did Oxford and Cambridge. By the same token, however, the new institutions became less capable of challenging the ancient universities as purveyors of social standing. Given the aristocratic bias against industrial pursuits, the more the civic universities produced specialists for industry, the more they could be depicted as second-rate institutions. As a 1914 Oxford broadsheet jibed:

> He gets degrees in making jam
> At Liverpool and Birmingham.[46]

The Cambridge University Appointments Board found that many firms that were favorable to technically trained university graduates in the late 1930s were of the opinion that equally good technical knowledge could be acquired at provincial universities or technical colleges "but that the Cambridge man of the right sort gets something beyond his technical training that is useful to him in industry." Quoting from firm responses, the report went on to say that " 'provided the individual has time for social activities,' a Cambridge course is good for technical posts in industry. It prevents a man from becoming 'too much a specialist and tends to develop his character.' " The Acton Society Trust study in the mid-1950s found that in terms of promotion within the firm, a degree from a civic university was inferior not only to attendance at Oxford, Cambridge, or a major public school but also to the possession of a nontechnical qualification or direct entry into the firm as a managerial trainee (presumably on the basis of personal connections). Even among civic-university graduates, those with arts degrees (less than one-sixth of the total) did significantly better than did those with science degrees.[47]

The failure of the civic universities to force change upon the elite institutions contrasts sharply with the way many of the land-grant colleges in the United States imposed their standards of useful knowledge and training on older colleges that had originally adopted the classical Oxbridge model of education. The result was that Britain developed a highly segmented university system that produced bureaucratic personnel for highly segmented managerial structures. The ancient universities supplied men thought to be suited for quick advancement to higher-level managerial positions, while the civic universities produced specialists tailored for lower-level salaried positions.

By the 1920s bureaucratic integration of specialized knowledge for the development, diffusion, and utilization of technology was already well underway in the U.S. corporate sector. Not so in Britain. Bureaucratic segmentation in British industry was, if anything, reinforced by the fact that the determination and control of technological standards and professional accreditation remained largely in the hands of people who did not see themselves as part of the "management team." The widespread persistence of highly competitive industry in Britain meant that many scientists and technologists were not even salaried employees of the industrial firms to which they provided specialist knowledge and advice. In British industries characterized by large numbers of relatively small firms, research and development was provided by separate, government-aided research associations rather than by in-house staff departments of industrial firms as was the practice in the United States.[48] Firms that were unwilling or unable to employ technical specialists directly could not even begin to implement a policy of management development designed to facilitate the coordination of the specialized division of labor.

But even technical specialists in the direct employ of larger British industrial firms could be resistant to coordination and control. Particularly in the mechanical technologies derivative of the first industrial revolution, much of the knowledge and decision making concerning the use of technology remained the prerogative of skilled blue-collar workers. As a result, in Britain the term "engineer" continued to connote a skilled craft worker well into the twentieth century, whereas in U.S. industry it had long since come to mean a college-educated member of a managerial team. In 1913 there were only 1,129 students in engineering in all the universities of England and Wales, none of them at the graduate level. In 1950 only 10% of the mechanical engineers in Britain were university educated. The engineering associations controlled access to the various branches of engineering, and even required university graduates to undergo apprenticeship. In some cases, as in the municipally run electricity supply industry, British electrical engineers maintained strong craftlike unions.[49]

Along with the very different socialization processes involved in apprenticeship as opposed to university education, a very different intellectual outlook distinguished the shop-culture from the school-culture engineer. To use the language of a British university-trained engineer visiting the United States in 1903, the distinction was between engineers who "could . . . apply rules, but not the principles upon which the rules were founded" and those who had had the opportunity for "the development of intellect—grasp, judgment, and ability to apply general principles to details."[50] The remarks of the editor of a British engineering journal confirm that shop culture so defined remained strong in British mechanical engineering in the late 1920s, well past the time when it had been superseded by school culture in the United States:

> In these days of organized college courses it is well to remember that in the last analysis the leaders in our industry are produced from one source—they are the products of the workshops or factories. . . . [I]t may be said that they are scientific without being scientists. A list of past presidents of our senior engineering institutions would include many names of distinguished leaders whose unique merit consisted in a highly developed mechanical instinct which was sufficient to guide them to the right point of view on any problem connected with their work. Without anything more than this valuable intuition many of our great engineers of the past would

continue to be eminent in these days. . . . A perusal of the correspondence and inquiry columns of engineering journals and the proceedings of institution meetings makes manifest the fact that the real difficulties of engineers are principally those of a practical character.[51]

As the heads of their own successful undertakings, some of the most outstanding shop-culture engineers sought unsuccessfully to continue to manage in the manner of the "practical man." For example, Charles Wilson and William Reader recount how, from the early nineteenth-century on, "three generations of a family each nobly endowed with engineering and inventive talent" permitted D. Napier & Son to remain a force in the British mechanical engineering industry. The Napiers, however, had "a dislike for the mass market and everything to do with it," an aversion that got them into periodic financial difficulties from the 1890s on. Struggling to stay in the game in the 1930s on the basis of past successes, financial setbacks thwarted any new engineering innovation, in part because "the best of [their] rising talent had been allowed to go."[52] In 1942 Napier's came under the control of English Electric.

The experience of a university-trained electrical engineer at Standard Telephones and Cables in the 1950s illustrates the persistence of shop-culture attitudes in Britain. The higher management of STC (the British subsidiary of ITT) was made up of shop-culture engineers "who in their time had made undeniable contributions to the progress and success of the company but who had now grown old together in a virtually closed society." Gordon Duddridge joined the firm in the early 1950s (he had been employed at ICI. before the war and then ran government factories) as "one of the first of the new breed of division managers [in charge of undersea cables] to have full responsibility embracing engineering, marketing, and manufacturing." But he had difficulty getting along with the chief engineer of the telephone cable division, who told him, "The whole trouble is you're a damned traitor, Gordon. You're working in manufacturing with a university degree. You're a traitor to the engineering cause."[53]

The family firm, aristocratic values, and control of technology by the "practical man" meant, therefore, that even by midcentury

British higher education did not as a rule provide a general technical and social training to future managers upon which firm-specific management development policies could build as was the case in the United States. By the 1940s, however, many British businessmen, consultants, and statesmen had come to recognize the economic superiority of American modes of management. Inspired by the success of technical and managerial education in the United States, the British sought to make their own system of higher education more relevant to business needs in the post-World War II period.

Active British interest in U.S. higher education goes back at least to the turn of the century, when the Moseley Educational Commission visited the United States. As the Commission reported, "The great industrial and commercial firms are abandoning the traditional methods of waiting for apprentices to 'come through,' and are attempting to manufacture the junior officers, by a rapid process, out of college graduates in technology and commerce."[54] In 1924 the Balfour Committee on Industry and Trade pointed out the tremendous disparity between the United States and Britain in the number of students in management education. The first important governmental initiative to reform British higher education was not undertaken until 1945, however, when the Committee on Education for Management (chaired by the well-known management consultant Lyndall Urwick) was appointed to make policy recommendations.[55]

The British Institute of Management was created in 1947, mainly to foster management education. British interest in the U.S. model of management education was sustained by two reports—one on education for executives and one on university training for engineers—issued by British "productivity teams" that had visited the United States.[56] In the 1950s attempts were made to expand and reorient the British system of higher education to provide managers and technical specialists to industry. But despite these efforts the relationship between education and industry remained underdeveloped in the 1960s and beyond.[57] Well into the post-World War II period the transformation of the system of higher education to provide the social and technical foundations of management development—a transformation that had occurred in the United States in the first decades of the twentieth century—had simply not taken place in Britain.

Under the National Scheme of Management Studies, most of the post-World War II expansion of higher education took place in technical colleges. T. M. Mosson argues:

> By the late 1950s the National Scheme . . . had fallen into a measure of disrepute. . . . Taken overall the scheme came to be associated by many with a low level of attainment and as a qualification with a lack of social prestige. It is probable that in the eyes of management the better courses run by the better colleges were degraded by association with the worst.[58]

Almost all the courses were taken part time, mainly in the evenings and often over a period of five years. In 1962 only two institutions offered full-time courses. The expansion of management education, therefore, was not designed to develop a new breed of management personnel but was, rather, an attempt to upgrade those already at work.[59]

Even then, middle managers who aspired to upward mobility did not make use of the colleges, viewing them as providing a form of working-class education that might provide satisfactory training for supervisors and foremen. Teachers at the technical colleges generally lacked university degrees, although many had business experience. Top business managers, however, were unwilling to give guest lectures at the colleges.[60]

As for the traditional universities, which had the social standing to appeal to middle and top managers, even by the mid-1960s management studies had not yet been deemed appropriate. Where management courses were taught, they focused on social skills and a widening of intellectual horizons. These courses were most useful to upper-level managers in their late thirties and early forties in transition from technical specialist to general management responsibilities. According to Mosson, "The objective is to enable the specialist turned generalist to use and control the work of specialists, or to enable him to understand the relationship between his firm and the environment."[61]

In terms of management careers, such training was probably too little too late. In the United States, the transformation of specialists into generalists was an essential purpose of management development *within* the firm that built upon the general *pre-employment* educational base, itself shaped by the evolving managerial structures' demands for bureaucratically integrated personnel. Well into the post-World War II period little if any comparable dynamic between corporate management structures and the system of higher education was evident in Britain.

It was not only the institutions but also the culture of management education that differed. In 1930 James A. Bowie, Director of the Department of Industrial Administration at Manchester, wrote, "To British eyes the most striking feature of the average American university is the highly organized character of daily life. . . . Except in some of the greatest universities, the American undergraduate is dominated by his time-table."[62] In his 1954 report *University Education for Business in the U.S.A.*, Norman Hunt, Professor of Organization of Industry and Commerce at Edinburgh, commented on his visit to the Harvard Business School:

> Students are frequently tested and graded, so that they are constantly subjected to pressure of work, shortage of time, and mental strain. This is quite deliberate and is part of the process of education for the hard competitive world of business. It is difficult for anyone with a background of British academic life to understand how this can be part of the activities of the university.[63]

In the 1950s Standard Telephones and Cables sent one of its managers to the Advanced Management Program at the Harvard Business School, but, according to the company historian, "he came back confused."[64]

By the late 1950s the only full-length postgraduate course in administration in a British university catered mainly to American and Canadian students. The Readership in Industrial Administration at Cambridge was endowed in 1954 with American matching funds. In 1968–69, there were only 300 students in M.B.A.-type courses (mostly of one-year duration) in Britain, compared with 19,000 in the United States.[65]

The lack of foundations of management development in the British educational system reflected the paucity of policies to transform specialists into generalists within British industrial firms. Of the 51 large companies included in the Acton Society Trust survey carried out in the mid-1950s, one-third had absolutely no organized system of management training, and only about 10% used internal job rotation as a mode of management development. Silberston argued that among specialists in the auto industry "job rotation is not . . . anything as widespread as it might be" and that the "practical difficulties are often considerable." As late as 1967, W. G. McClelland, Director and Professor of the Manchester Business School, argued the need for managerial job rotation to transform specialists into generalists and permit prospective leaders to escape dead-end jobs. But he went on to remark that it was "surprising how rarely such job rotation was arranged."[66]

The same study that found that the recruitment and training of top British managers had not changed much from the mid-1960s to the mid-1970s also found that production and site managers were drawn mainly from supervisory positions or craft occupations. Moreover, of those who had been classified as managers in 1965, 17% had been demoted to an operative occupation ten years later. Only 4% of the 2,637 managers in the 1975 sample had begun their careers in a managerial occupation. Across all managerial categories, the first jobs of at least one-fifth and perhaps as many as half of those in the sample were as semiskilled operatives.[67]

Throughout the twentieth century bureaucratic segmentation *has* been present in the United States, but it divides shop-floor and clerical workers from professional, managerial, and technical workers, with educational credentials serving as means of allocating people to segments and legitimizing the segmentation.[68] As a general rule, however, U.S. *managerial* structures have been characterized by bureaucratic integration. Conversely, in terms of training and promotion in British industrial bureaucracies, highly trained technical specialists were more closely integrated with shop-floor workers below than with general managers above. Within what we have come to think of as the corporate managerial structure, bureaucratic segmentation remained widespread in Britain as least through the 1950s, and apparently beyond.

IV.   Bureaucratic Integration and the Multidivisional Form

Previous comparative research into twentieth-century industrial development has shown that in the United States the multidivisional organizational form served as a potent means of enterprise expansion from the 1920s on, whereas in Britain this organizational form was rare even at midcentury.[69] The characteristic features of the multidivisional form are (1) centralized control over strategic decision making and long-run planning of enterprise activities, (2) the delegation of operational decision making to divisions that are monitored as profit centers, and (3) the rationalization and centralization of key staff functions. By enhancing the capability of top management to coordinate the specialized division of labor, the multidivisional form enables firms to extend the bounds of enterprise rationality, expanding the scope of their activities to a wider range of product lines and more far-reaching market locations.

In other words, the multidivisional form was very conducive to what I have called bureaucratic integration. Centralized control —a necessary but by no means sufficient condition for the success of the multidivisional capitalist corporation—facilitated management development programs that fostered bureaucratic integration. An important element of long-run planning was management development that was not confined to particular functional activities, product divisions, or geographic regions of the firm. Enterprise-wide management development programs made possible job-rotation schemes that involved the movement of people not only among divisions but also from divisions to centralized staff functions. Such career patterns were basic to a continuous process of transforming promising specialists into generalists. By enhancing the prospects for advancement within the firm, enterprise-wide management development programs provided an incentive to the junior or middle manager to identify more strongly with the enterprise as a whole than with a particular work group, specialist activity, or region.

Given centralized control, the key to the success of the multi-divisional form in the United States was the delegation of authority over operational decision making without loss of control by top management over enterprise strategy. The setting up of divisional profit centers and the monitoring of the performance of the divisions did not in and of itself create effective middle management. If middle managers were to be capable of directing the day-to-day operations of divisions along profitable lines, they themselves would have to be capable of coordinating and monitoring a specialized division of labor within their prescribed domains. The development of such generalist capability required the development of specialists who were more or less continuously in the process of becoming generalists. For such a training program to operate effectively the delegation of decision-making authority had to descend well down the managerial hierarchy, with the scope of coordination increasing as managers climbed the bureaucratic ladder.

Given the dependence of top management on employees to whom it had delegated considerable authority, positive incentives of advancement were much more powerful inducements to appropriate performance than were negative sanctions of dismissal. Just as the delegation of authority extended decision-making responsibility down the hierarchy, so open lines of promotion helped ensure that the loyalty of managerial personnel would extend up the hierarchy. Moreover, the very fact that managers could move up the hierarchy made them willing to pass on information and delegate authority to subordinates who might one day take their places, thus extending appropriate training and positive incentives further down the organizational structure. At the same time, by separating control of key staff functions from the divisions, top management ensured that critical information would not become the property of self-serving entities within the organization.

The importance of bureaucratic integration for the success of the multidivisional enterprise helps explain the relatively slow diffusion of the multidivisional form in British industry. By Derek F. Channon's account, in 1950 only 12 firms in Britain had adopted the multidivisional form, and only four of these were wholly British.[70] A necessary condition for long-run coordination of the firm's activities on the basis of the multidivisional form was the centralization of control within the firm. In cases of amalgamation of a number of family firms, the achievement of centralized coordination was often impeded by the persistence of separate family control over the various businesses within the amalgamated organization. It was only when control over strategic decision making had been centralized that top management had the power to delegate authority so that the firm could become involved in a wider array of products and regions.

But centralization of control over strategic decision making did not necessarily mean that top management would be able or willing to create an organizational structure that would permit the successful diversification and geographic expansion of the firm's activities.[71] Even for those large British firms where control over strategic decision making was centralized rather than fragmented, the aristocratic attitudes of the managerial elite combined with shop-culture control of technology made top management unwilling, and perhaps even unable, to delegate authority within the organization. Shop-culture control of technology, moreover, made it extremely difficult, if not impossible, for top management to rationalize and coordinate the functional activities of the firm.

Bureaucratic segmentation thus impeded the unbounding of rationality on the basis of a corporate hierarchy. It made top managers unwilling to delegate authority over operational decision making for fear of losing control of strategic decision making, and rendered them unable to coordinate the specialized division of labor. The evolution of British social institutions, moreover, did little to foster bureaucratic integration as did social institutions in the United States. If anything, twentieth-century expansion of the British educational system served more to reinforce bureaucratic segmentation than to break it down.

Prior to the 1950s, therefore, bureaucratic integration was very difficult in Britain. But it was not impossible. The case of Unilever, the product of the 1929 merger of British-based Lever Bros. with

Dutch-based Margarine Union, illustrates the conditions under which bureaucratic integration was possible even for a firm in which British management was dominant. The case of Unilever also supports the hypothesis that bureaucratic integration was a necessary condition for the success of the multidivisional form.

When Lever Bros. became part of Unilever in 1929, it brought with it 49 manufacturing concerns in the United Kingdom that maintained 48 separate sales organizations. Under Geoffrey Heyworth, who was to become chairman of Lever Bros. and Unilever in 1941, a process of reorganization was begun that continued throughout the 1930s and 1940s, resulting in one of Britain's first and few multidivisional enterprises in the first half of this century.[72]

Bureaucratic integration played an important role in the successful multidivisionalization of Unilever. Whether the founding Lever had himself been adept at delegating authority and developing managers is open to debate, although it does appear that Crosfield's, a pre-1920 acquisition of Lever Bros., had been in the forefront of management development in Britain. Next to Lever Bros., Crosfield's had become Britain's second largest soapmaker, a position that it had attained not so much by advertising effort as by pioneering scientific research. Early on, Crosfield's had begun to employ and promote British science graduates, while at the same time stressing upward mobility for all promising employees. Herbert Davis, who had joined Crosfield's in 1912, became a director of Unilever in the late 1930s and later a vice-chairman and member of the company's strategy-making committee. In general, Crosfield's management had little difficulty becoming integrated into the Unilever structure and supplied much in the way of managerial resources to the giant company.[73]

As part of its rationalization efforts in the 1930s, Unilever began a systematic management development program, apparently unhampered by either British or Dutch family influence.[74] According to Charles Wilson:

> [The 1930s] saw a steady infusion of recruits, a high proportion from the universities but some selected from inside the business. The recruits had to be tried and tested. All this meant continual experiment and interchange between the headquarters and factory

and between factory and factory. There was no room for a class of permanent central administrators. Men had to move, and the records show that they did move.

Within a multinational organization, the moves were often from country to country, so that "throughout the world . . . technicians and accountants of three or four different nationalities worked together."[75] Aside from the potential benefits of such movements for transforming specialists into generalists, the multinational context must have made difficult the survival of British aristocratic culture that contributed to bureaucratic segmentation in many large British-based firms.

In a rather thorough description of the multidivisional organizational structure at Unilever in 1950, Geoffrey Heyworth, the chairman, stated that "there are about 200 people who take on themselves the decisions which make or mar the success of the business as a whole," and he asserted that "the biggest job of top management is to ensure the quality of this 200." He continued:

> To do so it is necessary to know something of the quality of about three times that number in order to be able to make the best selection when vacancies arise. We not only have to know something of these 600, but we have to see that they get opportunities for gaining the necessary breadth of experience to be able to fill one of the 200 posts. This involves planning moves of promising people progressively. For example, a young production manager in England might be moved to an Advisory and Service Department in London or Rotterdam for a year or two before returning to a larger operating unit, perhaps abroad. He is observed by his immediate superior and by the travelling members of top management.

Heyworth went on to say that the war had interrupted the recruitment process, depleting the pool from which the 200 key managers could be drawn.

> In this situation our rule is that it is better to leave a vacancy unfilled than to lower the standard; and if we have to make a choice between filling a vacancy in an advisory department and filling one in an operating unit, priority is always given to the operating unit, because it is no use providing good advice if the operating units are not staffed with men of the ability required to carry it out effectively.[76]

By midcentury Unilever had apparently risen above the social institutions and cultural attitudes that shaped management-succession policies of most large British-based firms. Unilever's mode of management was clearly the exception rather than the rule in Britain. Even those firms that did try to adopt the multidivisional form in the post-World War II decades may not have been very successful in shedding detrimental institutional and cultural influences. Channon shows that there was considerable adoption of the multidivisional form in Britain in the 1950s and 1960s, typically on the advice of the ubiquitous McKinsey & Co. But he raises doubts about the extent of the concomitant changes in management structure and methods:

> Many of the internal characteristics of the corporations adopting multidivisional structure reflected prior structural forms. In particular there was little evidence of change in the reward system, especially as a mechanism to apply *internal* competition for divisional performance.[77]

Even in the context of an attempt at divisionalization of activities and decentralization of authority, the implementation of a bureaucratically integrated managerial structure in late postwar Britain may have faced severe institutional and cultural obstacles, such as (1) a system of higher education that had been shaped in part by the prevalence of bureaucratically segmented managerial structures, (2) the control of technology by shop-floor and shop-culture interest groups, and (3) the persistence of aristocratic values and social class distinctions in the hierarchical ordering of the managerial structure. In the face of these obstacles, insightful executives and experienced management consultants may not have been sufficient to transform the system of incentives, the lines of communication, and the loci of control within a large bureaucratic enterprise to permit managerial structure to make a success of the new organizational form.

NOTES

1. The major sources for the British-U.S. comparison are Alfred D. Chandler, Jr., *The Visible Hand: The Managerial Revolution in American Business*, Cambridge, Harvard University Press, 1977; Alfred D. Chandler, Jr., and Herman Daems, *Managerial Hierarchies: Comparative Perspectives on the Rise of the Modern Industrial Enterprise*, Cambridge, Harvard University Press, 1980; Peter L. Payne, "The Emergence of the Large-Scale Company in Great Britain, 1870–1914," *Economic History Review*, 2d ser., 20, December 1967; Alfred D. Chandler, Jr., "The Growth of the Transnational Firm in the United States and the United Kingdom: A Comparative Analysis," *Economic History Review*, 2d ser., 33, August 1980; Alfred D. Chandler, Jr., "The United Kingdom: The Persistence of Family Capitalism," unpublished manuscript, Graduate School of Business Administration, Harvard University, 1984; Derek F. Channon, *The Strategy and Structure of British Enterprise*, Boston, Graduate School of Business Administration, 1973; Leslie Hannah, *The Rise of the Corporate Economy*, 2d ed., London, Methuen, 1983; Bernard Elbaum and William Lazonick, "The Decline of the British Economy: An Institutional Perspective," *Journal of Economic History*, 44, 2, June 1984; Bernard Elbaum and William Lazonick, eds., *The Decline of the British Economy*, London, Oxford University Press, 1985.

2. Alfred Marshall, *Principles of Economics*, London, Macmillan, 1890. E. A. G. Robinson, *The Structure of Competitive Industry*, Cambridge, Cambridge University Press, 1933.

3. Herbert Simon, *Administrative Behavior*, 3d ed., New York, Free Press, 1976.

4. Chester Barnard, *The Functions of the Executive*, Cambridge, Harvard University Press, 1938.

5. "Should a Businessman Be Educated?" *Fortune*, 47, April 1953. Robert N. McMurry, "Man-Hunt for Top Executives," *Harvard Business Review*, 32, 1, January–February 1954.

6. The following summary draws upon Richard Hofstadter and C. DeWitt Hardy, *The Development and Scope of Higher Education in the United States*, New York, Columbia University Press, 1952; Frederick Rudolph, *The American College and University*, New York, Vintage, 1962; Laurance R. Veysey, *The Emergence of the American University*,

Chicago, University of Chicago Press, 1965; E. J. James, "The Origin of the Land Grant Act of 1862," *University of Illinois Bulletin*, 8, 10, 1910; A. C. True, *A History of Agricultural Education in the United States, 1785–1925*, Washington, Government Printing Office, 1929; William Lazonick, "The Integration of U.S. Higher Education into Agricultural Production," unpublished manuscript, Harvard University, 1977; David Noble, *America by Design*, New York, Oxford University Press, 1977.

7. Anglo-American Council on Productivity, *Education for Management*, London, Anglo-American Council on Productivity, 1951, pp. 48–51. Norman C. Hunt, *University Education for Business in the U.S.A.*, Management Education Series No. 1, European Productivity Agency, 1953, p. 11.

8. United States Bureau of the Census, *Historical Statistics of the United States, Colonial Times to 1970*, Washington, D.C., Government Printing Office, 1976, pp. 383, 385–86.

9. Cited in Suzanne Keller, *The Social Origins and Career Lines of Three Generations of American Business Leaders*, New York, Arno, 1980, pp. 133, 135n.

10. J. B. Taylor, "College Education and Business," *Educational Review*, 19, 1900. See also Charles F. Thwing, "College Training and the Business Man," *North American Review*, 177, October 1903; Irvin G. Wyllie, "The Businessman Looks at the Higher Learning," *Journal of Higher Education*, 23, 1952; Mabel Newcomer, *The Big Business Executive*, New York, Columbia University Press, 1955, p. 66.

11. Spurgeon Bell, *Productivity, Wages, and National Income*, Washington, D.C., Brookings Institution, 1940, p. 10; Seymour Melman, "The Rise of Administrative Overhead in the Manufacturing Industries of the United States, 1899–1947," *Oxford Economic Papers*, n.s. 3, February 1951, p. 66; United States Bureau of the Census, *Historical Statistics*, pp. 140–41.

12. Cited in Alfred Lief, *The Firestone Story*, New York, McGraw-Hill, 1951, p. 158. See also Hugh Allen, *The House of Goodyear*, Cleveland, Corday & Gross, 1943, p. 312; Alfred Lief, *"It Floats": The Story of Procter & Gamble*, New York, Rinehart, 1958, p. 157.

13. Boris Emmet and John E. Jeuck, *Catalogues and Counters*, Chicago, University of Chicago Press, 1950, p. 554. Alfred D. Chandler, Jr., *Strategy and Structure*, Cambridge, M.I.T. Press, 1962, p. 238.

14. Keller, *Social Origins*. Newcomer, *Big Business Executive*. "The Nine

Hundred," *Fortune*, 46, November 1952. W. Lloyd Warner and James C. Abegglen, *Occupational Mobility in American Business and Industry*, Minneapolis, University of Minnesota Press, 1955.

15. Noble, *America by Design.*

16. Cited in Noble, *America by Design*, p. 38.

17. *Ibid.*, p. 243.

18. Hunt, *University Education.* Melvin T. Copeland, *And Mark an Era*, Boston, Little, Brown, 1958, chaps. 2, 6.

19. Newcomer, *Big Business Executive*, p. 147.

20. McKinsey cited in Robert K. Merton, "Bureaucratic Structure and Personality," in Merton et. al., eds., *Reader in Bureaucracy*, New York, Free Press, 1952, p. 322. Barnard, *Functions*, p. 222, Newcomer, *Big Business Executive*, p. 135.

21. M. P. McNair, "The Harvard Experiment," in R. J. Mackay, ed., *Business and Science*, London, Sylvan Press, 1931, pp. 75–6.

22. For recent analyses along these lines, with the historical focus more on blue-collar workers, see Richard Edwards, *Contested Terrain*, New York, Basic Books, 1979; William Lazonick, "Technological Change and the Control of Work: The Development of Capital-Labor Relations in U.S. Manufacturing Industry," in Howard Gospel and Craig Littler, eds., *Managerial Strategies and Industrial Relations*, London, Heinemann, 1983.

23. Howard Lee Davis, *The Young Man in Business*, New York, Wiley, 1931, p. 35.

24. Litchfield cited in Allen, *Goodyear*, p. 312. Teagle cited in National Industrial Conference Board, *Company Programs of Executive Development*, Studies in Personnel Policy, No. 107, New York, National Industrial Conference Board, 1950, p. 19.

25. Newcomer, *Big Business Executive*, pp. 80, 112.

26. Keller, *Social Origins*, p. 98. "The Nine Hundred," *Fortune*. See also Warner and Abegglen, *Occupational Mobility*, p. 126.

27. Cited in National Industrial Conference Board, *Company Programs*, p. 23. See also *ibid.*, pp. 28–29, 34, 45–49, 53; John V. L. Morris, *Employee Training*, New York, McGraw-Hill, 1921; Emmet and Jeuck, *Catalogues*, p. 559; Allen, *Goodyear*, pp. 315, 322; Charles L. Walker, "Education and Training at International Harvester," *Harvard Business Review*, 27, September 1949, p. 554; Newcomer, *Big Business Executive*, p. 136; American Institute of Management, *How They Recruit and Develop Their Managers: A Survey of 168 Excel-*

lently Managed Companies, New York, American Institute of Management, 1965.

28. Marshall E. Dimock, *Administrative Vitality*, New York, Harper, 1959, pp. 212–13. On the potential ambiguity between demotion and promotion in "lateral" transfers, see Fred H. Goldner, "Demotion in Industrial Management," *American Sociological Review*, 30, October 1965.

29. Ralph J. Cordiner, "The Implications of Industrial Decentralization," *American Management Association General Management Series No. 134*, New York, 1945, pp. 26–8.

30. *Ibid.*, pp. 27–9.

31. Payne, "Emergence of the Large-Scale Company." Chandler, "Growth of the Transnational Firm." Chandler, "Persistence of Family Capitalism." Hannah, *Rise of the Corporate Economy*. Elbaum and Lazonick, eds., *Decline of the British Economy*.

32. T. C. Barker, *The Glassmakers*, London, Weidenfeld & Nicolson, 1977. B. W. E. Alford, *W.D. & H.O. Wills and the Development of the UK Tobacco Industry, 1786–1965*, London, Methuen, 1973. D. C. Coleman, *Courtaulds*, Vol. 1, Oxford, Clarendon Press, 1969. William Reader, *Imperial Chemical Industries*, Vol. 1, London, Oxford University Press, 1975. Charles Wilson, *The History of Unilever*, Vol. 1, New York, Praeger, 1968.

33. See references in note 31 as well as Leslie Hannah, "Strategy and Structure in the Manufacturing Sector," in Leslie Hannah, ed., *Management Strategy and Business Development*, London, Macmillan, 1976.

34. L. Urwick, "Promotion in Industry," *Public Administration*, 5, April 1927, p. 185.

35. Frank Plachy, Jr., *Britain's Economic Plight*, Boston, Little, Brown, 1926, p. 67.

36. Federation of British Industries, *Stocktaking on Management Education*, London, Federation of British Industries, 1961, p. 58, my emphasis. On these issues generally, see Julia Wrigley, "Seeds of Decline: Technical Education and Industry in Nineteenth Century Britain," in Elbaum and Lazonick, eds., *Decline of the British Economy*; Martin J. Weiner, *English Culture and the Decline of the Industrial Spirit, 1850–1980*, Cambridge, Cambridge University Press, 1981.

37. David Landes, *The Unbound Prometheus*, Cambridge, Cambridge University Press, 1969. Weiner, *English Culture*. David Ward, "The

Public Schools and Industry in Britain after 1871," in Walter
Laqueur and George L. Mosse, eds., *Education and Social Structure in
the Twentieth Century*, New York, Harper, 1967. Coleman, *Courtaulds*,
Vol. 1, pp. 271–72. D. C. Coleman, "Gentlemen and Players,"
Economic History Review, 26, February 1973.

38. Acton Society Trust, *Management Succession*, Acton Society Trust,
     1956, pp. 14, 22, 90.

39. Moseley Educational Commission, *Reports of the Moseley Educational
     Commission to the United States, October–December, 1903*, New York,
     Arno Press, 1969, p. 184.

40. Michael Sanderson, *The Universities and British Industry, 1850–1970*,
     London, Routledge & Kegan Paul, 1972, pp. 58–9. Acton Society
     Trust, *Management Succession*, pp. 8, 128. R. V. Clements, *Managers:
     A Study of Their Careers in Industry*, London, Allen & Unwin, 1958,
     pp. 142–48. I. C. McGivering, D. G. J. Matthews, and W. H.
     Scott, *Management in Britain*, Liverpool, Liverpool University Press,
     1960, pp. 65–71. Political and Economic Planning, *Graduates in In-
     dustry*, London, Allen & Unwin, 1967. But see the general evidence
     in D. G. Clark, *The Industrial Manager*, London, Business Publi-
     cations, 1966, pp. 37–42, as well as the specific case of Courtaulds
     in D. C. Coleman, *Courtaulds*, Vol. 3, Oxford, Clarendon Press,
     1980, pp. 132–37, and Arthur Knight, *Private Enterprise and Public
     Intervention*, London, Allen & Unwin, 1974, pp. 20, 72, 83, which
     indicate that the emphasis had shifted to science degrees by the
     early 1960s.

41. Reader, *Imperial Chemical Industries*, Vol. 1, pp. 92–3, 219. A. E.
     Musson, *Enterprise in Soap and Chemicals*, Manchester, Manchester
     University Press, 1965, p. 147. R. W. Ferrier, *The History of the
     British Petroleum Company*, Cambridge, Cambridge University Press,
     1982, p. 339; Barker, *Glassmakers*, p. 236.

42. Sanderson, *Universities*, p. 248. For an example of the impact of
     wartime loss on managerial succession, see Peter L. Payne, *Colvilles
     and the Scottish Steel Industry*, Oxford, Clarendon Press, 1979, p. 132.

43. Clements, *Managers*. McGivering, Matthews, and Scott, *Manage-
     ment*, chap. 2. Guy Hunter, *Studies in Management*, London, Uni-
     versity of London Press, 1961, pp. 20–1; British Institute of Man-
     agement, *New Trends in Management Training and Succession*, London,
     British Institute of Management, 1961. Geoffrey Crockett and Peter
     Elias, "British Managers: A Study of Their Education, Training,

Mobility, and Earnings," *British Journal of Industrial Relations*, 22, March 1984.

44. Sanderson, *Universities*, pp. 64–5. See also Alford, *Wills*, pp. 281–82.

45. Sanderson, *Universities*, p. 78. Massachusetts Institute of Technology, *Treasurer's Report*, 1913. Cornell University, *Treasurer's Report*, 1913–1914, p. 45. Percy Dunsheath, *The Graduate in Industry*, London, Hutchinson's, 1947, p. 42.

46. Cited in Sanderson, *Universities*, p. 95.

47. Cambridge University Appointments Board, *University Education and Business*, Cambridge, Cambridge University Press, 1945, pp. 39–40. Acton Society Trust, *Management Succession*, pp. 28–9.

48. David Mowery, "British and American Industrial Research: A Comparison 1900–1950," in Elbaum and Lazonick, eds., *Decline of the British Economy*.

49. Robert R. Locke, *The End of the Practical Man: Entrepreneurship and Higher Education in Germany, France, and Great Britain, 1880–1940*, Greenwood, JAI, 1984, pp. 51, 58, 101. Leslie Hannah, *Electricity before Nationalisation*, London, Macmillan, 1979, pp. 218–84.

50. Moseley Educational Commission, *Reports*, p. 57.

51. Cited in Locke, *End of Practical Man*, p. 101.

52. Charles Wilson and William Reader, *Men and Machines: A History of D. Napier & Son, Engineers, Ltd., 1808–1958*, London, Weidenfeld & Nicolson, 1958, pp. 156–59.

53. Peter Young, *Power of Speech*, London, Allen & Unwin, 1983, pp.125, 129–30.

54. Moseley Educational Commission, *Reports*, pp. 56–7.

55. Committee on Industry and Trade, *Factors in Industrial and Commercial Efficiency*, London, His Majesty's Stationery Office, 1924, p. 261. Ministry of Education, *Education for Management*, London, His Majesty's Stationery Office, 1947.

56. T. M. Mosson, *Management Education in Five European Countries*, London, Business Publications, 1965. Anglo-American Council on Productivity, *Education for Management*. Anglo-American Council on Productivity, *Universities and Industry*, London, Anglo-American Council on Productivity, 1951.

57. Mosson, *Management Education*. Weiner, *English Culture*, pp. 132–37. Channon, *Strategy and Structure*, pp. 212–13, 245–46.

58. . Mosson, *Management Education*, pp. 163–64.

59. David G. Clarke, "A Survey of Management Education in the United Kingdom," *Journal of Industrial Economics*, 4, February 1956.
60. Mosson, *Management Education*, p. 167. Aubrey Silberston, *Education and Training for Industrial Management*, London, Management Publications, 1955, p. 33.
61. Mosson, *Management Education*, p. 198.
62. James A. Bowie, *Education for Business Management*, London, Oxford University Press, 1930.
63. Hunt, *University Education*, p. 38.
64. Young, *Power of Speech*, p. 183.
65. Ronald S. Edwards and Harry Townsend, *Business Enterprise*, London, Macmillan, 1958, p. 546. Silberston, *Education and Training*, p. 80. Channon, *Strategy and Structure*, p. 246.
66. Acton Society Trust, *Management Succession*, pp. 95–107. Silberston, *Education and Training*, p. 52. W. G. McClelland, "Career Patterns and Organisational Needs," in R. J. Hacon, ed., *Organisational Necessities and Individual Needs*, Oxford, Blackwell, 1968, p. 30.
67. Crockett and Elias, "British Managers," pp. 36–7.
68. Samuel Bowles and Herbert Gintis, *Schooling in Capitalist America*, New York, Basic Books, 1976. Jerome Karabel, "Community Colleges and Stratification," *Harvard Educational Review*, 42, November 1972.
69. Chandler, *Strategy and Structure*. Channon, *Strategy and Structure*. Hannah, "Strategy and Structure," pp. 184–87.
70. Channon, *Strategy and Structure*.
71. For example, see the case of Courtaulds, as set forth in Coleman, *Courtaulds*, Vols. 2, 3.
72. Wilson, *History of Unilever*, Vol. 2, pp. 345ff, 380ff; Vol. 3, chap. 2. Musson, *Enterprise*, chap. 19. Geoffrey Heyworth, "Lever Brothers and Unilever Limited," in G. E. Milward, ed., *Large-Scale Organisation*, London, MacDonald and Evans, 1950.
73. Wilson, *History of Unilever*, Vol. 1, p. 48. D. K. Fieldhouse, *Unilever Overseas*, London, Croom Helm, 1978, p. 45. Musson, *Enterprise*, pp. 145–49, 343–45; chap. 20.
74. Wilson, *History of Unilever*, Vol. 1, chap. 20; Vol. 2, p. 48. Fieldhouse, *Unilever Overseas*, p. 39.
75. Wilson, *History of Unilever*, Vol. 2, p. 316.
76. Heyworth, "Lever Brothers," pp. 177–78.
77. Channon, *Strategy and Structure*, pp. 213–14, emphasis in original.

[9]

Organizational Capabilities in American Industry: The Rise and Decline of Managerial Capitalism

William Lazonick[1]
Barnard College, Columbia University
and
Institute for Advanced Study, Princeton

Organizational Capabilities

Organizational capabilities represent the power of planned and coordinated specialized divisions of labor to achieve organizational goals. Through planned coordination, the specialized productive activities of masses of individuals can coalesce into a coherent collective force. Through planned coordination, organizations can integrate the various types of knowledge needed to develop new products and processes. Through planned coordination, organizations can speed the flow of work from purchased inputs to sold outputs, thereby enabling the enterprise to achieve lower unit costs.

Over the past century the growing technical and social complexity of the specialized divisions of labor that must be planned and coordinated to achieve economic success have made organizational capabilities ever more critical for attaining and sustaining competitive advantage. Increasingly and across a widening range of industries, the benefits of planned coordination in developing and utilizing productive resources have justified the high fixed costs of building the organizations that can plan and coordinate.

Organization building is a social phenomenon that can be supported or hindered by the particular political, cultural, and economic environments in which any given business enterprise purchases its inputs, produces its goods, and markets its products. It is therefore possible to characterize not only particular enterprises but also the national economies in which those enterprises operate by the existence of more or less powerful organizational capabilities. From the late nineteenth century, when international industrial

---

[1]A version of this paper will appear in Howard Gospel, ed., *Industrial Training and Technological Innovations* (London, 1990).

BUSINESS AND ECONOMIC HISTORY, Second Series, Volume Nineteen, 1990.
Copyright (c) 1990 by the Business History Conference. ISSN 0849-6825.

36

leadership passed from Britain to the United States and Germany, superior organizational capabilities were critical. So too with the rise to dominance of Japan over Britain in cotton textiles in the 1920s and 1930s--a shift in international competitive advantage that rehearsed the more recent and more broad-based successes of Japanese industry against American and European competitors [6, 16, 17].

My purpose here is to provide an outline of the development and erosion of organizational capabilities in American industry during the twentieth century--a century that has witnessed the rise and relative decline of U.S. "managerial capitalism." The general historical perspective that I shall sketch out is by no means definitive. Only in recent years has scholarly research begun to discover and comprehend the internal evolution of business organizations. There is much more detailed research to be done. My hope is that a synthesis of existing knowledge on the development and erosion of organizational capabilities in the United States will be helpful for undertaking that research, as well as for stimulating debate over the institutional dynamics of capitalist development in the late twentieth century.

The Rise of Managerial Capitalism

Since the early nineteenth century, the geographic, occupational, and social mobility of labor in the United States has placed a premium on the building of managerial structures for successful industrial enterprise. The U.S. experience contrasted with that of Britain where geographic concentrations of skilled labor, reproduced on the job and in local communities from generation to generation, made it possible to conduct a successful business enterprise with little in the way of managerial planning and coordination. In Britain, capital could move to existing supplies of labor. In the United States, capital had to entice labor to move to it or alternatively develop and utilize technologies that made the enterprise less dependent on skilled manual labor that was in scarce supply. To solve the labor problem, U.S. industrialists had to build managerial structures that could ensure the sustained availability of the requisite labor services and that could plan and coordinate the development and utilization of labor-displacing technologies [4, 15, 16].

In the nineteenth century, as today, building a managerial structure meant training personnel in relevant industrial knowledge and motivating them to use that knowledge to further the goals of the enterprise. Higher education was as yet unimportant in the training of managers. They acquired relevant knowledge on the job--typically on the shop floor--and often moved from firm to firm to expand their knowledge base, bringing with them the skills as well as business connections that they already had acquired.

The interfirm, and interindustry, mobility of such technically trained personnel was a major factor in the diffusion of new technology in the nineteenth-century United States [10, 24]. With enough acquired experience, and some financial backing, some technologists would start their own firms. But if an entrepreneur wished to take advantage of expanding market opportunities in the nineteenth century, he had to create incentives for technical specialists to remain in his employ rather than go to work for the competition. To retain these specialists, and to ensure that they used their positions of responsibility and authority for the benefit of the firm, the entrepreneur often gave key personnel stakes in the enterprise in the forms of equity shares and promises of promotion to positions of greater power and pay. Gaining the commitment of managerial personnel to the firm was a cumulative dynamic process: the more successful the firm, the greater its ability to retain and reward key managerial personnel and the more the personnel would seek to further the interests of the firm [5, 6, 14].

The building of managerial structures was, therefore, both an effect and cause of the growth of American enterprises. Extensive managerial structures evolved in industries in which high fixed costs of technology and organization could, through planned coordination and the resultant achievement of large market shares, be transformed into low unit costs. The Lowell textile firms that launched the industrial revolution in the United States had managerial structures that were more extensive and costly than those that existed in the dominant British cotton industry. But it was the growth of the railroads from the 1840s that launched the managerial revolution in the United States. Particularly as the railroads evolved into regional and national systems, it became necessary to build managerial structures to plan and coordinate the flow of people and goods [5].

The railroads not only provided a school for industrial managers-- Andrew Carnegie was the most famous "graduate"--but also gave industrial enterprises the ready access to national supply and product markets that could make high fixed-cost investments in productive technology and managerial organization potentially worthwhile. Through planned coordination, enterprises that undertook these high fixed-cost investments in organization and technology could surge ahead of their rivals in the development and utilization of productive resources. For example, with railroads providing access to national markets for materials and finished products, the leading steel and oil refining companies--Carnegie Steel and Standard Oil in particular--made huge investments in plant and equipment as well as raw materials, and then, through the planned coordination of productive activities, captured the large market shares that enabled the transformation of these high fixed costs into low unit costs. As a result, these enterprises were able to underprice their competitors and emerge as dominant in their respective industries [5, 6].

Dominant firms also emerged in machinery manufacture, such as sewing machines (Singer) and agricultural equipment (McCormick). To compete in these industries required large investments not only in production facilities but also in marketing capabilities. To be competitive, companies had to invest in the training and motivation of knowledgeable and reliable salesmen who could provide after-sales service to the equipment users and who could also supply information from the field to manufacturing personnel concerning the need and potential for product development. As product innovation became central to successful industrial enterprise, the building of an effective marketing organization became as important, if not more important, to commercial success as the building of an effective

38

production organization. In a growing number of industries, the planned coordination of production and distribution activities within an organization provided the basis for attaining and sustaining competitive advantage. To accomplish the necessary planned coordination required the building of managerial structures--firm-specific investments in, and long-term commitments to, highly trained personnel [14].

The building of organizational capabilities became even more important in the next wave of managerial enterprises that emerged from the last decades of the nineteenth century in the science-based electrical and chemical industries. As these industries developed it became apparent that the integration of production and distribution facilities would not be sufficient for a firm to sustain whatever initial competitive advantage it may have had. The further growth of the enterprise required continuous innovation, which in turn required investments in research and development facilities. Firms such as General Electric, American Telephone and Telegraph, and Du Pont led the way in establishing R & D capabilities and integrating scientific personnel into the managerial structure [11, 23].

With the rise of the science-based industries came the growing need for personnel who had attained a conceptual comprehension of science and technology prior to taking up positions in industry. Following the successful German example of wedding higher education and industrial development, American businesspeople began to look to the educational system to provide their firms with the requisite personnel. Prior to the 1890s the U.S. system of higher education, like the British Oxbridge system on which it originally was modeled, was not integrated into the industrial sphere. Even the land-grant college system that had come into being in the 1860s and that would play a key role in the integration of higher education into the economy had been created primarily to enhance the social stature of America's farmers and artisans rather than to improve their productive capabilities. As individuals trying to make a living off the land or in their workshops, however, farmers and artisans had little use for the land-grant colleges [14].

These institutions only became integrated into economic activity from the late 1880s as the United States Department of Agriculture, with the subsequent support of rural bankers, agricultural machinery makers, and mail-order houses (all interested in rural prosperity), began using the land-grant colleges to develop new agricultural technologies and train agricultural "salesmen" who, through university extension courses, could help diffuse the new technologies to the farmers. At about the same time, some land-grant colleges--most notably M.I.T.--began training mechanical, electrical, and chemical engineers and scientists ready and willing to take up employment in managerial enterprises. Many of these engineers and scientists went on to climb the managerial hierarchy to positions of industrial leadership [14, 21].

Increasingly, after the turn of the century, major firms adopted the practice of regularly recruiting most new managerial personnel--and not just scientists and engineers--from the system of higher education. At the same time, dominant business interests--Carnegie and Rockefeller to name just two of the most important--pumped financial resources back into the system of higher education to ensure that, among other things, it would be able to fulfill its new-found function of peopling the burgeoning managerial structures. The competition for business funding ultimately forced the elite institutions such as Harvard and Yale to direct some of their educational attention toward servicing the personnel needs of managerial capitalism [14].

By the 1920s the U.S. system of higher education had taken its present form and had become deeply integrated into the economic system. Higher education provided future managerial personnel not only with the basic cognitive equipment needed to comprehend the nature of increasingly complex technology but also with the behavioral socialization needed to function within the new managerial organizations. As a result, higher education became a standard credential for embarking on a managerial career. It provided the pre-employment foundations for the development of managerial personnel within the firm. Educated recruits could be expected to have the cognitive capabilities for acquiring industry-specific technical knowledge as well as the behavioral characteristics required to interact within the organizational context and respond positively to organizational incentives.

American industry now had available the semi-processed human resources on which the organizational capabilities of U.S. corporate enterprises would be built. The graduates of higher education entered the firm as lower-level technical specialists, and over the next several years were rotated from one department and function to another to enable them to gain the experience necessary to move up the corporate ladder into positions requiring general managerial capabilities. In the process the corporation determined who would move up the hierarchy furthest and fastest. But even for the most promising of managers, the climb to the top was a career-long process, during which the employee had to demonstrate continuously his (until recent years rarely her) commitment to the organization. Compared to many of the fast tracks of today, rewards for devoted performance would come slowly, but steadily and surely. With the widespread separation of ownership from control that had occurred in American industry by the first decades of this century, moreover, an ambitious managerial employee ostensibly could envision ending his career at the pinnacle of the company's hierarchy of status and power [14].

In return for the employee's long-term commitment to the organization, the enterprise made a long-term commitment to the "organization man" to provide him with employment security and social status. The firm also had a strong incentive to invest in the productive potential of the career manager. A precondition for the firm to make this commitment was an entrenched position in its relevant product markets. The firm could only offer the employee long-term security, and would only make long-term investments in human resources, if the firm itself had sound prospects for long-term survival as a productive entity.

Enterprises that experienced sustained growth, moreover, could continually create new opportunities for the exercise of authority and responsibility that could be offered to loyal managerial employees. Hence the importance for personnel management of a diversification strategy that would continually take the firm into new product and geographic markets in which it could make use of the organizational capabilities it already had developed in capturing existing markets.   By generating not only employment stability but also new opportunities and rewards, the continuous growth of the firm was critical to creating incentives for career managers to contribute their skills and efforts to the pursuit of organizational goals. Success bred success.

The successful implementation of a diversification strategy required the building of an appropriate organization structure. The ability to integrate technical specialists into the organization and transform some of them into general managers was the key to the success of the multidivisional structures, which, as Alfred Chandler has shown, emerged in the 1920s and diffused rapidly in the 1930s and 1940s across dominant firms in American industry [4].   The multidivisional structure enabled the firm to augment its organizational capabilities for the purpose of expanding the scope of its activities to a wider range of product lines and more geographically extensive markets.

By separating strategic from operating decision-making, top management could focus all of its attention on planning long-term investment strategies.   But in focusing on strategic decision-making top management had to ensure that the operating divisions would respond to the overall goals of the firm--top management had to delegate authority to middle managers without losing control over the pursuit of the strategic objectives that had been set at the top.   Essential to the superior performance of the enterprise that adopted the multidivisional structure was the organizational integration of the managerial structure through the training and motivation of salaried personnel.

Centralized control facilitated the planning and coordination of management development programs that fostered organizational integration. Management development built on the pre-employment technical and social training that managerial personnel had acquired in the nation's education system.   The training acquired through management development was not confined to particular functional activities, product divisions, or geographic regions of the firm.   Enterprise-wide management development programs made it possible to adopt job-rotation schemes that were part of a continuous process of transforming specialists into generalists.   Often the schemes involved the movement of people not only between divisions but also from divisions to centralized staff functions and back.

Besides providing training, management development also became integral to the incentive system within the managerial structure. Management development programs expanded the potential for advancement within the firm, while encouraging junior and middle managers to conform to enterprise goals rather than to the goals of particular workgroups, functions, divisions, or regions.   Given the dependence of top management on salaried employees to whom it had delegated considerable authority and in whose training the firm had made significant investments, positive incentives of promotion up the hierarchy were much more powerful inducements to securing superior performance than were negative sanctions of demotion and dismissal.

Just as the delegation of authority extended decision-making responsibility down the firm's hierarchy, so did open lines of promotion help to ensure that the loyalty of managerial personnel would extend up the hierarchy. Moreover, the very possibility for moving up the hierarchy made middle managers willing to pass on information and delegate authority to subordinates who might one day take their places, thus extending appropriate training and effective incentives further down the organizational structure. At the same time, by separating control of key staff functions from the divisions, top management ensured that critical information would not become the property of self-serving entities within the firm [14].

The Managerial Structure and the Shop Floor

The long-term attachment of salaried employees to particular organizations in effect made managerial personnel members of the firm. Not so for shop-floor workers who, even to the present in the United States, generally have the status of hourly workers who are paid set rates for performing particular jobs. A blue-collar worker may spend a "lifetime" with the firm, especially when employment operates under seniority-based union rules. But American ideology has it that the shop-floor worker is a dispensable cog in the productive machine.

Indeed, since the late nineteenth century American management has sought to put this ideology into practice through the structuring of the hierarchical and technical divisions of labor [16]. The very formation of coherent managerial structures in U.S. firms created a clear-cut segmentation between salaried managers and wage workers that contrasted sharply with the integrated character of the managerial structures themselves. The process of segmentation between managers and workers began in the late nineteenth century, and its impetus was an obsession of American managers with taking skills off the shop floor. Up until the 1870s, American industrialists, and particularly those in metal and wood manufactures, relied extensively on craft workers to organize productive activities on the shop floor. These workers often were immigrants from Britain and Germany who had acquired their skills within the more traditional workplaces of Europe. But in the last decades of the nineteenth century, the combination of expanding national markets and rapid changes in process technology gave American managers both the incentive and ability to dispense with skilled craft workers [16].

Through the planned coordination of mechanized production processes, American managers could achieve the high rates of throughput that made it possible to gain competitive advantage or were essential just to remain competitive in capital-intensive industries. The attempts by craft workers to maintain their traditional shop-floor prerogatives, even in the face of deskilling technological change, threatened the achievement of what Alfred Chandler has called economies of speed [5]. Having invested in interconnected and expensive process technologies that were capable of high levels of throughput, management did not want to be bound by traditional craft norms concerning the allocation and pace of work as well as rates of pay.

It was the challenge to the position of craft control that prompted the workers to form the American Federation of Labor in the late 1880s.

The rise of craft unionism, however, only strengthened the resolve of U.S. mass producers to rid their workplaces of craft control. This they did not only by the violent suppression of strikes and the victimization of union labor but also by the cooptation of some of the more skilled craftsmen-- particularly those engaged in the set-up and maintenance of machinery--- into the managerial structure as engineers and supervisors. At the same time, American managers found ready at hand a massive influx of unskilled immigrant labor, primarily from southern and eastern Europe, eager to work in the mechanized factories.

A portion of these workers were assigned to unskilled heavy labor that had not yet been mechanized. But an increasing proportion found themselves assigned to "semi-skilled" operations. The cognitive requirements of semi-skilled jobs were minimal. Besides eliminating heavy labor, machines performed what for human minds and hands had previously been complex technical functions. Meanwhile a small group of elite, skilled personnel set up and maintained the machines. Left to semi-skilled workers were routine operative functions required to maintain the flow of work. What made these jobs demanding, both physically and mentally, was the pace of work, as managers tried to extract the maximum output from the high-throughput technologies in which their firms had invested. To avoid costly downtime on, and damage to, the expensive high-throughput machinery, it was essential that the semi-skilled operatives remain attentive and cooperative on the shop floor.

Not all machine operatives obliged. In the last two decades of the nineteenth century "scientific management" arose in enterprises that had invested in modern equipment. The goal of "scientific managers" was to get these workers to cooperate in the generation of high levels of throughput. The new technologies that were being put in place were not only skill- displacing but also *effort-saving*--the same amount of output could be produced with less effort on the part of the shop-floor worker, so that generating high levels of throughput no longer *necessarily* required that the operative actually work harder and longer. If only workers would trust "scientific managers" to set output norms consistent with the effort-saving capabilities of the new technologies and to fix piece rates that would give workers a fair share of the productivity gains, both capital and labor could, as Frederick Taylor put it, "together turn their attention toward increasing the size of the surplus until this surplus becomes so large that it is unnecessary to quarrel over how it shall be divided" [16, 19].

Taylor and his disciples had little success in gaining the cooperation of workers in the generation of high levels of throughput. Workers were disinclined to place their trust in the "scientific managers," because the industrial capitalists who really ran the factories were committed to extending and prolonging the "non-union era." The capitalists simply refused to bargain with the workers' representatives. Undermining even further the quest for high throughput was the rise after the turn of the century of a more militant labor movement, headed by the Industrial Workers of the World who advocated sabotage of the flow of work in order to pose a threat to the capitalists and thereby protect the interests of shop-floor labor.

With the struggle over "restriction of output" taking center stage in capital-labor relations, industrial managers became even more insistent that skill and initiative not be left on the shop floor, and that, by the same token, shop-floor workers not have control over the reproduction of relevant skills through craft-regulated apprenticeship training. Fearful that skilled shop-floor workers would use their scarce resources to reduce their effort and increase their pay, management deemed that knowledge of the shop-floor production process must reside within the managerial structure. In the short run, as already mentioned, management transformed skilled workers into managerial personnel. In the long run, management invested in new machine technologies that displaced shop-floor skills. In the process, the semi-skilled positions were increasingly filled by new immigrants who had arrived with few skills or by blacks who had left the South in search of a better living. Ethnically as well as organizationally and economically, a social gulf separated shop-floor workers from the managers who planned and coordinated their work [16, 19].

To get these increasingly alienated shop-floor workers to supply sufficient effort to maintain the flow of work, management turned in the early decades of this century to an extensive reliance on supervisory labor --a strategy that, however, often served to exacerbate the conflict on the shop floor, especially when labor markets were tight. In its reliance on the "drive system," moreover, management had not yet resolved the problem of how to ensure that supervisors, typically recruited from among the shop-floor workers and with meager prospects for rising further up the managerial hierarchy, would act in ways that furthered organizational goals [12, 16].

From the late 1910s, pressured by the exigencies of wartime labor shortage, the mass producers began to solve the problem of restriction of output on the shop floor. With the support of a repressive state, management attacked and eliminated the radical elements in the labor movement. In the aftermath of World War I, management also rebuffed large-scale efforts--in particular the Great Steel Strike of 1919--by the more conservative AFL to organize mass-production workers. By removing the possibility for workers to gain their ends through collective union voice, the demonstration of capitalist power set the stage for more progressive measures, particularly in firms that had attained dominant market shares, to gain a degree of cooperation from semi-skilled workers.

Personnel departments were put in place to rationalize labor policies, thereby eroding the autonomy of the foremen to whom management had been obliged to delegate substantial control. "Company unions" or "employee representation committees" were set up to provide an institutional context for workers to air their grievances to management. Attention was paid to the training of foremen to promote rather than undermine cooperative shop-floor relations, and lines of authority were put in place to ensure that foremen exercised control in accordance with company personnel policy [12].

Most important, during the boom of the 1920s, a significant number of dominant enterprises began to provide their shop-floor workers with "good jobs"--employment that offered higher pay and more job security than

44

could be found in the more competitive sectors of the economy. The managements of entrenched firms began, however modestly, to share with workers the huge surpluses that their firms were accumulating, and in an era during which the labor movement was in any case weakened, workers who landed the "good jobs" were inclined to cooperate in ensuring the rapid flow of work through the production process. With effective managerial coordination of high-throughput production processes now extending down to the shop floor, the 1920s saw phenomenal productivity growth in American manufacturing. Skills had been taken off the shop floor and production workers remained but "hourly," and ostensibly dispensable, labor. Nevertheless the planned coordination of the specialized division of labor was enabling dominant managerial enterprises to win a measure of cooperation from these workers. As a result, these firms were able to transform the high fixed costs of their investments in organization and technology into low unit costs, large market shares, and huge profits [16].

Managerial Capitalism in the Age of Mass-Production Unionism

With the depression of the 1930s, the "good jobs" of shop-floor workers vanished. At the beginning of the downturn, dominant enterprises sought to maintain employment for their shop-floor workers. But as the depression deepened in the early 1930s, massive layoffs of production workers became the rule. It appears, however, that dominant enterprises made greater efforts to keep their managerial structures intact. Top executives recognized that it would be difficult to recreate integrated managerial organizations that had taken decades to build if they were permitted to break apart. The economic success of the 1920s meant that most dominant firms had the financial power to take the long view in maintaining the integrity of their managerial organizations; they came into the 1930s with huge surpluses and little debt. It also appears that many dominant firms used the doldrums of the 1930s to create new products and search for new markets, and to implement multidivisional organizational structures to carry these strategies through. If, in the crisis of the 1930s, deskilled shop-floor workers were deemed dispensable, integrated managerial structures were not [15].

As good jobs vanished, shop-floor workers sought to remake their relations with their capitalist employers. Supported by a government that recognized the political and economic advantages of a viable union movement in the mass-production industries, workers successfully put an end to the "non-union era." The major objective of the mass-production unions that arose in the last half of the 1930s was "security"--the assurance that their members would enjoy both employment stability and substantial shares in their firms' prosperity.

The key to security was seniority. Unionized mass-production workers continued to be paid hourly rates attached to jobs, the form of payment suggesting that any individual worker was dispensable to the firm. But, barring another Great Depression, seniority provisions gave workers the prospects of steady employment as well as protection against discriminatory treatment for their involvement in unions. Indeed, over time, and typically through plant-level bargaining, seniority became the basis on which shop-floor workers moved up internal job ladders to positions that paid progressively higher hourly rates. Mass-production unionism gave workers substantially more collective power that could be used to challenge managerial prerogatives to control conditions of work and pay. But by giving workers employment security mass-production unionism also helped to overcome the legacy of workers' mistrust of corporate management created by the massive layoffs during the Great Depression. The accord between organized labor and corporate management created a basis for labor-management cooperation in creating value on the shop floor [3, 6].

U.S. industrial corporations also ensured that unionization did not extend too far up the organizational hierarchy. Specifically, in the mid-1940s attempts at unionization by foremen were stifled, helped by a legal ruling that declared that foremen were part of management, and hence could not demand union recognition under the National Labor Relations Act. With well-developed personnel departments in place--and extending a process of organizational integration that had already begun in the non-union era of the 1920s--corporate management was able to delegate supervisory authority to foremen without fear that these recruits from the shop floor would abuse their managerial power. By definitively according managerial status to foremen, moreover, corporations extended a powerful positive incentive to shop-floor workers by giving them the opportunity of rising to managerial positions, even if there was little chance of promotion beyond the level of first-line supervisor. In the 1940s the problem of "the man in the middle" was resolved in a way that established effective lines of authority and communication between the higher management levels and the shop floor. These organizational linkages enhanced managerial control [16, 18].

This modified structure of managerial capitalism enabled U.S. mass producers to take advantage of the propitious macroeconomic conditions of the 1940s and dominate the international economy into the 1960s. But it is important to note that the organizational structures available to U.S. mass producers were not creations of the post-World War II era. Rather they were extensions of a process of organization building that had begun in the late nineteenth century and that permitted most of the enterprises that had emerged as dominant in the rise of managerial capitalism to remain dominant into the second half of the twentieth century. Although unions now shared power with management in bargaining over shares of value gains, workers left investment decisions to management; unlike the earlier craft organizations, their unions were not inherently opposed to technological change and redivisions of labor on the shop floor. In the postwar era of economic growth and U.S. international dominance, mass-production unionism showed itself to be compatible with the transformation of high fixed costs into low unit costs in mass-production enterprises.

Ensuring the continued dominance of the U.S. economy in the 1940s and 1950s was the movement of many U.S. firms into new product and geographic markets. The growth of multinational operations would not have been possible if the U.S.-based enterprises that went multinational had not already developed the organizational capabilities needed to dominate the

46

vast U.S. domestic market. The continued growth of many of these firms, and their ability to share the gains of success with their managers and workers, would not have been possible without huge investments in research and development--activities that enabled enterprises to build on their existing technological capabilities to generate product innovations. In the United States during the 1940s and 1950s, these firm-level investments in R & D received substantial support from private and public funding that enabled a vast expansion of the system of higher education, as well as from direct government financial support, generally justified as military expenditures, but with apparently significant spillovers into commercial uses [20].

The Decline of Managerial Capitalism

Since the 1960s U.S. industry has entered into a period of long-term relative decline, not unlike the experience of British industry since the late nineteenth century. As both cause and effect of this decline has been the erosion of the organizational capabilities that U.S. industrial corporations had built up over the previous half century, if not longer. During the 1960s the erosion of the organizational capabilities of U.S. industrial enterprises began on the shop floor--the weakest link in the structure of organizational integration that had been achieved previously. Shop-floor workers had never been extended "membership" in the firms for which they labored; in their work they had been reduced to "appendages of the machines" (to use Karl Marx's apt phrase), and they belonged to powerful union organizations that could refuse to cooperate with management in the bargaining process if workers' interests were not being met. During the 1970s and 1980s, however, the erosion of the organizational capabilities of the major U.S. industrial corporations has gone much further than loss of control over the shop-floor labor force. As we shall see, the erosion of organizational capabilities has also occurred within the managerial structures themselves.

The result has been the waning of "managerial capitalism" as a dominant force in international industrial competition. The decline of managerial capitalism has not occurred in a competitive vacuum. The U.S. economy has been in *relative* decline. That is, the dominant managerial enterprises that form the core of the U.S. economy have continued to grow, and in many cases even innovate, but in their competitive capabilities, these enterprises have been surpassed by more powerful modes of business organization, particularly those emanating from the Japanese economy.

Elsewhere I have elaborated on the characteristics of the organizational capabilities of Japanese "collective capitalism" that have made the institutions of "managerial capitalism" obsolete [16, 17]. Suffice it to say here that the strength of Japanese enterprise derives from organizational integration that extends beyond the limits of the planned coordination of the specialized division of labor as practiced under U.S. managerial capitalism. First, organizational integration in Japan extends across horizontally and vertically related *firms* to a much greater extent than in the United States (where such integration is indeed often illegal) so that planned coordination spans units of financial control to encompass multifirm business organizations. Second, within dominant Japanese enterprises, organizational integration extends further down the organizational hierarchy, beyond the managerial structure itself, to include male blue-collar workers.

Both these extensions of organizational integration significantly enhance the organizational capability available to Japanese industry while significantly increasing the risks confronted by American firms that would attempt to make the huge investments in facilities and personnel necessary to remain competitive. Confronted by an international economy that they no longer dominate, many major U.S. enterprises have sought to adapt on the basis of the past successes, thereby reaping the returns on their prior investments without committing sufficient resources to ensure their future prosperity. Short-run adaptive responses inevitably lead to the erosion of organizational capabilities as the business enterprise can no longer maintain the incentives for key employees to remain committed to the organization --even if, as is increasingly less likely to be the case, these employees have the training and the physical facilities available that are necessary to enable the enterprise to remain at the forefront of innovation.

Deskilling on the Shop Floor

As already indicated, the vulnerability of American industrial enterprises to superior organizational capabilities from abroad was greatest on the shop floor. With a few exceptions such as IBM and Kodak, U.S. industrial enterprises had never made long-term employment *commitments* (as distinct from implicit promises) to their shop-floor workers. Inherent in insistence by American managers of their "right to manage" the shop floor was the ideology that, at any time and for any job, any individual shop-floor worker was dispensable--paid by the "hour" for the job at hand and no more.

In terms of workers' *skills*, managerial ideology could claim some relevance. Intent on taking skills off the shop floor where workers might use them to control the pace of work, U.S. managerial enterprises had not made significant investments in the skills of shop-floor workers. Management tended not to count the deskilled shop-floor worker among the firm's valued assets. But in terms of workers' *efforts*, this managerial ideology was much less well-founded. In practice, to gain the cooperation of shop-floor workers in maintaining the rapid and steady flow of work so essential to achieving low unit costs, management had to offer them a measure of employment security and a share (however indirect) in the prosperity of the enterprise [16].

Prior to the Great Depression, some of the more farsighted industrial managers had systematized their personnel policies to provide hardworking shop-floor workers with realistic promises of economic security. As we have seen, when the promises were not kept during the Great Depression, workers took the matter of economic security into their own hands. Once the major industrial corporations had recognized the new mass-production unions, it was not managerial personnel policy but rather the workers' own collective organizations with their emphasis on seniority rights that would provide workers with the employment security and economic gains critical for gaining their cooperation in the workplace. In effect managers of most of the great U.S. industrial corporations came to rely on independent union organizations to ensure the stability of the long-term relation between shop-floor workers and the firms for which they worked.

This institutional arrangement remained viable as long as the U.S. industrial corporations continued to dominate their markets. But when, in the 1960s and 1970s, the corporations stumbled in the face of international competition and sought to roll back the bargaining gains that workers had made over the previous decades, the adversarial character of U.S. labor-management relations broke through the cooperative veneer. In industries such as steel and automobiles that were dominated by adaptive (as distinct from innovative) oligopolists, the costs of the accord with labor that had been struck in the 1940s began to outstrip productivity gains. As long as there was no serious foreign competition and the U.S. national firms in an industry did not engage in significant price competition among themselves, U.S. corporations were able to pass off higher labor costs to consumers in the form of higher prices. By the late 1960s, however, the limits of the adaptive strategy had been reached. With powerful international competitors on the scene, domestic inflation only served to erode U.S. international competitive advantage [16].

The U.S. competitiveness problem was not only higher wages but also lagging productivity growth. High wages, tight labor markets, and the availability of unemployment benefits--not to mention the restiveness of younger blue-collar workers, both black and white, in the wake of the civil rights and antiwar movements--had weakened managerial control over shop-floor workers. Alienated in any case by the routine nature of their work and without any formal power to influence the nature of the work environment, blue-collar workers sought to control their expenditure of effort by unauthorized work stoppages, work to rule, and absenteeism, all of which had adverse consequences for productivity.

In the 1970s many observers of American industry pointed to the alienated shop-floor worker, confined to routine and repetitive tasks requiring little skill development, as an explanation of the slowdown in the growth of labor productivity in American manufacturing that had begun in the mid-1960s. In many plants around the country, experiments in job enlargement and job enrichment were undertaken to try to enhance "the quality of worklife" (as it was called) in order to elicit more effort from workers. Although the initial impacts of these programs were generally positive, many of the experiments in the early 1970s were cut short when the workers whose jobs had been enriched and enlarged began questioning traditional managerial prerogatives. In the long run, attempts such as these at piecemeal transformation of the organizational structure may well have reduced rather than enhanced organizational capability by creating expectations for more meaningful work which in the end were not fulfilled [13, 16, 25].

In the 1980s Japanese success in taking market share away from once-dominant U.S. mass producers made it clear that the prime source of Japanese competitive advantage was not low wages (as many Americans had chosen to believe in the 1970s) but superior organizational capabilities. Many American industrial managers also came to recognize that the major difference between the internal organization of U.S. and Japanese enterprises was the extent to which Japanese managers *developed* skills on the shop floor and delegated authority to blue-collar workers to use those skills to ensure a rapid flow of high-quality work. As a result of the Japanese challenge, American industrial managers began to realize that enhancing "the quality of worklife" was not just a means of eliciting effort from workers (as had been the case in the failed experiments of the 1970s).

Rather industrial managers came to recognize that upgrading the skills of the shop-floor labor force was an end in itself because it augmented the firm's human-resource "assets." To maintain the rapid flow of high-quality work using new, automated manufacturing technologies requires shop-floor workers with the cognitive capabilities to ensure that the machines work properly with a minimum of downtime. U.S. mass-production industries can no longer compete using workers whose own mechanical motions merely complement those of the machine, as previously has been the case. The effective use of the new technologies requires shop-floor workers who can ensure the quality, as well as the quantity, of work [16, 22].

As a precondition for technology-specific training for workers under the auspices of the employing enterprise itself, the large-scale adoption of new "flexible" technologies requires a supply of more highly educated shop-floor workers than U.S. industry has used or has had available in the past. To generate a large supply of workers capable of acquiring the requisite training both within and outside the manufacturing enterprise, institutional rigidities in the U.S. educational system must be confronted. When, in the early twentieth century, vocational schooling entered U.S. secondary education to track youths away from college and into the blue-collar labor force, the resultant segmentation of the labor force was consistent with the social division of labor between managers and workers in the world of work [2]. But in recent decades the same educational system has lost touch with the changing human-resource needs of an industrial era in which the potential for automation has created a new role for shop-floor workers in monitoring the quality, as well as ensuring the quantity, of work [22].

Mass Education and Deskilled Labor

What is now needed is an educational system that rejects the conception of the worker as a mere appendage of the machine and prepares future workers for active involvement in speeding the flow of work while maintaining its quality in the "flexible" factory. There is no point, however, in building new organizational structures and educational systems if those who run the largest industrial corporations eschew innovative investment strategies that can make use of skilled workers who are encouraged to exercise initiative on the shop floor. Yet prevailing organizational structures within U.S. manufacturing enterprises may be inhibiting the adoption of innovative investment strategies because they reflect a century-long managerial obsession with taking skills, and initiative, off the shop floor. It would appear that even entering the 1990s many, if not most, American managers are reluctant to develop skills on the shop floor for fear of losing control of the flow of work [16].

Despite conservative investment strategies in the mass-production industries, the 1980s witnessed, somewhat belatedly, the widespread recognition of the need to improve the quality of mass education in the United States. At the same time, however, blue-collar workers have experienced massive, and typically permanent, layoffs in the face of international competition. Good blue-collar jobs have vanished in the United States, not because of a lack of effective demand as in the 1930s but because of the supply-side effectiveness of international competitors. Youths in working-class schools and communities see that the good jobs are no longer there. Yet they are confronted with an educational system that is geared toward generating blue-collar workers who will be able and willing to spend their lives doing routine work. The system no longer has a hold on them. Particularly in black communities, class discipline, a modicum of which was previously secured by the prospects of steady and well-paying blue-collar jobs, has broken down.

The Decline of Innovation

Although mass education for blue-collar workers has been deteriorating, the United States still possesses a powerful system of higher education, capable of generating technical specialists required for innovation in the late twentieth century. But the system of higher education is less integrated into the U.S. industrial economy than it used to be. For one thing, international competitors, with their powerful organizational capabilities in place, are able to make ample use of the open U.S. system of higher education. One reason why U.S. industrial corporations are having increasing difficulty in maintaining control over intellectual property is that they have become too reliant on the publicly funded educational institutions to foot the bills for R & D, rather than, as they did in the past, use the higher educational system as the foundation for investments in in-house R & D. In addition, over the post-World War II decades, the spillover of military R & D expenditures to civilian uses appears to have diminished [20].

At the same time, the evolution of U.S. financial institutions has generated strong disincentives for highly educated Americans to become technical specialists and pursue the types of managerial careers with particular enterprises that, as outlined above, were critical to the building of organizational capabilities in the era of U.S. industrial dominance. The deregulation movement of the 1970s and the related financial revolution of the 1980s opened up new opportunities for the graduates of higher education to make large sums of money quickly with little experience in either technology or the organizations for which they worked. The new opportunities made the slow climb up the managerial hierarchy of an industrial corporation distinctly less attractive for these educated personnel. When combined with the rise of formidable international competition, moreover, the financial revolution has placed the long-term existence of many once-stable industrial corporations in jeopardy, so that the firm-specific career that a college graduate could once take for granted is now by no means assured [15].

More generally, the domination of financial interests over industrial interests has been eroding U.S. organizational capabilities even at the managerial level where historically organizational integration in the United States had been most complete. To be innovative in the late twentieth century requires not only appropriate human-resource development and far-reaching organizational integration but also massive financial commitments in the face of returns that are more uncertain than ever. In general, financial commitment means that those who, as employees, creditors, or owners, can lay claim to the revenues of the firm will not enforce those claims in ways that undermine the development and utilization of the firm's organizational capabilities [15]. In the private-sector enterprise, financial commitment generally means the retention of earnings for the sake of developing the resources of the firm. High degrees of financial commitment characterize those industrial enterprises in Japan and Germany that are the major international competitors in the late twentieth century. In international competition, financial commitment has become ever more critical to the development and utilization of organizational capabilities. Yet since the 1950s a number of forces in the U.S. economy have been eroding financial commitment.

The erosion began within the industrial enterprise itself. During the first half of the century when the major U.S. industrial corporations rose to international dominance, ownership was increasingly separated from control. Stockholding was widely dispersed among portfolio investors who, by virtue of the fragmentation of ownership, ceded to professional managers the right to determine the allocation of the firm's financial resources. The interests of these top managers were bound up with the interests of their managerial organizations. They had typically pursued their careers with the firms that they now ran. As salaried managers, moreover, their only claims to higher levels of remuneration derived from the long-run competitive performance of the enterprise.

During the 1950s, however, top managers ceased to be merely salaried employees. Through stock-based compensation systems, they became substantial owners, and hence the beneficiaries of the prolonged run up in stock prices that ended only at the close of the 1960s. During the 1950s and 1960s, the incentives increased for top managers of the major corporations to identify with the short-run market performance of their companies' stocks. The methods for improving short-run performance often conflicted with the long-term financial requirements for building organizational capability for the sake of sustained innovation.

By the same token, top managers now had vastly more scope than previously to use their positions of strategic management as the basis for their own individual aggrandizement rather than as the basis for the development of the organizational capabilities of their enterprises as a whole. Hence as an alternative to engaging in innovative investment strategies in their current or technologically related lines of business, many top managers of the 1960s became conglomerateurs, each one with financial control over a multitude of industrial enterprises in which he had neither

52

organizational roots nor technological expertise. These conglomerate managers controlled the financial resources required to undertake innovative investment strategies. But the planning and coordination of these strategies was the task of the new "middle" managers--often (initially at least) the former top managers of the acquired companies who now headed the conglomerate divisions and who had the requisite understanding of the division's organizational capabilities to manage the innovation process.

Besides knowledge of products, processes, and people, however, the management of innovation requires financial commitment--and more specifically control over the allocation of enterprise earnings--which is precisely what the new "middle" managers whose role it was to manage innovation within the conglomerate structure no longer had the power to provide. Moreover, evaluated by the head office on the basis of their short-term performance, the divisional heads who indeed pursued innovative investment strategies quickly learned (if they were still around to make use of their knowledge) that adaptive behavior--managerial behavior that did not make large and sustained demands on enterprise earnings--got a better reception from the conglomerate bosses.

Although the conglomerate movement abated and indeed reversed itself somewhat in the 1970s as many ill-managed divisions were sold off, considerable damage to the organizational capability of many U.S. industrial corporations had been done. At the same time, increasingly powerful international competitive challenges made the top managers of U.S. industrial enterprises think twice about committing their firms' resources to long-run innovative strategies. Instead the tendency was for these firms to try to adapt on the basis of their successful investments of the past. In this adaptive mode, the rewards of promotion to top management positions went to those who displayed the most talent for improving the "bottom line." We can conjecture that it was this type of top manager, driven by financial goals, who was most likely to cooperate with the raiders in the hostile takeover movement of the 1980s. The popularity of "golden parachutes" and other compensation schemes designed to bribe top management to make way for corporate raiders revealed that America's industrial leaders could pursue their own individual ends not only through the medium of the securities markets but also by selling their very offices of financial control.

The use of securities markets to buy and sell industrial enterprises for the sake of individual gain has often torn apart U.S. organizational capabilities without creating the conditions for putting more powerful organizational capabilities in their place. The problem is not mergers and acquisitions per se, but the purposes for which, and the conditions under which, they are undertaken. It may make strategic sense for an innovative firm to acquire or merge with other existing enterprises which have already developed unique capabilities rather than adopt the much slower and more uncertain strategy of developing these operations from the ground up. The success of such mergers and acquisitions in permitting the production of higher quality goods at lower unit costs depends on the willingness and the ability of the previously distinct and separate enterprises to integrate their capabilities so as to join forces in pursuit of a common organizational goal.

As demonstrated by the history of British economic decline, however, the simple vertical or horizontal amalgamation of firms or operations without organizational integration does not result in sustained competitive advantage--a lesson that was repeated in the United States with the rise and fall of the conglomerate movement in the 1960s and 1970s [6]. Financial integration does not imply organizational integration. And as demonstrated by the organizational advantages of the Japanese system of enterprise groups, organizational integration can occur across units of distinct financial control [1].

As financial commitment and organizational capability have eroded, the United States has lost competitive advantage not only in the "mature" industries of the Second Industrial Revolution but also in the high-technology industries of the Third Industrial Revolution [7, 8]. The formation of Sematech as a consortium of the major U.S. electronic firms to combine resources in the research and development of semiconductors was a step in the direction of a more collective capitalism that might have been able to respond to the new competition. Yet even IBM--the U.S. industrial organization par excellence--is so consumed with its struggles for restructuring its own product lines that it has been unable to provide effective leadership in restructuring the supply of its industry's vital capital inputs. The example of Japan suggests that the generation of innovation and the attainment of competitive advantage in such technologically complex and high fixed-cost industries require thoroughgoing vertical integration of the industry's productive capabilities as well as a degree of horizontal cooperation among major competitors in ensuring the supply of high-quality capital goods.

In the high fixed-cost, high-technology industries, it is only such collectivized organizations that can effectively nurture and sustain innovative new ventures into dynamic going concerns. The experience of the 1980s showed that the mode of venture capital that provided the financial commitment to innovative new ventures in the past is no longer adequate to meet the exigencies of the new international competition. Although the venture capital funds grew enormously during the 1980s, a plethora of venture capital firms competing for scarce high-technology personnel and eager for short-term returns have undermined the building of the organizational capabilities that the success of innovative investment strategies requires [15].

The comparative history of capitalist development--and in particular the successful Japanese challenge to the once-dominant United States, not to mention the previously dominant Britain--shows that now more than ever industrial leadership requires the long-term commitment of resources to organizations that can plan and coordinate the development and utilization of productive capabilities. In developed capitalist economies, however, those who control wealth can choose to live off the past rather than invest in the future. A necessary condition for continued investment in innovation, marked by the building of organizational capabilities, is that such adaptive behavior be constrained. A sufficient condition is that the economic uncertainty inherent in innovative investments be reduced by means of policies that educate the labor force, mobilize committed financial resources, and coordinate interdependent innovative efforts [17].

References

1. Michael Best, The New Competition (Cambridge, MA, 1990).
2. Samuel Bowles and Herbert Gintis, *Schooling in Capitalist America* (New York, 1976).
3. David Brody, *Workers in Industrial America* (New York, 1980).
4. Alfred D. Chandler Jr., *Strategy and Structure* (Cambridge, MA, 1962).
5. _____, *The Visible Hand* (Cambridge, MA, 1977).
6. _____, *Scale and Scope: The Dynamics of Industrial Capitalism* (Cambridge, MA, 1990).
7. Stephen S. Cohen and John Zysman, *Manufacturing Matters* (New York, 1987).
8. Michael L. Dertouzos, Richard K. Lester, and Robert M. Solow, *Made in America: Regaining the Productive Edge* (Cambridge MA, 1989).
9. Robert Hayes and William Abernathy, "Managing Our Way to Economic Decline," *Harvard Business Review*, 58 (July-August 1980).
10. David Hounshell, *From the American System to Mass Production 1800-1932* (Baltimore, 1984).
11. _____, and John K. Smith Jr., *Science and Corporate Strategy: Du Pont R & D, 1902-1980* (Cambridge, ENG, 1988).
12. Sanford Jacoby, *Employing Bureaucracy: Managers, Unions, and the Transformation of Work in American Industry, 1900-1945* (New York, 1985).
13. Thomas A. Kochan, Harry C. Katz, and Robert B. McKersie, *The Transformation of American Industrial Relations* (New York, 1986).
14. William Lazonick, "Strategy, Structure, and Management Development in the United States and Britain," in Kesaji Kobayashi and Hidemasa Morikawa, eds., *Development of Managerial Enterprise* (Tokyo, 1986).
15. _____, "Controlling the Market for Corporate Control: The Historical Significance of Managerial Capitalism." Paper presented to the Third International Joseph A. Schumpeter Society Meetings, Airlie, Virginia, June 3-5, 1990.
16. _____, *Competitive Advantage on the Shop Floor* (Cambridge, MA, 1990).
17. _____, *Business Organization and the Myth of the Market Economy* (Cambridge, ENG, 1991).
18. Nelson Lichtenstein and Stephen Meyer, eds., *On the Line: Essays in the History of Auto Work* (Urbana IL, 1989).
19. David Montgomery, *The Fall of the House of Labor* (Cambridge, ENG, 1987).
20. Richard R. Nelson, "U.S. Technology Leadership: Where Did It Come From and Where Did It Go?" Paper presented to the Third International Joseph A. Schumpeter Society Meetings, Airlie, Virginia, June 3-5, 1990.
21. David Noble, *America by Design* (New York, 1977).
22. Michael Piore and Charles Sabel, *The Second Industrial Divide* (New York, 1984).
23. Leonard Reich, *The Making of American Industrial Research* (Cambridge, ENG, 1985).
24. Ross Thomson, *The Path to Mechanized Shoe Production in the United States* (Chapel Hill, NC, 1989).
25. Richard E. Walton, "From Control to Commitment: Transforming Work Force Management in the United States," in Kim B. Clark, Robert H. Hayes, and Christopher Lorenz, eds., *The Uneasy Alliance: Managing the Productivity-Technology Dilemma* (Boston, 1985).

Index

Economists of the Twentieth Century

Monetarism and Macroeconomic Policy
Thomas Mayer

Studies in Fiscal Federalism
Wallace E. Oates

The World Economy in Perspective
Essays in International Trade and European Integration
Herbert Giersch

Towards a New Economics
Critical Essays on Ecology, Distribution and Other Themes
Kenneth E. Boulding

Studies in Positive and Normative Economics
Martin J. Bailey

The Collected Essays of Richard E. Quandt (2 volumes)
Richard E. Quandt

International Trade Theory and Policy
Selected Essays of W. Max Corden
W. Max Corden

Organization and Technology in Capitalist Development
William Lazonick

Studies in Human Capital
Collected Essays of Jacob Mincer, Volume 1
Jacob Mincer

Studies in Labor Supply
Collected Essays of Jacob Mincer, Volume 2
Jacob Mincer

Macroeconomics and Economic Policy
The Selected Essays of Assar Lindbeck, Volume 1
Assar Lindbeck

The Welfare State
The Selected Essays of Assar Lindbeck, Volume 2
Assar Lindbeck